PROPERTY MANAGEMENT

Walt Huber
Glendale College - Professor of Real Estate

William Pivar
College of the Desert - Professor Emeritus

Educational Textbook Company, Inc.
www.etcbooks.com
626-339-7733

COPYRIGHT © 1999, 2002 EDUCATIONAL TEXTBOOK COMPANY, INC.

EDUCATIONAL TEXTBOOK COMPANY, INC.
P. O. Box 3597
Covina, California 91722
(626) 339-7733
FAX (626) 332-4744
www. etcbooks. com

ISBN: 0-916772-32-2

Library of Congress Cataloging-in-Publication Data

Huber, Walt
Property Management, Walt Huber and William Pivar
2nd Edition

Summary: Covers all material in property management with special emphasis on managing a property management company. Very clear and simple language, easy-to-read format with photographs, charts, and graphs. Includes glossary and index; suitable for consumers, students, and teachers wishing information regarding personal real estate transactions.

1. Real Estate Business – California 2. Real Estate Property – California
332.7209   [332.72]

Preface

"You'd be hard pressed to find a successful property management company today that doesn't have its own Web Site." Walt Huber

Property Management by Walt Huber and William Pivar is a comprehensive, easy to read text that not only covers property management, but addresses the growing influence of the Internet on the field of real estate.

In order to bring the Internet to your students and make it user friendly, were introducing "Hubie the, R E Internet Mouse." We've not only simplified real estate legal concepts, but we've updated the format to include Internet addresses.

You'll find "Hubie" popping up throughout the book as a friendly indicator to clearly mark important Websites.

Who better to bring the Internet and real estate together, than authors William Pivar and Walter Huber. Pivar is not only a prominent real estate attorney, but has worked for one of the largest management companies in Wisconsin. Huber has authored numerous books on the subject of real estate and the Internet, and both authors have been teaching real estate and property management in California colleges for over twenty years.

Special thanks also to the people who helped design and produce this book: Philip Dockter,art director; Melinda Winters, cover design; and Rick Lee, executive editor.

Additions and revisions were made with the help of Ted Bartlett, CPM from Glendale College; Albert Ramseyer JD, Attorney, County Counsel, County of Los Angeles; and Steven A. Latour, property manager at Kaiser Permanante, all to whom we are very grateful.

ABOUT THE AUTHORS

Dr. William Pivar is Professor Emeritus at College of the Desert, Palm Desert, California. Dr. Pivar has a national reputation as an expert in real estate matters. He has been quoted in many major newspapers and national financial publications. His numerous books have received favorable reviews in publications such as *Money Magazine*, and he has authored a Fortune Book Club selection.

Dr. Pivar's property management experience goes beyond academia. He served as a property management officer for the General Services Administration, which is the real estate management agency of the federal government. As assistant chief of operations, he had the supervisory responsibility of several thousand government owned and leased properties in a five-state area. He served on property inspection teams and was directly responsible for contracting for maintenance, improvements, and security.

Dr. Pivar was general counsel and later president of a property management service that, under his direction, became the largest management firm in the state.

He has served as an expert witness in real estate matters and has been called on as both an American Arbitration Association and Federal Mediation and Conciliation Service arbitrator.

Walt Huber is a well known author and serves as Real Estate Coordinator at Glendale College. Mr. Huber has served on state education committees and has extensive property management experience in managing a varied portfolio of family-owned properties.

Table of Contents

Chapter 1   Property Management —
A Profession of Service..1
Chapter 2   Preparing for Management................................ 31
Chapter 3   Leases and Leasing... 63
Chapter 4   Lease Clauses... 97
Chapter 5   Residential Property Management.....................133
Chapter 6   Commercial, Office, and Industrial
Property Management..................................... 173
Chapter 7   Special Management Situations......................... 209
Chapter 8   Liability and Risk Management..........................249
Chapter 9   Security and Safety.. 277
Chapter 10 Maintenance and Energy Conservation.............. 309
Chapter 11 Records and Controls..................................... 345
Chapter 12 Promotion and Advertising................................ 373
Chapter 13 Fair Housing and Ethics.................................. 401
Chapter 14 Tenant and Owner Relations............................. 429
Chapter 15 Management Operations.................................. 455
Glossary.. 487
Index.. 494

Property Management— A Profession of Service

KEY WORDS AND TERMS

Accredited Management Goal Oriented Organization (AMO)
Accredited Marketing Director (AMD)
Accredited Residential Manager (ARM)
Accredited Shopping Center Manager (ASM)
American Industrial Real Estate Association
Association Management Specialist (AMS)
Building Owners and Managers Institute (BOMI)
Certified Leasing Specialist (CLS)
Certified Facility Manager (CFM)
Certified Manager of Community Associations (CMCA)
Certified Property Manager (CPM)
Certified Shopping Center Manager (SCSM)
Community Associations Institute
Completed Staff Work
Corporate Property Managers
Economic Life
Electric Elevator
Employee Manager
Facilities Management Administrator (FMA)
Franchises

Independent Property Manager
Industrial Revolution
International Council of Shopping Centers (ICSC)
International Design and Development Award
International Facility Management Association
International Real Estate Institute
MAXI Award
Moldboard Plow
Professional Community Association Manager (PCAM)
Property Management Association (PMA)
Real Estate Investment Trust
Real Property Administrator (RPA)
Senior Certified Marketing Director (SCMD)
Senior Certified Shopping Center Manager (SCSM)
Structural Steel
Systems Maintenance Technician (SMT)
System Maintenance Administrator (SMA)
Urban Land Institute (ULI)
Vacancy Factor

1

LEARNING OBJECTIVES

In this chapter, you will learn about the historical background of property management that has led to the present career opportunities in this field of service. You will understand why owners choose professional property management and how professional management can meet owner needs and goals. You will also learn what it takes to make a successful property manager. You will be able to evaluate how your personal attributes fit with those necessary for success. You will understand that preparation and education are lifetime activities and how professional organizations can aid your career growth.

The History of Property Management

A professor once said, "The first property management job was to assign living spaces on Noah's Ark!"

We aren't absolutely certain as to the accuracy of this statement, but we do know that property management has been around for several thousand years. The ancient Egyptians had overseers to manage their estates as did the Greeks and Romans. While they utilized mostly slave labor, their job was to supervise the upkeep of the estates which protected the value and to maximize the income. This isn't much different than the goals of modern day property management.

In the middle ages, property managers in Europe collected rents from the serfs for a lord or vassal. Part of the rent was kept by the lord or vassal and the rest was sent up along the feudal chain to another lord, vassal or king.

Later, in England, estate managers handled the affairs of vast estates including housing for workers, maintenance of improvements as well as agricultural supervision. In pre-revolutionary America, estate managers carried on much of these same duties, often for holders of land grants who were absentee owners.

There were a number of events which increased the importance of and changed the scope of property management.

Large cities were an early phenomena of the Mediterranean areas. Because of a warmer climate and long growing seasons, labor was able to produce more food per agricultural worker. This freed labor from agricultural pursuits and allowed the growth of major cities. In ancient Rome, there were many buildings six and seven stories high which were rented to citizens. Rome had its rent collectors and property managers. Large cities did not emerge in central Europe until hundreds of years later.

Property Management—A Profession of Service

THE MOLDBOARD PLOW

Prior to the moldboard plow, the earth was tilled with a stick or iron spike that was dragged by horse, oxen or a human being. These tools made a narrow furrow in the hard earth. Plantings were limited to their growth by the compaction of the soil.

The **MOLDBOARD PLOW** *had a curved plate attached to the spike that could lift and turn over a wide furrow of ground.* The yield from the land increased dramatically. In middle Europe, this freed labor for other pursuits. It allowed for a nonagricultural lifestyle and was a factor in the growth of the cities. The growth of the cities required housing, which was primarily rental housing, and with this housing the need for management.

THE INDUSTRIAL REVOLUTION

The industrial revolution in England, with the harnessing of first water power and then steam, allowed for factories to mass produce goods that were once produced by hand or otherwise unavailable. The needs of the factories for workers brought laborers in from farm communities leading to a rapid growth of cities and in rental housing. The industrial revolution spread from England to other European countries and the United States. Steam and later electric power allowed for horizontal growth of factories which earlier had power conveyed from water wheels by gears, drive shafts and belts which necessitated vertical factories.

THE ELECTRIC ELEVATOR

The Otis elevator was the first practical elevator and was powered by electricity.

It provided dependable vertical travel, thus allowing tall buildings to be constructed. This increased the value of land in the central cities as it allowed for greater utilization of ground space. Buildings were still limited as to height by the fact that the lower floors required extremely wide walls to support the masonary construction of the upper floors.

STRUCTURAL STEEL

The use of structural steel allowed for modern day skyscrapers. The steel frame allowed relatively light exterior sheathing which made tall buildings possible without the loss of space from massive supporting lower walls.

THE GREAT DEPRESSION

The depression that followed the stock market crash of 1929 resulted in thousands of properties being foreclosed and held by lenders who could not find buyers. The great depression was actually a boost for professional management.

Career Opportunities in Property Management

There is a present need for trained professional property managers in a number of areas. Numerous specialties are available within the property management field to utilize a wide range of talent.

Property managers fall into different categories:

Employee Manager. This manager is an employee of an owner or corporation and has management duties dealing with one or more properties.

Resident Manager. A manager of an apartment property who resides on the premises.

Independent Property Manager. These managers handle property individually or with the assistance of their employees. These managers handle property for more than one owner and have agency duties toward each client they represent.

There are a number of employment opportunities within the property management field.

THE GOVERNMENT

Federal, state, county and local governmental units as well as agencies of the government employ property managers. Although titles vary, property managers are responsible for maintenance, repair and protection of real property that is government owned or leased for governmental use. In some cases they actually lease government property to others.

The **GENERAL SERVICES ADMINISTRATION** is the real estate management agency for the federal government. It is the largest single employer of property management personnel in the world.

www.gsa.gov
(General Services Administration)

REITs

We are seeing a rapid growth in **REAL ESTATE INVESTMENT TRUSTS**. These trusts simply buy and manage income properties for the benefit of their stockholders.

Property Management—A Profession of Service

REITs are publicly traded and, by law, must distribute 95 percent of their funds from operation to the shareholders.

They have an advantage over corporate structures in that they are not taxed on earnings distributed to shareholders. Therefore, they avoid the double taxation of corporations.

Many large developers, limited partnerships and other property owners become REITS in order to have liquidity. REIT shares have a ready market. Many are listed on the stock exchange (New York, American or NASDAQ).

Today, REITs are the primary buyers of large income properties because of their easy access to capital. They can raise capital by selling common stock, preferred stock or bonds. They can also borrow from commercial lenders. Some REITs have open lines of credit approaching the billion dollar mark. While some REITs operate in just a few geographical markets, others operate nationwide.

 www.nareit.com
(National Association of Real Estate Investment Trusts - NAREITs)

Some REITs specialize in types of property. As an example, some REITs buy fast food restaurants of particular franchisees and lease them to the operators. There are a half dozen REITs that only own factory outlet shopping centers. Others own only apartments or shopping centers.

Many REITs operate based on opportunity. They may buy or even develop properties that are residential, office, commercial and industrial in nature. Some REITs look for distress properties with serious problems. They then solve the problems. Others only want quality properties.

Because of the significant ownership role of REITs, they are a prominent employer of property managers.

CEOs of REITs tend to have backgrounds in development or finance rather than property management.

A reason for this could be the fact that many REITs were development companies just a few years ago. These companies went public to be able to liquify assets (stocks) and because of the ability of REITs to both raise equity capital and to borrow funds. Some property managers are now rising to the top as executives retire.

REITs raid other REITs for employees by paying them what they are worth. Many property managers are now making executive salaries from $100,000 to one-half million per year.

> *The REITs have been one of the best things that ever happened for property management as far as increasing the manager's income is concerned.*

Because REITs are publicly traded, management is under tremendous pressure from large institutional stockholders to show significant growth in funds from operations. This is the standard measurement for REIT performance.

Because of this pressure, there is pressure to show improvements quarter by quarter. This is unfortunate, because in looking at the short-term, long-term goals tend to come secondary. Immediate expenses as to property upgrade might be put back. Maintenance expenses might also be reduced and staff might suffer layoffs. These short-term fixes to increase FFO (Funds From Operation) might in the long-term be detrimental to the shareholders even though they offer instant gratification.

Property managers in some instances know that growth rates of the past cannot be sustained. When growth rates slow or funds from operations actually show a decline, stocks tend to tumble.

Management often has income related to stock performance so management suffers as well. It is expected that a number of REITs, currently the darlings of Wall Street, will tumble as to stock prices. The REITS themselves are generally healthy. It is just that they cannot show the growth in earnings quarter after quarter that was expected by stock market analysts.

FINANCIAL INSTITUTIONS

Between foreclosure and disposition of property, it must be managed. While many financial institutions use independent property management firms, there are still thousands of property managers employed by financial institutions.

CORPORATIONS

> *Many large corporations have over one-half of their assets in real property.*

In recent years, they have begun to realize that property management is an executive function and not necessarily a blue-collar function. Property management has been raised to the Vice Presidential level in many corporations.

Corporate property management might include leasing space and the supervision of leases. The property manager working in a major corporate environment might have responsibilities as to space alterations and maintenance as to both corporate owned and leased space. In many cases, maintenance is separated from corporate property managerial duties and is given to plant superintendents or plant engineers.

Property Management—A Profession of Service

Corporate property managers are often responsible for the security of excess property until it is needed or disposed of. However, in many cases security is under the plant superintendent rather than a property management duty.

Corporate property managers may act as lessors as well as lessees in subleasing or leasing corporate leased or corporate owned property.

FRANCHISES

Franchises realize the importance of property management as to leasing and maintenance. Expansion would not be possible without good property management.

EMPLOYEES OF PRIVATE OWNERS

Some real estate brokers and non-licensees work as employees of individual owners rather than as agents. They manage one or a group of properties for the owner with employee responsibilities.

PRIVATE MANAGEMENT FIRMS

Many real estate brokerage offices operate property management services.

Some just handle a few properties while others are well staffed divisions handling hundreds of properties for dozens if not hundreds of separate owners.

There are many firms which handle property management exclusively. By not competing with general brokerage offices they are able to obtain a significant portion of their business from referrals.

Some property management firms specialize in particular types of property while others only perform a single property management function, such as leasing agents.

ON-SITE MANAGEMENT

The greatest number of property managers are on-site managers who live and/or work exclusively at a property where they have management duties.

They are generally employees of either the property owners or of a management firm. Most residential managers are employed to manage residential property but on-site managers are found in other areas, such as mini-warehouse management.

WOMEN IN PROPERTY MANAGEMENT

While there have always been many female leasing agents, women are just beginning to enter the field with full property management duties and responsibilities.

A past problem was that few women felt that they had knowledge of the physical plants as to maintenance, repair and improvements. This is slowly changing as we find more women in the trades and serving as general contractors. There are also many courses available which cover maintenance of the physical plant.

Women should realize that a great many men entered the property management field with the concept "if it's broken, tap it with a hammer and if that doesn't work, call a repairman." It doesn't take long for on-the-job training to take hold.

MINORITIES IN PROPERTY MANAGEMENT

Minorities have primarily served as resident managers although there are minority property managers and minority-controlled property management firms. Most African American property managers manage properties where tenants are primarily African American.

Corporate America has a number of African American property managers. A great many African American property managers work for government agencies.

Very few property managers working for REITs (other than resident managers) are African American. REITs seem to have a very solid steel ceiling for black advancement.

Asians and Hispanics seem to be better represented in the mid-management levels of property management, but relatively few rise to the corporate level working for REITs. We can only guess at the reasons why minorities fail to reach the upper level management positions within REITs.

Why Owners Choose Management

Many owners choose property management for economic and personal reasons.

ECONOMIC REASONS

Property managers can simply do a better job of management than most owners because of training and experience.

8

Property Management—A Profession of Service

A professional property manager has a better understanding of the rental market. They are more likely to locate tenants and negotiate leases having more favorable terms than are owners who relegate property management to a part-time business.

Even owners who have the training and ability to do an excellent management job of their own property, nevertheless, will use professional managers. The reason is the value of the owner's time. A surgeon can better use valuable time performing surgery than trying to collect rent from a delinquent tenant or making calls for repairs to a property.

The Main Financial Benefits of Hiring a Property Manager

Increased Rents. The property manager is less eager to give away rent or lower rents when the necessity to do so is not indicated by market conditions.

Reduced Vacancy Factor. By qualifying prospective tenants, the property manager can select tenants who will have a longer tenancy period. This can be aided by lease terms. This results in lower turnover of tenancy which equates to a lower vacancy factor.

Reduce Tenant Damage. Through qualifying tenants and requiring reasonable property damage bonds, the probability of damage to the premises is reduced and when damage does occur, the damage bond is usually sufficient to cover the damage.

Reduced Repair Costs. Good property management will include preventative maintenance programs which will reduce the likelihood of costly emergency repairs for operating systems.

Reduced Expenses. Because of purchasing power in managing a great many units, property managers can obtain services and supplies at significant discounts from the prices offered to an individual owner. In addition, a professional manager is less likely to be taken advantage of by a vendor or service provider.

Management Planning. A professional property manager will plan ahead for changes in tenant mix, changes in uses, changes in lease terms, etc. based on the goals of the owner.

Prolonging Economic Life. Property goes through a period of development and lease up. It then goes through what can be a lengthy period of maturity and, finally, it enters a period of decline usually resulting in abandonment or demolition.

Some properties go through these phases rapidly and others very slowly. There are apartment structures in Europe which have been desirable for several hundred years. Physically, nonresidential structures can maintain an economic life span far longer than the 39 1/2 years that the IRS offers for depreciation. Property management cannot only extend a property's life span, it can reverse the clock through remodeling or restoration.

PERSONAL REASONS

Many property owners realize that they don't have the temperament to deal with tenants or problems. Some let problems bother their peace of mind. Others are too nice and end up being taken advantage of by tenants. These property owners hesitate to get tough as to rule violations, rent collections and evictions. There are thousands of owners who give their tenants below-market rent. They're afraid to raise rents or just don't want to appear to be a bad person. In many cases, owners have run their properties as charitable institutions rather than in a businesslike manner.

Those owners who recognize their short comings choose professional management.

Attributes of a Successful Manager

While an estimated two-thirds of our national wealth is in real estate, we have far more stock brokers than property managers.

In recent years, we've come to realize the importance of professional property management. The stock market has played a significant part in this realization. The success of some Real Estate Investment Trusts (REITs) has led to the understanding that all managers are not the same. Professionals who plan their work and work their plan can out-perform the pack.

Property managers must be both detail and people-oriented.

They must be meticulous as to record keeping, follow through on tenant complaints and problems and continually strive to do things better.

Property managers must understand the needs and goals of both owners and tenants. While acting as an agent for the owner they must, nevertheless, treat tenants with fairness and understanding.

Specific qualities that a successful manager should possess include the following.

MENTAL STAMINA

The property manager must remain focused on a problem and seek a solution. The "hot shot" salesperson who wants to close a transaction and then forget it will not succeed in property management where the work just begins with the lease.

Property Management—A Profession of Service

INTEGRITY

A property manager's word must be his or her bond when dealing with owners, tenants and contractors. Those dealing with a property manager must know that they can rely on the manager to carry out what it is he or she said will be done.

ORGANIZATIONAL SKILLS

A property manager must be organized so that multiple problems can be addressed and followed at the same time.

BRAVERY

You may not view it as such, but property management is a field that requires bravery. The property manager cannot hesitate to deliver bad news to an owner or tenant. The property manager cannot be coerced by attorneys in lease negotiations or give in to unreasonable demands by irate tenants. This all requires bravery.

PEOPLE SKILLS

We normally view property management as simply a management of fixed assets. It is more than this. The manager deals with people as much as he or she does with property. Some writers talk about the property manager who manages people. We don't like this use of the word "managing." Managing denotes using. A good property manager does not use people.

The property manager works with people to create a harmonious and mutually beneficial relationship.

Interpersonal relation skills are important for success. However, these skills can be learned. Property managers must be able to correct problem behavior in a tenant or worker without generating resentment or personal animosity.

The property manager must become a listener more than a teller. The manager must strive to understand other people and what it is that they want. Don't view this as the manipulation of people. It is working with people for mutual advantages.

ABILITY TO PRIORITIZE

The property manager cannot allow him or herself to become focused on pennies and forget the dollars. The property manager must first focus his or her efforts and resources on the most important problems.

Priorities will differ among owners. The property manager CANNOT forget that he or she stands in the shoes of the owner as an agent of the owner.

GOAL ORIENTED

A property manager cannot manage by simply putting out fires or oiling the hinge when it squeaks. He or she must set goals for a property with the coordination of the owner. When the owner knows the goals and has been a part of their development, the manager will then remain focused on these goals. The manager must periodically review actions and policies as to reaching those goals.

Setting goals doesn't necessarily mean that those goals will be reached. However, the efforts of the property manager to reach them will only help the property and the owner.

COMMUNICATION SKILLS

The property manager must be able to clearly and succinctly explain an idea, problem or solution in writing as well as verbally.

In learning to outline a letter, a property manager will understand organization of thoughts and priority of messages to be conveyed. The property manager will then be able to use this organizational skill verbally by thinking through what has to be communicated before engaging his or her tongue.

TEAM ORIENTED

A property manager must realize that he or she is not a prima donna but part of a management team. The on-site manager, accountant and even maintenance personnel are part of the team and must be treated as team members. If one does not do his or her job, everyone will suffer.

ABILITY TO DELEGATE

Anyone can say, "Do This!" This is not delegation.

Delegation involves giving a person "authority" as well as "responsibility."

All too often, a person is held accountable without the authority to do something correctly.

Delegation also involves a system to monitor progress without appearing to look over a person's shoulder. Instead of asking, "Is it done yet?" a better way would be to ask, "What is the status of....?"

Some offices have short morning meetings where the status of all actions are reviewed. This helps persons feel that they are team members and also to understand what others are doing.

FLEXIBILITY

Property managers must be flexible. They must be able to think in terms of alternatives, "...if this happens" or, "Who could use this property?"

BE PART OF THE SOLUTION

Anyone can spell out a problem. However, no one likes the bearer of bad news. A good property manager looks at a problem as a challenge. The first thing he or she must analyze is:

1. What happened? Am I sure of the facts?
2. What will be the result of what happened?
3. What are the alternatives to alleviate the problem?
4. What is the best of these alternatives?
5. Why is it the best alternative?

Property managers must then communicate the problem, the alternatives and their recommendations to the owners or supervisors. This is known as **COMPLETED STAFF WORK**. Never present a problem without recommending a solution. Be prepared to defend your solution.

Completed staff work is what management is all about.

If you cannot think or analyze, you become redundant and may very well be replaced by a computer. Once you become involved in completed staff work, you will find that people will be more willing to listen to you and follow your advice.

ACCEPT RESPONSIBILITY

Instead of blaming others or using the bland excuse of "It just happened," be willing instead to accept responsibility.

BENEFIT ORIENTED

Property management is concerned with maximizing the long-term benefits that can be derived from real estate.

AGENCY FOCUSED

Instead of being "me" focused, a property manager must think about his or her principal as being the primary purpose of business. The interest of the client must always come first. If you can adopt this attitude, you will serve your principal well and in turn you will be successful.

> *Doing for others rather than to others will result in referral business, long-term relationships and prosperity.*

A MONEY MANAGER

Property managers can best meet owners' needs by fully understanding their needs and financial situation. This would include making payments on debt service, and even arranging financing for improvements and renovations. A property manager should periodically review an owner's debt service and consider refinancing if it would be in the best interest of that owner.

Completed staff work would involve knowing the interest rates, locating a lender and preparing a loan application for the owner to sign. A number of property management contracts provide for a fee involving this service.

Licensing Requirements

> *Generally, renting or leasing real property in an agency capacity for others requires a real estate broker's license.*

This license requirement extends to offering to rent, soliciting rental listings and negotiation of leases and/or rental terms.

There are exemptions to the licensing requirement.

OWNERS

An owner need not be licensed to manage his or her own property.

WITHOUT COMPENSATION

Doing acts without compensation may exempt a person from licensing requirements.

The California Attorney General 32 Ops Atty Gen. 210 stated that "for a compensation" is critical to require licensing. According to the Attorney General, unless the buying and selling of promissory notes secured by a deed of trust is done "tor a compensation," the person buying and selling such notes is not a real estate broker within the requirements of the real estate law. Based on this reasoning, compensation would also be a critical requirement for licensing of property managers.

POWER OF ATTORNEY

Persons holding an executed power of attorney from an owner of real property can sell or lease the property under the power of attorney.

This is based on the legal concept that if a person can deal with their property, then they can transfer that right to another. Courts have not allowed this exception to be used by a non-licensee to conduct an ongoing property management business.

In some states, employees of licensed property management firms are allowed to show property accept rental applications and deposits as well as to provide rental information to others without being licensed.

Case Example

Sheetz v. Edmonds (1988) 201 C.A. 3d 143

Sheetz managed 23 separate properties for compensation. All of the properties were owned by a friend. Sheetz was not licensed, although engaged full time in property management. Sheetz was operating under a power of attorney which he claimed allowed him an exemption from Department of Real Estate licensing.

The Real Estate Commissioner issued a cease and desist order for Sheetz to stop managing these properties. Sheetz was the plaintiff in this action against Edmonds (the Real Estate Commissioner).

The Court of Appeals upheld the action of the real estate commissioner. The court determined that the exemption for a power of attorney applied to particular transactions or very limited periods. The exemption cannot be used as a substitute for obtaining a broker's license.

In this case, it was clear that the power of attorney was given for the purpose of evading licensing requirements.

HOTEL MANAGER

A manager of a hotel, motel or auto and trailer park, resident manager of an apartment building, apartment complex, or court, or to an employee of any such manager generally need not hold a broker's license.

TRANSIENT OCCUPANCY

Any person or entity (including an employee of a broker) who solicits or arranges and accepts reservations and/or money for transient occupancies is generally exempt from licensing.

RESIDENT MANAGERS

Resident managers of apartment buildings generally need not be licensed as real estate brokers even though they handle rentals as part of their duties.

Professionalism in Property Management

Property managers realize the need to improve their current skills and to learn new skills to meet the needs created by today's property management requirements. The professionalism of the industry has grown from within the industry itself and was not mandated by others.

"Professional trade associations" meet the needs of property management for today and tomorrow.

INSTITUTE OF REAL ESTATE MANAGEMENT (IREM)

The address of IREM is: Institute of Real Estate Management, 430 North Michigan Avenue, Chicago, IL 60611-4090.

IREM is an institute of the National Association of Realtors®. IREM offers educational and professional programs in property management.

IREM was founded in 1933. Guidelines were established that members agreed to adhere to. The basic guidelines covered protection of clients by using trust funds and employee bonding as well as agreeing not to accept any form of kickbacks from contractors and suppliers without full disclosure to the clients.

Property Management—A Profession of Service

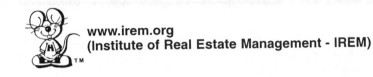

www.irem.org
(Institute of Real Estate Management - IREM)

In 1938, IREM set qualification standards for its professional designations.

Certified Property Manager (CPM)

The Certified Property Manager (CPM) designation is likely the most prestigious and widely recognized designation for professional property management.

To become a CPM, candidates must meet criteria set forth by IREM and obtain 260 points, 160 of which are required.

Criteria

1. Be a candidate for at least one year.
2. Be currently in the real estate management business.
3. Either hold a real estate license or certify that you are not required to have one.
4. Be a member or affiliated with a local board of Realtors®.
5. Be approved by your local IREM chapter.
6. Continue to subscribe to the Code of Ethics of the Certified Property Managers.
7. Be current with all national and chapter service fees.
8. Have at least a high school diploma and complete an application.

160 Required Points

These points are received from three areas:

1. IREM courses.
2. Management plan (developed for an actual property).
3. Experience.

100 Elective Points

Elective points are earned by completing elective courses as well as attaining other professional designations.

Accredited Residential Manager (ARM)

Specialists in residential property management are designated as Accredited Residential Managers (ARM).

Unlike the CPM designation which covers various types of property, the ARM designation is strictly for residential property. Candidates must:

1. submit letters of recommendation;
2. pass a designated examination;
3. meet experience requirements.

Accredited Management Organization (AMO)

The Accredited Management Organization (AMO) designation is given to firms rather than to individuals.

To attain the AMO designation, the firm must have a person with a CPM designation in charge of the firm's management operations and must have authority and responsibility in a number of designated areas. The executive CPM must also complete an IREM course covering "Managing The Management Company."

Educational Courses

IREM offers educational courses in over 85 cities as well as correspondence courses covering a wide range of management and management-related topics. Besides national courses, there are also local chapter network courses. Course offerings include:

MKL402 Marketing and Leasing Strategies for Multifamily Properties.
MKL403 Marketing and Leasing Strategies for Office Buildings.
MKL404 Marketing and Leasing Strategies for Retail Property.
BDM601 Expanding Your Business.
HRS402 Managing Human Resources for Optional Results.
HRS603 Enhancing Your Leadership Style.
FIN402 Identifying Financial Alternatives at the Property Level.
ASM401 Transforming Client Expectations into Business Success.
ASM402 Improving Income Property Performance.
ASM603 Financing and Valuation Strategies for Real Estate Assets.
ASM604 Measuring Performance of Real Estate Assets.
ASM605 Applying Investment Criteria to Real Estate Asset Decisions.
LRM402 Risk Management: Protecting People, Property and Profits.
LRM603 Avoiding Surprises: Trends in Regulation and Legislation.
MKL201 Mastering the Essentials of Marketing and Leasing.
FIN201 Mastering Property Budgeting and Accounting.
HRS201 Managing and Motivating a Property Team.
LRM201 Do's and Don'ts of Fair Housing Practice.
MNT201 Managing Maintenance Operations.

CLM201 Managing Small Commercial Properties.
MTF201 Managing Public Housing.
MTF202 Managing Government-Insured Multifamily Housing.
MTF203 Managing Community Associations.
MTF204 Managing Single-Family Homes and Small Residential Properties.
ETH800 Ethics for the Real Estate Manager.

IREM also offers a binder of 57 forms for leasing, occupancy, recordkeeping and reporting, maintenance, personnel management, etc., with the right to print these forms on your photo copiers.

They also (for a nominal fee) offer General Management Contract forms, condominium association management forms, as well as forms for both office building inspection and office building management.

BUILDING OWNERS AND MANAGERS ASSOCIATION INTERNATIONAL (BOMA)

The address of BOMA is: Building Owners and Managers Association International, 1201 New York Avenue, N.W. Suite 300, Washington, D.C. 20005.

Founded in 1907, BOMA is a federation of 94 local associations with over 16,000 members representing more than six billion square feet of commercial property in North America.

BOMA has local chapters in all major cities. BOMA holds an annual convention which is a major event as well as an important office building show.

BOMA has an educational institute (BOMI) which promotes the interests of the real estate industry through programs of personal development and by collecting, analyzing and disseminating information.

www.boma.org
(Building Owners and Managers Association International - BOMA)

BOMI offers several important designations:

Real Property Administrator (RPA)

To earn the prestigious designation RPA, a candidate must complete the following courses that are offered by the Institute:

1. The Design, Operation and Maintenance of Building Systems, Part I.
2. The Design, Operation and Maintenance of Building Systems, Part II.
3. Property Manager's Guide to Commercial Real Estate Law.
4. Real Estate Investment and Finance.
5. Environmental Health and Safety Issues.
6. Ethics is Good Business - Short Course.

In addition to the above required courses, the RPA also requires two of the following electives:

1. Risk Management and Insurance.
2. Fundamentals of Real Property Administration.
3. Leasing and Marketing for Property Managers.
4. Asset Management.

Facilities Management Administrator (FMA)

BOMI offers a Facilities Management Administrator (FMA) designation that requires completion of seven mandatory courses and an ethics course.

Additional Designations

BOMI also offers a Systems Maintenance Technician (SMT) and Systems Maintenance Administrator (SMA) designation upon completion of required courses.

BOMI courses prepare individuals NOT only for top management positions but also for hands-on operating positions working in the trenches.

PROPERTY MANAGEMENT ASSOCIATION (PMA)

The address of this organization is: Property Management Association, 7900 Wisconsin Avenue, Suite 204, Bethesda, MD 20814.

Founded in 1952, this professional group consists primarily of property managers in the Washington, D.C. area. There are monthly meetings and special seminars. They do have members in other areas of the country.

www.npma.org
(National Property Management Association - NPMA)

Property Management—A Profession of Service

PMA has a number of excellent publications, such as:

1. Lighting for Safety and Security.
2. Roofing: A Guide to Specifying and Obtaining Services by Contract.
3. Safety and Security: A Guide to Obtaining Services by Contract.
4. Swimming Pool Management: A Guide to Specifying and Obtaining Services by Contract.
5. Pest Control: A Guide to Specifying and Obtaining Services by Contract.
6. Risk Management and Insurance: A Guide to Specifying and Obtaining Services by Contract.
7. Elevator Maintenance: A Guide to Specifying and Obtaining Services by Contract.
8. Grounds Care: A Guide to Specifying and Obtaining Services by Contract.
9. Painting: A Guide to Specifying and Obtaining Services by Contract.

From the above partial list of publications (which are also available to nonmembers) you can see that PMA is a "hands on" type of organization. They also have a monthly bulletin with informative articles about upcoming seminars. "How To Collect Rent" is an example of one of the PMA's more practical seminars.

INTERNATIONAL REAL ESTATE INSTITUTE

To contact, write: International Real Estate Institute, 8383 East Evans Road, Scottsdale, AZ 85260, or they can be reached at 1-602-998-8267, or on-line at e-mail: irei@iami.org.

Membership in the association includes the professional designation RPM (Registered Property Manager). There are no educational requirements for this designation, but the institute does offer educational programs and numerous publications including the Global Real Estate News.

URBAN LAND INSTITUTE (ULI)

The institute can be reached by writing: Urban Land Institute, 1025 Thomas Jefferson Street, N.W. Suite 500 West, Washington, D.C. 20007-5201 or by calling 1-800-321-5011.

The Urban Land Institute was founded in 1926 as a nonprofit education and research institute. Its 13,000 members cover the entire spectrum of land use and development. The ULI sells over 50,000 books annually offering professional information. They also conduct seminars. While primary emphasis is on development, the ULI also researches and publishes excellent material on the leasing and management of both residential and commercial properties.

www.uli.org
(Urgan Land Institute)

AMERICAN INDUSTRIAL REAL ESTATE ASSOCIATION

The association can be reached by writing: American Industrial Real Estate Association, MCI Center, Suite 600, 700 South Flower Street, Los Angeles, CA 90017.

The association has available excellent lease and contract forms for both industrial and commercial property. We have included a number of their forms in this book.

Another organization that offers a complete set of property management forms is Professional Publishing. For sample forms you can call this company at 1-800-288-2006.

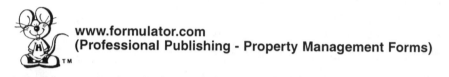

www.formulator.com
(Professional Publishing - Property Management Forms)

INTERNATIONAL COUNCIL OF SHOPPING CENTERS (ICSC)

Write them at: International Council of Shopping Centers, 665 Fifth Avenue, New York, NY 10022-5370.

This is a specialty organization which offers a number of excellent educational programs as well as professional designations and marketing awards. They also publish an extensive array of books covering all aspects of shopping center management.

www.icsc.org
(International Council of Shopping Centers - ICSC)

Certified Leasing Specialist (CLS)

This award is obtained by meeting experience and educational requirements as well as passing a written examination.

1. Experience requirements include full-time (85 percent) experience in shopping center leasing for at least four of the prior six years.

2. Completion of ICSC Leasing I and Leasing II certificate courses as well as the ICSC Leasing II Advanced Certificate Program, including 30 hours of college-level continuing education courses in approved areas.

3. Pass the written CLS examination.

4. Continue a mandated program of continuing education after achieving the CLS designation.

Property Management—A Profession of Service

Certified Shopping Center Manager (CSM)

Over 2,400 professionals from all over the world have achieved this prestigious designation. Requirements include experience, education substitution and passing a comprehensive examination:

1. A candidate for the CSM designation must have had four years experience as a manager of a shopping center. Experience must include maintenance, leasing, marketing and promotions. An applicant can substitute designated course completions for the fourth year of experience.

2. Pass a six-hour, two-part examination.

Accredited Shopping Center Manager (ASM)

The **ACCREDITED SHOPPING CENTER MANAGEMENT (ASM)** designation is only available to international members practicing outside the United States. Requirements for this designation are similar to the CSM designation requirements and the examination is parallel to the CSM examination.

Accredited Marketing Director (AMD)

The **AMD** designation is available for candidates who have served as a shopping center marketing director for four years or served as a shopping center manager with duties encompassing those of a shopping center marketing director.

Educational requirements may be substituted for the fourth year of experience.

The AMD examination consisting of 100 items and is administered over a period of four and one-half hours.

Senior Level Accreditation

Senior level designation is available for Certified Shopping Center Managers (SCSM) and Certified Marketing Directors (SCMD).

Qualifications include achievement of the CSM or CMD designations plus continued educational requirements. They must have held their CSM or CMD designations for three years.

Awards

ICSC has an award program based on an International Marketing Competition (The MAXI Award) as well as International Design and Development Awards.

The MAXI award is given in a number of categories:

1. community service;
2. public relations;
3. consumer or trade advertising;
4. sales promotion and merchandizing;
5. grand opening, expansion and renovation;
6. retailer development;
7. center productivity.

The International Design and Development Awards Program has two general categories:

1. innovative design and construction of a project;
2. renovation or expansion of an existing project.

COMMUNITY ASSOCIATIONS INSTITUTE

Community Associations Institute, 1630 Duke Street, Alexandria, VA 22314.

www.caionline.org
(Community Association Institute)

The **COMMUNITY ASSOCIATIONS INSTITUTE (CAI)** *acts as a clearinghouse for ideas and practices for successful operations and management of all types of residential common-interest housing.* Membership includes homeowner associations, property management firms and service providers.

CAI offers workshops, conferences, educational programs, as well as books, periodicals, and newsletters. They also have a website for subjects relating to common-interest developments. There are currently 59 local chapters including 10 chapters in California.

CAI offers a number of professional designations.

Certified Manager of Community Associations (CMCA)

> *The CMCA designations certifies that a manager has the basic knowledge necessary to manage any type of community association.*

Requirements for the CMCA designation include completion of the M-100 Essentials of Community Association Management course, pass the M-100 examination and pass the National Certification Exam. Recertification is required every two years.

Property Management—A Profession of Service

Association Management Specialist (AMS)

This designation is available for candidates who have passed the M-100 course and have had at least two years of association management experience in specific functional areas. The certification must be renewed every three years.

Professional Community Association Manager (PCAM)

This is the highest professional designation available from CAI.

To achieve this designation, candidates are required to have at least three years of experience in common-interest development management plus having graduated from an extensive educational program set forth by CAI. The designation must be renewed every three years through work experience, service activities and continuing education.

INTERNATIONAL FACILITY MANAGEMENT ASSOCIATION

1 E. Greenway Plaza, Suite 1100, Houston, TX 77046-0194.

IFMA is an international organization of management involved in coordinating the physical workplace with the people and work of the firm. They primarily deal with managing industrial and commercial facilities. Membership is available to professionals and educators involved in at least two of the following activities:

1. Long-range facility planning;
2. Annual facility planning;
3. Facility financial forecasting and budgeting;
4. Real estate acquisition and/or disposal;
5. Interior space planning;
6. Architectural and engineering planning and design;
7. Environmental health and safety;
8. New construction and/or renovation work;
9. Maintenance and operations management of the physical plant;
10. Facility business functions.

www.ifma.org
(International Facility Management Association - IFMA)

IFMA has programs and conventions around the world and offers specialized councils for specialized management that include health care facilities, academic facilities, museums/cultural institutions, religious facilities, research and development facilities, sports and recreational facilities, etc.

Members can earn the Certified Facility Manager (CFM) designation through education and testing.

═══════ CHAPTER 1 SUMMARY ═══════

Property management originally evolved from the needs of the wealthy to have someone care for their estates. The moldboard plow was a factor in the growth of the cities because it dramatically increased crop production allowing labor to be freed from agricultural duties.

Property managers fall into a number of categories:

1. Employee managers.
2. Resident managers.
3. Independent property managers.

There are a variety of employment opportunities for property managers at the present time. They include:

1. Government.
2. Real Estate Investment Trusts.
3. Financial institutions.
4. Corporations.
5. Franchises.
6. Employees of private owners.
7. Private management firms.
8. On-site management.

Women are just beginning to enter top positions in property management although many women are engaged in leasing activities. African Americans have not cracked the upper levels of property management in significant numbers.

Owners choose professional management for various reasons including:

1. Increasing rents.
2. Reducing vacancy factors.
3. Reducing repair costs.
4. Reducing tenant damage.
5. Reducing expenses.
6. Management planning.
7. Prolonging economic life.

Property Management—A Profession of Service

Attributes of a successful property manager, include:

1. Mental stamina.
2. Integrity.
3. Organizational skills.
4. Bravery.
5. People skills.
6. Ability to prioritize.
7. Goal oriented.
8. Communication skills.
9. Team oriented.
10. Ability to delegate.
11. Flexibility.
12. Be part of the solution.
13. Benefit oriented.
14. Agency focused.
15. A money manager.

A number of professional organizations provide important management training, have excellent publications and recognize career development with professional awards and recognition.

The Institute of Real Estate Management (IREM) is affiliated with the National Association of Realtors®.

The IREM offers many programs and classes. It also offers professional designations of Certified Property Manager (CPM), Accredited Residential Manager (ARM) and Accredited Management Organization (AMD).

The Building Owners and Managers Association International (BOMA) has an extensive educational program and offers a number of professional designations including Real Property Administrator (RPA), Facilities Management Administrator (FMA), Systems Maintenance Technician (SMT) and Systems Maintenance Administrator (SMA).

The Property Management Association has a number of excellent publications available to members and non-members.

The International Real Estate Institute offers the Registered Property Manager (RPM) designation. They also provide worldwide contacts for members.

The Urban Land Institute provides books, studies and seminars. They sponsor research in many areas concerning property management.

The American Industrial Real Estate Association has developed lease and contract forms for industrial, office and commercial property.

The International Council of Shopping Centers offers a variety of educational programs and offers professional designations including Certified Leasing Specialist (CLS), Certified Shopping Center Manager (CSM), Accredited Shopping Center Manager (ASM), Accredited Marketing Director (AMD), Senior Certified Shopping Center Manager (SCSM) and Senior Certified Marketing Director (SCMD).

The Community Associations Institute is involved in common ownership residential management. They offer professional designations including Certified Manager of Community Associations (CMCA), Association Management Specialist (AMS) and Professional Community Association Manager (PCAM).

The International Facility Management Association (IFMA) specializes in the evolution of the office.

CLASS DISCUSSION TOPICS

1. Name some of the larger property management firms in your areas. What types of property do they manage?

2. Go through the "Help Wanted" ads in your local Sunday newspaper. Identify ads covering property management functions. Are they all labeled "Property Managers"?

3. Which firms headquartered in your area would have need for a property management professional? Why?

4. Identify property in your area that appears in need of professional property management. Why?

5. From the yellow pages of your local telephone book, identify those property managers and firms which have professional designations.

6. What areas, if any, of property management are of particular interest to you? Why?

CHAPTER 1 QUIZ

1. The high-rise office buildings were made possible because of:
   - A. the moldboard plow
   - B. structural steel
   - C. the electric elevator
   - D. both B and C

2. Which of the following property management areas employ the largest number of people?
   - A. Franchise leasing
   - B. Resident managers
   - C. Government
   - D. REIT management

3. Characteristics of REITs include:
   A. publicly traded
   B. purchasers of large properties
   C. not taxed on profits passed on as dividends
   D. all of the above

4. Benefits offered by professional property management include:
   A. lower vacancy factors
   B. higher rents
   C. prolonging economic life
   D. all of the above

5. Personal attributes for success in property management include:
   A. people skills
   B. goal oriented
   C. flexibility
   D. all of the above

6. CPM stands for:
   A. Certificate in Property Management
   B. Corporate Property Manager
   C. Certified Property Manager
   D. Consumer Protection Marketing

7. ARM stands for:
   A. Association of Retail Managers
   B. Accredited Residential Manager
   C. American Restaurant Management
   D. Alliance of Residential Managers

8. AMO stands for:
   A. Accredited Management Organization
   B. American Maintenance Organization
   C. Association of Management Officers
   D. Alliance of Management Organizations

9. BOMA stands for:
   A. Benevolent Order of Managing Agents
   B. Building Owners and Managers Association
   C. Builders, Operators and Managers Alliance
   D. Building Operators Maintenance Association

10. RPA stands for:
    A. Real Property Administrator
    B. Residential Property Administrator
    C. Real Estate Professional Alliance
    D. Repair, Protect and Administer

Answers: 1. D; 2. B; 3. D; 4. D; 5. D; 6. C; 7. B; 8. A; 9. B; 10. A

Preparing for Management

KEY WORDS AND TERMS

Agency
Appreciation
Bonding
Capital Gains
Cash Flow
Depreciation
Gross Multiplier
Hedge Against Inflation
Hold-Harmless Clause
Impossibility of Performance
Incapacity
Indemnification
Inventory List
Lease File
Leveraged
Management Plan

Mutual Agreement
Negative Cash Flow
Occupancy Rules and Regulations
Operating Account
Operating Procedures
Psychic Income
Pro forma Statement
Rent Rolls
Resident Manager
Service Contracts
Slumlord
Stabilization
Takeover Checklist
Waiver of Subrogation
Zero-based Budgeting

LEARNING OBJECTIVES

In this chapter you will learn how benefits of ownership and owner goals relate to a management plan. The management plan analyzes a property as it presently is and includes the changes in operation and physical aspects of the property that are recommended to best maximize owner desired benefits.

You will learn when to refuse property management opportunities. There are situations when negative aspects will outweigh fees and commissions.

By going through a comprehensive property management contract, you will understand the importance and relevance of the various contractual provisions. You will learn when property management contracts can be terminated with and without further obligation.

You will understand the necessity of having a takeover checklist and the necessity of obtaining documents and information upon obtaining a management contract. A smooth transition requires a great deal of effort and you will understand the nature of this effort.

Owner Benefits

You must understand what an owner wants in order to develop a management plan. There are a number of benefits that real property offers to investors. One or more of these benefits will be owner goals.

INCOME

CASH FLOW is the cash left over after cash expenses. It is money that an owner can spend. Since cash flow does not deal with non-cash expenses (depreciation), cash flow is greater than net income.

Some owners concerns are with immediate cash flow while other owners are more concerned with long-term cash flow benefits. An owner who has the greatest concern for immediate cash would be reluctant to make improvements or changes in use or tenancy that could have a short-term negative effect on the cash flow. Owners who take a long-term approach are generally more secure financially. They will make improvements, change use and type of tenant if it makes economic sense as a long-term investment.

If an owner is highly leveraged (a high loan-to-value ratio) it usually doesn't take much to turn a positive cash flow into a negative cash flow or vice versa. Such owners might resist improvements or more than minimum maintenance.

> *Because rents appear higher, gross income shown on the books is more important than cash flow to some owners.*

The owner wants high scheduled rents to show a low *GROSS MULTIPLIER (sale price divided by gross rent).* Such owners are interested in selling the property at the maximum price or obtaining a maximum loan on the property. Therefore, they want you to get the highest rent possible even if it requires rent concessions.

SECURITY

Historically, real estate has acted as a hedge against inflation.

While prices in particular areas may decline, generally over the long term, real estate values have risen at a greater rate than inflation. Besides values, rents, on the whole, have also risen at a rate above the inflation rate as measured by the Consumer Price Index.

Even though real estate is less risky than most other forms of investment, there nevertheless are risks. Owners differ as to the risks they are willing to accept. As an example, an owner who wished to avoid risks might want a long-term lease at a below-market fixed rent from a financially secure national firm over a lease offering higher rents and rent escalation from a local firm. The degree of risk an owner is willing to accept would be reflected in the management plan for the property.

MAINTAINING THE PROPERTY

Most owners want their properties maintained to protect their investment. They realize that proper maintenance directly relates to both vacancy factors and rents.

Managing property for an owner who is the occupant of the property would not involve renting or rent collection. Management would focus around maintaining the property and possibly property improvements.

DEPRECIATION AND CAPITAL GAINS

Some owners like the fact that part of their income can be sheltered from taxation by depreciating the building and improvements. The fact that real estate is one of the last tax shelters appeals to them.

Capital gains taxes have been reduced to 20 percent. This makes a shorter term hold and sale more attractive to some owners. We can expect to see more speculators involved in real estate in the future. Without the capital gains advantage, most real estate investors have been buying with the idea of a relatively long holding period.

APPRECIATION

Because real estate has risen in value so dramatically since World War II, many owners expect the values to continue to rise. Some owners are willing to accept negative cash flows in order to gain future appreciation.

If an owner expects the appreciation as to land value and eventually expects to demolish the structure, then this would affect the management plan, as the owner would resist improvements to the property.

PSYCHIC INCOME

Some owners don't care what the building looks like, it's the profit and loss statement that matters to them. *Other owners are very concerned as to the image that their property conveys. They want* **PSYCHIC INCOME***, the prestige that goes with being able to say they own a trophy property.* Some even want their name on the building even though they don't occupy a unit, and despite the fact that the name could be a valuable commodity when negotiating a long-term lease.

Owners who seek prestige want their property to shine as to maintenance. Usually these owners are not highly leveraged. Therefore, it doesn't take too much to produce a positive bottom line. While the return on equity for such an owner might be less than for other investment properties, this type of owner will probably be happy if the property has good tenants and is well maintained.

COMBINATION OF BENEFITS

> *The benefits that an owner expects from ownership are likely a combination of benefits listed with greater emphasis on just one or two of them.*

What owners don't want is aggravation. They want a relatively problem-free investment. If there is a problem, they want to know you will solve it for them.

The Management Plan

Your **PROPERTY MANAGEMENT PLAN** *is an analysis of the present state of the property as to physical condition, nature of tenants, rents, lease provisions, etc., and what you expect to achieve and how you will achieve it.* The management plan should seek to fill the owner's goals.

The property management plan might be prepared prior to obtaining management. The prepared plan would be used as a tool to persuade owners that the property manager understands their property and their goals and will be able to meet those goals.

> *What owners want must be an integral part of the management plan.*

If you regard your management plan as an important document, owners will treat it in a similar manner. Therefore, many property managers place their management plans in a finished binder and indicate on the cover that it was prepared for a particular property and owner.

We recommend that the management plan be formally presented to the owner at a time and place where it can be explained in detail without interruption.

PROPERTY ANALYSIS

Your analysis of the property should include the following:

Location of The Property

The strengths and weaknesses of the location should be considered. Location is one factor that cannot be changed.

The Physical Structure

This would include construction type and quality, age and general conditions of the property including deferred maintenance.

Grounds and Parking

The condition of the grounds and adequacy of parking should be considered.

Current Tenants

Who the current tenants are, rent levels and current vacancies should be covered. This should include strengths and weaknesses of current tenants and the relationship of current rent to market rent.

Area Analysis

The analysis should include the demographics and changes in the area, as well as the vacancy factor for similar property in the area. New construction in the area and changes in property use should be covered as to how it will affect the subject property.

Chamber of Commerce information can be valuable in that it will probably have supporting data. Major banks have economists who prepare a variety of reports as to regions and particular cities. This information can be invaluable in supporting your management plan.

Other Possible Uses

Different uses of the property should be considered if applicable.

Photos

Include photos to emphasize points being made such as deferred maintenance, competing properties, etc.

GOALS

The "management plan" might include one-year goals as well as longer term five-year goals.

The goals should be measurable and meaningful. The intermediate steps proposed in the management plan should lead naturally toward those goals.

Goals might include control as to growth of expenses or to actually reducing expenses. Goals might be to increase rents, obtain longer-term leases as well as to reduce the vacancy factor.

Showing a desired rent schedule is NOT enough. Your management plan must show how you will arrive at this goal.

Your plan might actually call for increasing expenses to upgrade the physical plant. This would in turn result in an immediate reduction in cash flow in order to insure later benefits of greater cash flow and property value.

Your management plan might include prioritizing corrective action as to condition of the property. It would include a time table for corrective action. You plan might even include financing arrangements to cover corrective action and/or property improvements.

Suggested improvements should include estimated costs for the work. You have to realize that your plan must sell the owner on the benefits of making the improvements and any change in operations.

You must keep in mind that your management plan involves much more than planning. It is a tool for action. The plan is worthless if not implemented.

PRO-FORMA STATEMENT

*Your property management plan should include a budget for the first year based on anticipated expenses and anticipated revenue which is your **PRO-FORMA STATEMENT**. Assumptions made in your pro-forma statement should be clearly explained. The owner must realize that your anticipated income will be directly related to the anticipated expenses, and that a change in net income might not be possible without a change in the budget. In some cases, a pro-forma statement can be based on a change in use.*

Your desired rent schedule should be included and your figures should consider current lease restraints on rent adjustments.

Zero based budgeting can be used effectively to show owners what can be done. **ZERO BASED BUDGETING** *requires every expense to be justified as well as every staffing position. It starts from scratch rather than with the prior year's budget.* All too often, managers simply add on inflationary adjustments to prior years of expenses to estimate the next year's expenses. This common approach does not consider if the last year's budget was excessive, or too lean and, if so, where is the fat or inadequacies in the budget.

STAFFING

Your management plan should include present staffing and any recommended changes in staffing. Any changes should be supported.

COST SAVINGS

If savings are possible through your purchasing power, use of contract work, etc., your management plan should spell out just what these savings will be.

RESERVE REQUIREMENTS

Your management plan should justify the amount of funds to be held as a reserve against unbudgeted expenses.

ECONOMIC CHANGES

> *Property is NOT managed in a vacuum. National and local economic conditions will affect your plan. They affect rents, vacancy factors and costs.*

Any assumption that you make should be clearly covered in your management plan. You must be as realistic as possible. Owners know if the neighborhood where the property is located is declining. They want the truth, not a "Pollyanna" approach.

MARKETING PLAN

The management plan should cover how you intend to market the vacant space. This could include:

1. Signs;
2. Press releases;
3. Preparation of property briefs and brochures;

4. Advertising preparation;
5. Advertising budget and media selections;
6. Open houses (residential);
7. Providing information to cooperating brokers;
8. Phone contacts;
9. Personal contacts;
10. Using present tenants as a source of leads.

MANAGEMENT PLAN PRIOR TO CONSTRUCTION

Property management can actually begin prior to construction.

Persons having extensive experience in leasing will have a good feel for which amenities will have little if any effect on rents for the unit being planned and which amenities will have significant economic effects.

As an example, a trash compactor might add little if any as to rent, but it could add additional maintenance costs to a particular rental range and area. A convertible den might be more important than a formal dining area where there is a kitchen dining nook. Tennis courts might not be economical amenities in some areas but in other areas they would be economically very viable additions.

Besides amenities, at least one developer of high rise office structures has the initial blueprints reviewed for maintenance purposes. Some of the suggestions the developer adopted were wall-hung stools and partitions to reduce cleaning time, washbasins accessible for the handicapped, redesigned janitorial closets to permit cleaning carts and electrical hall outlets for vacuums and floor polishers. Small details of operation and use can be easily provided for in the planning stages but, if not solved, can create problems in operation.

For large projects, the leasing start-up and applicable maintenance contracts and staffing decisions should be made prior to completion.

Some large apartment developments spend almost a year for stabilization (a reasonable occupant level). Shortening the time frame can mean significant savings to the owners.

Refusing Management

Just as a sale listing should be refused when the agent feels he or she cannot adequately represent the owner or where the problems associated with listing outweigh the reward, property managers must evaluate whether or not they want to manage a property for an owner.

SPECIALIZATION

A property management firm may refuse to manage a property because of its geographical location. A property outside of the area where the firm is operating might require more effort to manage the property than the rewards justify.

A firm that specializes in residential management might turn down the opportunity to manage a small industrial complex knowing that they lack the expertise to handle industrial leases.

UNREALISTIC FEES

Abraham Lincoln said, "A lawyer's time is his stock in trade." What Lincoln meant was that a lawyer's advice and experience is what the lawyer is selling and therefore his or her time requires compensation. The same holds true for property management.

> *A property manager is NOT going to remain in business if he or she is NOT adequately compensated.*

Don't try to buy a management contract by cutting fee schedules or agreeing to accept what an owner offers if you do not feel the compensation is adequate. Accepting bargain-basement fees will affect your efforts. It will also affect your reputation if you perform at less than maximum effectiveness.

When you allow one owner a significant break on fees, that owner may brag about how he or she beat you down. When other property owners discover your two-tier fee schedule, they're going to be unhappy even though you are doing an excellent job for them. The owners will feel you have taken advantage of them.

> *In competitive situations where you have shown what you can do, always compete on a professional basis and NOT because of lower prices.*

You may have seen a famous cartoon of two hobos sitting in an open boxcar. The caption reads, "You too! I was always the low bidder!" You must be fair to yourself as well as others.

If you stick to your fee schedule, you'll find that when an owner asks you to cut your fee they generally have already decided that you will handle their property. They're just trying to see if they can save at your expense.

SLUMLORDING

> *Don't accept a management position where an owner wants to milk a property for rents without regard to tenant services.*

Property owners with large numbers of aliens as tenants often take advantage of them as the owner knows the tenant won't complain about uninhabitable conditions. These owners will want you to act in their place and carry on as they would. By taking the management position you open yourself to liability under the law and lose your own self respect in the process. You're damaging your professional reputation in the community and it will negatively affect your economic status because other owners will be unwilling to entrust their properties to you.

There could be other reasons for the owner to milk a property and not do reasonable repairs and maintenance. An owner may intend to demolish the structure to use the site for a more productive purpose. The owner could be facing foreclosure and simply wants to grab the last few months rent before the property is lost to the lender. The effect is the same for whatever reason. You don't want to be a party to an attempt by the owner to maximize income at the expense of reasonable treatment of tenants.

NEGATIVE CASH FLOWS

Management of rental property that can be expected to result in a negative cash flow for an owner should be avoided unless the owner fully understands the financial picture and has the resources and willingness to support the property. **NEGATIVE CASH FLOW** *exists when cash disbursements exceed cash (rental) income, requiring the owner to continue to put more money in the property.*

Some owners of negative cash flow properties are reluctant to approve necessary repairs, are slow to make payments to the management company and can create a nightmare for the property manager.

CODE VIOLATIONS

You should avoid getting involved in property that is currently in violation of codes or zoning ordinances unless the owner has shown the ability and willingness to correct any problems.

Some owners offer management so that the manager appears as a buffer between the owner and public authorities. You don't want to be the one who has to answer to a judge regarding any violations of the property. The problems of such properties can far outweigh the benefits of what otherwise appears to be a very lucrative management contract.

We know of a property manager who returned a new management contract where the owner had already accepted the tenant. The manager was to merely consummate the lease and collect the rent. The manager discovered that the tenant, who was to pay an extremely high rent, had a criminal record and planned to use the property for an illegal purpose.

PLAYING SCROOGE

Owners who otherwise manage their own property might offer you the management because they don't want to get involved in particularly unpleasant tasks. As an example, several management firms declined an offer to manage an apartment building that had received approval for condominium conversion. The owner wanted the manager to collect rents for one month and give 30-day notices to all the tenants. Management was to cease when the tenants left. A management contract of this sort makes the manager a "bastard" and provides no real benefits.

In this case, had the owners been willing to provide adequate funding to assist the tenants in relocating, and your managerial duties included tenant relocation, then handling this would not reflect negatively on your firm.

OWNERS WANT TO CONTROL

Management can be a disaster when owners refuse to give up control. Sometimes it can be a lack of complete trust in you and other times it is just the personalities of the owners. Owners may want you to react more as an employee than as their agent. You're asking for trouble if you accept the management contract with untenable conditions placed on your actions that allow the owner to become a co-manager.

To give back a management contract is better than trying to share management duties.

The Chinese have a proverb, "A pig with two masters shall surely starve." Owners who constantly visit their property and give orders to maintenance personnel and onsite managers tend to interfere with proper management. Orders from owners tend to prioritize what they want rather than what good management would dictate. Confusion sets in and it becomes a situation for the resident manager and staff of "dammed if you do and dammed if you don't."

Some owners want approval of very minor expenses or want you to deal only with particular service providers. In one case, an owner required a particular service provider who gave exorbitant billings. The owner then received cash rebates from that service provider.

You don't want to get involved in tax fraud.

Even where there is no fraud involved, when you are dictated as to which contractors or service providers you must use, you lose control over these people and end up with no say in requiring quality and the timeliness of job completion. Some owners want to do their repairs or contract for them. This affects the manager's ability to properly deal with tenants.

> *A property manager should avoid involvement with an owner unless an atmosphere of trust and respect exists between them.*

You can readily see that changes are required if 10 percent of your management income is derived from property that takes 50 percent of your management time.

The Property Management Contract

The **PROPERTY MANAGEMENT CONTRACT** *is the agency agreement between an owner and a property manager and must clearly set forth the obligations of the parties.*

We have included the Building Owner's and Manager's Association (BOMA) International Standard Agency Management Agreement as Figure 2-1. This management agreement can be adapted for commercial, industrial, or office property. (In Chapter 5, we have included a shorter management agreement form which we feel is better suited for residential property although the BOMA form could be used.)

Pay attention to the notation on the cover page of the BOMA contract. It is intended as a guide in preparing management agreements and should not be used without the assistance of legal counsel. Revisions to the contract may be required to comply with state law or to meet the requirements of specific transactions.

ARTICLE I

Article I of the form clearly states that this is an exclusive agency for managing and leasing the described property.

ARTICLE II

Article II of the form sets forth the term of this management contract. This particular contract provides for automatic one-year renewals (after the original term) unless a 60-day written notice is given prior to the end of the contract or any renewal period. The contract provides that the owners shall be obligated for contracts for services, supplies and alterations entered into by the property manager while the contract is in effect.

Figure 2-1

MANAGEMENT AGREEMENT

THIS AGREEMENT made as of the _____ day of _____, 19_____,

by and between _____,

(hereinafter referred to as "Owner"), and _____

(hereinafter referred to as "Manager"),

WITNESSETH:

In consideration of the mutual promises and covenants contained herein, Owner and Manager agree as follows:

ARTICLE I

Exclusive Agency. Owner hereby appoints Manager as the sole and exclusive leasing, rental agent and manager of the property described on Schedule 1 attached hereto (hereinafter referred to as the "Building") and Manager hereby accepts such employment.

ARTICLE II

Term of Agreement. The term of this agreement shall commence _____, 19_____, and shall continue for a period of _____ years until _____, 19_____, and is automatically renewed thereafter for successive periods of one year each until terminated by either party upon not less than 60 days' written notice prior to the end of the initial term or any renewal period. Upon termination, Owner shall remain bound by the obligations of all contracts for services, supplies and alterations Manager has entered into in connection with the performance of its obligations hereunder.

ARTICLE III

a. *Rental of Building.* Manager shall use its best efforts to rent all space in the Building which is now vacant or may become vacant during the term of this agreement. When appropriate, Manager shall engage the services of other real estate brokers to lease space in the Building who shall be paid from such commissions as may become due to Manager under the terms of this agreement.

b. *Negotiation of Leases.* Owner shall refer all inquiries concerning the rental of space in the Building to Manager. All negotiations with prospective tenants shall be conducted by Manager or under its direction. Manager shall have the authority to execute on behalf of Owner all leases or rental agreements for periods of less than _____ year(s). Manager shall execute all leases covering a term of _____ year(s) or more with the prior written approval of Owner.

c. *Advertising.* Subject to the approval of Owner and at Owner's expense, Manager shall advertise such space as is available for rent and arrange for such signs, renting plans, brochures and other forms of advertising as may appear advisable. Owner agrees to reimburse Manager for all out-of-pocket expenses, including, but not limited to, long distance telephone calls and, with Owner's prior approval, the cost of out-of-town travel.

d. *Rental Rates.* Rental rates for space in the Building shall be established by Owner. Manager shall, promptly following the execution of this agreement and from time to time thereafter, make recommendations to Owner with respect to rental rates.

e. *Compensation.* As compensation for renting and leasing space in the Building, Owner shall pay Manager as set forth in Schedule 1.

ARTICLE IV

a. *Management of Building.* Manager shall manage the Building in an efficient and businesslike manner having due regard for the age and physical condition of the Building. Manager, through its employees and independent contractors, shall supply complete operational services for the Building.

BOMA International Standard Agency Management Agreement

b. *Repairs.* Manager shall, in the name of and at the expense of Owner, make or cause to be made such ordinary repairs and alterations as Manager may deem advisable or necessary. However, not more than $_____ shall be expended for any one item of repair or alteration without Owner's prior written approval, except emergency repairs if, in the opinion of Manager, such repairs are necessary to protect the Building from damage or to maintain services to tenants as called for in their leases.

c. *Service Contracts.* Manager shall, in the name of and at the expense of Owner, contract for those utilities and other building operation and maintenance services Manager shall deem advisable; provided that, no service contract shall be for a term exceeding one year without the prior written approval of Owner. Manager shall, at Owner's expense, purchase and keep the Building furnished with all necessary supplies. All expenses shall be charged to Owner at net cost and Owner shall be credited with all rebates, refunds, allowances and discounts allowed to Manager.

d. *Reimbursement.* Owner agrees to reimburse Manager for all out-of-pocket expenses, including, but not limited to, long distance telephone calls and, with Owner's prior approval, the cost of out-of-town travel.

e. *Employees.* Except as provided on Schedule 1, all persons employed in the operation of the Building shall be employees of Manager or a legal entity owned or controlled by Manager. Manager shall make disbursements and deposits for all compensation and other amounts payable with respect to persons who are employed in the operation of the Building, including, but not limited to, unemployment insurance, social security, workmen's compensation and other charges imposed by a governmental authority or provided for in a union agreement. Manager shall maintain complete payroll records. All payroll costs, including, but not limited to, those enumerated herein, are operating expenses to be reimbursed to Manager from Owner's funds received by Manager.

f. *Expenditures.* All expenditures authorized by this agreement shall be considered operating expenses to be paid from Owner's funds received by Manager. In the event disbursements shall be in excess of the rents collected, Owner agrees to pay such excess promptly on demand.

g. *Monthly Statements.* Manager shall, by the _____ day of each month, render to Owner a statement of receipts and disbursements for the preceding month. Manager shall, after deducting its compensation and any other sums due it from Owner, hold or expend such sums as Owner may have directed herein or otherwise and remit the balance to Owner.

h. *Collection and Segregation of Funds.* Manager shall collect the rent and other income from tenants of the Building. All funds received by Manager for or on behalf of Owner (less any sums properly deducted by Manager pursuant to any of the provisions of this agreement) shall be deposited in a bank in a special account maintained by Manager for the deposit of funds of Owner and not mingled with the funds of Manager.

i. *Bonding Employees.* All employees of Manager who handle or are responsible for Owner's funds shall be bonded by a fidelity bond in an adequate amount.

j. *Interest and Tax Payments.* Manager shall pay interest or amortization on mortgages, taxes, assessments, premiums on insurance or reserves for such items only as designated on Schedule 1.

k. *Special Services.* At the request of Owner, Manager will perform the following special services for Owner: (i) supervise remodeling, (ii) provide special accounting, and (iii) act as property consultant. If such special services are provided, additional fees shall be payable in an amount agreed upon between the parties.

l. *Legal Proceedings.* Manager shall, at Owner's request and expense, engage counsel and cause such legal proceedings to be instituted as may be necessary to enforce payment of rent or to dispossess tenants. Manager shall have the authority to compromise disputes with tenants involving setoffs or damage claims so long as the amount involved does not exceed one month's rent payable by such tenant.

m. *Compensation.* As compensation for management of the Building, Owner shall pay Manager as set forth in Schedule 1.

ARTICLE V

a. *Indemnification.* Owner agrees: (i) to hold and save Manager free and harmless from any damage or injuries to persons or property by reason of any cause whatsoever either in and about the Building or elsewhere when Manager is carrying out the provisions of this agreement or acting under the express or implied directions of Owner, (ii) to reimburse Manager upon demand for any moneys which Manager is required to pay out for any reason whatsoever, under this agreement or in connection with, or as an expense in defense of any claim, civil or criminal action, proceeding, charge or prosecution made, instituted or maintained against Manager or Owner and Manager, jointly or severally, affecting or due to the conditions or use of the Building or acts or omissions of Manager or employees of Owner or Manager, or arising out of or based upon any law, regulation, requirement, contract or award relating to the hours of employment, working conditions, wages or compensaton of employees or former employees, and (iii) to defend promptly and diligently, at Owner's sole expense, any claim, action or proceeding brought against Manager or Manager and Owner jointly or severally arising out of or connected with any of the foregoing, and to hold harmless and fully indemnify Manager from any judgment, loss or settlement on account thereof. The foregoing provisions of this Article shall survive the termination of this agreement, but this shall not be construed to mean that Owner's liability does not survive as to other provisions of this agreement. Nothing contained in this Article shall relieve Manager from responsibility to Owner for gross negligence or willful misconduct, unless such gross negligence or willful misconduct is covered by Owner's insurance on behalf of Manager.

b. *Compliance with Laws.* If Owner shall fail or refuse to comply with or abide by any rule, order, determination, ordinance or law of any federal, state or municipal authority, Manager, upon giving twenty-four hours' written notice mailed to Owner at its address as hereinafter set forth, may terminate this agreement.

c. *Insurance.* Owner agrees to carry public liability, elevator liability and contractual liability (specifically insuring the indemnity provisions contained in Article IIIa), steam boiler (if applicable), and such other insurance as the parties agree to be necessary or desirable for the protection of the interests of Owner and Manager. In each such policy of insurance, Owner agrees to designate Manager as a party insured with Owner, the carrier and the amount of coverage in each policy shall be mutually agreed upon by Owner and Manager. A certificate of each policy issued by the carrier shall be delivered promptly to Manager by Owner. All policies shall provide for 10 days' written notice to Manager prior to cancellation.

d. *Waiver of Subrogation.* Owner shall procure an appropriate clause in, or endorsement on, each of its policies for fire or extended coverage insurance and on all other forms of property damage insurance including, but not limited to, coverage such as water damage, property damage, boiler and machinery insurance and sprinkler leakage insurance, covering the Building or personal property, fixture or equipment located thereon whereby the insurer waives subrogation or consents to a waiver of the right of recovery against Manager, and having obtained such clause or endorsement of waiver of subrogation or consent to a waiver of right of recovery, Owner hereby agrees that it will not make any claim against or seek to recover from Manager for any loss or damage to property of the type covered by such insurance.

ARTICLE VI

If the Building is sold prior to termination of this agreement, Manager shall represent Owner in connection with the sale. Owner shall pay Manager a commission for these services in accordance with Schedule 1.

ARTICLE VII

a. *Bankruptcy and Insolvency.* In the event a petition in bankruptcy is filed by or against either Owner or Manager, or in the event that either shall make an assignment for the benefit of creditors or take advantage of any insolvency act, either party hereto may immediately terminate this agreement by written notice. Remedies set forth hereinabove shall be in addition to and shall not exclude any other remedy available under applicable law to the parties hereto.

b. *Independent Contractors.* It is expressly understood and agreed that Manager will act as an independent contractor in performance of this agreement. No provision hereunder shall be intended to create a partnership or a joint venture with respect to the Building or otherwise.

c. *Notice.* Any notice required or permitted under this agreement shall be given when actually delivered or when deposited in the United States mail as certified mail addressed as follows:

To Owner:

To Manager:

or to such other address as may be specified from time to time by either party in writing.

d. *Suit or Action.* If suit or action is instituted in connection with any controversy arising out of this agreement, the prevailing party shall be entitled to recover, in addition to costs, such sum as the court may adjudge reasonable as attorneys' fees in such suit or acton and on any appeal from any judgment or decree entered therein.

BOMA International Standard Agency Management Agreement

e. *Assignment and Amendment.* All terms and conditions of this agreement shall be binding upon the parties hereto and their respective successors and assigns. This agreement may not be modified or amended except by written agreement of the parties.

IN WITNESS WHEREOF the parties hereto have executed this agreement in duplicate as of the date first hereinabove written.

_____
Owner

_____
Manager

**BOMA INTERNATIONAL
STANDARD
AGENCY MANAGEMENT
AGREEMENT**

NOTE: The foregoing form has been distributed by the Agency Management Committee of Building Owners and Managers Association International as a guide to members to assist in preparing management agreements. It is likely that revisions will be needed to comply with the laws of various jurisdictions and to meet the requirements of individual transactions. The foregoing form should not be used without the assistance of legal counsel.

BOMA International Standard Agency Management Agreement

SCHEDULE 1 TO MANAGEMENT AGREEMENT

DATED _____

1. The property covered by the management agreement is described as follows:

2. Owner shall compensate Manager for renting and leasing space in the Building, including expansion of space occupied by existing tenants, as follows:

For lease renewals, Manager shall be compensated as follows:

Manager shall be entitled to compensation for expansion space and renewals at the rates specified above upon the exercise of options contained in leases negotiated by Manager, even though such options are exercised after the termination or expiration of the agreement. Upon termination of the agreement pursuant to the provisions of Article II, Owner shall recognize Manager as the broker in any pending negotiations for lease of space in the Building. In the event of the consummation of a lease with a person with whom Manager was negotiating at the date of termination of the agreement, Owner shall pay Manager a commission at the rate prescribed above.

3. Manager's compensation for management of the Building shall be as follows:

4. In the event of a sale of the Building, the commission payable to Manager shall be as follows:

5. Manager shall pay, subject to availability of Owner's funds, mortgage payments, BOMA dues, taxes, assessments, premiums on insurance or reserves for such items as follows:

6. The following persons engaged in the operation of the Building shall be employees of Owner:

SCHEDULE 1

BOMA International Standard Agency Management Agreement

A management contract length should be related to the services provided and the owner reimbursement.

As an example, a short-term contract, even one for one year, would not be appropriate if the contract provided only a percentage of the rents received (no rental fees) if there were a significant number of vacancies. In such a contract, the owner could take advantage of you and let you stabilize the property. You would do the hard work and the owner would take over when the property was fully leased.

A straight percentage might be appropriate for a one-year contract if the property had a reasonable vacancy factor and was relatively well run. Similarly, if you only received a short-term management contract you would not want to take on trying to get a poorly managed building in shape. This could mean changing the tenant mix and on-site personnel, instituting new rules and regulations, evicting problem tenants, changing rents, etc.

When things are done right and you have policies and procedures in place with relatively stable tenants, then you stand to profit from past efforts. Don't accept an obligation without the rewards.

ARTICLE III

Rental

The manager agrees to use his or her best efforts to rent all space and keep the space rented during the duration of the management contract. The manager has the authority to use other real estate brokers in leasing the space, however, the property manager shall be responsible for paying their commissions out of the commissions received by the property manager.

Lease Negotiation

The owner agrees to refer all rental inquiries to the manager who will have the authority to execute leases on behalf of the owner. The period of leases that can be executed by the manager would be set forth. Leases for longer periods require the prior written approval of the owner.

Advertising

The manager has the authority to place signs on the property for rentals and prepare advertising material. This contract calls for owner reimbursement of all of the manager's out-of-pocket expenses, including long distance telephone calls. The owner's prior approval is required for out-of-town travel.

Residential property management contracts generally do NOT provide for the owner to pay for advertising costs.

Rental Rates

This clause clearly provides for rental rates to be established by the owner. The manager can merely make recommendations.

Compensation

The managers compensation is set forth in Schedule I.

ARTICLE IV

Management of Building

The property manager agrees to manage the property in an efficient and businesslike manner, considering the age and physical condition of the property, supplying complete operational services.

Repairs

Acting for the owner, the manager can make ordinary repairs and alterations. Owner's prior written approval is required for any one item of repair or alteration that exceeds a specified dollar limit. This limit should be reasonably high enough so that constant owner approval is not necessary. Too low a limit would indicate an owner's lack of trust in the manager.

The dollar limit can be exceeded in emergencies where repairs are required to protect the building or to maintain tenant services.

Service Contracts

The manager is authorized to contract for services and utilities. Contracts exceeding one year shall require the prior written approval of the owner.

This clause also authorizes the manager, at the owner's expense, to keep the building furnished with necessary supplies.

The owner is to be charged the net costs and shall be credited with any rebates, refunds, allowances and discounts allowed to the manager (no secret profits).

Reimbursement

The owner agrees to reimburse the manager for out-of-pocket expenses.

Employees

Schedule I to this contract specifies those employees who shall be employees of the owner. All other employees are employees of the manager. The manager will be responsible for unemployment insurance, workers compensation, payroll deductions, social security contributions, etc., for the manager's employees. Payroll costs for employees of the manager shall be reimbursed from owner funds.

> *Note: The parties can therefore agree as to who will be the employer, the manager or the owner.*

Expenditures

Expenditures provided for in the management contract are operating expenses that may be paid from funds of the owner received by the manager (rents). Any expenses in excess of rents shall be paid on demand by the owner.

Monthly Statement

This clause provides the date during the following month for the monthly statement. The amount due the owner after the deduction of management compensation shall be sent to the owner unless agreed otherwise.

Collection and Segregation of Funds

The manager has responsibility for rent collections and rents shall be deposited in a bank account and not commingled with the manager's own funds. (See Chapter 11.)

Bonding of Employees

All employees of the manager who handle or are responsible for owner funds shall be bonded by a fidelity bond of an adequate amount.

Interest and Tax Payments

The manager shall make mortgage, tax, special assessment and insurance payments or set up reserves for the payments if designated in Schedule I.

Special Services

Special services such as supervision of remodeling, special accounting and property consulting shall be performed by the manager at the owner's request. Additional fees shall be agreed upon for special services.

Legal Proceedings

At the owner's request and consent, the manager shall hire attorneys and commence legal proceedings to enforce payment of rent or to dispossess tenants. The manager has the power to settle disputes with tenants involving set-offs or damage claims providing the amount does not exceed one month's rent for such tenant.

Compensation

The manager's compensation is set forth in Schedule I.

ARTICLE V

Indemnification

The owner agrees to hold the manager harmless (hold harmless clause) for damages or injuries to persons or property when the manager is carrying out provisions of this contract and to reimburse the manager for defense costs regarding such claims.

The manager is NOT relieved of gross negligence or willful misconduct unless covered by owner's insurance.

Compliance With Laws

Failure of the owner to comply with a rule, order, determination, ordinance or law (federal, state or municipal) shall allow the manager to terminate the agreement upon 24-hour written notice.

Insurance

The owner agrees to carry public liability, elevator liability, contractual liability, steam boiler and other insurance agreed to be necessary to protect the owner and manager's interests. The owner agrees to name the manager as a party insured. The amount of coverage shall be agreed by the parties. Policies of insurance shall provide for 10-day written notice to the manager prior to cancellation.

Waiver of Subrogation

The property insurance coverage shall provide that the insurer waives any subrogation rights against the manager. Otherwise the insurer, after paying a claim, could go against the manager for reimbursement if the insurer believed that the manager was responsible for the loss.

ARTICLE VI

This clause provides that a sale of the property prior to termination of the management contract shall entitle the manager to a commission for services in accordance with Schedule I.

ARTICLE VII

Bankruptcy and Insolvency

In the event of bankruptcy or an assignment to benefit creditors by one party, the other party may terminate the contract by written notice.

> *Termination would NOT exclude any other remedy available under the law. (Could still sue for damages.)*

Independent Contractor

The parties agree that the property manager is an independent contractor in the performance of this contract. The property manager is not a partner or joint venturer.

Notice

This provision provides as to where owner and manager notices are to be sent.

Suit or Action

If a lawsuit is instigated concerning the performance of this contract, the prevailing party shall be entitled to costs plus reasonable attorney fees. (This provision will reduce the likelihood of a frivolous lawsuit.)

> *Note: Some management contracts provide for either consensual or mandatory arbitration of disputes.*

Assignment or Amendment

The terms of this agreement are binding on the successor and assigns of the parties.

> *Any modification or amendment to the contract must be in writing.*

SCHEDULE I

Schedule I includes the following.

Description of the Property

The description must be clear and unambiguous.

Manager Compensation for Leasing

The leasing commission would be set forth. It would ordinarily be a percentage of rent received for the entire lease. The fee for lease renewal might be the same as for leasing but it could be less.

The leasing fees apply to expansion space as well as renewal options exercised after the expiration of the management agreement.

If the manager was negotiating with a prospective tenant when the management contract was terminated and a lease was later consummated, the manager shall be entitled to a leasing commission.

Management Commission

The management commission is separate from the leasing commission and would ordinarily include a minimum commission against a percentage of gross receipts.

Sale Commission

This clause provides a separate commission to be paid to the manager if the property is sold.

> *The manager need NOT have been a party to the sale to be entitled to this commission.*

Payments by Manager

This clause sets forth what payments the manager shall make on behalf of the owner such as insurance, taxes, mortgage payments, etc.

Employees of Owner

This paragraph would specify which employees or categories of employees will be employees of the owner.

Agency Termination

Agencies, such as management contracts, can be terminated in a number of ways. These include:

1. Expiration of the term of the agency.
2. Impossibility of performance such as the taking of the property under management contract by eminent domain.
3. Mutual agreement. Parties can agree to end the agency.
4. Bankruptcy of the principal or agent.
5. Incapacity of principal or agent. An example would be a party being declared incompetent.

Either the principal or the agent can cancel a management contract since courts will not force an agency relationship on anyone. However, if either party cancels without just cause, they can be held liable for damages resulting from the wrongful cancellation.

An exception to the right to cancel is an agency coupled with an interest. As an example, if the management company would loan an owner money to make renovations as part of a management contract, then the agent would have a financial interest in the property and the agency could not be unilaterally canceled.

Case Example

Pacific Landmark Hotel, Ltd. v. Marriott Hotels, Inc. **(1993) 19 C.A. 4th 615**

In order to obtain a 50-year management contract from a hotel, Marriott Hotels, Inc. had a subsidiary corporation make a $23 million loan to the hotel.

The owners of the hotel sued Marriott to cancel the management contract because of breach of contract. Marriott prevailed in Superior Court based on the finding that Marriott had an agency coupled with an interest since they had made a substantial loan to the hotel.

This decision was reversed by the Court of Appeals which held that because a corporation is a separate entity and the loan was made by a separate corporation, Marriott did not have an agency coupled with an interest so the management contract could be cancelled.

Takeout Checklists

Your work begins when you receive a signed management contract. There are many things that must be done quickly for a smooth transition of management from an owner or another manager to you.

A formal checklist is important or you are almost certain to miss something.

Things you want or information required would include:

1. Names of all owners as well as social security numbers.
2. Owner's home address.
3. Owner's home telephone number.
4. Owner's business address.
5. Owner's business telephone number.
6. Name, address and telephone number of the person authorized to act as agent of the owner in the event the owner is unavailable or cannot be located.
7. Resident manager's name.
8. Resident manager's telephone number. (Resident manager must be notified as to their status and who to contact. They must also be given information as to accepting lease deposits, lists of contractors, etc.)
9. Resident manager compensation as well as any contract of employment.
10. Resident manager's social security number.
11. Names, addresses, telephone numbers and social security numbers of other employees as well as their compensation.
12. Payroll records of all employees.
13. Copies of all existing service contracts. (Service providers will have to be notified as to where to send billings.)
14. Information and/or contracts for any work in progress. (Contractors will have to be notified as to billings.)
15. Copies of all leases (lease file). (Tenants will have to be notified as to where to send rents.)
16. Security deposits should be turned over to you and deposited in your trust account.
17. Information on vacancies and rent schedules. (You want to review current marketing procedures and rents and institute a new marketing plan if and/or rent adjustments are called for.)
18. Keys. You want copies of all keys now kept by the resident manager.
19. Inventory lists. (If there is an inventory or owner-owned personal property, including maintenance equipment, you will need a copy. If there is none, one should be prepared.)
20. Occupancy rules and regulations. (You want a copy of present rules and regulations which might need to be modified. If there are none, you should consider what is required.)
21. Copies of insurance policies. (You'll want to review present coverage and make recommendations for change if needed. You'll also want to notify insurance agents that future correspondence should go to you as well as being named as an insured under liability policies.)
22. Copies of last tax statement. (You will want the tax parcel number to have future tax statements sent to you. If taxes appear too high, you should consider an appeal.)

23. Mortgage payment book. (If you are to make mortgage payments you will need the payment book. You should also notify the mortgagee that you are managing the property and payment receipts or other correspondence should be to you.)
24. Leases in progress. (You will want copies of rental applications and information as to their status as to verifications and credit checks.)
25. Evictions in progress. (You want to know the status of any three-day or 30-day notices as well as unlawful detainer actions.)
26. Rent rolls and back rent. (You want copies of rent rolls and the amount of back rent or security deposits that are due.)
27. Files. (You want the tenant files, contractor files and other records kept. The records may have to be placed in a compatible format with your record keeping system.)
28. Monies owed by former tenants. (If the debts have not been turned over to collection, you should make a decision as to what should be done. If the owner or prior manager has turned over any collections to a collection agency, they should be notified that checks and correspondence should go to you.)
29. Last utility bills. (You want to notify utility providers that future billings shall be sent to you.)
30. Washer - Dryer/Vending Machines. You need to know who owns any coin operated machines. If owned by others, you want copies of the contracts (to notify vending companies that checks go to you). If owned by the property owner, you want to know how receipts are presently being handled.
31. Trash removal information. You want to know the name, address and telephone numbers of the trash carrier and if there is a written contract. (You should notify the trash company of any change as to billing.)
32. Unpaid past due or presently due bills and any contested charges. (You want to be able to pay just bills as well as defend against improper charges).
33. Building plans. (If available, building plans could be helpful for renovation or improvements.)
34. Operating account. (You will likely require a check from the owner to set up an immediate operating account so bills can be paid and the reserve amount agree upon can be kept in the account.)
35. Copies of last year's operating statement. (This can be used to analyze progress or discover problems.)

As soon as possible, the property manager should:

1. Meet with the resident manager and review all current operating procedures. The manager should be instructed verbally and in writing as to your specific requirements.
2. The resident manager should be given a copy of his or her job description.
3. All vacant units should be inspected by the property manager and any resident manager.

4. Repairs, renovations and present maintenance should be reviewed with the resident manager and maintenance staff.
5. A property inspection, with a written report, should be conducted with the resident manager, maintenance supervisor (if applicable) and the property manager.
6. Review the tentative management plan with the resident manager. If none was prepared, work should commence on the management plan. The tentative plan might require some revisions.
7. Tasks that require immediate attention should be prioritized with the resident manager and the maintenance supervisor.

Additional requirements for property takeover will be dictated by the nature of the property.

CHAPTER 2 SUMMARY

Benefits that owners obtain by the ownership of rental property include:

1. Income.
2. Security.
3. Depreciation.
4. Capital gains taxation.
5. Appreciation.
6. Pride of ownership (Psychic income).

By understanding benefits of ownership and what an individual owner of a particular property is seeking, you can prepare a management plan. A management plan would include an analysis of the plus and minus features of a property as to:

1. Location.
2. Physical structure.
3. Current tenants.
4. Current rents and lease terms.
5. Area analysis.
6. Other possible uses.
7. Photographs.
8. Goals of management.
9. Prioritization of actions.
10. Pro-forma statement.
11. Proposed staffing.
12. Areas of cost savings.
13. Financial reserve requirements.
14. Economic changes likely to effect management.

There are times when good business practices would dictate that a property manager should refuse management opportunities.

1. Specialization. Management situations removed from the manager's physical area of activity and/or outside his or her area of expertise.
2. Unrealistic fees offered by an owner.
3. Slumlord opportunities where expenses are to be severely restrained and the object is to milk the property.
4. Negative cash flow situations where the owner is reluctant to subsidize proper management activities.
5. Property with code violations where the owner is unwilling or unable to correct the situation.
6. Short-term management opportunities to relieve the owner of an unpleasant task.
7. Situations where the owner doesn't have enough faith in you to give up control.

The BOMA property management contract included in this Chapter can be used for commercial, industrial and office properties. It is intended as a guide, not to be used without legal counsel review. Elements of this contract, include:

1. Exclusive agency to lease and manage.
2. Term of the contract with an automatic renewal unless notice is given.
3. Managers agreement to use best efforts.
4. Manager to handle leases. The authority as to lease term without owner's approval is set forth.
5. Owner's obligation for advertising costs.
6. Owner sets the rentals, the manager advises.
7. Property manager agrees to manage in an efficient manner.
8. Owner's permission is required for repairs above a set amount.
9. Manager is not to enter into service contracts beyond one year without owner's permission.
10. The owner agrees to reimburse the manager for out-of-pocket expenses.
11. Employees not designated as employees of the owner are employees of the manager who is responsible for insurance and withholding although costs are to be reimbursed by the owner.
12. The manager may use rent money for owner-obligated expenses.
13. The manager will supply owner with a monthly statement and remittance.
14. The manager will not commingle funds of owner with manager's funds.
15. Employees responsible for funds will be bonded.
16. The manager shall make designated payments from rent receipts.
17. Special services provided by the manager will be performed at agreed upon fees.

18. The manager shall commence legal action at owner's direction and expense. Manager has authority to settle disputes without owner's concurrence for up to one month's rent paid by the tenant involved.
19. The owner agrees to hold the manager harmless as to property damage and personal injury arising from the management contract.
20. Landlords breach or failure to comply with a law or legal order shall allow manager to terminate the agreement.
21. The owner agrees to carry designated liability coverage to protect the manager.
22. The owner's insurance carrier shall waive subrogation rights.
23. The sale of the property shall entitle the manager to a stated commission.
24. Bankruptcy or insolvency acts of one party shall allow the other party to terminate the agreement.
25. The property manager is to be an independent contractor.
26. The location where notices are to be sent is set forth.
27. In the event of a lawsuit, the prevailing party is entitled to costs and attorney fees.
28. The contract shall be binding on assigns and successors in interest.

The schedule attached to the contracts describes the property and sets forth lease commissions, lease renewal commissions, management commissions and sales commissions if property is sold. The payments that the manager shall make on behalf of the owner are set forth and who shall be an owner employee is covered.

Agencies such as management contracts can be terminated by:

1. Expiration of term.
2. Impossibility of performance.
3. Mutual agreement.
4. Bankruptcy.
5. Incapacity.
6. Unilateral action by either party.

The one contract that cannot be terminated unilaterally is an agency coupled with an interest.

When taking over management, there should be a checklist because documents and information is needed by the manager for a smooth transition.

CLASS DISCUSSION TOPICS

1. Using the Saturday or Sunday classified ads in a local paper, find ads for investment properties that emphasize benefits. What benefits are represented?

2. Picking a local property, how would you analyze location, physical structure, current tenants, the area?

3. Give an example of a local property that could be used for purposes other than the present use.

4. Give an example of a local property where you would refuse management. Why?

5. Estimate the management fees and leasing fees for a particular local property. Why do you think those fees are fair?

CHAPTER 2 QUIZ

1. Benefits of ownership of investment property include all EXCEPT:

    A. risk
    B. appreciation
    C. pride of ownership
    D. capital gains tax on sale profits

2. A property analysis included in a management plan would cover:

    A. the locational advantages and disadvantages of the property
    B. the physical structure
    C. current tenants and rents
    D. all of the above

3. What is a Pro-Forma Statement?

    A. The current rent schedule
    B. An audited operating statement
    C. A statement as to anticipated rents and expenses
    D. A chart showing the changes in vacancies

4. Zero-based budgeting is based on:

    A. no expenses for maintenance
    B. 100 percent occupancy
    C. starting with zero and justifying every budgeted item
    D. anticipated revenue equaling anticipated expenses

5. A property manager should consider refusal of management when:
    A. the manager lacks the expertise to properly handle management
    B. the owner refuses to allow the manager to take any action without prior approval
    C. the owner wants the manager to avoid making repairs
    D. for all of the above situations

6. A slumlord wants:
    A. maximum rents with minimum tenant services
    B. minimum rents and minimum tenant services
    C. maintenance to take precedence over revenue
    D. the manager to think in terms of long-term benefits of properly maintaining property

7. Negative cash flow management involves:
    A. tax free income
    B. continued infusion of cash by the owner
    C. unreported cash income
    D. preparing records showing cash expenses that were not actually paid

8. The length of a management contract should:
    A. never be less than five years
    B. be under one year
    C. ideally be on a month-to-month basis
    D. be related to problems to be corrected and services to be provided

9. A management contract can be terminated because of:
    A. bankruptcy of either party
    B. mutual agreement between owner and manager
    C. impossibility of performance
    D. any of the above

10. A management contract cannot be unilaterally canceled by an owner when:
    A. the manager does not wish cancellation
    B. the manager has an interest coupled with an agency
    C. the owner owes the manager an outstanding debt
    D. the contract is for a stated period and it has yet to expire

Answers: 1. A; 2. D; 3. C; 4. C; 5. D; 6. A; 7. B; 8. D; 9. D; 10. B

Leases and Leasing

KEY WORDS AND TERMS

AIDS (Prior Occupant)
Assignment of Lease
Capacity
Compensation
Consumer Price Index
Contracts of Adhesion
Credit Reports
Death on Property
Estate for Years
Flat Lease
Flood Hazard Area
Gross Lease
Hazardous Substances
Lead-Based Paint
Lease
Lease Renewals
Legal Purpose
Lessee

Lessor
Letter of Intent
Master Lease
Military Ordinance
Mutuality
Net Lease
Options to Renew
Percentage Lease
Periodic Tenancy
Proposal to Lease
Qualifying Tenants
Recording
Rent Incentives
Statute of Frauds
Sublease
Sublessee
Sublessor
Win/Win Negotiating

LEARNING OBJECTIVES

The American Indians did not consider themselves to be owners. They did not grasp the concept of private ownership. They regarded land as something that was just there for anyone to use. They stayed in an area until they decided to move based on the hunting, fishing and seasons of the year. When the Indians received colorful trinkets for Manhattan, they did not realize that they had given up the right to use the land.

With private ownership came owners who could not or did not want to directly use and possess their property.

A lease is the only way an owner can profit by property ownership if the owner does not use the property for his or her own business, agricultural or housing needs.

In this chapter you will learn what a lease is and the requirements of all types of leases, as well as the difference between assignment of a lease and subleasing. You will understand the necessity of qualifying prospective tenants and the process. You will understand the role of the property manager in drafting leases and the dangers in using lessee prepared leases. You will understand the dangers and benefits as to the length of the lease. This chapter will also prepare you for reaching a win/win objective in lease negotiations. You will also understand your disclosure obligation to tenants.

Lease - Definition

A **LEASE** *is a contract which transfers possession from an owner (lessor) to a tenant (lessee).* While the tenant is entitled to exclusive possession during the term of the lease, the lessor retains title and reversionary rights to take possession at the end of the lease.

Since a lease is a contract, the four basic contractual requirements apply.

Mutuality. This refers to a meeting of the minds. The lease must be clear and unambiguous as to its terms, compensation and property to be leased.

Capacity. The parties must be of legal age and have the mental capacity to contract.

Legal Purpose. To be enforceable, the lease must be for a legal purpose. A lease that specifies an illegal use is void.

Consideration. While courts seldom are concerned with the adequacy of consideration, there must be consideration flowing from the lessee to the lessor. It is usually money but it could be anything of value.

Note: Adequacy of consideration could be used to show that the lease was NOT freely entered into (undue influence) or the presence of fraud, both of which would allow the injured party to void the lease.

Statute of Frauds

Every state has a statute of frauds indicating which documents must be in writing.

The statute of frauds requires certain instruments to be in writing. They must be signed by the person who is being held to the instrument. Generally included among the instruments that must be in writing are leases for more than one year. Therefore, oral leases one year or less need not be in writing.

State **STATUTES OF FRAUDS** usually require contracts (leases) to be in writing if, by their terms, they cannot be fully performed within one year. Therefore, an oral six-month lease, which could ordinarily be enforceable, would be unenforceable if it were not to commence for seven months. By the terms of such a lease, it would take more than one year for full performance (13 months).

Even though a lease might NOT have to be in writing, it "should" be in writing.

By setting forth lease terms as a written contract you are protected against a situation where the lessee claims the verbal agreement was different from the agreement you claim it to be. Actually, both parties are protected by writing since people tend to have convenient memories and remember agreements in a manner beneficial to them.

Types of Leases

ESTATE FOR YEARS

*Leases can be for a fixed term. Such leases are known by the legal term **ESTATE FOR YEARS**.* A one-month vacation rental would be an estate for years in that it has a definite termination date when possession must be returned to the lessor.

PERIODIC TENANCY

*A lease that automatically renews itself, unless notice is given by either party to cancel it, is known as a **PERIODIC TENANCY**.* In most states, the notice requirements to cancel a periodic tenancy would be the length of the rent paying period, but no more than 30 days.

Do NOT confuse 30 days with one month—they are NOT the same.

A weekly rental would only require seven days notice, which is the length of the rent paying period. A one year lease that automatically renews itself would generally require a 30-day notice of termination.

A 30-day notice is not universal for ending a periodic tenancy. As an example, the notice period is 45 days in Hawaii.

In some states, the notice to terminate must expire on the end of the rent paying period. This is not the case in some states such as California, where the notice can be given at any time.

Just as a notice must be given to terminate an estate for years, the same notice requirement must be given by the lessor to change the terms of the lease, such as a rent increase.

> *Month-to-month tenancies are the most common of the periodic tenancies.*

RENT-PAYING PROVISIONS

Rent can be a fixed sum or a variable sum according to some formula. Several types of leases are based on rent-paying provisions.

Gross Lease

A *GROSS LEASE, also known as a "flat lease," is a lease where the tenant pays a fixed rent.* Generally, residential leases are gross leases, although many commercial and industrial leases also provide for a fixed rental. With a gross lease the lessor pays the taxes and insurance. Maintenance costs can be either the responsibility of lessor or lessee based on the provisions of the lease. A gross lease for a long term, such as five years, might have a provision for rent increases at various times over the period of the lease.

Net Lease

A *NET LEASE is a lease where the lessor is given a flat amount of rent each month and the tenant pays taxes, insurance, maintenance and other expenses that would otherwise be the owner's responsibility.* Investors love net leases because they have no operational responsibilities. All they need to do is collect their rent.

> *Net leases are generally for commercial or industrial property.*

SALE-LEASEBACKS *usually provide for net leases where the investor buys the property from the seller and the seller becomes the buyer's tenant.* There can be many variations as to net leases where the lessor is responsible for some costs.

Net leases are usually long-term leases and often contain provisions for rent increases. The most common provision ties the rent to the Consumer Price Index (CPI).

The lessor is able to maintain the same purchasing power from the rent money. It would otherwise be reduced because of cheaper dollars due to inflation. Net leases are covered in Chapters 4 and 7.

Percentage Leases

A **PERCENTAGE LEASE** *is where the rent is tied to the gross income of a business.* They are generally used for shopping centers. Percentage leases require a minimum rent coupled with the percentage of the gross. Generally, businesses with a higher markup pay higher percentages as rent under percentage leases. Percentage leases and the applicable clauses protecting the lessor are covered in Chapters 4 and 7.

CORPORATION LEASES

Where either the lessor or lessee is a corporation, the board of directors must give approval to corporate officers to sign the lease or management contract.

Should a corporation lease out all of its corporate property, the lease must be approved by a majority of the stockholders, since the corporation could be putting itself out of the business that is set forth in its corporate charter.

GROUND LEASE

A **GROUND LEASE** *is a lease of land only.* Ground leases are used extensively by Indian tribes in leasing their land. They are also used for commercial property.

Ground leases are usually long-term leases.

At the end of the lease, the lessor gets possession of the property and generally the improvements placed on the property by the tenant. Many of the free standing sites in shopping centers, such as those pads for fast food restaurants, are ground leases. The tenant puts up the building and is responsible for all improvements. The owner keeps title to the property and pays no capital gains taxes, although he or she is taxed on the rent.

Ground leases are usually net leases where the tenant pays taxes as well as all other expenses. They may also have a percentage of the rent feature where they include a percentage of the gross in addition to the net amount. This may be in conjunction with a Consumer Price Index feature of the net lease. The CPI and the additional percentage serve to give the owner protection against inflation.

Many large chains like ground leases since they avoid tying up huge sums of cash in land. Another advantage is that some owners will accept a much lower rent than the cash value of the land would normally dictate because they realize that they are going to own the tenant's improvements at the end of the lease.

As an example, it is hard for an owner of land worth $1,000,000 to turn down a net lease offer of $45,000 a year when the owner will not only get back the property in 25 years, but will own the improvements as well. In addition, the appreciation in value will belong to the owner who did not have any taxes or other carrying costs until that point in time. After 25 years, the owner knows that he or she can sell the property, lease it to others or lease it to the original lessee from a position of great strength.

From the viewpoint of the tenant, the use of the land is only costing them four and one-half percent a year. The improvements will be fully amortized over the term of the lease. It is a win/win situation.

Assignment and Subletting

Unless a lease prohibits assignment or subleasing, a lease can be assigned or subleased.

ASSIGNMENT

In an **ASSIGNMENT**, *the lessee becomes an assignor and assigns or transfers all of his or her interest in the property to another party, the assignee.* While the assignee becomes primarily liable to the original lessor for complying with the lease terms and the payment of rent, the assignor remains secondarily liable. Therefore, should the assignee default on the rent, the original lessee can be held liable for the rent. (See Figure 3-1.)

SUBLEASE

Under a **SUBLEASE**, *the lessee under a lease becomes a landlord and leases to his or her own tenant.* The sublessee pays the sublessor (original lessee) who then pays rent to the lessor (owner). Unlike an assignment, the lessee remains primarily liable on the lease. The sublessee is not liable under the original lease and has no contractual obligation to the lessor (owner). The sublessee is only liable to the sublessor.

Figure 3-1

Lease Assignment

Lessor/Owner

Lessee/Tenant

Becomes Assignor but remains liable on the lease

Rent

Assignee

Takes obligations under lease (primary liability)

The advantage to a lessee that a sublease offers is that it is possible to make money on the difference between what the sublessee is paying and what is due under the original lease. As an example, assume a tenant has a long-term lease at $1,000 per month but no longer wants to occupy the property. If the leased value of the premises had increased the lessee would be economically ahead to sublease rather than assign the lease. If the lessee could sublease for $2,000 per month then he or she could keep $1,000 per month and pay the original lessor the $1,000 rent. (See Figure 3-2.)

Qualifying Tenants

Having a poor or problem tenant is not necessarily better than not having a tenant. A poor tenant can mean rent not collected, damage to the property, lawsuits, general aggravation and the loss of rental opportunities to other tenants. With a tenant in possession you cannot rent to a qualified tenant.

Figure 3-2

Advantage to Lessee of a Sublease

Finding out about problems with tenants after they take possession is too late. You want to qualify the tenant before a lease is signed and possession is given.

Qualifying means that you want to determine not only the tenants character problems and habits that could make him or her undesirable, but also the tenants ability and willingness to meet lease obligations.

For residential leases, the prospective tenant should fill out an application to lease. The application should give you a basis for investigating and determining if the application to rent shall be approved or rejected. Qualification of tenants is covered in greater detail in Chapter 5.

INCOME DETERMINATION

As part of the application you should request a pay stub showing the present employer and gross income. You would also want to see the applicants photo identification (driver's license). There have been many cases of persons using other person's names in order to qualify for a rental which they would not be able to qualify for had they used their own names.

You should check with the present employer and past employers as indicated on the application. While they might not want to verify present or past income, they will verify period of employment. A significant discrepancy between what the applicant has stated and what the employer states would indicate a problem.

The length of employment is important as is the length of past employment. A person who has had relatively short periods of employment with significant gaps between the employment periods coupled with a present recent employment would appear to present significant risks.

You might want to use a ratio of income to rent to determine qualifications of a tenant. A ratio is not very good to use because you might make exceptions. If you made an exception for one person and turned down an applicant with a similar income ratio, you could become involved in a civil rights case if the person turned down was a member of a minority or protected group (See Chapter 13).

Hard and fast rules do not take into account income which might not appear on a pay stub, such as gifts from family.

> *While income should be checked, the character of the prospecting tenant is more important.*

CHARACTER

A persons credit history, how they honored prior financial commitments, is a good indicator as to how they will honor their lease obligation. A person who is constantly late in paying other bills will likely be late in paying rent as well.

You can run a credit check with one of the credit agencies if your office is a member. There is a problem with using only one credit reporting agency. Because the three national services are independent of each other, one service might give a prospective tenant a clean bill of health as to credit while another agency might have information about a judgment entered for unpaid rent due a prior landlord.

There are firms which will supply you with credit information from more than one reporting service.

Advantage Credit Services provides a tenant screening service for real estate brokers. They will supply credit reports using two of the three services (TRW,

Transunion and Equi-Fax). Brokers may obtain applications for the services at no charge. They simply need to complete the application, fax it to Advantage Credit Services and wait for the reply (usually within 20 minutes). The broker will be faxed two credit reports with problems highlighted. The fee for this service is currently $18 for each screening (individual owners pay a higher fee than do brokers). For information on Advantage Credit Service call 1-800-296-5050.

www.acs.pf.com
(Advantage Credit Service)

If a credit report service does not have any information about a prospective tenant, you should treat it as a red flag. Check prior landlords and references. A good approach is to contact references and ask them names of other persons who are familiar with the prospective tenant. These people are less likely to have been coached as to what to say.

By checking with prior landlords you will find out about problems in paying rent as well as character problems. Landlords prior to the present landlord will likely be more forthcoming with information. If a present landlord has had no problems with a tenant and you indicate that he or she wants to rent from you, it would be contrary to the landlord's best interests to be honest. On the other hand, former landlords will have no such interests and are more likely to be honest with you. In some cases they will be eager to tell you about unpleasant relations that they have had with a tenant.

A tenant's Personal And Credit Information Form (See Figure 3-3) can be used to obtain the information you will need for qualifying a tenant.

Proposal to Lease

When lessor and lessee are serious about leasing, but many of the terms have not yet been agreed upon, they may exercise a letter of intent which shows the parties intent to negotiate in good faith to effectuate a lease.

> *A letter of intent with a major tenant would influence lesser tenants to commence negotiations for space.*

It would also be a factor in obtaining permanent financing for the project. Financing could be arranged contingent upon finalizing a particular lease or leases.

Figure 3-4 is a Proposal to Lease. This proposal includes rent, terms of the lease, good faith deposits, etc. This proposal is not a binding contract as to either party until they have both signed a mutually agreeable lease.

Figure 3-3

NCR (No Carbon Required)

TENANT'S PERSONAL AND CREDIT INFORMATION
(Use separate sheet for each tenant.)

PERSONAL INFORMATION

Name	Social Security No.
Present Address	Drivers Lic. No.
City/State/Zip Birthdate	Res. Phone

GENERAL INFORMATION

Other Occupants?	Number	Relationship	
Animals?	Number	Type	Smoker ☐ Yes ☐ No
Car Make	Year	Model Color	License No.

EMPLOYMENT INFORMATION

If employed less than two years, give same information on prior occupation

Present Occupation	Bus. Phone
Employer	Supervisor
Self Employed d.b.a.	Title
Business Address	From To
Type of Business	Monthly Gross Income
Prior Occupation	Bus. Phone
Employer	Supervisor
Self Employed d.b.a.	Title
Business Address	From To
Type of Business	Monthly Gross Income

REFERENCES

Housing

Current Address	From To
Landlord/Agent	Phone
Address	
Previous Address	From To
Landlord/Agent	Phone
Address	

Credit

Bank	☐ Checking ☐ Savings	Acct. No.
Address		Phone
Credit Reference	Highest amount owed $	Acct. No.
Address		Phone
Purpose of Credit		Acct. Opened Closed
Credit Reference	Highest amount owed $	Acct. No.
Address		Phone
Purpose of Credit		Acct. Opened Closed

Personal

Name	Phone
Address	Length of acquaintance
Nearest Relative	Phone
Address	Relationship

Have you ever filed a petition of bankruptcy? _____ Have you ever been evicted from any tenancy or had an eviction notice served on you? _____
Have you ever willfully and intentionally refused to pay any rent when due ? _____ Have you ever been convicted of a misdemeanor or felony other than a traffic or parking violation? _____ Are you a current illegal abuser or addict of a controlled substance? _____ Have you ever been convicted of the illegal manufacture or distribution of a controlled substance? _____
If you to any of the above, please indicate date of assurance: ▬▬▬▬▬▬

I DECLARE THAT THE FOREGOING IS TRUE AND CORRECT, AUTHORIZE ITS VERIFICATION AND THE OBTAINING OF A CREDIT REPORT. I agree to pay to the Landlord a non-refundable screening fee not to exceed $30.00. I understand that I am entitled to a copy of any consumer credit report obtained by the Landlord. I further agree that the Landlord may terminate any agreement entered into in reliance on any misrepresentation made above.

Applicant _____ Date _____

FORM 105-TA (10-97)   COPYRIGHT © 1994–97 BY PROFESSIONAL PUBLISHING, 880 LAS GALLINAS AVE., SAN RAFAEL, CA 94903   (415) 472-1964   FAX (415) 472-2069

PROFESSIONAL PUBLISHING

Figure 3-4

AIR AMERICAN INDUSTRIAL REAL ESTATE ASSOCIATION

STANDARD PROPOSAL TO LEASE

_____, California   _____
(City)   (Date)

1.   Lessee. _____, ("Lessee")
hereby proposes to lease the real property (the "Premises") hereinafter described upon the terms and conditions herein set forth.

2.   Premises. The Premises which are the subject of this proposal are located in the County of _____,
State of _____, commonly known as _____
and described as _____
_____
_____

3.   Broker.
        3.1   This proposal is being submitted to Lessor through _____
("Broker") who is the procuring cause of this proposal. Lessee agrees to use the services of Broker exclusively in connection with any and all
negotiations and offers with respect to the Premises for a period of one year from the above date.
        3.2   Notwithstanding whether or not the Parties ultimately enter into a lease of the Premises, the Parties acknowledge that the
following real estate brokerage relationship exists:
                ☐ (Check if applicable) Broker represents both Lessor and Lessee; or
                ☐ (Check if applicable) Broker represents Lessee exclusively and shall not be considered the subagent and/or representative
of Lessor's broker.

4.   Deposit.
        4.1   (A) ☐ (Check if applicable) Lessee hereby delivers to Broker a check in the amount of $_____
("Deposit"). ☐ Broker is to hold said check uncashed in Trust. Lessee hereby acknowledges this instruction (_____Lessee's initials).
        4.1   (B) ☐ (Check if applicable) Lessee hereby delivers to Broker a check in the amount of $_____
("Deposit"). Broker is instructed to hold check uncashed until acceptance hereof and by his/her initials. Broker hereby acknowledges this
instruction. (_____Broker's initials).
        4.2   Upon execution of the lease agreement contemplated hereby, Broker is authorized by Lessee to deliver the Deposit to Lessor.

5.   Term. The term of the lease shall be _____months and shall begin on _____
and shall end on _____

6.   Rent.
        6.1   Monthly rent during the initial lease term shall be $_____payable, in advance, on the _____ day
of each month of the term hereof.
        6.2   On execution of lease, Lessee shall pay to Lessor $_____ representing rent for _____
_____

7.   Security Deposit. The Security Deposit shall be in the amount of $_____.

| Total monies due upon execution of Lease (security deposit plus advance rent): $_____ |

8.   Agreed Use. The Premises shall be used only for _____
_____
_____

9.   Possession and Condition of Premises. Lessor warrants that the Premises, without regard to the purpose for which Lessee will
use them, do not violate any covenant or restriction of record or any applicable governmental requirement. If Lessee is not already in possession,
Lessor shall deliver the Premises on _____broom clean and free of debris with the plumbing, lighting, heating,
ventilating and air conditioning, and loading doors in good operating condition. Subject to the preceding two sentences, Lessee accepts the
Premises in an "AS IS" condition and in its present condition.

10.   Maintenance and Repairs. The foundations, exterior walls, and exterior roof shall be maintained by _____
_____
Lessee shall repair and maintain all other parts of the Premises and adjacent areas.

11.   Insurance.
        11.1   Property Insurance (i.e., all perils included within the classification of fire and extended coverage, vandalism, and malicious
mischief - see paragraph 8.3 of the appropriate American Industrial Real Estate Association Standard Lease Form for a more detailed
description) shall be paid for by _____
If paid for by Lessor, Lessee shall pay any increase in premiums over those paid in the "Base Period".
        11.2   Liability insurance naming Lessee and Lessor as co-insured or "additional insured," shall be paid for by Lessee.

12.   Property Taxes. Real property taxes shall be paid by _____ .
If paid by Lessor, Lessee shall pay increases over the taxes payable for the 19____-19____ real estate tax year.

13.   Proportion and Share of Expenses. If the Premises are part of a larger building or a complex of buildings, Lessee shall pay its
proportionate share, i.e. _____%, of the operating expenses, if any, of the property of which the Premises are a part, including, but not limited
to, real property taxes, insurance, maintenance, and security costs.

14.   Lease Agreement. The Lease which is to be ultimately executed by the Parties shall contain the provisions of the most recent
edition of the ☐ Net ☐ Gross ☐ Other (specify) _____
American Industrial Real Estate Association Standard Lease Form subject to such modifications, other than the terms as specifically set forth
herein, as may be mutually agreed upon by the parties in writing.

15.   Sublease Proposal.
                ☐ If this box is checked, this is a proposal to sublease, and
        15.1   All references herein to Lease, Lessor, and Lessee shall be construed to mean Sublease, Sublessor, and Sublessee,
respectively.
        15.2   The sublease shall be subject to and subordinate to the Master Lease and, except for those matters which are directly
contradicted by this proposal, the terms and conditions of the parties shall be the terms and conditions of the Master Lease.
        15.3   Within three business days following acceptance of this proposal, Sublessor shall deliver to Sublessee a complete and
accurate copy of the Master Lease.
        15.4   If this transaction requires the approval of the Master Lessor, Sublessee shall provide to the Master Lessor all information
reasonably required by Master Lessor. Sublessor shall use its best reasonable efforts to obtain Master Lessor's approval, and if within
_____ business days following acceptance of this proposal, the Master Lessor has not approved this transaction, this transaction shall, at

Page 1 of 2

©1997 – American Industrial Real Estate Association

the option of Sublessee, be terminated and all amounts deposited by Sublessee shall be returned to Sublessee.

16. No Broker Representations. Lessor and Lessee acknowledge that Broker has made no representations or warranties regarding the physical condition of the Premises, or its suitability for Lessee's intended use, and that neither Party has made any representations or warranties to the other (except as expressly set forth in this proposal) and that Lessor and Lessee are relying upon their own independent investigations in making or accepting this offer.

17. Disclosure. This Proposal is contingent upon Lessee's receipt and written approval, within five days after delivery to Lessee, of a completed American Industrial Real Estate Association "Property Information Sheet" duly executed by or on behalf of Lessor.

18. Assignment and Subletting. Lessee shall have the right to sublease or assign the lease with Lessor's prior written consent, which consent shall not be unreasonably withheld.

19. Attorneys' Fees. Should litigation arise between Lessor, Lessee and Broker, or any of them, concerning this transaction, the prevailing party shall be entitled to reasonable attorneys' fees.

20. Expiration. Unless accepted in writing by Lessor on or before _____, this proposal shall expire and be of no further force or effect, and Lessee's deposit shall be returned to Lessee.

21. Time. Time is of the essence with respect to this proposal.

22. Addendum. Any Addendum attached hereto is hereby incorporated in this proposal by this reference.

Addendum attached: Yes: ☐ (Paragraphs _____ through_____)
No: ☐

LESSEE HAS READ, AND FULLY UNDERSTANDS THE FOREGOING AND ACKNOWLEDGES RECEIPT OF A COPY HEREOF.

THIS PROPOSAL IS NOT BINDING ON EITHER PARTY. IT IS INSTEAD INTENDED TO FACILITATE NEGOTIATIONS BETWEEN THE PARTIES. THE PARTIES SHALL NOT BE OBLIGATED TO LEASE THE PREMISES UNTIL BOTH HAVE SIGNED A MUTUALLY AGREEABLE LEASE AGREEMENT.

ATTENTION: NO REPRESENTATION OR RECOMMENDATION IS MADE BY THE AMERICAN INDUSTRIAL REAL ESTATE ASSOCIATION OR BY ANY REAL ESTATE BROKER AS TO THE LEGAL SUFFICIENCY, LEGAL EFFECT, OR TAX CONSEQUENCES OF THIS PROPOSAL OR THE TRANSACTION TO WHICH IT RELATES. THE PARTIES ARE URGED TO SEEK ADVICE OF COUNSEL AS TO THE LEGAL AND TAX CONSEQUENCES OF THIS TRANSACTION.

DATED: _____

LESSEE:

By _____

Street Address _____

City, State, Zip _____

Telephone Number of Lessee _____

Broker: _____

By _____

Street Address _____

City, State, Zip _____

Telephone Number of Lessee _____

23. Lessor's Acceptance. Lessor accepts the foregoing proposal to Lease the Premises and authorizes Broker to communicate to Lessee Lessor's acceptance hereof and to deliver an executed copy of this Agreement to Lessee.

LESSOR:

DATED: _____

_____

By _____

Street Address _____

City, State, Zip _____

Telephone Number of Lessor _____

COMMISSION AGREEMENT

In consideration of the real estate brokerage services rendered by Broker to Lessor, the undersigned Lessor agrees that if Lessee leases, purchases, or acquires any other rights to the Premises or other premises owned by Lessor within six months of the date of this Proposal, then, Lessor shall pay Broker a fee in accordance with Broker's current Schedule of Commissions. If Lessor has appointed an exclusive agent other than the Broker named herein, the brokerage commission shall be as mutually agreed between the brokers.

LESSOR:

DATED: _____

By _____

NOTE: These forms are often modified to meet changing requirements of law and needs of the industry. Always write or call to make sure you are utilizing the most current form: AMERICAN INDUSTRIAL REAL ESTATE ASSOCIATION, 700 So. Flower St., Suite 600, Los Angeles, CA 90017. (213) 687-8777.

©1997 – American Industrial Real Estate Association

Drafting Leases

USE OF STANDARD FORMS

A property manager should not attempt to modify standard clauses in a lease, prepare new clauses or prepare complex leases by the cut-and-paste method utilizing clauses from other leases. First of all, it exposes the property manager to liability should his or her draftsmanship create results not contemplated that work to the detriment of the owner.

Secondly, preparing a lease using other than what is regarded as a standard industry lease could be construed as the unauthorized practice of law. (You are doing it for another and are compensated in the form of management and/or leasing fees.) Giving legal advise to others in the course of management could also be regarded as the unauthorized practice of law.

Case Example

People v. Landlords Professional Services (1989) 215 C.A. 3d 1599

The Court of Appeals in affirming a judgment against the defendant pointed out that the sale of legal forms and detailed manuals on how to complete the forms was legal. However, in this case the defendant advertised that they accomplished evictions. Clients discussed evictions with counselors who offered specific legal information. This action constituted the practice of law.

Don't attempt to use a standard lease that is NOT appropriate for the tenancy.

As an example, you should not use a residential lease form for a property including both residential and commercial areas.

While there are a great many standardized lease forms covering commercial and industrial properties, if any lease form is to be materially altered or a new lease drafted, competent legal counsel should be sought.

A point to remember is that lease ambiguities are generally resolved against the party drafting the lease. Therefore, it behooves the property manager to make certain that the lease is clear. If a lease form includes a clause you do not understand, see an attorney; don't take chances.

Care must be taken so that the original lease plus all possible options will NOT exceed any statutory limitation.

In most states, statutes provide maximum periods for leasing. In California, and a number of other states, the maximum period is 99 years. A one year lease with unlimited options to renew for one year periods could exceed 99 years. Such a lease should be avoided since the courts in some states would not enforce the lease.

TITLE OF LEASE

Some lessors entitle their lease "Proposal to Lease." It is a proposal by the tenant to lease which includes all the lease terms and conditions. When signed by the lessor, it becomes a binding lease.

The title "Proposal to Lease" is used simply to make the document less menacing to a tenant than "Lease." However, it is clear that this in fact is a lease when signed by the lessor.

The authors consider this practice deceptive and unprofessional.

LEASES PREPARED BY LESSEES

You should be on your guard when a tenant or tenant's attorney has prepared a lease on a form you are not familiar with. While it may appear clear, you should protect yourself from liability by having the lease reviewed by an attorney. The attorney should also review your customary lease form so that any differences can be noted.

With the advent of laser printers, some landlords (and even tenants) will prepare leases which appear to be standard form leases.

Some will also include a form number. Unfortunately, some people will use this technique to try to take advantage of the other party.

You do not want to be a party to any deception. Even if the lease was prepared by your client, you want to make certain the tenant fully understands the lease provisions, especially any unusual provisions in the lessor's favor. You may wish to suggest to the lessee that he or she also have the lease reviewed by an attorney.

CONTRACTS OF ADHESION

A **CONTRACT OF ADHESION** *is a one-sided contract where one party has superior bargaining ability and will not allow any modification. It is a take-it-or-leave-it proposition.*

A contract of adhesion, such as a lease, that a court determines to be so unfair as to be oppressive, will not be enforced. The courts will consider the agreement unconscionable.

Oil companies offer "take-it-or-leave-it leases" to lessees, as do franchisors.

EXPIRATION DATE

For residential property, you want your leases to expire when rentals are in most demand in your area.

In a college area, you would want one-bedroom rentals to expire before the beginning of the next term when there will be peak demand. This will avoid lengthy vacancy periods.

Three-bedroom units are normally sought by families with children of school age. Leases expiring after the end of the school year and prior to the coming school year, such as July 1 and August 1, will likely be at a time of greatest demand.

In cold climates, apartments having pools would be most desirable for tenants June 1, July 1 and August 1, when the pool is a positive feature. On December 1, the renter is not likely to be greatly influenced by the presence of a swimming pool.

When you do rent a property during a period of low rental activity, such as December 1, you should consider having the initial lease for a period other than one year so that the lease will expire during a more desirable rental period, such as September 1. Subsequent lease extensions or renewals can be for a one-year or multi-year period.

If a tenant takes occupancy on October 8, you would want the October rent prorated so that November rent comes due on November 1. Having all rents due on the same date allows ease in record keeping and late fee calculations. You are less likely to overlook a delinquency.

LENGTH OF THE LEASE

A number of years ago an attorney realized there was a need for offices for young attorneys that were furnished and offered the required support services. He started a business which quickly made him a multimillionaire. He leased whole floors of large office buildings. He then offered attorneys a private office, telephone answering, secretarial services, support services such as copy machines and fax, use of shared conference rooms and a well equipped law library.

The business prospered and he had operations in dozens of cities serving thousands of attorneys. At the time, the economy was growing and rents were high. He locked in his space rentals with long-term leases at close to the peak of the market in the mid to late 1980s. In order to maximize his income he took a risk that led to financial disaster. He only subleased for one year periods.

Office space became overbuilt, building developers went bankrupt. Lenders were left with vacant space so rentals went down drastically. The glut of office space provided opportunities for others. Newcomers were able to lease space for much less than the innovator of the space for attorneys was paying. They were able to steal his tenants by offering rents which he could not match because of the terms of his master leases. What could he have done to protect himself?

He could have negotiated shorter term master leases with multiple options to extend (with his tenant leases ending at the end of each extension period). This way he could be in a position to not exercise the option to renew, but instead renegotiate the rent downward based on competitive space available. Few building owners would not consider concessions at a time building vacancies rates were over 20 percent.

Of course, hindsight is always 20/20. Nevertheless a person should consider the "what ifs" when negotiating leases.

As a lessor, if you feel that rents will go up significantly and there will be a relatively low vacancy factor, then shorter term leases would be in your best interest. However, it you believe that overbuilding or other market factors will increase the vacancy factor which will result in lower rents, then you would want to lock in tenants with long-term leases. The tenant, on the other hand, would prefer a short-term lease with options to renew. As in the case example given, the tenant could either extend, if rents were advantageous, or renegotiate from a position of strength if rents dropped.

Case Example

Bed, Bath & Beyond of La Jolla, Inc. v. La Jolla Village Square 52 C.A. 4th 867

The plaintiffs negotiated a lease at a new shopping center. The defendant sent the plaintiff a lease for signature which the plaintiff signed and returned. Meanwhile, Linens 'N Things offered the defendant more rent for the space which the landlord accepted.

The Court of Appeals upheld the trial court's decision in favor of the defendant since the Statute of Frauds required a written lease. The lease was never signed by both parties so the contract was never entered into. The landlord was free to negotiate with others until they had committed themselves in writing.

Lease Negotiations

There is NO lease until the lease has been agreed to.

Parties can change their minds any time during the negotiation process.

The advantage of using a printed lease form prepared by a form company is that tenants feel it is standard boiler plate and they are less likely to insist on changes.

When you have a great many leases in one building, it is preferable for management to have lease terms as identical as possible. When each lease is negotiated from scratch, it can lead to a management nightmare if each of the many clauses are different.

While residential leases are usually contracts of adhesion because the tenant must accept the lease offered or walk away, leases for commercial and industrial property are likely to be the result of negotiation as to price and/or terms.

UNDERSTANDING POSITIONS AND EXPECTATIONS

When negotiating a lease, as an agent of the lessor you want to make the best deal possible for your client. The tenant and/or the tenant's representative wants to make the best deal possible for the tenant.

Each party is likely to have an opening position advantageous to them as well as an idea as to how low or how high they can go. As an example, see Figure 3-5.

As you can see from Figure 3-5, an agreement should be reached. This is not always the case because a tenant who does not know if a lessor will come down to his or her price range might look elsewhere.

Figure 3-5

Tenant's Position

LOW	HIGH
$800	$1,200

Compromise in the Middle at $1,200

Lessor's Position

LOW	HIGH
$1,200	$1,800

A different situation is set forth in Figure 3-6.

Figure 3-6

Tenant's Position

LOW	HIGH

$800	$1,500

**No Middle = No Compromise
No Agreement**

Lessor's Position

LOW	HIGH

$1,700	$2,200

It would appear that in this situation an agreement is impossible. This is not necessarily the case. Negotiations will often convince or influence a person to justify a change in position. One party may reduce expectations or both parties might change positions so that a positive agreement can be reached.

Don't expect to always get the maximum possible in negotiations, as negotiations are NOT carried out in complete sunlight.

Each party has motivating factors that are not apparent to the other party. As an example, buyers who have purchased property will often reveal that they would have paid more if they had to and sellers in the same transaction have revealed that they would have accepted less.

When you experience many vacancies and/or there is competition in the marketplace from similar property that has been vacant for some time, the tenants have a great deal of leverage in negotiations. Sometimes tenants don't perceive this power and fail to use it. On other occasions, they assume that they have leverage power when in actuality they do not. If the negotiations are to be successful, this perception of power has to be deflated.

An example of deflating the tenant's perception of power would be in negotiating a lease extension. If the tenant believes you need the tenant more than the tenant needs you, then the tenant might demand a reduction in rent for a lease extension. You might be able to reduce the tenant's expectations by notifying the tenant that you will be showing the premises to a prospective tenant. Always use a real person interested in the rental you will be showing. A tactic like this can change a current tenant's attitude from, "I'll get a reduction in rent" to "I don't want to relocate because it means a loss in business." If you can reduce the tenant's expectations, then the tenant asking for major rent concessions might end up happy with only minor concessions or even a slight rent increase.

> *Again, care must be taken to avoid appearing too tough or you could end up losing your tenant.*

In a market situation where there is a very low vacancy factor for similar properties and you have several prospective tenants, it is a lessor's market that is advantageous to your client. Nevertheless, in preparing for negotiations you should determine:

1. What you want;
2. What you must have;
3. What is not too important.

You should consider the market to determine what you want. In Chapter 5 you will find that tenants, not owners, make the ultimate decision as to rents. You must consider the supply and demand features of the marketplace. If a particular tenant is important to you, you must consider the fact that too high a rent will mean a marginal or loss operation.

> *You can expect vacancies if your commercial tenants are NOT making a reasonable profit.*

GIVE A LITTLE

In residential leases there are usually many tenants and few if any items to be negotiated. Tenants expect to either accept the lease offered or to look elsewhere. Owners know that to negotiate different rents for different tenants will create ill will among tenants who are paying more than others. There is little room, if any, for negotiations. Commercial and industrial leases are far different in that different tenants offer various advantages to a lessor. There are usually many areas subject to negotiation, including rent.

> *Always let the tenant gain something by the negotiation process.*

This is especially important when an attorney represents the tenant. The tenant and/or attorney should go away from the negotiations feeling as if they are winners; that you have given them something they otherwise would not have had. Even when you are dealing from a position of strength and you know you don't have to give any concessions, you still want the tenant to be a winner. You can do this by asking for terms or clauses which, while favorable for you, you're willing to forgo. In setting forth your position, you will have built in concessions to be made during the negotiation process.

This is win/win negotiating. If the negotiations result in a lease, your working relationship with the tenant will be better because the tenant will regard you as reasonable.

On the other hand, if you adopt a win/lose philosophy where you convey a take-it-or-leave-it approach, you will lose lease opportunities even though you could have gained almost everything you wanted. Even though the owner's position was reasonable, the inability to give any concessions during negotiations will result in tenants looking elsewhere. As an example, assume a dealer wanted $8,000 for a used car. You would be pleased with yourself for saving $1,000 if you could buy the car for $7,000. On the other hand, if the dealer wanted $7,000 for the car and was unwilling to lower the price, you would probably shop elsewhere even though it may not be in your best interest to do so.

> *If a tenant feels that you're unreasonable but gives in to your position, you will have generated ill will which could come back to haunt you at a later date.*

A lease extension might come at a time when the tenant is in a position of strength and may want to humiliate you.

In negotiating a lease, keep in mind that an overall objective can often be reached by alternative paths. Examples would be items such as basic rents, graduated lease terms, what is included or not included with the rent, the period of the lease, minimum rent on percentage leases, and percentage of the gross.

Assume a prospective tenant indicates that he or she will not pay more than $2,000 per month. The tenant might nevertheless agree to a $1,700 per month lease plus a pro-rata share of parking lot maintenance and security costs, even though the total might be $2,300 per month.

> *Never get personal in negotiations.*

While you may feel that the tenant's position is unreasonable and that the attorney representing the tenant is the most obnoxious person you have ever met, don't let them know it. Show respect for the other party as a person but disagree as to position.

Although you may be treated rudely during what is otherwise a successful negotiation, you may have to deal with the party in the future so you want the other party to regard you as a fair and reasonable person.

DO IT QUICKLY

The advantage of face-to-face negotiations is that you can sense agreement or hostility and agreements can be made quickly. You want a quick negotiation.

The longer a period of lease negotiations, the greater the tenant's apprehension.

They are likely to look elsewhere in the event that they are unsuccessful in reaching an agreement. Often a tenant will obligate himself or herself to other space when an agreement with that tenant could have been quickly made. The longer the negotiations process the greater the likelihood the negotiations will fail.

You should continue on other points of the negotiations even though you seem to have reached an impasse on a particular point. Write down the terms of which you agree or check them off indicating agreement. When everything is agreed upon except for the impasse item, you should define the problem. As an example:

"Except as to the amount of base rent, the other aspects of the lease are acceptable to you, is that correct?"

Now that the problem has been clearly defined as a single item (or several), you should make the prospective tenant justify his or her position.

"Why do you feel that the base rent of $1,200 per month that I have proposed is excessive?"

You want the tenant to justify his or her objection. This will give you an opportunity to reinforce the advantages that the property offers.

If it is clear that a concession is necessary, you must have the tenant's position if he or she has not given it. As an example:

"Based on what you have expressed, What is the highest figure you would pay as to base rent?"

You need a tenant's position from which to negotiate up. Even though it was stated as a maximum, it seldom is and should not be assumed as a maximum. Any position set forth should be treated as a position from which to negotiate.

If a lease is to be prepared by others and is not to be signed at the conclusion of negotiations, prepare a memo of understanding which sets forth the provisions agreed to and have the memo signed by the prospective tenant and yourself. Copies go to both parties. This reduces the chance of a tenant claiming that the lease does not reflect what was agreed to. A memo of understanding reduces the probability that the tenant will go elsewhere or try to renege on any agreement. The memo could be a binding contract if it is complete. The memo should clearly set forth:

1. rent and any escalation;
2. costs to be paid by lessor and/or lessee;
3. services to be provided by lessor;
4. period of the lease and any renewal periods and their terms;
5. deposits;
6. any concessions such as modifications by the owner or free rent;
7. responsibilities of the tenant;
8. each lease clause (reference a standard lease if a standard clause is to be used);
9. late rent;
10. assignment and sublease;
11. use of premises.

RENT INCENTIVES

Owners like to show high rents to bankers for refinancing as well as to prospective buyers when they wish to sell and to establish a base rent in the event of subsequent rent control.

The only way to get above market rents is to offer something special.

Rental concessions should be considered for several other reasons. If you are taking over a new structure or one that has recently been rehabilitated, you would want to stabilize the structure (fill vacancies) as soon as possible. This could eliminate a negative cash flow for the owner. Rental concessions can give you an edge on the competition.

Rental concessions should be considered where there are many vacancies or there has been a vacancy for a long period of time, such as a commercial building vacant over a year.

Rental concessions might be absolutely necessary if the rent being asked is more than market rent for similar available properties. Rental concessions can take several forms:

Free Rent

Free rent is the most common concession offered.

While a first month's free rent is more effective than the 12th month's free rent on a one-year lease, it does tend to attract renters who have a greater likelihood of defaulting on lease obligations. However, don't reduce property damage bonds or other deposits. If tenants move in without money, you risk never seeing any money even when you thought you properly qualified them.

An effective variation on free rent is to offer it to your present tenants. As an example, offer one month's free rent if the new tenant can bring in someone else to lease a unit. Since the tenant does not get a rental incentive, he or she is less likely to move when the lease expires.

> *Tenants who received rental incentives are more likely to leave at the end of their leases than are tenants who do NOT receive incentives. The likelihood of moving increases directly with the amount of incentives given.*

A Desirable Premium

One landlord offered a free 31-inch color television set as a rental concession. Her costs were less than half the month's rent. It enabled the landlord to rent out the new building in record time.

A promotion in a golf course community offered a Callaway custom fitted driver in exchange for leases signed by a particular date.

A different incentive offered by a developer is one year's prepaid cable television with all the premium channels. The developer's costs were less than offering a month's free rent. He reported greater rental success with this promotional incentive.

Instead of giveaways, some lessors advertise a very attractive rent to bring in prospective tenants. In addition to the rent, they charge for parking, trash removal, etc. We consider this practice deceptive and recommend it be avoided.

Name That Building

For single-tenant and multi-tenant buildings, offering the building name can be a tremendous incentive for a tenant to sign a lease. A tenant's name on a structure or complex adds prestige to the tenant's firm.

Names such as "The Superior Insurance Building," "Thompson, Inc." or "The Hydraulic, Inc. Industrial Center" will mean a great deal to tenants and it doesn't cost the owner one dime.

Giving away the name should only be done when the tenant is leasing a significant portion of the space under a long-term lease. The name will give you leverage for all of the lease terms.

One successful property management firm uses doctored photographs of buildings to show the name of the prospective tenant on the entrance to the building as well as large letters across the front of the structure.

Of course, the owners concurrence should be obtained before you give away the name, especially if it currently bears the owner's name.

Give Them the Building

Several national corporations have demanded and received equity positions in the buildings they occupy when negotiating a lease for a significant amount of office space located in areas where a high vacancy rate exists.

Typically, they would take around 10 percent in corporate stock or as a limited partnership. Giving away part of the building can make economic sense if it turns a negative cash flow situation into an investment having a significant positive cash flow.

Some lessors have come up with a variation of this idea. When a building has a high debt and is vacant, an owner realizes he has an asset with questionable value. By offering a prospective tenant an equity position up to 50 percent to sign a reasonably long-term lease, the offer becomes nearly impossible to turn down.

The tenant pays a rent which pays the mortgage and more. The tenant gets one-half of the cash flow from the building, and income increases as lease payments escalate. When the mortgage is paid off the tenant still has the equity position in the property. The tenant is tied to the property because leaving would mean the equity value would greatly diminish.

LEASE RENEWALS

When negotiating renewals or extensions you should consider the fact that it cost money to move. Besides the time and expense of moving and the indirect expenses associated with new stationery, decorating items, etc., commercial tenants are likely to suffer a loss in business both during and after their relocation.

Because of the bother and costs associated with moving, a tenant will generally be willing to pay a premium over comparable vacant units to remain at a location.

> *Residential tenants are more likely to move because of rent increases than are commercial tenants.*

A rent increase from five percent to ten percent, even though not indicated by market conditions, will generally be accepted by a commercial tenant. However, you could end up with a vacancy if you get too greedy.

You want to make the increase seem reasonable rather than arbitrary when you offer a tenant a new lease at a higher rent. As an example, you can show cost increases such as taxes and insurance as the reason. There is always some rise in costs.

You might be in a situation where you have several vacancies and a commercial tenant needs a downward adjustment in the rent to survive. Rather than lowering the rent, offer to defer a portion of the rent. As an example, instead of paying $1,800 per month rent, a tenant may pay $1,000 per month and sign a note for $9,600 for the balance of the one-year lease. You haven't reduced rents and there is a possibility that the tenant will recover financially and make good on the note. Later if the tenant is able to pay the full rent you have the tenant pretty well locked in until the arrearage can be paid off.

Don't offer to defer rent without owner's written concurrence.

DEALING WITH IMPASSE

There are several ways to overcome an apparent impasse. You can go on to other points. However, if the impasse remains, try one of the the following methods.

Break Bread

You can defuse a tightening situation over coffee or a meal. Ask questions about the prospective tenant, his or her interests and family. Try to be physically close, but always give the other person space. Coming within three feet of a someone's face is considered an intrusion and places that person on the defensive.

At the end of the break, ask the prospective tenant,

> **"Let's turn positive for a few moments. What is there about the property that you like?"**

You can follow this up with,

> **"You like the property and I would like to rent it to you. What will it take to reach an agreement?"**

The response would allow you three choices:

1. Acceptance;

2. A counter offer such as "Make it [$] and we have a deal." Whenever you give what appears to be the final agreement, put your hand forward for a handshake. A person will often easily and almost automatically extend his or her hand. A handshake is a universal acknowledgment of an agreement.

3. There are several other options when a prospective tenant has come up with terms which differ from yours:

A. A split-the-difference approach is based on emotion rather than reason, but from an early age we have learned that splitting the difference is fair.

"Let's make a deal. We'll split the difference and make [the basic rent $1,700 per month]. Do we have a deal?" Again, prompting a handshake.

B. Giving in on something else to get approval is a good approach.

"I'll give you two underground parking spaces at no cost plus rent at $1,750 per month. Do we have a deal?" Again, extend your hand. Having concessions in reserve helps with this approach.

FOREIGN LANGUAGE NEGOTIATIONS

If you negotiate a lease in any language other than English, make certain the tenant fully understands the lease as written.

You should provide the tenant with a copy of the lease in the language in which it was negotiated.

In several states, if a residential lease is negotiated primarily in Spanish, or if the lessee request it, a Spanish translation of the lease must be provided to the lessee. Most form companies have lease forms in Spanish and some have translations in several languages

RECORDING LEASES

Generally, possession is considered constructive notice that a person has an interest in real estate.

If a lender made a loan on a property where a tenant was in possession, a foreclosure of the loan would leave the lender owning the property subject to the lease rights of the tenant. However, if the lease had been signed but the tenant had not yet taken possession of the property, a lender would not have constructive notice of the tenant's rights. So a later foreclosure of a loan could leave a tenant subject to eviction by the foreclosing lender.

Property managers for franchises and corporations, which lease a great deal of space, generally record their leases as soon as they are completed.

This is especially important if there is going to be a significant time lapse between the time the lease is entered into and the time the lessee will be taking possession. Recording also gives a later lienholder constructive notice so a foreclosure of a trust deed or mortgage entered into after the lease was recorded would result in the foreclosing lienholder taking possession subject to the rights of the tenant.

DISCLOSURES

While a property manager is generally the agent of the owner and has duties to the owner to obtain the most advantageous lease possible, the property manager has duties of fair play and honesty towards prospective tenants.

If a property manager knows that a property is unsuited or cannot be used for the intended purpose of the prospective tenant, then the prospective property manager must disclose this information. As an example, an intended use might be prohibited by zoning or restrictive covenants. Disclosure would be required if the property manager knew of these restrictions. Similarly, the property manager should disclose any negative information he or she possesses which a prospective tenant would want to know.

Other disclosures are mandated by state statutes in addition to those mentioned above. These types of disclosures might include the following.

Hazardous Substance

If hazardous substances were known to have been released or present on the property or if the owner has reasonable cause to believe hazardous substances are on the property, then lessees might have to be notified of this fact.

Failure to notify the prospective tenant about any hazardous substance could be the basis for the tenant voiding the lease and possibly obtaining damages.

Lead-Based Paint

When leasing residential property, the lessor must provide the lessee with a pamphlet warning of the hazards from lead-based paint.

Providing the lead-based paint pamphlet is a federal requirement.

Flood Hazard Area

The lessor might be required to disclose to the lessee the fact that the leased premises are within a flood hazard area.

Military Ordnance

Leases of residential property might require the lessor to disclose to the lessee any knowledge of a former military ordnance location which might contain explosive materials within a stated distance of the rental.

Death

Some states exempt lessors from any liability for failure to disclose to a lessee a death that occurred on the property more than a designated time period prior to entering a lease agreement.

> *Note: If you feel that the death or manner of death is information which a prospective tenant would want to know, we recommend disclosure even if the disclosure is NOT required by state law.*

AIDS

In a number of states, statutes provide that a lessor is under no obligation to disclose to a lessee that a previous occupant was HIV positive or had AIDS.

> *Note: The statutes generally do NOT prohibit disclosure but states that you need NOT disclose. You should be aware that if you make such a disclosure, you could be held responsible for slander or libel if you are incorrect.*

You have a duty to answer honestly, based on knowledge which you possess, if a prospective tenant asks about the death or affliction of a prior tenant. If you don't know, then that should be your answer.

Stigmatized Property

Stigmatized property is property which has developed an undesirable reputation in the community. As an example, if a property had been written up in a national tabloid as being haunted or this belief was held in the community, then the property would be stigmatized. If the property was the scene of a particularly brutal murder, it could be stigmatized to the point where many people would not want to occupy it, even at a reduced rent.

An apartment would be stigmatized where three separate renters died in violent accidents over a one-year period.

If over its 10-year life span, nine occupants of a commercial business location had gone bankrupt, the location would be considered unlucky by many. Some people believe strongly in luck and will NOT want to occupy any structure that they consider unlucky.

You have a duty to an owner to use your best efforts to lease property when you are acting as an agent. You also have a duty to prospective tenants as to fair dealing. Placing yourself in the prospective tenants shoes, if you would want to know particular facts or beliefs about a property prior to leasing it, then you should disclose this information to your tenant. This is nothing more than the application of the Golden Rule.

CHAPTER 3 SUMMARY

A lease is a contract. The four basic requirements of a contract apply:

1. Mutuality - clear meeting of the minds as to the essential terms of the lease;
2. Capacity to contract;
3. Legal Purpose;
4. Consideration.

A fifth requirement writing applies to leases of over one year and leases which, by their terms, cannot be completed within one year (**Statute of Frauds**).

Leases for a fixed term are estates for years while leases that renew themselves unless terminated are periodic tenancies.

A gross or flat lease has a fixed level rental amount. In a net lease, the lessor receives a fixed amount and the lessee pays all property expenses including taxes and insurance. With a percentage lease, the tenant pays a minimum rent (usually) plus a percentage of the gross income.

Leases that do not prohibit assignment or sublease can be assigned or subleased. An assignment is a transfer of all of a lessor's interest although the lessor remains secondarily liable on the lease. A sublease is a new lease between the original lessee and a sublessee. The sublessee is the tenant of the original lessee.
Tenants should be qualified by checking income, credit history and rental history.

A real estate broker should not prepare a lease other than a standard form as it could be regarded as an unauthorized practice of law.

The court might regard a one-sided, take-it-or-leave-it lease as unconscionable and refuse to enforce it (**Contract of Adhesion**).

Leases should be written to expire in prime rental periods. With a long-term lease, the lessor risks not being able to take advantage of escalating rents that are not reflected in the lease or its escalations.

In lease negotiations, a win/win attitude results in a greater chance of a favorable conclusion as well as better tenant relations. As lessor, you should try to have an area for concession.

Rent incentives can be used to rent projects quickly, obtain a competitive edge on the market and even obtain an otherwise above market rent. Incentives don't have to be monetary.

Tenants in possession are more likely to accept an increase above the market rental for a lease renewal than a prospective tenant who is considering the rental.

Leases may be recorded. They give constructive notice of the tenant's interest and would thus take priority over later mortgages and trust deeds.

While a property manager has agency duties to an owner he or she represents, the property manager has a duty of fair play and disclosure to the prospective tenant. If the property manager knows of problems with the property that could effect the tenancy or intended use, then the problems should be revealed to the tenant. The lessor should also reveal hazardous substances that may have been released on the premises and if the property is located in a flood hazard zone.

If it is known that residential property is within a distance specified by statute of a facility where explosive ordnance may be found, then this must be disclosed.

By law, a lead-based paint pamphlet is to be provided to tenants for residential rentals.

A lessor need not reveal death from any cause on the premises if disclosure is not required by state statute. The fact that a prior resident had AIDS or was HIV positive is usually exempt from disclosure.

CLASS DISCUSSION TOPICS

1. Which properties in your area could use rental incentives? Why?

2. Go through ads for apartments for rent in your local newspapers. Discuss the types of rental incentives offered in the ads.

3. If you or your office is currently handling rentals, how are prospective tenants screened? What could be done to improve the screening process?

4. Give examples of local tenants who prepare the leases (or tenants you feel prepare their own leases). Why do landlords accept this tenant practice?

5. In your area, what would be the best time for leases to expire? Why?

6. Which tenants in your area are on net leases? Why do you suppose this type of lease was chosen?

7. Which tenants in your area are on percentage leases? Do you know what percentages particular businesses are paying?

8. Which tenants in your area would suffer economically if they had to relocate? Why?

CHAPTER 3 QUIZ

1. Which of the following is NOT a requirement for every lease?

    A. Mutuality
    B. Legal purpose
    C. In writing
    D. Consideration

2. A lease that automatically renews itself, in the absence of notification by either party, is what kind of lease?

    A. A gross lease
    B. A percentage lease
    C. A periodic tenancy
    D. An estate for years

3. A tenant pays taxes, insurance and all maintenance expenses. What kind of lease does she have?

    A. Net lease
    B. Gross lease
    C. Percentage lease
    D. Flat lease

4. Which of the following tenants would be MOST LIKELY to have a percentage lease?

    A. Residential tenant
    B. Manufacturer
    C. Government agency
    D. Jewelry store

5. A transfer by a lessor of all interest in a lease to a third party, who agrees to accept the lease obligations, would be a:

    A. sublease
    B. assignment
    C. contract of adhesion
    D. percentage lease

6. When the value of the premises has increased significantly above the rent specified in the lease, an economic tenant would be better off to:

    A. assign the lease
    B. sublease the premises
    C. void the lease
    D. renegotiate a higher rent

7. In qualifying a prospective tenant, you should be interested in the tenants:

    A. income
    B. credit history
    C. rental history
    D. all of the above

8. If you believe that rents will increase significantly in the near future, the leases you negotiate for owners, should:

    A. prohibit assignment
    B. be for relatively short terms
    C. include renewal options
    D. be estates for years

9. Rent incentives are most likely to be given when:

    A. there is low unemployment
    B. the rent is set below market rent
    C. there is a high vacancy factor
    D. the tenant only marginally qualifies

10. When could a lessor have a goal of obtaining an above market rent?

    A. When giving rent incentives
    B. When negotiating a lease renewal
    C. Both A and B
    D. Neither A nor B

Answers: 1. C; 2. C; 3. A; 4. D; 5. B; 6. B; 7. D; 8. D; 9. C; 10. C

Chapter 4

Lease Clauses

KEY WORDS AND TERMS

Accelerated Payments
Arbitration
Assignment
Attorney Fees
Automatic Renewal
Bad Checks
Bankruptcy
Breach of Lease
COLA
Common Areas
Competition Clause
Complete Agreement
Covenant to Remain in Business
CPI
Destruction of Premises
Eminent Domain
Estoppel Certificate
Escalator Clause
Excuse from Performance
Extension of Lease
Fixtures
Grace Period
Guarantors
Hold Harmless Clause
Holdover Clause
HVAC
Joint and Several Liability
Late Charges

Lead-Based Paint Disclosure
Limitation on Occupants
Merchant Associations
Minimum Rent
Net Sales
Noncompetition Clause
Non-Disturbance Clause
Nonwaiver Clause
Notice of Nonresponsibility
Option to Purchase
Option to Rebuild
Option to Renew
Partial Destruction
Percentage Lease
Possession Clause
Quiet Enjoyment
Radius Clause
Recapture Clause
Renewal of Lease
Rental Interruption Insurance
Rent Tolled
Right of First Refusal
Security Deposit
Sublease
Surrender
Time is of the Essence
Trade Fixtures
Zero Tolerance Drug Clause

LEARNING OBJECTIVES

In this chapter you will learn about the many clauses which may be included in leases. You will learn what they mean and their applicability to the specific needs of lessors and lessees.

By understanding what can be included in a lease, you will be better able to meet the needs of your clients while performing property management duties.

Administration of Lease Clauses

In order to administer a great many leases, a property manager should attempt to use standard clauses wherever possible.

This is not always possible. A synopsis of each lease can be prepared to indicate the standard clauses for each lease, renewal dates, any options as well as those clauses which have been rewritten or added with the substance of the changes and additions. For easy access, this data can be in a computer file. The entire lease can also be included in the computer file for reference purposes by use of a scanner.

Again, when new clauses are added or changed, legal assistance should be sought. Commercial and industrial leases are more likely to have specially written clauses and alterations to clauses than would residential leases.

Lease Clauses

Following are some of the specific clauses utilized in leases. In Chapters 5 and 6, you will find lease forms that include many of the clauses described in this chapter as well as variations of these clauses.

Some of the clauses and material set forth applies only to residential property, only to commercial or industrial property, to various types of property or for specific types of leases.

The clauses covered are not all-inclusive as new clauses can be formulated to cover any situation. These are simply clauses that are more commonly encountered.

Accelerated Payments. Leases frequently state that a breach of the lease, as to rent payments, shall accelerate all payments under the lease. What this means is that if there are four years remaining on the lease, the rent for the remaining four years becomes immediately due if the lessee becomes delinquent in rent.

Despite the fact that accelerated payment clauses can be found in many preprinted lease forms, rent acceleration in residential leases is unenforceable in most states.

The fact that a residential tenant agreed to the clause does not make it enforceable. Depending upon state law, the clause may be enforceable for nonresidential leases.

Acknowledgment. Lessee acknowledges that disclosures as to the condition of the premises, suitability of the premises for lessee purposes and environmental matters were made to lessee by lessor and/or broker and that no oral representation was made as to the suitability of the premises. The lessee further acknowledges that he or she has investigated the premises and assumes any responsibility as to any patent defects. The lessor could still be liable as to latent defects which were known but not disclosed.

Advertising. Percentage leases for shopping centers often have advertising requirements for tenants who are to share in joint advertising for the shopping center based on a formula. In some cases, management might also share in such expenses. This obligation would be spelled out in the lease.

Air Conditioning/Heating. This clause would set forth landlords and tenants obligations as to supplying air conditioning heating and ventilation. In some cases air conditioning may be included, in others the tenant might be supplied with chilled water for the tenants own equipment (commercial leases).

Heating obligations would also be set forth in this clause. *The term* **HVAC** *is frequently used. It stands for Heating, Ventilating and Air Conditioning.*

Alterations.

This clause would likely prohibit alterations without lessor's consent.

Some commercial and industrial leases give the lessor the right to elect to be the owner of lessee installed alterations and utilities or to require their removal at the end of the lease.

Amendments. The only way the lease can be modified is through a written agreement signed by the parties involved.

Arbitration. An **ARBITRATION CLAUSE** *may provide for either mandatory or consensual binding arbitration of disputes arising under the lease.* The manner of choosing an arbitrator shall be set forth. One method is to obtain a list of three arbitrators from an arbitration service. Each party eliminates one arbitrator and the remaining arbitrator is chosen for the arbitration.

> *By agreeing to binding arbitration, the parties agree to give up the right to sue in a court of law.*

However, the advantages are lower litigation costs and a quick resolution of a dispute without right to an appeal.

Assignment and Subleasing.

> *Generally, this clause prohibits assignment or subletting by the tenant without the consent of the lessor.*

When agreeing to long-term leases, most large commercial tenants want the right to assign the lease. Generally, they will agree to an assignment subject to the consent of the owner. They will do so because the lessor (landlord) cannot be unreasonable in his or her refusal to consent to a lease assignment.

The clause would likely state that acceptance of rent from a third party does not constitute agreement to an assignment and that lessor's acceptance of one assignment or sublease may not be considered acceptance of subsequent assignments or subleases.

The clause may provide for a fee to accompany a request for an approval of assignment or sublease. It may even provide that the lessor has an option to terminate the lease upon receipt of a request for assignment or sublease.

> *Note: There is some disagreement as to the enforcement of this termination right.*

The lease might provide that in the event of default the lessor can go against the assignee or guarantor without first going against any other person liable on the lease. Upon default, the clause might provide that sublessee and assignees will be bound by all lease obligations but that lessor shall not be bound as to any deposits made by sublessee or assignee to the original lessee. (The lessor is not responsible for security deposits or other monies sublessees or assignees paid to the original lessee.)

Some commercial and industrial leases provide that the lessor shall have the option to cancel the lease if all or a designated portion of the leased premises is assigned or sublet.

Figure 4-1 is a Lessor Lease Assignment And Assumption Of Obligations by the assignee.

Case Example

John Hogan Enters, Inc. v. Kellogg **(1987) 187 C.A. 3d 589**

A tenant paid a base monthly rent of $2,750 plus an overage based on gross monthly sales. In 1981, the average monthly rent paid was $4,200. In 1982, it was $4,000 and in 1983, it was $3,700. The tenant assigned the remaining nine years of the lease to Phipps for a consideration of $150,000. Phipps wanted the premises for an antique shop which he intended to operate as a hobby. Phipps admitted that the business would not result in rent over the $2,750 base rental because of the nature of the business. The landlord refused to consent to the assignment and Phipps sued for damages.

The Court of Appeals held that the landlord was justified in rejecting the tenant. The landlord does not have to agree to a lease where they will receive less rent. "Refusing to consent to highway robbery cannot be deemed commercially unjustified."

The court referenced Kendall v. Ernest Pestana, Inc. (1985), 40 C. 3d 488 where the California Supreme Court held that a landlord might only refuse to consent to a lease assignment when there is a commercially reasonable objection (which there was in this case). A landlord might not withhold consent for the purpose of charging a higher rent or part of the monies paid for the assignment.

Note: Because a tenant can benefit by an assignment of a lease (in the case above, the assignee paid $150,000 for the lease), many leases provide that in the event of an assignment (or sublease), the lessor shall be entitled to a portion of the profits derived by the tenant giving the assignment (or sublease). By sharing in any compensation the tenant would negotiate for the greatest compensation possible. If the lease provided that all the compensation from an assignment go to the landlord, the tenant would likely assign the lease without any charge, thus eliminating possible additional income to the landlord. Both parties are likely to benefit by sharing the compensation.

Figure 4-1

AIR AMERICAN INDUSTRIAL REAL ESTATE ASSOCIATION

ASSIGNMENT AND ASSUMPTION OF LESSOR'S INTEREST IN LEASE

1. _____ ("Assignor")

hereby assigns and transfers to _____ ("Assignee")

the interest of Assignor under that certain Lease (the "Lease") dated _____, by and between

_____, as Lessor,

and _____, as Lessee,

concerning the real property commonly known as _____

_____ (the "Premises").

2.   Assignor also assigns to Assignee the security deposit under said Lease in the sum of $ _____
and the interest of Lessor in any applicable guaranty of said Lease.

3.   This Assignment shall be effective from and after the recordation, in the county where the Premises are located, of the deed passing fee
title to the Premises to Assignee.

Dated: _____

ASSIGNOR:

_____

_____

_____

By _____

Name Printed: _____

Title: _____

By _____

Name Printed: _____

Title: _____

ACCEPTANCE AND ASSUMPTION

Assignee hereby accepts the above Assignment and assumes all of the rights and obligations of the Lessor accruing from and after the
recordation, in the county where the Premises are located, of the deed passing fee title to the Premises to Assignee. Assignee shall defend,
indemnify, and hold Assignor harmless with respect to the obligations of Lessor under said Lease accruing from and after said date.

Dated: _____

ASSIGNEE:

_____

_____

By _____

Name Printed: _____

Title: _____

By _____

Name Printed: _____

Title: _____

For this form, write: American Industrial Real Estate Association, 700 S. Flower Street, Suite 600, Los Angeles, Calif. 90017
©1996 – American Industrial Real Estate Association   FORM AA-8701

Lease Clauses

Case Example

CARMA Developers Inc. v. Marathon Dev. CAL Inc. (1989) 211 C.A. 3d 1360

A commercial lease required consent to any assignment or sublease. It also provided that should the tenant request consent to assign or sublet, the lessor could, at its option, terminate the lease and enter into its own lease with the assignee or sublessee.

The tenant requested to sublet a portion of the property and the landlord then exercised the recapture clause which terminated the lease. After the tenant vacated, the tenant sued for breach of contract.

The court held that the clause was an invalid restraint on alienation. There was no justification for the clause. The termination was purely to obtain a higher rent. The court, in finding for the plaintiff, also pointed out that it violated the covenant of good faith and fair dealing.

Note: The clause was inconsistent with another clause in the lease that the landlord's consent to assignment or subleasing would not be unreasonably withheld.

Case Example

Artesia Medical Dev. Co. v. Regency Assocs. Ltd. (1989) 214 C.A. 3d 957

A commercial lease prohibited assignment without the landlord's approval. A tenant assigned the lease without seeking approval and the first notice the landlord received was that the assignee was in possession. The landlord sued the tenant and the assignee for unlawful detainer.

The Court of Appeals determined that the assignment was illegal and that there was no contractual relationship between the assignee and landlord. The unlawful detainer was upheld based on wrongful possession, not the lease.

Note: If consent for assignment had been requested, then the landlord could not have unreasonably refused to accept the assignment.

Attorney Fees. This provision provides that should there be legal action under the lease, the prevailing party in the lawsuit will be entitled to reasonable attorney fees. This clause reduces the possibility of a frivolous lawsuit.

Authority. Officers of corporations signing the lease acknowledge that they have authority to sign the lease and obligate the corporation based on a resolution of the board of directors.

Bad Checks. Your lease should set forth a charge that will be imposed for any check returned because of insufficient funds as well as for a check where the issuer has placed a stop payment. The lease should make it clear that this charge will be in addition to any late payment charge which might be applicable.

A bad check charge should apply to checks written by the tenant as well as third-party checks (checks written by others and endorsed to the property management).

> *Many property management company offices will NOT accept third-party checks with the exception of social security and government checks.*

If a bad check is replaced by another bad check, your policy should be to immediately start eviction proceedings against the tenant.

Many offices have a policy of evicting tenants who submit two bad checks while other firms have a modified policy of eviction for two bad checks in one, 12-month period. If the tenant is on a lease for one year or more, your lease should provide for termination upon receipt of a bad check. It should also provide that failure to evict does not waive your rights to evict for any later bad check.

Bankruptcy. A clause might provide that tenant bankruptcy or assignment of the lease to creditors shall allow the lessor to, at its option, terminate the lease and if so terminated, the tenant or assigns will vacate the premises. Generally, the clause would state that the tenant would still be obligated for any losses suffered by the lessor by the default of the lessees. (Guarantors would still be liable.) The lease might also provide that bankruptcy of the lessor would not terminate the lease.

Breach by Lessor. Lessee's rights are set forth for lessor breach. A lessee might have the right to cure a lessor default and deduct costs from the rent up to an amount set forth in the clause.

Broker. In this clause, the tenant either claims that he or she negotiated with a specific broker or without a broker and does not know of any broker who would be entitled to any commission. This statement by a tenant could make it difficult for a leasing agent with an open listing to claim they are entitled to a commission from the lessor if not named by the tenant.

The clause might name the brokers involved in the transaction and provide for the amount of compensation they are to receive. The amount of commission might also be provided for exercising any options.

Cleaning. This clause will specify responsibility for cleaning. Some office space is rented with cleaning included in the rent. In large office structures having several hundred tenants, if each tenant hired his or her own cleaner it could provide a logistical nightmare and could also compromise security. This clause could specify the firm or firms authorized to clean in the building and the tenant agrees not to employ any cleaning firm other than those listed.

Codes. The tenant agrees to comply with all building safety, health and fire codes.

Common Areas. This clause sets forth maintenance responsibilities and use of common areas. In many office buildings, there are law libraries available for use by all the tenants. The clause might provide that the use is subject to posted regulations (and charges, if any). The common areas would be defined for the rental.

Competition Clause. This clause would be used in a percentage lease and would prohibit the tenant from opening a competing location within a reasonable radius (expressed in miles) of the location.

This clause is sometimes called a "radius clause."

If a tenant did open a competing location, it would siphon off gross income from the other location. One would think that an owner would not wish to compete with his or her own business competition. It could make economic sense if the volume was high and the new location had a low fixed rent rather than a percentage lease.

Complete Agreement. There will usually be a clause indicating that the lease is the complete agreement and there are no verbal understandings or separate agreements affecting the tenancy that are not set forth therein or referenced by the lease.

When persons negotiate, many items might be discussed. Items have not been agreed upon unless they have been set forth in the lease.

Condition of the Premises. This provision would require the premises to be free of debris and all systems (HVAC, electrical, plumbing, elevator, freight doors, etc.) are operational at commencement of the lease.

Construction/Contractors.

Commercial leases generally include a requirement that any contractor used by the tenant will be licensed.

There might also be a requirement for pre-approval of any contractor by the lessor.

There might be a limitation on the time which a tenant on a commercial lease can spend for construction, remodeling and fixturing. Otherwise, the tenant could end up paying just the minimum rent for an extended period of time when there is a percentage lease.

The landlord's obligations and/or lack of obligations for tenant alterations and construction would be set forth. In some commercial leases, the lessor agrees to take over an agreed portion of alteration and construction costs.

Covenant to Remain in Business. Commercial leases, especially percentage leases, often have this clause printed in the lease. This prevents the tenant from leaving an empty store and paying the minimum rent under the lease. An empty store hurts other tenants and reduces the lessor's income on percentage leases.

While the clause "remain in business" is frequently printed, courts have determined that it is an implied covenant in percentage leases.

Case Example

College Block v. Atlantic Richfield Co. (1988) 200 C.A. 3d 524

A tenant signed a 20-year lease to build and operate a gas station on the plaintiff's land. The lease provided for a minimum rent plus a percentage of the gross income. After 17 years, the defendant closed the gas station and paid the minimum rent. The landlord brought action based on an implied covenant in the lease to operate the gas station for the term of the lease. If the gas station were operating, the lessor's income would have exceeded the minimum rent by more than 200 percent.

The Court of Appeals affirmed the trial court which ruled in favor of the landlord. The court held that a covenant to operate a business is implied in a percentage lease in which the minimum rent is not substantial. The court pointed out that the lease prohibited the landlord from operating gas stations on other sites owned by the landlord.

Default by Tenant. This clause would provide what would constitute a default and lessor's rights to bring suit, reenter premises, terminate lease, etc.

The rights could include rights in any assignment of the lessee or rights in any subleases entered into by the lessee.

Destruction of Premises. This clause sets forth what happens if the premises are destroyed. This could include one of the following:

1. Termination. Tenant and/or lessor could have the right to lease termination.

2. **Rent Tolled.** The rent could be waived until the premises are available to be used. The period of the lease could also be tolled (lease would be extended for the period premises were not available. This clause could be based on total and/or partial destruction.

3. **Option to Rebuild.** Lessor might have the option to rebuild or terminate lease. If lessor decides to rebuild, the period to rebuild is set.

4. **Partial Destruction.** The lease could provide for a rent adjustment based on the portion that is useable.

Drugs. A zero-tolerance drug clause might be included in a residential lease. The presence of illegal drugs on the premises shall be treated as proper cause for eviction. This would apply even though the drugs were brought on the premises by a guest.

Note: A California court has upheld the right to evict when the tenant's son was found to have drugs in their apartment.

Earthquake Ordinance. If an earthquake ordinance requires extensive structural work, the lessor shall have the option of performing the required work or terminating the lease and demolishing the structure. If the lessor chooses to make the repairs, the clause could provide for rent abatement while the premises cannot be occupied.

Easements. Lessor shall be permitted to grant easements (such as for utilities) providing such easement do not impair lessee's use of the premises.

Eminent Domain. This provision might provide that the tenant shall have no claim against the landlord if the premises are taken by a public entity by eminent domain. Unless the tenant agrees to waive any claim as to the public agency, the tenant would be entitled to receive compensation under eminent domain for the value of the leasehold, costs of relocation and fixtures. This sum could be considerable.

Entry. Leases should provide for situations when the landlord might enter the premises as well as any notice requirements. These situations could include:

1. insurance inspection;
2. inspect for repairs or to make repairs;
3. check for hazardous material and/or disposal of such material;
4. for appraisal purposes;
5. show premises to prospective tenants, purchasers and lenders;
6. emergency situations.

Escalator Clause. This clause would provide for periodic rent increases. It might be a set increase or an increase determined by the consumer price or other index.

Estoppel Agreement. This clause provides that the lessee will complete an estoppel certificate upon request by the lessor. The certificate sets forth that the lease has not been modified. The tenant has no option to purchase or right of first refusal, the amount of rent, the date the rent has been paid to, the amount of security or lease deposits and that the tenant is not in default.

Estoppel certificates might be required by a buyer if the lessor decides to sell the property. If the lessee fails (or refuses) to exercise an Estoppel Certificate, the lessor can exercise such a certificate.

Eviction. This clause would provide that should the tenant be evicted for the breach of any lease covenant, the tenant agrees to reimburse the landlord for all costs associated with the eviction. Costs would include reasonable attorney fees as well as any rental loss suffered by the landlord through the entire term of the lease.

Excuse from Performance. Lessor's obligations under the lease might be excused by Act of God (Act of God Clause), labor problems or other problems beyond the control of the lessor, that impair the lessor's ability to meet contractual obligations. Unless provided for in the lease, the lessee's obligations would not be excused for these reasons. The lease might provide that if the lessor is unable to give the tenant possession on the date indicated, and this delay is for a reason outside the lessor's control, then the rent would be tolled until possession could be given.

Financial Statement. Lessee and any guarantor agree to provide a financial statement to a prospective lender or purchaser if lessor requests same.

Fixtures. *FIXTURES were once items of personal property that had become so attached to the property that they were now considered part of the real estate.* A residential tenant cannot remove fixtures he or she installed unless the lease gave him or her that right. Generally, if there is a question as to an item being a fixture or real property, the courts will side with the tenant rather than the landlord. Three basic tests are used to determine if an item has become a fixture:

1. **Intent of the Parties.** Did the parties intend the item to stay? This is the most important test. In the lease, parties can agree if items might be removed by the tenant or shall remain as part of the realty.

2. **Adaptability**. If the property is particularly adapted to the property it would likely be a fixture.

3. **Attachment.** Permanent attachment is evidence that the item is a fixture.

A court might determine that a ceiling fan installed by a tenant is not a fixture, but a shower over the bath installed by the tenant is a fixture and must remain.

> *For commercial and industrial tenants, fixtures would likely be regarded as "trade fixtures" or fixtures that were installed for the purpose of conducting a business or trade.*

This could include signs, machinery encased in concrete, special cooling systems, etc. The tenant can remove trade fixtures at the end of the tenancy and for a reasonable period thereafter. A tenant would be liable for any property damage that results from the removal of the trade fixtures.

Even though the law on trade fixtures allows removal, leases often specify this right or might take away this right. The parties can agree that particular trade fixtures shall remain with the building.

Grace Period. This lease might provide a grace period for meeting obligations under the lease.

Guarantors. When a tenant does not appear to have the ability to meet lease obligations or has had serious credit difficulties in the past, landlords would be reluctant to rent to such a tenant unless there is a guarantor. A **GUARANTOR** *agrees to be liable under a lease if the tenant defaults*. A guarantor could be a supplier or purchaser from the tenant or even a relative of the tenant.

If the tenant defaults on the lease the landlord still has a duty to **MITIGATE DAMAGES**. *This means that the landlord must use due diligence to keep damages low.* This would include prompt action upon the default of the tenant, including eviction and a reasonable attempt to again rent the premises.

> *Failure of the guarantor to execute the guaranty agreement can be considered a default.*

Hazardous Substances. The clause might require lessor approval before hazardous substances are used on the premises.

If hazardous substances come onto the premises or are discovered on the premises by the tenant, then the tenant shall immediately notify the lessor.

Anytime hazardous material is to be placed on a site you want to make certain that there is an adequate guaranty to cover any loss which may be sustained because the material enters the soil or is not otherwise properly disposed of.

Case Example

Bennett v. Leatherby (1992) 3 C.A. 4th 449

LMI leased commercial property for 10 years. The lease contemplated that LMI would sublease the premises to a restaurant franchisee. Leatherby guaranteed the lease for five years after an assignment or subletting. The sublessee defaulted on the lease. The lessor settled with the general partners of the sublessee for $50,000, releasing them from all further claims under the lease. The lessor then brought action against the guarantors (Leatherby) for $228,000 which covered the remainder due under the lease.

The Appeals Court upheld the trial court's judgment in favor of Leatherby. By releasing the debtor, the plaintiff, the guarantors were effectively released. They guaranteed performance by a sublessee and the lessor accepted $50,000 for all amounts due by the sublessee. Since there was nothing further due, the guarantor was released.

Note: In a guarantor situation, do not release the person primarily liable unless the guarantor agreement specifically states that a release or settlement with the lessee (or sublessee) will not eliminate the guarantor's liability for any remainder due.

The clause would likely provide that the lessee would agree to indemnify the lessor for any loss suffered by the lessor because of hazardous substances coming onto the property during the lease period.

The lease might provide that if hazardous substances are discovered on the property (not due to use or negligence of lessee) and remedial action is required, the lessor shall have the option to terminate the lease if the cost of remedial action exceeds a stated dollar amount. However, the lessee would have the right to pay the excess costs and retain lease rights.

Hold Harmless Clause. A *HOLD HARMLESS CLAUSE is when the tenant agrees that he or she will not hold the lessor responsible for any personal injury or damages.* The clause could provide that the tenant shall indemnify the lessor for any damages suffered by the lessor because of the tenancy. The tenant could also agree to defend the lessor in any lawsuit resulting from the tenancy.

The hold harmless clause can be limited to water damage or it can be all inclusive. For commercial leases, hold harmless clauses are generally held to be valid. Generally, hold harmless clauses are not enforceable for residential leases.

Why do residential lessors continue to insert this clause in a lease? The reason is simple. If a tenant thinks that a landlord is not liable then they are unlikely to seek legal action against the landlord.

The hold harmless clause usually will NOT protect the property manager from damages where the injury resulted from the manager's negligence.

Holdover Clause. Should the tenant remain in possession at the end of the lease or after giving notice to vacate and failing to vacate, the landlord may, at his or her option, consider the tenant to be on a month-to-month tenancy. (Of course the landlord also has the option of ejecting the holdover tenant.) The holdover clause generally sets forth a rent for the holdover period which is significantly higher than the rent the tenant was paying. This serves to encourage the tenant to either vacate or negotiate a new lease.

Hours of Operation. The leases of many shopping centers specify hours that the store must be open. In this way, they will not have some stores opening on Sunday at noon and others closed all day and other irregular hours. Shoppers want all the stores open during similar hours and this is what attracts them to shopping centers.

Improvements (Lessor). If lessor improvements are to be made and the costs will be in excess of the limit set, lessee shall pay the excess prior to the commencement of work.

Insurance. The lease might require that all insurance carriers who provide required insurance be licensed in the state.

Who is responsible for property insurance would be specified in a net lease.

While the lessee would ordinarily be responsible in such a lease, a modified net lease might provide for lessor responsibility.

If the lessee's use of the premises causes increased insurance rates for the structure or adjacent structures owned by the lessor, the insurance clause could require that the lessee pay these increased costs.

Some commercial net leases require that the lessee carry rental interruption insurance so that rent is paid to the lessor if the premises are destroyed or materially damaged. This provision would customarily protect both lessor and any mortgagor for up to one year's rent.

The insurance clause might require the lessor to carry property insurance up to a percentage of the replacement cost (usually 80 percent). The lessor might also be required to carry coverage for sprinkle system damage.

> *Commercial leases frequently require tenants to carry high limit liability protection naming both the lessor and lessee.*

Normally, the lease will require that evidence of the insurance coverage be provided to the property owner.

The lessor might require the tenant to also carry plate glass insurance for the windows and coverage for equipment that is exclusive to the use of the premises.

The tenant might be required to carry a policy of boiler insurance if the boiler is under the tenant's control. Boiler insurance covers damages and liability from a boiler explosion. What the insurance actually does is it provides professional inspection which checks boiler operations and safety devices to protect against explosion. Hartford Insurance has much of this business as they have developed a great deal of experience in this field.

Case Example

Morales v. Fanster (1989) 209 C.A. 3d 1581

A lease required that a tenant carry liability insurance covering the premises in a minimum amount of $500,000. In fact, the tenant only carried $300,000 in protection.

A child was injured on the premises and the tenant insurance carrier paid the limit of its policy ($300,000) to the child's parents. The parents then sued the landlord because the landlord had failed to enforce the lease provision as to the amount of insurance coverage.

The court ruled for the landlord since the landlord had no duty to require a tenant to carry insurance for the benefit of third parties. The fact that the lease required the insurance created no duty on the part of the landlord to enforce the clause.

The court pointed out that if a landlord had a duty to enforce tenant insurance coverage clauses, then landlords would likely respond by not requiring insurance at all. This would not be in the public's interest.

Invalid Provision. This clause provides that if any portion of the lease is held to be invalid, it shall not affect the validity of the remainder of the lease.

Interest. Any amount owed on the lease shall bear interest. The interest rate might be stated or it might be a formula such as prime rate plus a designated percentage. A common provision is at the maximum legal rate. The clause would make it clear that interest is in addition to any late charges.

Joint and Several Liability. When there is more than one tenant signing the lease, this clause provides that the tenant shall be *JOINTLY AND SEVERALLY LIABLE. This means that in the event the lease is breached, the landlord can sue one tenant separately or all the tenants, and a suit against one tenant will not act to discharge the obligations of the other tenants.*

Law Governing Agreement. This clause would specify which state laws would govern any contract interpretation or dispute. It would likely be the state where the property is located or the law of the state where the landlord is headquartered.

Lead-Based Paint Disclosure.

> *Lead-based paint hasn't been used in residential property since 1978.*

The Federal Real Estate Disclosure and Notification Act requires that owners disclose to buyers and renters the presence of lead-based paint and/or lead-based paint hazards for residential dwellings. These are single-family dwellings or single-family dwelling units (apartments) intended for residential use.

The law requires known information or reports of lead-based paint for housing built prior to 1978. It is unlikely you would have knowledge or records of lead-based paint, but generally most old oil-based paint used prior to the mid-1970s had a lead base.

> *The lessor (or agent) must supply prospective tenants of housing built prior to 1978 with a copy of the Environmental Protection Agency's pamphlet entitled, "Protect Your Family From Lead-Based Paint."*

The lessee must acknowledge receipt of the pamphlet and the agent must sign and date it. Agents must maintain records of the notice for three years after commencement of the rental.

Violation of the rule can lead to civil and criminal penalties. For more information about lead-based paint, you can call the **Environmental Protection Agency at 1-800-424-LEAD**. In lieu of the federal disclosure, state disclosure, such as the California pamphlet entitled *Environmental Hazards: A Guide for Homeowners, Buyers, Landlords, and Tenants*, might be supplied to prospective tenants. A lead-based paint disclosure form can be found in Chapter 5.

Liability for Damages. This clause might provide that the landlord shall not be liable for damages to or loss of tenant property caused by acts of third persons (including theft), acts of God, plumbing breaks and leaks, electrical problems, etc. This clause would advise the tenant to obtain insurance coverage if they desire to have their property protected against loss.

Limitations on Occupants. A landlord can limit the number of persons that can occupy a property. However, the number of persons must be reasonable.

The general rule of HUD is that limiting occupancy to two persons per bedroom is being reasonable.

Occupancy is of importance to a lessor because the greater the number of occupants, the greater the wear and tear on the unit and common areas. In addition, if the landlord supplies any utilities or water, the usage increases with higher occupancy.

Besides limiting the number of persons allowed, the clause can limit the period for which guests can remain in the unit. This protects the lessor as to the claim that permanent residents are actually guests. As an example, guests stays could be limited to 30 days.

Locks. This clause would set forth the tenant rights, if any, to make duplicate keys and put in additional locks. If tenants are allowed to change locks the clause might specify the type of lock and the duty to provide keys to the lessor for emergency entry. This clause would also make tenants liable for damages to any locks.

Merchant Association. This shopping center and mall clause requires tenants to join a merchants association and be subject, as additional rent, to the dues and assessments of the association as well as the maintenance of a marketing and public relations staff.

Noise Levels. Malls and shopping center leases would likely prohibit the use of outside speakers. The lease might also include a maximum decibel level for noise emanating from the premises.

Noncompetition. Just as an owner doesn't want tenants to compete in another location (See Competition Clause), tenants don't want other tenants to compete with them. Some tenants, like greeting card stores, might want lease provisions that restrict the lessor to leasing to a competitor. A delicatessen may want a clause prohibiting the lessor from opening a delicatessen in the shopping center or leasing another delicatessen.

A tenant with significant economic clout will often negotiate noncompetition clauses.

Nonwaiver. This clause basically says that the lessor's failure to declare a lessee default shall not waive the lessor's right to declare a default for a subsequent breach. The lessor has not waived the obligation of the tenant.

Notice of Nonresponsibility. The landlord shall have the right to post a notice of nonresponsibility on the premises.

In some states, such as California, the failure of the lessor to post such a notice within ten days of knowledge that the tenant has authorized construction work on the premises would make the property subject to mechanics' liens.

Notices. This clause provides that all notices shall be in writing and designates the person(s) who they shall be served on. It might provide for service by registered mail.

Operating Costs. A lease might provide that certain operational costs such as parking lot maintenance, exterior lights, security services, etc., be paid by the tenants. The lease would have to specify which operational costs the tenants would bear and how the costs would be apportioned to the various tenants. It might also provide for adjustments when costs increase.

Option to Purchase. It is often necessary for lessors of commercial buildings to give a tenant an option to purchase. If the landlord wants the tenant and the tenant insists on the option, then completion of the lease agreement hinges on giving the tenant the option to purchase.

In an option to purchase, an owner is giving up something of value. The absolute requirement that the owner convey the property at an agreed price to a purchaser should the purchaser exercise it. On the other hand, purchasers are not required to exercise this power.

Options to purchase, to be enforceable, require that consideration be given to the optionor (the owner).

Options are often given at prices that are so high that neither the lessor nor leasing agent believe that the option will ever be exercised. Changing situations as well as market changes can result in the exercise of the option. Unless the management contract or a separate document provides for commission upon the option being exercised, the broker would have located a buyer for just management and/or rental fees.

A clause similar to the following could be set forth in the lease (if not covered in the property management contract):

"In the event that the option to purchase is exercised during the period of or during any extension of this lease, then the lessor or agrees to pay [broker] [   ] percent of the option price at close of escrow. The lessor also irrevocably assigns such commission rights to the broker and hereby instructs the escrow holder to disburse such funds to the broker upon close of escrow."

The option to purchase could be set forth as an addendum to the lease such as Figure 4-2, which is an addendum prepared by the American Industrial Real Estate Association.

Option to Renew (or Extend). Options don't have to be for purchase, they can be for lease extensions. They might allow the tenant to extend the lease for one or more periods of time at the same rent or at a higher rent. Courts have held that options to extend leases at market rent are enforceable because market rent is ascertainable. Some leases provide that the parties choose a third party to determine what the market rent will be. However, the authors strongly recommend rent be specified or a formula for determining the rent be set forth in the lease.

A notice to renew should be timely or the right would ordinarily be lost. However, there are exceptions where a late notice to renew might be excused.

Case Example

Herbst v. Santa Monica Swim & Health Club, Inc. **(1987) 192 C.A. 3d 916**

A lease required that notice to renew be given at least 90 days prior to the termination of the lease. The notice to exercise the renewal option was actually given one week after the original lease had expired.

The trial court ruled that the landlord had waived the notice deadline since the landlord obviously knew that the tenant intended to remain on the premises. The landlord was aware that the tenant had spent a great deal of money ($250,000) to upgrade the facilities. In addition, the tenant had requested that the landlord install a new permanent sign reflecting a change of name. The court regarded this as another showing of intent to renew the lease. The court commented on the fact that the landlord was aware of the failure of the tenant to give timely notice and intended to use this failure as the basis of demanding a rental increase.

The Court of Appeals affirmed the trial court's decision.

Figure 4-2

AMERICAN INDUSTRIAL REAL ESTATE ASSOCIATION

OPTION TO PURCHASE
STANDARD LEASE ADDENDUM

Dated _____

By and Between (Lessor) _____

(Lessee) _____

Address of Premises: _____

Paragraph _____

(a) Lessor hereby grants to Lessee an option to purchase the Premises upon the terms and conditions herein set forth.

(b) In order to exercise this option to purchase, Lessee must give written notice of the exercise of the option to Lessor during the period from _____ to _____ (the **"Option Period"**), time being of the essence. If such notice is not so given, this option shall automatically expire. At the same time the option is exercised, Lessee must deliver to Lessor a cashier's check in the amount of _____ payable to _____, to be part of the purchase price.

(c) The provisions of paragraph 39, including those relating to Lessee's Default set forth in paragraph 39.4 of this Lease are conditions of this Option.

(d) If Lessee elects to exercise this option to purchase as provided above, the transfer of title to Lessee shall occur on the close of escrow on_____, and until that time the terms of this Lease shall remain in full force and effect.

(e) If Lessee elects to exercise this option to purchase, the purchase price to be paid by Lessee shall be _____
_____
_____

(f) Within ten days after this option to purchase is exercised, Lessor and Lessee shall give instructions to consummate the sale to _____, located at _____
_____, who shall act as escrow holder, on the normal and usual escrow forms then used by such escrow holder, as follows:

(i) Escrow shall close on the date set forth in paragraph (d) above;

(ii) Lessor shall deposit the check referred to in paragraph (b) into escrow upon opening thereof, with the balance of the purchase price to be deposited into escrow no later than 11:00 a.m. on the business day prior to the expected closing date;

(iii) The parties agree to execute any additional instructions as are normal and usual;

(iv) The balance of the terms and conditions of sale shall be as set forth in the American Industrial Real Estate Association "STANDARD OFFER, AGREEMENT AND ESCROW INSTRUCTIONS FOR THE PURCHASE OF REAL ESTATE", a copy of which is attached hereto, except for the following: _____
_____

and paragraphs 4.2; 5; 6; 9.1 a,b,c,d,e,h,i,j, and k; and 20, which do not apply.

Initials: _____   Initials: _____

_____   _____

©1996 – American Industrial Real Estate Association

NOTE: These forms are often modified to meet changing requirements of law and needs of the industry. Always write or call to make sure you are utilizing the most current form: AMERICAN INDUSTRIAL REAL ESTATE ASSOCIATION, 700 So. Flower St., Suite 600, Los Angeles, CA 90017. (213) 687-8777.

OPTION TO PURCHASE   FORM OP-2-780

Parking. Leases for both commercial and residential properties might have parking clauses specifying reserved parking areas for tenants and/or customers. If the lease is subject to any parking rules or charges they will be referenced in this clause.

The tenant may be protected in that the lease might prohibit the lessor from reducing parking by placing additional structures in the present parking area. (Often a lessor will place a kiosk, such as for photo services, in the parking area to increase income.)

The parking clause might specify lessor and/or lessee responsibilities for maintenance of the parking areas.

Parking rules and regulations might include:

1. right to issue parking stickers as well as to refuse to re-issue stickers for vehicles violating rules;
2. right to have violating vehicles towed away at lessee's expense;
3. limitation on size of vehicles allowed (such as full size sedans);
4. parking charges and validation procedures;
5. agreement that lessor shall not be liable for damage to or theft from parked vehicles;
6. prohibition against washing or waxing vehicles in parking areas;
7. rights of lessor to modify parking rules and regulations.

Performance Under Protest. The parties might pay amounts due under the lease without waiving any rights to dispute the amounts by indicating that payment is made under protest. In this way they retain the rights to seek arbitration or legal remedies.

Pets. A pet provision might allow pets, prohibit pets completely or allow pets subject to certain restrictions.

> *Even though a landlord has a no-pet prohibition in the lease, the landlord CANNOT exclude seeing-eye dogs and support animals utilized by handicapped tenants.*

Possession. The lease would specify when possession is to be delivered to the tenant. Because a tenant in possession might not vacate, which would require legal action, the lease should provide that neither the owner nor agent will be liable for any damages resulting from the lessor being unable to provide possession when due. While the lease will remain in effect and cannot be voided by the tenant, the clause would provide that rent shall not start until possession is given.

Prohibited Use. This clause would prohibit any illegal use of the premises. It might also prohibit any use that would increase the lessor's insurance premiums without the lessor's consent or a use that interferes with other tenant's rights to quiet enjoyment of the premises. The clause could also prohibit specific activities such as topless entertainment or adult bookstores.

Quiet Enjoyment.

There is an implied covenant in every lease of quiet enjoyment.

QUIET ENJOYMENT means that the landlord will not interfere with the tenants rightful use of the premises. Some leases, nevertheless, set forth the rights of these tenants.

A breach of quiet enjoyment could be a landlord's making noisy repairs late at night, landlord's wrongful entry into the tenant's rental unit, a landlord's failure to provide heat when required to do so by the lease, etc.

A tenant can treat a landlord's failure to provide quiet enjoyment of the premises as a breach of the lease (constructive eviction), and can vacate the premises and be excused from further rent obligations. Tenants will often look for some fault to find a basis to claim constructive eviction. If a court determined that the landlord's actions (or failure to act) were not sufficient to justify the tenant's breaking the lease, then the tenant would still remain liable for rent under the lease even though he or she has vacated the property.

Renewal of Lease. A lease might provide for renewal as well as a time period to exercise the renewal. A tenant's failure to exercise the renewal right by a specified date might be forgiven if the tenant had made significant improvements to the property and the lessor knew that the tenant intended to renew. To allow the lessor to refuse a renewal and demand higher rent in such a case would result in unconscionable damage to the tenant. The late renewal should be excused.

A lease with unlimited renewal options is not necessarily invalid, however, it cannot exceed any statutory limit (Shaver v. Clanton (1994) 26 C.A. 4th 568).

Other Leases. This clause provides that the lessee will not hold the lessor liable for any lease violation of any other tenant.

Outside Displays. This clause might be used to prohibit or require lessor approval to place merchandise or displays outside the premises, such as walkways.

Recapture Clause. A *RECAPTURE CLAUSE in percentage leases provides the lessor with the opportunity to cancel the lease after a stated period of time unless a particular annual volume of gross sales is reached.* As an example, if a store strives for full markups and avoids clearing-inventory sales, the volume is likely to be less than expected from the type of business and square feet leased. If your shopping center has a number of potential tenants who have more sales aggressive histories, then termination of an under performing tenant's lease might be in order.

Receipt of Lease (Rules). By signing the lease the lessee acknowledges receipt of a copy of the lease. The clause might also cover tenant rules and regulations. The tenant also acknowledges that he or she has read the lease and rules (if applicable).

Recording. The lessor and lessee agree to acknowledge the lease (before a notary) if requested by the other party so that the lease can be recorded. Recording would give constructive notice of the lease interests.

Remedies. The lessor remedies in the event of lessee default are set forth. They include termination of tenant's right to possession and re-renting to mitigate damages, suing for damages, leaving the tenant in possession and suing as the rent becomes due, etc.

Removal of Property. If a tenant abandons the premises leaving behind personal property, this clause authorizes the lessor to remove personal property left behind and store it. Generally, the property can be sold if not claimed, and storage fees paid, after a statutory period (90 days in California). The proceeds would first apply to the cost of the sale, then the cost of storage and removal and the balance then applied to any monies owed to the lessor under the lease. Any balance should go to the lessee.

Renewal. A lease might contain a clause that provides for automatic renewal of the lease. This places the burden of nonrenewal upon the tenant. The lease would provide that unless the tenant notifies the lessor to the contrary within a stated period prior to the expiration of the lease, it would automatically be renewed.

> *In some states, such as California, the clause is voidable by the party who did NOT prepare the lease unless the renewal or extension clause appears in at least eight point boldface type immediately prior to the place where the lessee signs the lease.*

In California, the tenant cannot waive the boldface type requirements. Other states have similar limitations on automatic residential lease renewals or extensions. The protection of the requirement for boldface notice for automatic renewal does not generally apply to nonresidential tenants. They are considered more sophisticated so are not afforded this protection.

Note: A "lease renewal" is considered a new lease and it could provide for a change in terms. A "lease extension" is the same lease but the term is stretched out.

Rent Clause. The lease will specify the amount of rent or provide a formula or means to determine the amount of rent. Generally, the total rent shall be stated for the term of the lease and that it will be paid monthly in advance in a stated amount. For a percentage lease it would list the rent as minimum rent. The lease clause might indicate that the dollars are U.S. dollars. (Note: other nations also use the dollar designation.)

The clause might prohibit the tenant from using any set-offs he or she might have against the amount due. (If the tenant claimed the lessor owed them money they could not deduct the amount owed from their rent payment.)

The clause would include any late charges and the length of any grace period that was provided the tenant before the late charge is assessed.

Most leases do NOT allow any grace period, although state laws might provide a grace period for residential tenants.

Care should be used in setting late charges. If there is rent control, the late charge could result in rent that exceeds the maximum allowed.

The lease might provide that the last month's rent shall be paid in advance. Because last month's rent is taxed to an owner when it is received, but a security deposit is not taxed unless forfeited, many owners prefer increased security deposits to last month's rent.

Percentage leases generally provide for a minimum rent plus a percentage of the net sales. The lease might define net sales as the gross sales less:

1. returns where credit is given;
2. settlements to customers for defective goods;
3. delivery charges;
4. interest charges (paid by the customer);
5. bad checks;
6. sales taxes;
7. gift certificates sold (until redeemed).

As an encouragement to retail stores to go for a volume business, percentage leases often provide for a decreasing percentage of the gross as volume increases. For instance, a furniture store has 18 percent rent for the first $1,000,000 in sales in a calendar year and 14 percent for the next $1,000,000 and 10 percent for all over $2,000,000. This graduated rent would encourage lower markups and sales. The lower percentages should begin at a figure you would estimate for an annual volume. In this manner, a tenant who achieves lower rent percentages really provides gravy income to the lessor.

Case Example

Wu v. Interstate Consol. Indus. (1991) 226 C.A. 3d 11511

A renewal option in a lease provided that appraisers should set the fair market rental value if the parties could not agree as to the rent for the renewal period. The property which was leased as a movie theater was given a fair rental value of $3,000. However, the appraiser pointed out that the fair rental value as shops would be $8,500. The landlord demanded the higher figure.

The Court of Appeals affirmed the trial court which held that the property was leased as a theater and the tenant could not change the use without the consent of the landlord. The purpose of an option was to allow the business to continue not to force the tenant to abandon the premises. This was a theater lease and theater rent should apply.

Provisions for rent adjustments can be set forth in an addendum to the lease.

Rental Inducements. Any inducements such as free rent given to the lessee to lease the premises shall be canceled if lessee is in default and such inducements shall immediately become due, even if cured by the lessee. (This acts as an inducement against lessee default.)

Repairs. This clause might provide that the tenant indicates an inspection of the premises and acknowledges that they are in good condition and agrees that they will not be altered, repaired or changed without the written consent of the lessor.

The clause might also require that repairs be under the control of the lessor but at the lessee's expense. Some clauses provide that improvements to the premises will remain with the premises at the end of the lease. (See fixture's clause.)

Restoration. Lessee agrees to restore premises to the condition it was when rented. If lessee has responsibilities for maintenance of systems, they shall be in good and proper operating condition. Damage from removal of fixtures and equipment shall be repaired, unless it has been agreed that they shall remain. This clause could require removal and replacement of contaminated soil.

Right of First Refusal.

While an owner gives up something when he or she gives a tenant an option, a right of first refusal (or preemptive right) gives absolutely nothing.

This means that should the owner wish to accept a bona fide purchase offer from another party, the owner must first allow the tenant to match the offer during a specified time period. If the tenant does not match the offer, then the purchase can proceed. The owner is under no obligation to sell and can refuse any purchase offer.

A right of first refusal can be included as to a lease extension. The tenant has the right to match any lease terms offered by another prospective tenant. This clause gives the tenant some peace of mind when an owner is unwilling to give the tenant an option to renew the lease.

If a right of first refusal is included in a lease, is the property manager entitled to a sales commission if the right of first refusal is exercised? If the property management agreement or other agreement does not cover this contingency, the property management broker loses a management fee and receives nothing for the sale. The property manager should consider providing for consideration should a right of first refusal be exercised.

Case Example

Ellis v. Chevron U.S.A., Inc. (1988) 201 C.A. 3d 132

A lease was prepared by Chevron for a service station. The lease gave Chevron a right of first refusal as to any new lease when the lease expired. The landlord sought other lease proposals prior to expiration of the lease. A proposal received and which was conveyed to Chevron was:

1. $3,000 per month rent.
2. lessee to construct a new facility on that site,
3. lessee to acquire an adjacent site (for a larger station) and give the owner the option to buy the adjacent site at the end of the lease.

Chevron wished to exercise their right of first refusal but would not agree to build a new building or acquire the adjacent site, neither of which they needed.

The court did not agree that the owners had breached an implied covenant of good faith and fair dealing by not restricting the terms as to offers they would entertain. The offer was considered reasonable and if Chevron did not wish to meet it, they could not exercise their right of first refusal.

The court also pointed out that the lease was prepared by Chevron so any ambiguities in the lease should be resolved against Chevron.

Note: Courts are more likely to excuse a late option to renew than a late option to purchase. Generally, options to purchase must be exercised in a timely manner.

There have been cases where an owner has given one tenant a right of first refusal and another an option to purchase. There have been other cases where an owner has given more than one tenant a right of first refusal. The reason has been poor lease administration where an owner (or manager) had forgotten or didn't know of a provision buried in a lease given either long ago or by a previous owner or manager. In such cases, the owner and/or manager would be subject to legal expenses and what could be significant damages.

Rules and Regulations. This clause clearly states that rules and regulations are incorporated into the lease. (To avoid problems the rules and regulations should be identified and initialed by the parties to the lease and included as an attachment.)

Sale by Lessor. This clause provides that if the lessor sells the premises the lessor shall be relieved of all liability under the lease (no secondary liability if the buyer breaches any provision of the lease).

Security. This clause might provide that the lessor is not obligated to employ any security personnel or security services and that the malfunction of any existing security system or the discontinuance of any security service shall not obligate the lessor in any manner.

Security Deposit. The amount of any security deposit will be set forth as well as the tenant's right to the return of the deposit and landlords right to use the deposit for tenant damage, unauthorized alteration removal, back rent, etc.

Services. Which services will be performed or supplied by the lessor shall be set forth in the lease. As an example, the lease may provide that the lessor will provide a reasonable amount of hot and cold water, heat, air conditioning, janitorial services in common areas, exterior maintenance, etc.

The provision would generally provide that the landlord's failure to provide any of the services would not be grounds for a tenant's defense of constructive eviction. (This would probably not be enforceable on residential leases.)

The clause might provide that the lessor shall not be liable if failure to provide services results from conditions beyond the control of the lessor.

On net leases, the lessor might require that the lessee shall be obligated to provide service contracts for HVAC, boiler, elevator, pools, landscaping, etc. This would provide the lessor with some assurance that the facilities will be properly maintained.

Signatures. The lease might indicate that it is offered to the tenant, but it shall not be binding on the owner until signed by the owner or an authorized representative of the owner.

Signs. This clause might set forth the right of the tenant to place signs on the premises. These signs may be limited to size, shape, construction, color and lighting.

The clause could require that the lessor be responsible for installation of all signs (at lessee's expense).

Smoking. The lease could require the lessee to enforce a no-smoking regulation on the leased premises.

Surrender. Lessee agrees to turn over the premises to the lessor at the termination of the tenancy in the same state as received other than normal wear and tear.

The surrender clause might require a notice of surrender.

This notice must usually be given at least 30 days prior to the end of the lease which the tenant intends to surrender possession to the landlord at the termination of the lease. This notice lets the lessor know that the tenant does not intend to negotiate an extension or a new lease so that the lessor can begin activities to release the premises.

Taxes. Net leases will have a clause which requires that the tenant pay property taxes and insurance. Preferably, this clause will require the tenant to pay one-twelfth of the annual estimated taxes and insurance costs with each monthly payment. This protects a lessor against a tenant default when taxes are due. The lease might require the lessee to pay personal property taxes on property owned by the lessee prior to delinquency.

Term. This clause would spell out the beginning and ending dates of the lease.

Time Is of the Essence. This clause indicates dates and times set forth in the lease shall be strictly adhered to. In the absence of this clause a court would likely allow a "reasonable period" beyond a time specified.

Use. The use for which the premises are rented should be set forth. You would likely also want to spell out that the premises may not be used for any other use or purpose without the written consent of the lessor.

Many commercial leases specify what the tenant can sell.

Some even specify items that the tenant cannot sell. In addition, some leases protect tenants in providing that competing stores will not be allowed in the particular shopping center.

Case Example

Pay 'N Pak v. Superior Court (1989) 210 C.A. 3d 1404

Tenants, who leased a store in a shopping center, had a lease that restricted the use to the sale of baby-related items. The tenants wished to go out of business and wanted to assign their lease to stores specializing in the sale of ceiling fans and fireplace accessories. The landlord, Pay 'N Pak operated a home improvement store in the center and refused the assignment since it would bring in stores in competition with them. The tenants sued for compensatory and punitive damages. The trial court sided with the tenants pointing out that only a minor portion of Pay 'N Pak's business was derived from the sale of fans or fireplace accessories.

The Court of Appeals reversed the trial court holding that the volume of sales for these items should not have been the sole determinant of whether the refusal to accept an assignment was unreasonably withheld. While a landlord cannot use a clause against assignment for its own economic gain by attempting to charge higher rents, reasonable use restrictions in a shopping center are valid. A landlord may protect itself from competition.

Utilities. Tenant obligation as to utility costs would be set forth in this clause. If the tenants are to pay utilities, and there aren't separate meters, then leases should be clear as to each tenant's share. As an example, it could be based per unit or on the proportion of square feet occupied by each tenant.

Waiver. A waiver of one term by the lessor shall not be regarded as a waiver of any other term.

Waterbed. While waterbeds are not allowed above the ground floor in some older buildings because the weight could cause structural damage, the reason lessors do not want waterbeds is because of potential damage to walls, ceilings and carpeting from leakage of the waterbed.

You can protect yourself by requiring that the tenant carry waterbed insurance to protect your property against damage.

CHAPTER 4 SUMMARY

Standard form leases simplify the administration of leases. However, additional clauses and clause alternations might be necessary and may include the following:

Advertising. Sets forth advertising requirements for tenant. Usually cooperative with other tenant with percentage leases.

Assignment and Subleasing. This would either prohibit or require lessor approval for assignments or subleases.

Arbitration. It would provide for mandatory on consensual binding arbitration of lessor/lessee disputes.

Bad Checks. It provides for charges for bad checks. Bankruptcy.

Broker. Lessee states that no broker or a named broker helped to negotiate the lease. (Entitlement to commission.)

Codes. Tenant agrees to comply with municipal and state codes.

Common Areas. Covers maintenance and/or use of common areas.

Complete Agreement. The parties acknowledge that there is no agreement other than is set forth in the lease.

Covenant to Remain in Business. This clause requires tenant to remain in business. Otherwise, on a percentage lease, tenant could cease operations and pay the minimum rent.

Default by Tenant. This clause might define default and set forth the lessor's remedies.

Eminent Domain. Tenant rights, if any, if property is taken by eminent domain.

Escalator Clause. Provides for graduated increase in payments for the lease.

Fixtures. It may provide what is or isn't a fixture and removal rights, if any.

Guarantors. Other party agrees to be liable on the lease.

Hold Harmless Clause. Provides that tenant will not hold lessor liable for any injury or property damage caused by the condition of the property.

Hours of Operation. It specifies the hours and days a business must be kept open.

Insurance. Specifies the insurance coverage that the tenant must carry.

Law Governing Agreement. This clause specifies which state law shall apply.

Lead-Based Paint Disclosure. This is a federally mandated disclosure.

Noncompetition. Restrictions are placed on tenants and/or the owner as to competing businesses or products.

Notice of Nonresponsibility. Lessor's right to post the notice for protection as to mechanics' liens.

Operating Costs. Sets forth tenant's responsibility as to operating costs, such as maintenance of common areas and common area utilities.

Option to Renew. Tenant option to renew the lease on stated terms.

Possession. The time possession is to be given.

Prohibited Use. Uses that are not allowed.

Quiet Enjoyment. Lessor agrees not to interfere with tenants proper use of premises.

Receipt of Lease. Tenant acknowledges receipt of lease and applicable occupancy rules.

Renewal. Covers an automatic renewal of the lease unless lessor or lessee gives notice.

Rent. The amount of rent and/or any formulas for determining rent and other charges.

Repairs. Tenant acknowledges the property is in good condition and agrees that alterations and repairs will only be performed with the lessor's approval.

Rules and Regulations. Rules and regulations are incorporated into the lease.

Security Deposit. The amount of any deposit and its purpose.

Services. Specifies what, if any, services shall be supplied by the lessor.

Signatures. The lessor is not obligated until the lessor signs the lease.

Surrender. Lessee agrees to turn over premises to lessor at termination of the lease.

Taxes. Lessee agrees to pay property taxes on a net lease.

Time is of the Essence. Dates stated are considered essential and lateness would breach the agreement.

Use. Sets forth the specified use for which property may be used.

Utilities. Obligations as to utility costs are set forth.

CLASS DISCUSSION TOPICS

1. If your office handles any leasing, are form leases used? Are they ever altered? What is the extent of the alteration? Are leases ever put together by the cut-and-paste method using clauses from previous leases and/or other forms? Are leases, other than form leases, prepared or reviewed by attorneys?

2. Assume you are managing a shopping mall. One of the tenants, a retailer of womens' clothing, wants to assign her percentage lease to another party. You would probably withhold your consent for what types of businesses?

3. Which apartment complexes in your area allow pets? Are there any restrictions? What do you feel is the economic effect of allowing pets?

4. If a local shopping center or mall had percentage leases, which tenants, if any, do you feel are unlikely to be pulling their weight? How could the lessor have provided corrective measures for an underperforming tenant?

5. At your local shopping centers are there any stores closed while others are open? What does this do for the shopping center?

CHAPTER 4 QUIZ

1. A purchaser of a commercial building would want the tenant to furnish a:

    A. estoppel certificate
    B. notice of nonresponsibility
    C. right of first refusal
    D. lead-base paint disclosure

2. When a prospective tenant has had credit problems, a lessor is MOST LIKELY to request a(n):

    A. accelerated payment clause
    B. guarantor
    C. holdover provision
    D. recapture clause

3. A hold harmless clause would likely be unenforceable by a lessor of:

    A. a retail store
    B. office space
    C. industrial property
    D. a residential property

4. A clause that discourages a tenant from remaining in possession after the lease expires, would be a:

    A. holdover clause
    B. right of first refusal
    C. estoppel certificate
    D. nonwaiver clause

5. Tenants A and B sign a lease in which they agree to be jointly and severally liable. If past rent is due, who can the lessor sue?

   A. Tenant A alone
   B. Tenant B alone
   C. Tenants A and B together
   D. Any of the above

6. A tenant hires a contractor to remodel a store. The lessor would be concerned with:

   A. attornment
   B. the recapture clause
   C. a notice of nonresponsibility
   D. a nonwaiver clause

7. The right to cancel a lease, when the tenant's sales are not up to expectations, would be set forth in the:

   A. quiet enjoyment clause
   B. attornment clause
   C. recapture clause
   D. accelerated payments clause

8. Boldface eight point type face would most likely be required in a residential lease that provides for:

   A. lead paint removal
   B. automatic renewal if no notice is given
   C. a purchase option
   D. any of the above

9. A furniture store had a percentage lease specifying rent at 16 percent of net sales for the first $1,000,000 of sales. Sales over $1,000,000 would MOST LIKELY have a percentage of:

   A. 13 percent
   B. 18 percent
   C. 24 percent
   D. 32 percent

10. A tenant has a right to buy the property from the lessor, but this right only applies should the lessor decide to sell to another. If the lessor is not obligated to sell, this right would be a(n):

   A. option
   B. right of first refusal
   C. attornment
   D. nonwaiver agreement

Answers: 1. A; 2. B; 3. D; 4. A; 5. D; 6. C; 7. C; 8. B; 9. A; 10. B

Residential Property Management

KEY WORDS AND TERMS

Comparative Market Analysis
Confirmation of Lease
Constructive Eviction
Development Fees
Habitability
Lead Paint Disclosure
Moratorium
Population Bulge
Prequalification of Tenants
Qualification of Tenants
Quiet Enjoyment
Quit or Cure

Quit or Pay Rent
Rent Control
Self-Help Eviction
Stratified Housing Market
Supply and Demand
Thirty-Day Notice
Three-Day Notice
Turnover Rate
Uniform Residential Landlords and Tenant Act
Unlawful Detainer Action
Zoning

LEARNING OBJECTIVES

In this chapter you will learn about the factors which influence housing needs within a community.

You will discover what should be included in a residential property management contract by analyzing an actual contract.

You will learn about the necessity of developing policies for managing a residential property and the necessity for those policies.

You will learn that setting rents is both art and science. You will be able to analyze rents in a community to make informed decisions as to economic adjustments.

You will learn how to prepare a property for lease, the prequalifications and qualification process, showing the property, obtaining the lease application and getting the lease signed.

You will find learn about lessor disclosure requirements and both tenant and lessor obligations.

You will understand the necessity of rent collection procedures and the process of eviction as well as how to handle tenant problems and use charges.

Residential Defined

Residential property is property where people live.

For the purpose of this text we have included in this chapter the management of homes and apartments. In Chapter 7, we will cover additional residential management property types including mobile home parks, housing for the elderly, single-room occupancy, condominium association housing, etc.

Residential Housing Need

FAMILY UNITS

The need for residential units is determined more by the number of family units than raw population.

As an example, seven people in one family require but one housing unit, but seven persons who each desire to live alone would mean seven units.

ECONOMIC CONDITIONS

While the national economy is important as to housing needs, the local economy is more important as the local economy can run counter to the national economy. As an example, while housing starts were down during the early 1960s, there were areas where new housing was in great demand, such as areas of government spending for defense programs. In the early 1990s, there was a strong housing market nationally but most of California's housing market was weak. Layoffs, hiring, plant openings, closings, new public facilities, military base openings or closures will have a significant effect on the housing need within a local economy.

Economic conditions can influence coupling and uncoupling of family units. In times of high unemployment or high housing costs families are more willing to share a housing unit then they are when employment is low and/or they are able to afford their separate residences.

Where parents live within commuting distance of their jobs, children will often decide that living with their parents is not so bad after all if they find that taxes, rent and car payments leave them nothing left for the good life.

SOCIETY CHANGES

> *At one time care for seniors was both a moral responsibility and an economic necessity thrust upon children.*

Some of the senior readers may remember three and four generations living within the same household but we seldom see that today. Because of social security and pension plans, many senior citizens now have the means to live separately from their children. We have also seen the growth of divorce and with it the erosion of duty towards parents. Today it is more probable that adult offspring sponge off their parents than the other way around.

> *Differences in lifestyles between parents and children as well as the desire for privacy contribute to the demise of extended family households.*

INTEREST CYCLES

There is a rental housing need cycle which is closely related to interest rates. When interest rates are low, ownership becomes more affordable and families leave the rental market in favor of ownership. When interest rates rise, the affordability of ownership drops which keeps many families as renters when they would much prefer ownership.

POPULATION BULGES

Bulges in population age groups have effected housing needs. When the baby boomers born after World War II reached marriage age, they created an unprecedented demand for housing which fueled the inflation of the 1970s. This class of baby boomers created a second-home demand in the 1980s which we can expect to result in an increased demand for retirement housing in the not to distant future.

POLITICAL CHANGES

Changes in ordinances, statutes and taxes will effect residential housing needs and costs as well as the likelihood of fulfillment of those needs.

Taxes

> *Low property taxes in a community will encourage people to live and own property within that community.*

This encourages renters to then become owners. Low taxes also encourage development of residential rental projects. Lower taxes mean lower costs to owners.

High property taxes have a negative effect on new residential rental developments which in turn limits new construction.

Moratoriums and Limits

Because of problems in supplying services, many communities have placed moratoriums on new housing developments. The effect of moratoriums has been to limit supply of new units to existing housing. This tends to reduce the vacancy factor of existing housing and raises rents.

The same results are achieved by limits on growth. We are witnessing a great deal of the, "I'm aboard, lets raise the drawbridge" mentality. Growth limits are a reality in many communities.

In some areas, growth limits are supported by property owners who realize that growth limits will increase the value of developed property as well as rents. Other supporters just want to keep others out of their areas so that they can continue the lifestyle they currently enjoy. The proponents of no or-slow growth often claim to be acting out of a respect for the environment.

Communities experience greater housing pricing when they slow the growth rate below the housing demand for their area.

Development Fees

Development fees in many communities have been instituted for schools, police, fire, social services, etc.

These advanced fees must be paid to obtain a residential building permit. In some communities, these permits exceed $10,000 per unit.

> *Higher development costs result in higher costs for new construction and tend to increase market values of existing residential properties.*

New residential rental properties will not be built unless the developers anticipate rents sufficient to cover the higher costs.

Because high development fees tend to limit development, the demand for housing will probably result in higher rents.

Rent Control

Rent control is legal although it shifts a society burden of providing reasonable rents or rents that are below market level from the community to individual landlords.

Some rent control ordinances are much more lenient than others. As an example, any rent can be charged when a property in Los Angeles becomes vacant because rent control only applies to subsequent increases in rent.

In some areas like San Francisco, the rent control basis remains the same between tenancies.

One of the problems of rent control is that it works against many of its original purposes. It restricts the new housing supply rather than meeting the needs of lower income people. It becomes obvious which area a developer will prefer if the choice is developing in a rent-controlled area or a non-rent controlled area.

Rent control also creates deteriorating structures because landlords have little interest in pride of ownership and will only provide minimum maintenance to avoid code violations.

In New York, rent control has resulted in a poor utilization of property. Single persons will not give up six and-seven room apartments to move into one bedroom units when their large rent-controlled unit has a monthly rent less than what would pay for a smaller unit.

Those who can afford to buy show no incentive to purchase homes when housing costs are so reasonable. Many who reside in rent controlled buildings own vacation homes. Some own homes in the suburbs and only use their rent-controlled units for work-related purposes.

As a property manager, you should NOT be concerned about the fairness of rent control, but what the controls allow or don't allow as to the properties you manage.

In some cases, improving the property or renting units furnished will allow a higher rent. There is normally an appeal process to implement the rent increase. You should be aware of this process and understand when an appeal has a reasonable chance of success.

Besides local ordinances, some properties financed under special government loan programs are also limited to rent control. However, you should be aware that many of these programs have escape clauses. Rents may no longer be subject to control if you refinance the property without a government loan. This provides an opportunity to significantly increase income.

Communities with rent control usually establish rent control committees who hear complaints. Unfortunately, some of these committees have gone far beyond the statues in interpreting what can be allowed. You should be aware of the statutes in an area so that you will know when to seek legal counsel.

Case Example

City of Santa Monica v. Yarmark (1988) 203 C.A. 3d 133

After the California Supreme Court upheld a Santa Monica ordinance that prohibited owners from demolishing residential property, the California Legislature passed the Ellis Act which prohibited local government from requiring a residential landlord to continue to keep residential properties available for leasing. In other words, the state said that a landlord, like any other business, can go out of business.

Santa Monica subsequently passed a measure that a tenant could not be evicted when the purpose was demolition unless the landlord had a demolition permit (a permit would only be granted if the city determined that the building was uninhabitable and beyond any remedy or the landlord agreed to build new rent controlled units).

The court held that the provision against eviction was invalid. Santa Monica had gone too far. The purpose of the legislation was to evade the Ellis Act. The court pointed out that when local and state law conflict, then the local ordinance is preempted by state law.

Note: Santa Monica has been involved in hundreds of lawsuits involving rent control. The persons protected by Santa Monica's rent control ordinance are not low income people. In fact, the average household income of tenants under rent control was estimated to be around $60,000 in 1990.

Zoning

ZONING is public control of land use. Value drops when too much land is designated for a particular use. When not enough land has been zoned for a particular use, then the value would increase based upon the limited supply.

You should be aware that the zoning codes and symbols are not the same between communities. A C-4 zoning in one community might prohibit uses allowed by a C-4 zoning in another community.

> *By using requirements of parking, setback, height and green space, communities can zone as to density.*

Areas requiring more space per unit means that developers will have higher costs per unit because of the need for more land. This discourages new rental housing unless the developer feels that the additional costs will be met by increased rents.

> ### Case Example
>
> **Berman v. City of West Hollywood Rent Stabilization** (1988) 197 C.A. 3d 837
>
> A rent control ordinance required landlords to paint all rental units at least once every four years. Berman refused to paint a unit claiming it was rented "as is."
>
> The rent control board ordered Berman to reduce rents based on the decrease in maintenance.
>
> The court held that the ordinance was constitutional. The choice of painting or reducing rents was a reasonable means of providing for well maintained, affordable housing.

Zoning can be appealed to a zoning appeals board and then to the courts. The courts will only overrule zoning if they find that it is to arbitrary or capricious.

Zoning that is changed on existing property to disallow a current use generally allows the current use to continue as a nonconforming use. However, the use generally cannot be expanded nor allowed to restart after the use was discontinued.

TIME FOR DEVELOPMENT

It takes time for new housing to be developed to fill housing needs. It can take several years to go through the process from land acquisition to renting because of approval and construction time. The housing market could change in this period of time. Other new projects could become available for rental thus reducing the need for housing.

Due to costs involved, once land is acquired and approvals and financing obtained, projects can take on a life of their own and must be continued despite any changes in the economy.

STRATIFIED NEED

The need for housing is stratified by type of housing and rental price. As an example, there may be a glut of available condominium rental units but an unfulfilled demand for rentals of single-family homes. There might be a tremendous demand for two bedroom rentals under $500 per month, but a glut of available units at $2,000 per month or more.

New housing might fill one need but leave another need unfulfilled.

Residential Management Contracts

There are a number of property management contracts that have been developed by various professional organizations and form companies such as the BOMA form we included in Chapter 2.

The form we have included in this chapter was prepared by Professional Publishing. We like it for its readability and simplicity and we feel it is better suited to residential management situations. The contract describes the property and has a commencement and termination date.

> *We would NOT recommend any management agreement for less than one year.*

If the property has problems, we would not recommend any contract for less than three years. This longer term would allow you to recoup some of the benefits from the hard work of solving the property problems. Otherwise, owners could seek to reduce costs by going to another manager or manage the property themselves. You want to be compensated with higher fees for the work you are to do if you're using a short-term management contract.

The contract included as Figure 5-1 has eight basic sections shown here as A-H:

AUTHORITIES AND OBLIGATIONS OF BROKERS

By initiating each subparagraph, the parties agree that these are to be broker obligations and that the owner is granting the authority for their performance.

Advertising and Tenant Selection. The broker might advertise property that is for rent, display signs and screen and select tenants.

Negotiate Leases. The authority to negotiate leases is up to a limited period of time expressed as months.

Execute Leases. The property manager may sign leases as the representative of the owner.

Rent Collections. The manager may collect rents and deposits connected with rentals. They shall be placed in a bank trust account.

Terminate Tenancies. The property manager may terminate tenancies and give notices such as to quit or pay rent.

Figure 5-1

MANAGEMENT AGREEMENT

_____ "Owner," agrees to employ
_____ "Broker," to rent, lease, operate and manage
the real property in the City of _____, County of _____,
State of _____, commonly known as _____
_____
for a period commencing _____, and terminating at midnight on _____,
upon the following Terms and Conditions:

1. **BROKER'S AUTHORITIES AND OBLIGATIONS.** The following authorities and obligations, if initialed by both parties, are conferred upon and accepted by Broker:

   (a) [_____] [_____] To advertise the availability of the property "for rent" or "for lease", and to display "For Rent" or "For Lease" signs; to screen and use diligence in the selection of prospective tenants; and to abide by all fair housing laws.

   (b) [_____] [_____] To negotiate leases on terms established by Owner. Lease periods will not exceed _____ months.

   (c) [_____] [_____] To execute leases and rental agreements on behalf of Owner.

   (d) [_____] [_____] To collect rents, security deposits, and all other receipts connected with the property, and to deposit same in a trust account with a qualified banking institution.

   (e) [_____] [_____] To serve notice of termination of tenancies, notices to pay rent or quit, and other notices as are appropriate in Broker's discretion.

   (f) [_____] [_____] To employ attorneys approved by Owner for the purpose of enforcing Owner's rights under leases and rental agreements, and instituting legal action on behalf of Owner.

   (g) [_____] [_____] To provide all services reasonably necessary for the proper management of the property including periodic inspections, supervision of maintenance, alterations, and repairs as may be reasonably required.

   (h) [_____] [_____] To hire, supervise, and discharge all employees and independent contractors required in the operation and maintenance of the property. Compensation will be approved by Owner. The employment of any employee will be terminable at will. It is agreed that all employees are employees of Owner and not of the Broker. Broker will prepare payroll tax returns for Owner, where applicable, and make payments of payroll taxes to appropriate agencies from gross revenues.

   (i) [_____] [_____] To contract for repairs or alterations at a cost to Owner not to exceed $_____

   (j) [_____] [_____] To execute service contracts for utilities and services for the operation, maintenance, and safety of the property as Broker deems reasonably necessary. The terms of any such contract will not exceed _____ months, and the amount payable each month will not exceed $_____ without the prior written approval of Owner.

   (k) [_____] [_____] To pay from gross receipts all operating expenses and such other expenses as may be authorized by Owner, including mortgage payments, property taxes, insurance premiums, and _____

   (l) [_____] [_____] To maintain accurate records of all monies received and disbursed in connection with the management of the property. The records will be open for inspection by Owner during regular business hours and upon reasonable notice.

   (m) [_____] [_____] To submit monthly statements of all receipts and disbursements not later than the _____ day of the following month.

   (n) [_____] [_____] Other: _____
   _____

2. **OWNER'S OBLIGATIONS.** Owner agrees to pay Broker compensation for services rendered as follows (Broker's compensation is due and payable on demand and may be deducted by the Broker from gross receipts):

   (a) **Compensation for Management Services:**
   - [ ] $_____ per month for each single family residence.
   - [ ] _____% of gross monthly collections, provided that the minimum compensation will not be less than $_____ per month.
   - [ ] $_____ flat fee per month.

   (b) **Compensation for Leasing**
   - [ ] New leases _____
   - [ ] Renegotiated leases _____

   (c) **Compensation for Supervising Capital Improvements**
   - [ ] _____

   (d) **Compensation for Refinancing**
   - [ ] _____

   (e) **Compensation for Other Services**
   - [ ] _____
   - [ ] _____

3. **OWNER FURTHER AGREES**

   (a) To indemnify and hold Broker harmless from any and all costs, expenses, attorney fees, and damages from, or arising out of, the management of the property by Broker, or the performance or exercise of any of the duties, obligations, powers, or authorities granted in this Agreement, except where the damage is legally due to the negligent or intentional misconduct of the Broker.

Page 1 of 2
FORM 115.1 (10-97)   COPYRIGHT © 1985-97 BY PROFESSIONAL PUBLISHING, 880 LAS GALLINAS AVE., SAN RAFAEL, CA 94903   (415) 472-1964   FAX (415) 472-2069

PROFESSIONAL PUBLISHING

(b) To carry, at Owner's expense, bodily injury, property damage, and public liability insurance with customary limits for like property. The policy will be written on a comprehensive general liability form and will name the Broker as an additional insured. A certificate of insurance will be furnished to Broker on demand.

(c) To carry, at Owner's expense, worker's compensation insurance as may be required by law.

(d) To assume full responsibility for the payment of any expenses and obligations incurred in connection with the exercise of Broker's duties set forth in this Agreement.

(e) To deposit with Broker the sum of $_____ as an initial operating reserve, and to cover any excess of expenses over income within ten (10) days after a request by Broker. Broker may terminate this Agreement immediately if the request for additional funds is not paid. Owner understands that Broker is under no obligation to advance its own funds for payment of Owner's operating expenses.

4. NOTICE. All notices and demands will be in writing, and delivered either by personal delivery, overnight courier, or facsimile transmission with the original subsequently delivered by other means, or by certified mail, postage prepaid. In the event of mailing, delivery will be deemed to have been made on the third (3rd) day following the day of the mailing. Other notices will be effective upon delivery. Unless either party receives notice of a change of address, notices will be addressed as set forth in the signature blocks.

5. ATTORNEY FEES. In any action or proceeding involving a dispute between Owner and Broker arising out of this Agreement, the prevailing party will be entitled to receive from the other party a reasonable attorney fee to be determined by the court or arbitrator.

6. TIME. Time is of the essence of this Agreement.

7. ENTIRE AGREEMENT. This document contains the entire agreement of the parties and supersedes all prior agreements or representations with respect to the property which are not expressly set forth. This Agreement may be modified only in writing, signed and dated by both parties.

8. ADDITIONAL TERMS: _____

_____

_____

_____

_____

_____

_____

_____

_____

_____

_____

_____

_____

_____

_____

_____

_____

The undersigned acknowledge that they have thoroughly read and approve each of the provisions of this Agreement.

Broker _____ Date _____

By _____

Title _____

Address _____

Phone _____ Fax _____

Owner _____ Date _____

Owner _____ Date _____

Fed. ID Number _____

Address _____

Phone _____ Fax _____

Rev. by _____
Date _____

Page 2 of 2

FORM 115.2 (10-97)   COPYRIGHT © 1985–97 BY PROFESSIONAL PUBLISHING, 880 LAS GALLINAS AVE., SAN RAFAEL, CA 94903 (415) 472-1964 FAX (415) 472-2069

 PROFESSIONAL PUBLISHING

Attorneys. The property manager might employ attorneys approved by the owner to enforce the owner's lease rights and to commence legal action.

Note: Commercial management contracts might authorize employing attorneys for lease preparation and/or review.

Management Services. The property manager is to provide all reasonably necessary services for proper management (inspection, supervision of maintenance, alterations and repairs, etc.).

Hire and Discharge Employees. The property manager may hire, supervise and discharge required employees and independent contractors. Employee agreements shall be terminable at will. Employees will be owner employees and not the employees of the manager. Broker shall pay employees with appropriate contribution deductions from the gross revenue.

Contract Repairs. The property manager has authority to make repairs and alterations up to an agreed dollar limit. Exceptions would be owner agreement and emergencies where the owner cannot be contacted and the property must be protected.

Service Contracts. The property manager is authorized to enter service contracts up to a stated period of time and up to a dollar limit unless approved by the owner.

Operating Expenses. The property manager shall pay necessary operating expenses as well as expenses authorized by owner. (These could include mortgage payments, taxes and insurance). Payments shall be made from gross receipts.

Records. The property manager shall maintain records of money received and disbursed. The records shall be available for the owner's inspection.

Monthly Statements. The property manager shall submit monthly statements to the owner by a stated date after the end of the prior month.

Other. Any desired provision can be inserted such as "Manager can retain a balance of up to [$] in the owner's account." The provision would allow enough funds to pay taxes when they are due or extraordinary expenses.

OWNER'S OBLIGATIONS

This section provides for broker compensation. Fees could be in the following categories.

Compensation for Management Services. There could be a flat monthly fee for a property or a fee could be a percentage of gross monthly income and may be coupled with a minimum. The flat fee and percentage could be included in the management contract.

Compensation for Leasing.

Leasing compensation is usually a percentage of the total lease rent paid in the year received for the term of the lease.

Some contracts provide for higher percentages in the early years. Fees for renegotiated leases could be lower than for new leases. The leasing fee may be lowered or eliminated if a contract has a higher percentage of the gross.

Compensation for Supervising Capital Improvements. This would be a percentage of the cost of the improvements such as 10 percent. **Note:** it does not apply to maintenance or repair.

Compensation for Refinancing. If the property manager arranges refinancing of loans, a fee for this effort would be appropriate

Compensation for Other Services. The owner might agree to pay advertising costs or additional costs and/or fees.

ADDITIONAL OWNER OBLIGATIONS

Hold Harmless Provision. The owner agrees to hold the broker harmless for any costs expenses, attorney fees, damages, etc., arising from the contract and pay the broker these costs. As an example, if a broker was fined for a code violation, the owner would indemnify the broker for the cost of the fine. The owner would not be liable if costs were due to negligence or intentional misconduct of the broker.

Insurance (Property and Liability). The owner agrees to carry insurance as indicated including liability coverage naming the broker as an additional insured.

Insurance (Worker's Compensation). The owner agrees to carry worker's compensation insurance.

Responsibility for Obligations. The owner agrees to be responsible for expenses and obligations incurred in managing the property in accordance with this contract.

Initial Deposit. The owner shall make an initial deposit into an operating expense reserve. The broker is not obligated to advance broker funds for any obligation of the owner.

NOTICE

This provision requires all notices to be in writing and specifies manner of delivery and place of delivery.

ATTORNEY FEES

In any legal dispute between owner and broker, the prevailing party shall be entitled to reasonable attorney fees. This provision reduces the likelihood of frivolous lawsuits.

TIME

TIME IS OF THE ESSENCE, *which means that the time set forth in this agreement means the times stated and not within a reasonable period thereafter.*

ENTIRE AGREEMENT

The parties agree that this is the entire agreement and any prior representations have no effect on it. The contract may be modified in writing.

ADDITIONAL TERMS

Additional items of concern by property manager and/or owner may be set forth. As an example, the contract may spell out that the contract ceases upon sale of the property or death of the owner, although this is basic agency law.

Policies

Existing policies should be reviewed when a firm takes over management of a property.

The property manager may wish to make changes to the policies based on the owner's needs, demands of the marketplace, vacancy factor, etc.

SECURITY DEPOSITS

You will have to decide as to the types of security deposits and amount of security deposits for new leases. You might consider asking for the first and last month's rent in advance plus a security deposit.

If tenants tell you that they intend to use their security deposit for the last month's rent, you might ask them if they really want to do this. Point out to them that the rental records will show that they did not pay the last month's rent as agreed and that you were forced to take the rent out of their security deposit. You might also mention that these facts could be detrimental to their credit report.

Note: Don't threaten to report this information. It is enough to indicate that an investigation may bring this information to light.

> *In most states, the amount of a residential security deposits is limited by law.*

The **UNIFORM RESIDENTIAL LANDLORD AND TENANT ACT**, *adopted by many states, limits security deposits to one month's rent.* A number of states have greater limits. In California, a security deposit cannot exceed two month's rent for an unfurnished unit and three month's rent for a furnished unit. The California Code of Civil Procedure allows landlords to take three weeks to account for the security deposit. (It was formerly two weeks). Failure to do so within the allotted time could subject the landlord to $600 in damages.

> *Security deposits may be applied to damages as well as unpaid rent. However, they CANNOT apply to normal wear and tear.*

In many states nonrefundable deposits, such as a general cleaning charge or move-in fee, are not allowed. In most states, interest need not be paid on security deposits unless agreed to by the parties.

Besides the security deposit, you should require a key deposit (such as $10) sufficient to ensure that the key will be returned at the end of the lease. You should also require a deposit for any garage door openers.

Case Example

Korens v. R.W. Zukin Corp. (1989) 212 C.A. 3d 1054

Tenants brought a class action against a landlord for failure to pay interest on their security deposits. In ruling for the landlord, the court pointed out that neither the lease nor California statute requires interest on security deposits. If the tenants had expected interest, they should have negotiated this fact in their leases.

PETS

> *Allowing pets will reduce the vacancy factor for many apartments as well as increase the average tenancy period.*

An increased tenancy period reduces the costs associated with preparing a property for rental and related rental costs. In addition, property that accepts pets may rent at a premium compared to similar property where pets are not allowed. One of the

---

Case Example

People v. Parkmerced Co. (1988) 198 C.A. 3d 683

The owners of a 3,400 unit apartment complex charged tenants a first month's rent which was $65 higher than the rent for the remaining 11 months on the one-year leases. In addition, tenants wishing to change apartments were charged a $50 transfer fee.

This action was brought by the District Attorney based on California law requiring the refunding of all security deposits (California prohibits nonrefundable security deposits). The trial court ruled that Parkmerced should pay $222,000 in civil penalties, $40,000 in attorneys' fees and notify tenants of their right to have these fees refunded.

The Court of Appeals affirmed the award by the trial court. The court pointed out that the charges were not rent but were intended to cover front-end costs associated with moving a tenant in. The court indicated that the penalty charged was not excessive, in fact it was very lenient.

---

authors of this text agreed to pay an owner an additional $100 per month as an inducement to allow him to keep a dog.

If you allow pets, you might want to increase property damage bond requirements. Pets can ruin carpeting and damage hardwood floors. Older animals are subject to inoontinonco problems.

While an owner can decide not to allow pets, this refusal cannot apply to seeing eye dogs or support animals. In fact, a greater property damage bond cannot be charged than is required of tenants who do not own pets.

> *Handicapped persons are protected by the Americans With Disabilities Act.*

LEASE PERIOD

You might want one-year leases or even three-year leases.

> *Market demand would determine the length of the lease.*

While longer leases tend to reduce the vacancy factor, in an inflationary period the owner must wait until the lease has expired to raise rents.

You might want leases to expire in the months when it is easiest to rent. As an example, you would want a beach area unit to have a lease expiring on May 1, June 1, or July 1.

FURNISHED UNITS

Furnished units can demand significantly higher rents than unfurnished units.

Generally, bachelor and one-bedroom furnished units have the highest demand since such units appeal strongly to singles.

> *A problem with furnished units is that the turnover is normally greater than for unfurnished units, as moving for the tenants only involves a few trips to their vehicles with personal effects.*

Management fees for furnished units are normally higher than for unfurnished units because of the shorter occupancy periods and greater maintenance, cleaning and inventory expenses.

Kitchen appliances are usually included in a residential lease, even those for unfurnished units. Don't let tenants use their own appliances unless the benefits exceed the problems involved in moving out the owner's appliances and storing them until they will be required again.

OCCUPANCY

You cannot discriminate as to family status when renting. However, you can limit the number of occupants providing you are reasonable in that request. (See Chapter 13 .)

QUALIFICATION REQUIREMENTS

You can set qualification standards for your tenants but the standards must be reasonable and applied uniformly to all applicants for rental.

WHO NOT TO RENT TO

> *A property manager should NOT rent to a relative or close friend.*

Besides giving the appearance of a conflict of interest, a personal relationship with a tenant can cause significant problems. For instance, a tenant may think that he or she is an exception to the rules. You might hesitate to evict or take legal action because of your personal relationship with the tenant. On the other hand, if you treat this tenant the same as any other tenant, you could ruin an otherwise good relationship or cause family-related problems.

In New York, many lessors refuse to rent to attorneys because of their litigious nature. While we don't know of any similar cases, attorneys are not one of the protected groups under Civil Rights law.

Case Example

Harris v. Capital Growth Investors XIV (1991) 52 C.A. 3d 1142

This case involved a landlord who had a minimum income policy. The landlord required that a tenant's gross income be at least three times greater than the rent for the unit.

The plaintiff claimed that the income was arbitrary and not based on the actual ability to pay. The plaintiff also alleged that the policy was discriminatory as to sex because women generally have lower incomes than men.

In ruling for the defendant, the California Supreme Court recognized that businesses can justifiably place limitations on their businesses to insure full and timely payment for goods and services. The court held that a minimum income standard was a reasonable means to achieve this goal. The landlord's policy is only economic and did not make distinctions as to any protected category.

Note: While economic discrimination is not a violation of fair housing act, the standards should be reasonable. The dissenting opinions seem to indicate that the limitations as to income standard should be evaluated by the court.

Studies show that attorneys are far more likely to sue landlords than any other occupational group.

In addition, some property managers complain about the demanding nature of attorneys as tenants. One of the authors is appalled at rental discrimination against attorneys, However, he is an attorney.

Setting Rents

USING COMPARABLES

Setting rents is part art and part science. You should consider comparables when setting rents for any property. What are similar size units of similar desirability currently renting for? We are concerned with developments having a vacancy rate which is not overly low or overly high. As an example, if apartment rentals experience a seven percent vacancy factor within a community, we would not use comparables of units only having a two percent vacancy factor. Such a vacancy factor would indicate rents charged are too low since the vacancy factor would be practically nil. Similarly, if we used as a comparable units having a 20 percent vacancy factor, we could be setting rents too high. We would not then hope to meet the area average as to vacancies. Actually, meeting the average should not be a goal.

NO property manager wants to be average. They expect to be better because they are professionals.

Just as market values for sales prices can be estimated using a comparative market analysis, the same analysis can be performed for setting rental rates. Use the rental of each comparable and add or subtract from the comparable rental for any difference in location and amenities present or lacking in your rental.

In some cases, it is difficult to find comparables. As an example, units with a view generally command a significant rental premium over units without a desirable view. The premium might be as much as 100 percent. We find such premiums on some water-view properties. Check on data to determine what you feel is a fair premium for the view. If in renting apartment units you discover that the view property is renting faster than non-view property, it would indicate your rents are too low for property with a view or too high for non-view property.

As a general rule, you should reevaluate your rents if your rentals in a new structure are going much slower or faster than anticipated.

In determining a rent schedule or any change in that schedule, you should not be concerned at what price similar units are renting. You are not concerned with competition from occupied units. The only comparison should be with units currently available for rent.

What is NOT available does NOT compete with what is available.

SUPPLY AND DEMAND

What does determine rents? It is simply supply and demand.

If demand for a particular type of property exceeds supply, then rents should rise. If demand is less than supply, rents should drop. It is the basic capitalistic market system in action and it works. More products (rentals) will be added to the marketplace as demand increases and rents increase.

The real estate marketplace is different from economic models set forth in textbooks because it is a stratified marketplace. What this means is that there can be a high vacancy factor as to high rent units and a very low vacancy factor as to middle-income and low-income units.

Another economic factor to consider is that real estate is immobile but people are mobile. When rents get too high in one area, people will be willing to commute greater distances to residences in other areas. Rents and housing costs are extremely high in Orange County California. This has led to the growth in housing and tens of thousands of Orange County workers commuting from communities in Riverside County, where costs are significantly less.

THE IDEAL RENT

As a rule of thumb, if the vacancy factor in an area for a type of property is less than five percent, then the rents are considered too low and can be raised.

What a property manager is concerned about is that combination of rents and vacancy factor that will result in the highest net. As an example, assume a property has 100 units each rented at $1,000 per month for a total of $100,000 gross per month. Assume the rents are raised 10 percent and the property goes from full occupancy to a 10 percent vacancy factor. On the face of these facts, raising the rent 10 percent is not a smart economic decision. Now there are 90 units each rented at $1,100 per month or a gross income of $99,000 per month. The gross income declined one percent with the rise in rent.

Using the same situation, assume the rents were raised five percent and resulted in a three percent vacancy factor. You would now have 97 units rented at $1,050 with a total gross income of $101,850. The gross has increased by $1,850 per month so it would seem to be a good economic decision.

There are other factors to consider in setting rents. If higher rents result in a shorter average tenancy, then savings could erode by necessary costs incurred between tenants such as professionally cleaning carpets, repainting, etc. Such costs, above the normal wear and tear covered by the property damage bond, can easily average $500 per move, depending on the area and size of the rental. There can also be costs to rerent, such as advertising and even commissions.

> *Therefore, a property manager is more interested in long-term net income than in gross income.*

WHAT NOT TO USE IN SETTING RENTS

Owner Costs

> *What an owner paid only affects his or her price, NOT what the marketplace will allow him or her to receive.*

Simply because an owner desires a particular rate of return on an investment does not mean that rental should be set to yield that rate. The owner's desired rate of return is only a wish. In renting we are concerned with the realities of the marketplace. The owner's desired return might be more or even less than the market will allow.

Appraisals

Appraisals are simply one person's estimate of value.

Because a person uses a rental figure in the appraisal does not mean that such a rent is the proper rental for the property.

Appraisers too often use rentals based on what other properties are renting for which, as previously stated, are not the competition. The competition is other vacant units.

Appraisers also may lack the grasp of a particular stratified marketplace in a particular community. Appraisers also use figures which are fixed as to a point in time. They don't consider any changes which might influence rents since that date.

RAISING RENT

The rental marketplace is NOT a perfect economic model.

People will not move simply because an equally desirable unit can be rented for a few dollars less than they are currently paying. As an example, assume that rents in an apartment complex were to rise from $500 per month to $520 per month, a four percent rent increase. It is unlikely that tenants would leave simply because they could rent a similarly desirable unit elsewhere for $500. It costs money to move so moving would not be an economic decision for such a small difference. Of course, there is a point where rent increases will result in lower total revenue because of tenants moving.

It is possible to raise rents above what is being asked for similar units, but too much difference will make it extremely difficult to rent vacant units unless a rental incentive is provided. Another alternative is to make your units appear more desirable by properly preparing vacant units for rent.

WHEN RENTS ARE TOO HIGH

It is possible to get rents which are so high that they are economically unsound for the property owner.

Assume you are asking $500 in rent for a property which should rent for $375. You might find uninformed tenants who will agree to the rent or you might have to give rental incentives. Chances are, the time period to find tenants will be longer than it would normally take. This would mean vacant units until they are rented. Your costs to fill those vacancies, such as ads, commissions and incentives, will also be considerably higher than for market-rate rentals.

Tenants will eventually realize that they are paying too much in rent. Unhappy tenants are far more likely to abandon the premises before the lease expires than are tenants who realize that the rent is fair.

You can expect many of the tenants when their leases expire to look elsewhere for rentals unless you give enough in incentives to become competitive with other available rentals. Those tenants who leave increase your costs to prepare the premises for renting, advertising and other rental related expenses. In addition, it will be a relatively long period until a new tenant will be found at the rent desired.

The bottom line for the lessor would likely be far less in net income than a lower rent would provide.

INFLATION AND RENT

Rents can generally be raised to cover inflation. If they can be raised, then the purchasing value of the rent received is NOT diminished.

Rents usually increase with inflation and provide the landlord with an increase in the net income in excess of the inflationary increase. The reason is that normally debt service is a fixed expense. Look at the following situation before and after a 10 percent inflationary increase. The assumption is that expenses and rent will increase by 10 percent:

	Before Inflation	After Inflation
Gross rents	$1,000,000.00	$1,100,000.00
Debt Service	-650,000.00	-650,000.00
Operational Expenses	-300,000.00	-330,000.00
Positive Cash Flow	$50,000.00	$120,000.00

You can see that in the above example a 10 percent increase in the rent coupled with a 10 percent increase in operational expenses (including taxes and insurance) would result in a 140 percent increase in net spendable income for the owner.

However, inflation can increase expenses and not result in a rent increase since rent is determined by forces of supply and demand.

Keep in mind: inflationary rent increases are NOT a certainty.

Supply and demand of the marketplace indicates what you can get. Historically, though, rent increases have been able to exceed inflation in most parts of the country.

The Rental Process

PREPARING TO LEASE

When a unit becomes vacant, any delay in preparing for a rental is costly because every day delayed is a day's rent which can never be recovered.

Waiting two weeks for a crew to remove junk left in an apartment, touch up the painting and clean the carpet could exceed the cost of preparing the unit for rental. It might have been better to pay a premium to people who would get in immediately when a unit becomes vacant and finish the work in a few days.

You want the unit sparkling to rent it. That means a shine on tile, clean carpets, walls that look freshly painted, clean light fixtures and spotless windows as well as appliances that sparkle. Some property managers use car wax on appliances and fixtures. There can be no unpleasant odors in the apartment.

All light fixtures should have enough wattage to flood the apartment with light. Window shades, blinds and curtains should be pulled back to have natural light. You want the unit to appear bright and cheerful. Keep in mind that people are not entirely economic when renting. Emotion can trigger desire and you want your properties to evoke positive emotions.

When there are a number of identical-unit vacancies, you can prepare one as a sample unit. It might even be decorator furnished. This is an excellent rental tool when units have recently been completed. You must be certain that all units will be prepared for rental in an identical manner or you will end up with some unhappy short-term tenants.

PREQUALIFYING YOUR PROSPECTIVE TENANTS

Before you take prospects into a unit, you should determine if the unit is within their budget and if the size of the unit meets their needs. You should have also gone over with them all deposit requirements and the policy about pets.

If they can't afford the unit or it is too small, you are just wasting your time and theirs. In the end, you could lose a tenant for a unit which better suits their needs.

Be certain that you obtain names and telephone numbers before showing prospective tenants units.

SHOWING TO PROSPECTIVE TENANTS

Resident managers and leasing agents should turn on all the lights when showing a property.

They should be showing property to prospective renters who are satisfied with location and size requirements of the property and can meet the financial requirements.

A straight-forward approach is best even if the rental agent is not receiving any feedback from the prospective renters as to their satisfaction with the unit. Resident managers and leasing agents should be trained to present a closing similar to the following:

"This apartment is available [now/on July 1st] for [$610] per month [which includes one garage space and one parking space]. It requires a property damage bond of [$500 plus a $15 key deposit]. If you like this apartment, I can take your application for rent with a [refundable] deposit of [$50]. I will be able to notify you within [24 hours] if your rental application is accepted. Is this satisfactory with you?"

Their answer will be either yes or no. If the answer is yes, begin filling out the rental application which the prospects will then sign. They will also give you their check.

Ask to see a photo ID. You want to be certain that your renters are who they say they are.

There are a number of rental application forms available. See *Tenants Personal and Credit Information* form prepared by Professional Publishing which is included in Chapter 3.

THE QUALIFICATION PROCESS

As covered in Chapter 3, you should check the applicant's credit as well as check the accuracy of the current employment data. You also want to check with past landlords.

Don't take short cuts or assume because a person drives a fancy car and dresses well that they will be good tenants.

Be leery of tenants who need immediate occupancy.

If your check of a prospective tenant's employment and/or prior landlords cannot be verified, you should go further and check with references. Ask the references to give you the names of two other people who know the applicants. These are more likely to provide you with honest information about the applicants.

The qualification process should be regarded as a priority. Process your inquiries quickly.

THE LEASE SIGNING

Notify the applicants as soon as they have been approved. Set up an appointment for them to pay the balance of the first month's rent and any deposits due. The applicants should understand the total financial obligation at the time they sign any lease.

Carefully go over every provision of the lease with the tenant as well as any applicable occupancy rules. Tenants need to understand that the rules are important. The better the tenants understand the rules, the fewer problems management will encounter. The tenants then sign the lease and accompanying rules. They should know where they will obtain the key to the unit. Figure 5-2 is a sample of a Residential Lease prepared by Professional Publishing.

You should consider giving your tenants a check list with telephone numbers for utilities, post office, school registration, etc.

You might want to sign the lease on the premises where furnished rentals are involved. The tenants should also sign an inventory list of items furnished in the units. We recommend taking polaroid photos of the furnished units prior to renting and have the tenants sign and date each photo. This will help you should there be a dispute later as to damage to the units.

LESSOR DISCLOSURES

A number of lessor disclosures are required. These include the following:

Name and Address on Notices. Tenants of multi-unit dwellings generally must be provided with the name and address of persons who have management responsibility and on whom notices and demands may be served. This provision should be provided in writing if it is not provided in the lease.

Lead Paint Disclosure. For property that was built prior to 1978, tenants must be provide with a Disclosure on Lead Paint.

Uniform Residential Landlord and Tenant Act

In addition to obligations set forth in the lease there are legally mandated rights and obligations.

Figure 5-2

NCR (No Carbon Required) **RESIDENTIAL LEASE-RENTAL AGREEMENT AND DEPOSIT RECEIPT**

RECEIVED FROM _____, hereinafter referred to as Tenant,
the sum of $_____ (_____ dollars),
evidenced by _____, as a deposit. Upon acceptance of this Agreement, the Owner of the premises,
will apply the deposit as follows:

	TOTAL	RECEIVED	BALANCE DUE PRIOR TO OCCUPANCY
Rent for the period from _____ to _____ .	$ _____	$ _____	$ _____
Security deposit (**not** applicable toward last month's rent)	$ _____	$ _____	$ _____
Other	$ _____	$ _____	$ _____
TOTAL	$ _____	$ _____	$ _____

In the event this Agreement is not accepted by the Owner, **within** _____ **days**, the total deposit received will be refunded.
Tenant offers to rent from the Owner the premises situated in the City of _____,
County of _____, State of _____, described as _____
_____
_____

upon the following **terms and conditions**:
1. **TERM:** The term will commence on _____, and continue (**check one of the two following alternatives**):
   LEASE ☐ until _____, for a total rent of $_____ (_____
   _____ dollars).

   RENTAL ☐ on a month-to-month basis, until either party terminates this Agreement by giving the other party **30 days written notice.**
2. **RENT:** Rent will be $_____, per month, payable in advance, upon the _____ day of each calendar month to Owner or his or her
   authorized agent, at the following address: _____,
   or at such other places as may be designated by Owner from time to time. In the event rent is not paid **within** _____ **days** after due date,
   Tenant agrees that it would be impracticable or extremely difficult to fix the actual damages to Owner caused by that failure, and
   Tenant agrees to pay a **late charge** of $_____. Tenant further agrees to pay $_____ for each dishonored bank check. The
   late charge period is **not** a grace period, and Owner is entitled to make written demand for any rent if not paid when due. Any unpaid
   balance including late charges, will bear interest at 10% per annum, or the maximum rate allowed by law, whichever is less.
3. **MULTIPLE OCCUPANCY:** It is expressly understood that this Agreement is between the Owner and each signatory jointly and severally.
   Each signatory will be responsible for timely payment of rent and performance of all other provisions of this Agreement.
4. **UTILITIES:** Tenant will be responsible for the payment of all utilities and services, except: _____
   _____, which will be paid by Owner.
5. **USE:** The premises will be used exclusively as a residence for no more than _____ persons. Guests staying more than a total of
   _____ days in a calendar year without written consent of Owner will constitute a violation of this Agreement.
6. **ANIMALS:** No animals will be brought on the premises without the prior consent of the Owner; except _____
7. **HOUSE RULES:** In the event that the premises is a portion of a building containing more than one unit, Tenant agrees to abide by all
   house rules, whether adopted before or after the date of this Agreement, including rules with respect to noise, odors, disposal of
   refuse, animals, parking, and use of common areas. Tenant will not have a waterbed on the premises without prior written consent of
   the Owner.
8. **ORDINANCES AND STATUTES:** Tenant will comply with all statutes, ordinances, and requirements of all municipal, state and federal
   authorities now in force, or which may later be in force, regarding the use of the premises. If the premises are located in a rent control
   area, the Tenant should contact the Rent and Arbitration Board for his or her legal rights.
9. **ASSIGNMENT AND SUBLETTING:** Tenant will not assign this Agreement or sublet any portion of the premises without prior written
   consent of the Owner.
10. **MAINTENANCE, REPAIRS, OR ALTERATIONS:** Tenant acknowledges that the premises are in good order and repair, unless otherwise
    indicated. Tenant will, at his or her own expense, maintain the premises in good repair and in a clean and sanitary manner including all
    equipment, appliances, smoke detectors, plumbing, heating and air conditioning, and will surrender the same, at termination, in as
    good condition as received, normal wear and tear excepted. Tenant will be responsible for damages caused by his or her negligence
    and that of his or her family, invitees, and guests. Tenant will not paint, paper or otherwise redecorate or make alterations to the
    premises without the prior written consent of the Owner. Tenant will irrigate and maintain any surrounding grounds, including lawns
    and shrubbery, if they are for the Tenant's exclusive use. Tenant will not commit any waste upon the premises, or any nuisance or act
    which may disturb the quiet enjoyment of any tenant in the building. Owner will be responsible for the cost of any retrofitting required
    by governmental agencies.
11. **INVENTORY:** Any furnishings and/or equipment to be furnished by Owner will be listed in a special inventory. The inventory will be
    signed by both Tenant and Owner concurrently with this Lease. Tenant will keep the furnishings and equipment in good condition and
    repair, and will be responsible for any damage to them other than normal wear and tear. Tenant acknowledges receipt of _____ sets of
    keys, _____ garage door openers, other: _____

Tenant [_____] [_____] has read this page.

Page 1 of 3
FORM 105.1 (6-97)   COPYRIGHT © 1994–97 BY PROFESSIONAL PUBLISHING, 880 LAS GALLINAS AVE., SAN RAFAEL, CA 94903   (415) 472-1964 FAX (415) 472-2069

PROFESSIONAL PUBLISHING

Property Address _____

12. **DAMAGES TO PREMISES:** If the premises are damaged by fire or from any other cause which renders the premises untenantable, either party will have the right to terminate this Agreement as of the date on which the damage occurs. Written notice of termination will be given to the other party **within fifteen (15) days after occurrence** of such damage. Should such damage or destruction occur as the result of the negligence of Tenant, or his or her invitees, then only the Owner will have the right to terminate. Should this right be exercised by either Owner or Tenant, then rent for the current month will be prorated between the parties as of the date the damage occurred. Any prepaid rent and unused security deposit will be refunded to Tenant. If this Agreement is not terminated, then Owner will promptly repair the premises and there will be a proportionate reduction of rent until the premises are repaired and ready for Tenant's occupancy. The proportionate reduction will be based on the extent which repairs interfere with Tenant's reasonable use of the premises.

13. **ENTRY AND INSPECTION:** Owner will have the right to enter the premises: (a) in case of emergency; (b) to make necessary or agreed repairs, decorations, alterations, improvements, supply necessary or agreed services, show the premises to prospective or actual buyers, lenders, tenants, workers, or contractors; (c) when tenant has abandoned or surrendered the premises. Except under (a) and (c), entry may be made only during normal business hours, and with at least 24 hours prior notice to Tenant.

14. **INDEMNIFICATION:** Owner will not be liable for any damage or injury to Tenant, or any other person, or to any property, occurring on the premises, or in common areas, unless such damage is the legal result of the negligence or willful misconduct of Owner, his or her agents, or employees. Tenant agrees to hold Owner harmless from any claims for damages, no matter how caused, except for injury or damages caused by negligence or willful misconduct of Owner, his or her agents or employees. It is understood that Owner's insurance does not cover Tenant's personal property or improvements.

15. **PHYSICAL POSSESSION:** If Owner is unable to deliver possession of the premises at the commencement date set forth above, Owner will not be liable for any damage caused, nor will this Agreement be void or voidable, but Tenant will not be liable for any rent until possession is delivered. Tenant may terminate this Agreement if possession is not delivered **within _____ days** of the commencement of the term in Item 1.

16. **DEFAULT:** If Tenant fails to pay rent when due, or perform any provision of this Agreement, after not less than **three (3) days written notice** of such default given in the manner required by law, the Owner, at his or her option, may terminate all rights of Tenant, unless Tenant, within said time, cures such default. If Tenant abandons or vacates the property while in default of the payment of rent, Owner may consider any property left on the premises to be abandoned and may dispose of the same in any manner allowed by law. In the event the Owner reasonably believes that such abandoned property has no value, it may be discarded. All property on the premises will be subject to a lien for the benefit of Owner securing the payment of all sums due, to the maximum extent allowed by law.

   In the event of a default by Tenant, Owner may elect to: (a) continue the lease in effect and enforce all his rights and remedies, including the right to recover the rent as it becomes due, provided that Owner's consent to assignment or subletting by the Tenant will not be unreasonably withheld; or (b) at any time, terminate all of Tenant's rights and recover from Tenant all damages he or she may incur by reason of the breach of the lease, including the cost of recovering the premises, and including the worth at the time of such termination, or at the time of an award if suit be instituted to enforce this provision, of the amount by which the unpaid rent for the balance of the term exceeds the amount of such rental loss which the Tenant proves could be reasonably avoided.

17. **SECURITY:** The security deposit will secure the performance of Tenant's obligations. Owner may, but will not be obligated to, apply all portions of said deposit on account of Tenant's obligations. Any balance remaining upon termination will be returned to Tenant. Tenant will not have the right to apply the security deposit in payment of the last month's rent. Security deposit held at _____

18. **DEPOSIT REFUNDS:** The balance of all deposits will be refunded **within three weeks** (or as otherwise required by law), from date possession is delivered to Owner or his or her authorized agent, together with a statement showing any charges made against such deposits.

19. **WAIVER:** Failure of Owner to enforce any provision of this Agreement will not be deemed a waiver. The acceptance of rent by Owner will not waive his or her right to enforce any provision of this Agreement.

20. **NOTICES:** Unless otherwise provided, any notice which either party may give or is required to give, may be given personally or by mailing the same, postage prepaid, certified to Tenant at the premises or to Owner at the address shown in the signature block or at such other places as may be designated by the parties from time to time. Notice will be deemed effective five (5) days after mailing, or on personal delivery, or when receipt is acknowledged in writing.

21. **HOLDING OVER:** Any holding over after expiration of this Agreement, with the consent of Owner, will be a month-to-month tenancy at a monthly rent of $_____ payable in advance and otherwise subject to the terms of this Agreement, as applicable, until either party terminates the same by giving the other party **thirty (30) days written notice.**

22. **TIME:** Time is of the essence of this Agreement.

23. **ATTORNEY'S FEES:** In any action or proceeding involving a dispute between Owner and Tenant arising out of this Agreement, the prevailing party will be entitled to reasonable attorney fees and any costs incurred.

24. **FAIR HOUSING:** Owner and Tenant understand that the state and federal housing laws prohibit discrimination in the sale, rental, appraisal, financing or advertising of housing on the basis of race, religion, color, sex, familial status, sexual preference, handicap, or national origin.

Tenant [_____] [_____] **has read this page.**

Page 2 of 3
FORM 105.2 (6-97)   COPYRIGHT © 1994–97 BY PROFESSIONAL PUBLISHING, 880 LAS GALLINAS AVE., SAN RAFAEL, CA 94903   (415) 472-1964 FAX (415) 472-2069

PROFESSIONAL PUBLISHING

Property Address _____

25. ADDITIONAL TERMS AND CONDITIONS: _____

_____

_____

_____

_____

_____

_____

_____

_____

_____

_____

26. ☐ This unit is subject to rent control and the agency responsible to adjudicate claims is: _____

27. ENTIRE AGREEMENT: The foregoing constitutes the entire agreement between the parties and may be modified only in writing signed by all parties. This Agreement and any modifications, including any photocopy or facsimile, may be signed in one or more counterparts, each of which will be deemed an original and all of which taken together will constitute one and the same instrument. The following exhibits, if checked, have been made a part of this Agreement before the parties' execution:

☐ Exhibit _____ : Lead-Based Paint Disclosure (Required by Law for Rental Property Built Prior to 1978)

☐ Exhibit _____ : _____

☐ Exhibit _____ : _____

The Tenant hereby acknowledges receipt of a copy of this Agreement.

Tenant _____ Date _____   Owner _____ Date _____

Tenant _____ Date _____   Owner's Address _____

_____

Receipt for deposit acknowledged by _____ Date _____

COMMISSION AGREEMENT ON LEASE

NOTICE: The amount or rate of real estate commissions is not fixed by law. They are set by each broker individually and may be negotiable between the owner and broker.

The Owner agrees to pay to _____, the Broker in this transaction, the sum of $_____ for services rendered and authorizes Broker to deduct said sum from the deposit received from Tenant.

In the event the Lease is extended for a definite period of time or on a month-to-month basis after expiration of the original term, Owner will pay to Broker an additional commission of _____% of the total rental for the extended period. This commission will be due and payable at the commencement of the extended period if for a fixed term, or if on a month-to-month basis, at the termination of Tenant's occupancy or one year, whichever is earlier.

In any action for commission, the prevailing party will be entitled to reasonable attorney fees.

Owner _____ Date _____

COMMISSION AGREEMENT ON SALE

NOTICE: The amount or rate of real estate commissions is not fixed by law. They are set by each broker individually and may be negotiable between the owner and broker.

If a sale or exchange of the real property subject to this lease is made to the Tenant or any member of Tenant's family during the term of the lease or **within 180 days after termination of occupancy**, Owner agrees to pay Broker named above a commission of _____% of the sale price or exchange value. This Agreement will not limit any other rights of the Broker provided for in any listing or other agreement which may be in effect between Owner and Broker.

In any action for commission, the prevailing party will be entitled to reasonable attorney fees.

Owner _____ Date _____

| Rev. by _____ |
| Date _____ |

Page 3 of 3

FORM 105.3 (6-97)   COPYRIGHT © 1994–97 BY PROFESSIONAL PUBLISHING, 880 LAS GALLINAS AVE., SAN RAFAEL, CA 94903   (415) 472-1964 FAX (415) 472-2069

PROFESSIONAL PUBLISHING

The Uniform Residential Landlord and Tenants Act has been adopted in whole or in part in most states.

In adopting the act, many states such as California have made some modifications to this act.

GENERAL PROVISIONS

Unconscionable Leases. Leases that are considered unconscionable will not be enforced. (A lease where a tenant waives his or her legal rights would be considered unconscionable.)

Failure of Lessor to Sign. If a rental agreement is signed by the tenant and delivered to the landlord who fails to sign but accepts rent without reservation, the lease has the same effect as if it were signed and delivered.

> *If the term of the lease is longer than one year, the unsigned lease would only be valid for one year.*

Confession of Judgment. A lease provision where a tenant confesses judgment, if in default, is prohibited.

> *A confession of judgment gives up the right to defend actions in court.*

Attorney Fees. A provision where the tenant agrees to pay a landlord's attorney fees, regardless of a court decision, is prohibited.

> *Note: Attorney fees to the prevailing party would be proper.*

Hold Harmless. A provision where the tenant agrees to hold the landlord harmless for any personal injury or property loss, regardless of landlord fault, would be prohibited.

Knowingly Including Prohibited Provisions. If a landlord knows a provision is prohibited but knowingly includes it in a lease, the tenant is entitled to actual damages plus up to three month's rent and attorney's fees.

Security Deposits Limit. While there is no limit as to prepaid rent, residential security deposits are limited to one month's rent. (In California, it is two month's rent for unfurnished units and three month's rent for furnished units.)

Accounting for Deposits.

> *The landlord must account for funds within 21 days of termination of tenancy.*

Failure to return a deposit can result in return of the deposit plus twice the amount wrongfully held as well as attorney's fees. (In California, the lessor has 21 days to account for and return funds owed and damages are limited to actual damages plus $600 in exemplary damages.)

Name of Manager. The landlord must give the tenant the name and address of the manager or person authorized to receive notices and legal service.

Possession. The landlord must deliver possession of the premises at commencement of the lease.

LESSOR'S DUTIES

Codes. The landlord must comply with applicable health and safety codes.

Repairs. The landlord must make repairs necessary to keep the premises in a fit and habitable condition. The landlord is not responsible to make repairs for damage caused by the tenant's carelessness, such as a child's toy clogging a toilet.

If the tenant's improper conduct caused a problem making the premises uninhabitable, the tenant cannot require the landlord to repair. If the tenant interferes with the landlord's ability to make repairs the tenant cannot require the landlord to make repairs.

Common Areas. The landlord must keep common areas in a clean and safe condition.

Maintenance. The landlord must maintain electrical, plumbing, sanitary, heating, ventilating, air conditioning and other facilities (including elevators) in good and safe working order.

Garbage Receptacles. The landlord shall provide and maintain garbage receptacles and arrange for garbage removal.

Water and Heat. The landlord shall provide water and a reasonable amount of hot water as well as heat, the latter generally between October 1 and May 1. Exceptions to this period of time would be situations where the facilities are under the exclusive control of the tenant.

Working Toilet. There must be a working toilet, washbasin and bathtub or shower. The toilet, bathtub or shower must be in a ventilated room and the room must provide privacy.

Kitchen Sink. The kitchen must have a sink which cannot be made of absorbent material such as wood.

Natural Lighting. There must be natural lighting in every room (window or skylight). If the windows do not open, there must be ventilation.

Emergency Exits. There must be fire or emergency exits leading to a street or hallway.

Smoke Detectors. There must be smoke detectors in common stairwells and within the dwelling unit when there is more than one unit.

Agreements. Agreements otherwise as to garbage repair, etc., are proper as long as such agreements are made in good faith.

Quiet Enjoyment.

The lessor shall NOT interfere with a tenant's quiet enjoyment of the premises.

Violation of a lessor's covenant of quiet enjoyment could include:

1. wrongful entry into tenant's space;
2. barring tenant access to his or her space;
3. numerous and/or needless repairs that disturbs the tenant's peace;
4. leasing the property to a third party and giving possession while the tenant has a right of possession.

The breach of the covenant of quiet possession could allow a tenant to terminate the lease without further obligation.

TENANT'S DUTIES

Code Compliance. The tenant must comply with tenant obligations under building and health codes.

Cleanliness. The tenant must keep the premises clean and safe as conditions permit.

Garbage. The tenant must dispose of garbage and waste in a clean and safe manner.

Use of Fixtures and Appliances. The tenant must use electrical, plumbing and gas fixtures and appliances in a proper manner and maintain them in a clean manner.

Protection of Premises. The tenant shall not deliberately or negligently damage, deface, destroy or remove parts of the premises or permit others to do so.

Use of Premises. Tenant shall use the premises only as a dwelling unless agree otherwise.

Conduct. The tenants shall conduct themselves in a manner that will not disturb the peaceful enjoyment of other tenants.

Rules. The tenant shall abide by rules and regulations that promote the safety and welfare of tenants if they apply equally and fairly to all tenants.

End of Tenancy. The tenant shall surrender the premises to the landlord at the termination of the tenancy in a clean and proper manner.

After Occupancy

RENT COLLECTIONS

As a matter of security (see Chapter 9), rent should only be accepted in the form of a check or money order.

Cash creates a security problem and places property management personnel at risk.

Rent should be either paid at the resident manager's office or at the central office of the management firm. A procedure needs to be in place for rental collection problems.

Late Payment. Fees charged for late payments set forth in the lease must be strictly and uniformly enforced.

Tenant Promises. One tenant promise to pay by a specific date might be allowed but no further promises should be allowed to deter taking eviction action.

Three-Day Notice. When rent is 15 days late (some firms allow longer periods), the tenant should be served with a notice, generally a three-day notice to quit or pay rent. (See Figure 5-3.)

Unlawful Detainer Action. A three-day notice normally results in tenant compliance. In the event the tenant does not comply, an *UNLAWFUL DETAINER ACTION follows the three-day notice. It is the legal action to evict a tenant who is in default.*

No rent should be accepted (unless payment is in full) after the three-day notice is given or acceptance will defeat the unlawful detainer action. The specific rent due must be set forth.

Asking for more than what is due could also defeat the action.

A tenant has a period to respond to an unlawful detainer action. In California, the tenant has five days to file an answer. If the tenant fails to answer the complaint, a judgment will be entered against the tenant. This will authorize the sheriff to remove the tenant and his or her possessions from the property.

Tenant Defenses. The tenant can defend against an unlawful detainer action for the following:

1. That the action is invalid (three-day notice not served, only two days passed before unlawful detainer was served on tenant, etc.).

Figure 5-3

NCR (No Carbon Required)

THREE-DAY NOTICE TO PAY RENT OR QUIT

To _____, Tenants, Subtenants,
Occupants in Possession, of the premises commonly known as _____,
City of _____, County of, _____, State of California.

NOTICE IS HEREBY GIVEN that under the lease or rental agreement by which you hold possession of the above described premises, there is now due and unpaid rent in the total sum of $_____
(_____ dollars), which represents the rent due for the months of:

$_____ Due From _____, 19_____ To _____, 19_____
$_____ Due From _____, 19_____ To _____, 19_____
$_____ Due From _____, 19_____ To _____, 19_____

WITHIN THREE (3) DAYS after service of this notice, you are required to pay the rent in full, or surrender possession of the premises to the undersigned. If you do not, legal proceedings will be commenced against you to recover (a) possession of the premises; (b) actual damages, and (c) statutory damages of up to six hundred dollars ($600.00).

Owner ▭ does, ▭ does not elect to forfeit your lease or rental agreement.

As required by law, you are hereby notified that a negative credit report reflecting on your credit record may be submitted to a credit reporting agency if you fail to fulfill the terms of your credit obligations.

▭ This unit is subject to rent control and the agency responsible to adjudicate a claim is:_____
_____

Owner _____ Date _____
By _____
      (Manager)

PROOF OF SERVICE

I, the UNDERSIGNED, being at least eighteen (18) years of age, served the above THREE-DAY NOTICE TO PAY RENT OR QUIT, of which this is a true copy, on the above named tenant, in the manner indicated below:

1. I personally delivered a copy to the tenant at _____,
                                               (Address)
   on _____, 19_____, at _____ o'clock ▭ a.m. ▭ p.m.

2. The tenant was absent from his or her residence and business address. I personally delivered a copy to _____, a person of suitable age and discretion at tenant's residence or
                   (Name)
   business address, on _____, 19_____, at _____ o'clock ▭ a.m. ▭ p.m. and mailed a copy addressed to tenant at his or her place of residence.

3. There being no person at the leased premises, I affixed a copy of the notice in a conspicuous place on the property on _____, 19_____, at _____ o'clock ▭ a.m. ▭ p.m. and mailed a copy to tenant at the leased premises.

I declare under penalty of perjury under the laws of the State of California, that the foregoing is true and correct.

Signature _____ Date _____
_____
      (Please print name)

FORM 105-C CAL (7-97)   COPYRIGHT © 1987–97 BY PROFESSIONAL PUBLISHING, 880 LAS GALLINAS AVE., SAN RAFAEL, CA 94903   (415) 472-1964   FAX (415) 472-2069

PROFESSIONAL PUBLISHING

2. The property was not inhabitable. If a lessor breaches the covenant of habitability, an unlawful detainer will generally not be enforced against a tenant. The landlord has failed to provide a habitable dwelling.

3. The court will not allow the enforcement of an eviction when it is retaliatory. If a lessor evicts a tenant (for other than failure to pay rent) within a designated period of a tenant complaining to a public authority as to violations by the landlord or for tenant organizing activities, the court would view such action as retaliatory eviction and refuse to enforce the action. (California statutes provide a 180-day period.)

4. If the tenant can show that the eviction was based on the fact that the tenant was a member of a protected group, then the eviction could be a civil rights violation. (See Chapter 13.) The action would not be enforced.

Self-Help Evictions. A lessor cannot generally force a tenant to move by removing the door, cutting off utilities, threatening force, changing locks or by physically removing the tenant's possessions. All such actions would expose the lessor to compensatory and likely punitive damages. California Civil Code Section 789.3 provides for damages of $100 per day for cutting off utilities as well as other self-help eviction action.

ENFORCEMENT OF CONTRACT PROVISIONS OR RULES AND REGULATIONS

If a tenant fails to meet the requirements of the lease or rules as agreed to by the tenant, he or she may be served with a notice to Quit or Cure.

This notice sets forth the tenant's breach and provides that failure to cure the breach within a period of time (generally three days) would result in an action to recover possession (Unlawful Detainer Action). Figure 5-4 is a sample form of one such notice.

30-DAY NOTICE

To end a periodic tenancy either the lessor or lessee can give a notice to the other party. The notice is generally 30 days. In addition, some leases provide that in the absence of a 30-day notice, the lease would automatically renew itself. (See Chapter 3 and 4.)

CHANGE IN RENT/COVENANTS

A lessor can change the rent or covenants of the lease, when it is a periodic tenancy, by giving the tenant a notice as to the new rent and/or lease terms (generally 30 days).

Figure 5-4

NCR (No Carbon Required)

THREE-DAY NOTICE TO PERFORM CONDITIONS
AND/OR COVENANTS OR QUIT

To _____, Tenants of the premises commonly known as _____

City of _____, County of _____, State of California.

NOTICE IS HEREBY GIVEN that, under the lease or rental agreement by which you hold possession of the above described premises, the condition or covenant set forth below is being breached as follows:

1. Condition or covenant breached: _____
   _____
   _____
   _____
   _____
   _____

2. Specific facts of breach or violation: _____
   _____
   _____
   _____
   _____
   _____

WITHIN THREE (3) DAYS after service of this notice, you are required to perform and comply with the above mentioned condition or covenant, or to deliver possession of the premises to the owner. If you do not, legal proceedings will be commenced against you to recover possession of the premises, and for statutory and actual damages.

Owner ☐ does, ☐ does not elect to forfeit your lease or rental agreement.

☐ This unit is subject to rent control and the agency responsible to adjudicate claims is: _____

Owner _____   Date _____

By _____
      (Manager)

PROOF OF SERVICE

I, the UNDERSIGNED, being at least eighteen (18) years of age, served the above THREE-DAY NOTICE TO PERFORM CONDITIONS AND/OR COVENANTS OR QUIT, of which this is a true copy, on the above named tenant, in the manner indicated below

1. I personally delivered a copy to the tenant at _____
                                                          (Address)
   on _____, 19___, at _____ o'clock ☐ a.m. ☐ p.m.

2. The tenant was absent from his or her residence and business address. I personally delivered a copy to _____, a person of suitable age and discretion at tenant's residence or
   (Name)
   business address, on _____, 19___, at _____ o'clock ☐ a.m. ☐ p.m. and mailed a copy addressed to tenant at his or her place of residence.

3. There being no person at the leased premises, I affixed a copy of the notice in a conspicuous place on the property on _____, 19___, at _____ o'clock ☐ a.m. ☐ p.m. and mailed a copy to tenant at the leased premises.

I declare under penalty of perjury under the laws of the State of California, that the foregoing is true and correct.

Signature _____   Date _____

_____
          (Please print name)

FORM 105-G CAL (8-97)   COPYRIGHT © 1989–97 BY PROFESSIONAL PUBLISHING, 880 LAS GALLINAS AVE., SAN RAFAEL, CA 94903   (415) 472-1964   FAX (415) 472-2069

PROFESSIONAL PUBLISHING

CONFIRMATION OF LEASE

The lease may provide that the tenant will complete a lease confirmation (an estoppel certificate) setting forth the tenant's lease rights. This would be for purchasers or lender. If a tenant had an option to purchase it could effect the rights of lenders or purchaser if such a right were not disclosed.

CHAPTER 5 SUMMARY

The need for housing is affected by a number of factors:

1. The number of family units is more important than the raw population figures.

2. Economic conditions cause coupling and uncoupling of families.

3. Society changes with the decline of extended family residences encouraged by social security and pension plans.

4. Interest rates affect rental housing needs in that lower interest rates make ownership possible for more renters.

5. Population bulges result in need for starter housing as well as family and then elderly housing as bulges move through various age brackets.

6. Political changes such as taxes, growth limitations, development fees, rent control and zoning affect the number of new units which will be built to replace deteriorating housing stock.

7. The fact that development from land acquisition to renting can take as much as several years means that there can be a significant lag period between housing need developing and the meeting of that need.

8. Since the housing market is stratified by type of housing and amount of rent, there can be a need for one type of housing at one rental price and a housing surplus at another price.

Property management contracts are the owner/agent contracts. They should be for several years because of the time and effort required to turn around poorly managed property. Contracts would include:

1. The authority and obligations of the broker.
2. The broker's rights as to advertising and tenant selection.
3. The broker's power to negotiate and execute leases.
4. Rent collection authority.
5. Authority to terminate tenancies and give notices.

6. The authority to employ attorneys to enforce owners' rights.

7. Power to provide all management services.

8. Authority to hire and discharge employees.

9. Authority to contract for repairs and to enter service contracts (there may be dollar and time limits).

10. Authority to pay operational expenses, mortgage payments, taxes, insurance, etc.

11. The requirement for proper record keeping.

12. The requirement to submit monthly statements.

13. Special requirements would be added for specific owner or property needs.

Owner obligations would also be set forth in the property management contract. These obligations include:

1. Compensation to property manager as to a percentage of gross revenue, minimum fee or a flat fee.

2. Leasing compensation.

3. Compensation for supervision of improvements.

4. Compensation for obtaining refinancing.

5. Compensation for other services.

Other provisions of the property management contract would include an agreement to hold the property manager harmless from expenses and damages arising from the contract, as well as the owner's duty to carry designated insurance coverage. In the event of any dispute, the parties would agree that the prevailing party would be entitled to attorney's fees.

When a property management firm takes over management of a property they should review property policies and make changes where necessary. Areas of change to consider could include rent schedule, security deposits, allowing pets, periods of leases and expiration dates, furnishings of units, occupancy and qualification requirements, etc.

Rents should be competitive with other vacant units on the market, not units already rented. Rents should be set so that the rental rate and vacancy factor combine to produce the maximum net return to the owner. Too high a rent results in too high a vacancy factor and rents too low result in less than a maximization of income which is a disservice to an owner.

Property should sparkle when placed on the rental market. Prospective tenants should be prequalified before being shown a vacancy. A rental application should be the result of a successful showing. The applicant's credit, work history and rental history should be checked during the qualification process. If the applicant is qualified, the lease should be explained in detail as well as rules of the property. All deposits should be received at the time the applicant signs the lease.

By law the lessor is responsible for:

1. A weather-tight unit.
2. Proper plumbing and gas.
3. Water. Hot and cold water supply.
4. Heating facilities.
5. Proper wiring.
6. Clean and sanitary buildings and ground.
7. Sufficiently clean garbage receptacles.
8. Stairs, floors and railings in good repair.
9. A working toilet.
10. A kitchen sink of non-absorbent material.
11. Natural lighting in each room.
12. Emergency exits.
13. Smoke detectors.

The landlord must also not interfere with a tenant's quiet enjoyment of the premises.

The tenant's legal responsibilities include:

1. Cleanliness.
2. Proper garbage disposal.
3. Proper utilization of fixtures and appliances.
4. Not permitting damage to the property.
5. Use as residence only.
6. Surrendering the premises at the end of the lease.

Property management duties, in addition to leasing and maintenance, include setting forth procedure for rent collection and following those procedures, enforcement of contract provisions as well as property rules, adjustments to rents and eviction notices.

The quality of the interpersonal relationships between tenants and with tenants are one determinant of successful management. Tenant problems must be handled promptly.

CLASS DISCUSSION TOPICS

1. Describe any stratification differences in your local rental market.

2. Are a significant number of new residential rental properties being built in your area? Why?

3. Does your area have rent control? If yes, how has it affected the rental housing supply?

4. Are there residential units in your area that have rents which you regard as being below-market rents? If so, why do you suppose the rents have not been raised?

5. Are there apartment units in your area that have waiting lists? If yes, what does that tell you?

6. Do you know of any rental housing in your area which fails to meet minimum standards?

CHAPTER 5 QUIZ

1. Which of the following would be a factor of rental housing needs in an area?
    A. The growth in the number of family units.
    B. Changes in the local economy
    C. A lowering of interest rates
    D. All of the above

2. A moratorium on new construction could be expected to:
    A. reduce the vacancy factor
    B. result in rent increases
    C. both A and B
    D. neither A nor B

3. Rent control can be expected to result in:
    A. reducing new construction
    B. minimum maintenance of rent controlled units
    C. uneconomic utilization of property
    D. all of the above

4. A property management contract is likely to provide for compensation based on all of the following EXCEPT:
    A. a percentage of an owner's net income
    B. a percentage of an owner's gross income
    C. a fee for leasing
    D. a fee for supervision of improvements

5. A residential lease may properly:
    A. provide for the tenants to waive legal rights
    B. provide for a confession of judgment should the tenant default
    C. provide that the tenant pay the lessor's legal fees in any dispute, regardless of fault
    D. none of the above

6. Reasons why an owner would allow pets would include:

    A. to reduce the vacancy factor
    B. to increase rents
    C. to increase the average tenancy period
    D. all of the above

7. Which of the following is TRUE when comparing furnished and unfurnished residential units?

    A. Unfurnished units command higher rents
    B. People stay for longer periods of time in furnished units
    C. Maintenance costs are greater for furnished units
    D. Management fees are lower for furnished units

8. The best way to set rents would be to consider:

    A. the cost of the property
    B. the return that is desired by the property owner
    C. operational costs
    D. rents asked for comparable properties having reasonable vacancy factors

9. If the vacancy rate remains the same when rents and expenses both increase by 10 percent, the owner's net income should:

    A. remain the same
    B. increase less than 10 percent
    C. increase 10 percent
    D. increase more than 10 percent

10. Lessors of residential units have certain legal duties. They include all EXCEPT:

    A. the duty to supply heating facilities
    B. the duty to provide air conditioning facilities
    C. the duty to provide a working toilet
    D. the duty to provide for natural lighting in every room

Answers: 1. D; 2. C; 3. D; 4. A; 5. D; 6. D; 7. C; 8. D; 9. D; 10. B

Chapter 6

Commercial, Office and Industrial Property Management

KEY WORDS AND TERMS

Absorption Rate
Anchor Tenants
Class A Buildings
Class B Buildings
Class C Buildings
Class D Buildings
Clear Span
Combination Building
Commercial Property
Community Shopping Center
Demographics
Discretionary Purchasing Power
Economic Life
Excess Parking
Factory Outlet
Fire Suppression Systems
Fixturing Allowance
Foot-loose Industries
Free-standing Retailers
Garden Office Buildings
High-Rise Office Buildings
Industrial Parks
Intelligent Building
Labor Oriented Location
Loading Docks

Low-Rise Office Buildings
Market Oriented Location
Mega Mall
Mid-Rise Office Building
Mini Mall
Neighborhood Shopping Center
Overbuilding
Pedestrian Shopping Streets
Quality of Life
R & D Facilities
Regional Shopping Center
Sick Buildings
Special Use Structures
Square Footage
Stores
Supply Oriented Location
Symbiotic Relationship
Tenant Mix
Tenant Quality
Theme Buildings
Transportation Oriented Location
Trophy Building
Urban Pedestrian Mall
Utility Oriented Location

LEARNING OBJECTIVES

In this chapter you will learn how commercial, office and industrial property management differs from residential property management as well as management concerns in these areas. You will have the opportunity to review leases tailored for these properties. You will understand commercial, office and industrial property from the viewpoint of owner, manager and tenant.

Commercial Property Management

COMMERCIAL PROPERTY *involves the buying and selling of commodities or goods.* Primarily, commercial property would be involved in retail sales. A lesser amount of space would be devoted to wholesale operations, restaurants, and service providers, such as lenders who deal with the general public.

HOW MUCH COMMERCIAL SPACE?

The requirements for commercial space are not based on raw population figures alone. Other community factors include the following.

Number of Households. The number of households affects the demand for furniture and appliances as well as many other household purchases.

Discretionary Purchasing Power. After fixed expenses, such as mortgage or rent payments, car payments, insurance, basic food purchases, etc., what is left is discretionary income.

> *The greater the discretionary income, the better the business is for the sale of nonessential goods and services.*

Demographics. The age of the residents of an area affects saving and spending. For a large percentage of people in the 45 to 55 age group, a significant portion of their discretionary income is put into savings. On the other hand, the 25 to 35 age group spends a higher percentage of its discretionary income.

> *As a general rule, the need for commercial space within a community is inverse to the average age of its residents.*

Exceptions would be affluent retirement communities. Older populations require less commercial square footage while a younger population would need more commercial square footage.

Drawing Power of Area. The commercial areas in many communities have drawing power far greater than would ordinarily be expected. As an example, tourists from around the world who come to Los Angeles often want to shop on Rodeo Drive.

Many individual retailers and shopping centers draw customers from a wide geographical area.

In the 1960s, there was a chain of discount department stores in Southern California known as White Front. The chain went through an expansion stage and not only did the volume of the new stores fail to meet expectations, but a number of existing stores also suffered a significant decline in volume. It has been suggested that the failure of White Front was partially based on the fact that the management did not understand fully that the stores were drawing customers from a wide area. While new stores made it more convenient for customers, a loyal customer base was now spread over more stores.

TYPES OF PROPERTIES

Pedestrian Shopping Streets

PEDESTRIAN SHOPPING STREETS tend to be lined with buildings having no side-yard setbacks, just stores side-by-side.

> *Corner locations command the highest rent in pedestrian shopping streets because of greater window display area as well as signage.*

The corner locations are also more visible from vehicular traffic, especially if there is a traffic stop sign or traffic signal.

As a general rule, the closer a location is to the corner on a pedestrian shopping street, the higher the rent. The lowest rent would be in the center of the block. An exception would be a store next to another extremely successful store. Being close to a desired shopping location could bolster sales and allow for greater rent.

In The Sunbelt, the south and west sides of streets tend to have greater sales volume than do north and east sides of the street if other factors are equal. The reason for this is that the greatest volume of sales tend to be after 12 Noon when the south and west sides of the street are shaded from the hot sun.

The volume of foot traffic on pedestrian shopping streets would affect sales volume and rents. Often a few businesses mixed with other uses will cause pedestrians to cross a street and return on the other side of the street. Banks, savings institutions, brokerage offices, churches, etc., are of little interest to shoppers. A block with few if any retail stores is dead space for shoppers and will affect pedestrian traffic.

Chapter 6

Urban Pedestrian Mall

An **URBAN PEDESTRIAN MALL** *is a foot-traffic-only open mall.* By eliminating vehicular traffic on a street, an urban pedestrian mall can revitalize an urban shopping area. This has been successful in Santa Monica and in Santa Barbara. However, the Fulton Mall in Fresno was not a success. Problems with the Fulton Mall were attributed to a great deal of crime in the area, the opening of an enclosed mall which captured many of the upscale shops plus the fact that there was only one anchor tenant on the street.

Strip Centers

A **STRIP CENTER** *is a line of shops which attract vehicular traffic rather than foot traffic.*

Stores in many strip centers fail to support each other. Shopping at one store does not bring the shopper into neighboring stores. Customers tend to park close to the store they are interested in.

Volume would increase if strip center stores offered similar appeal to shoppers so that each store "fed" the other with customers, such as a four-store building selling women's shoes, dresses, women's sportswear and a beauty parlor. This is a **SYMBIOTIC RELATIONSHIP,** *where each store helps the other,* which means success for the merchants and for the owner of the building.

Mini-Malls (Convenience Center)

MINI-MALLS *are small centers with an anchor tenant that is a fast food store or convenience store, such as a 7-11 store.* A mini-mall would generally have less than 10,000 square feet and other shops could include a dry cleaner, donut shop, delicatessen, etc. The center would provide for quick ingress and egress.

Neighborhood Shopping Center

Neighborhood shopping centers would have a supermarket as a primary anchor tenant. **ANCHOR TENANTS** *are the primary draw for a shopping center.* Stores between the anchor tenants benefit from the foot traffic.

Additional anchor tenants for neighborhood shopping centers could be a chain drug store or variety store. Customers would frequent this type of anchor tenant at least once per week. A supermarket may have the same foot traffic at least three times per week. A neighborhood shopping center might consist of 10 to approximately 30 stores.

Community Shopping Center

A **COMMUNITY SHOPPING CENTER** *might have as the primary anchor tenant a department store or a discount store such as K-Mart or WALMART.* A major food store might be the other anchor with all types of shops between the anchor stores. There may be 30 to 75 stores in a community shopping center, including some free standing pads for fast food outlets, quick lube operations, banks, etc.

If a community shopping center (or a neighborhood shopping center) has as an anchor tenant a large home improvement center, other tenants could include carpet stores, tile stores, stores offering drapes, blinds and shutters, fireplace accessories, etc. These stores would probably be willing to pay a premium rent to be near the home improvement center.

Regional Shopping Center

A **REGIONAL SHOPPING CENTER**, *which could be in excess of one-half million square feet and house several department stores, is likely to be a mall*. The anchor tenants are usually placed at the end of wings in the mall. Shoppers must pass stores between the anchor tenants. The smaller stores would pay a premium rent for this foot traffic generated by the anchor tenants.

> *The greater the draw by anchor tenants, the higher the rent other tenants are able to pay.*

Because of the size of the center and distance shoppers have to park from stores, regional shopping centers seldom include major food stores. This eliminates shopping carts and makes store traffic flow smoothly.

When a developer or manager wants a particular high-profile anchor tenant in the shopping center, they may give a sweetheart deal of below-market rent schedule to entice the prospective tenant. In some cases the offer is free rent for one year followed by a percentage lease beginning at below-market level and only reaching market rental in five to seven years. This, of course, would be an extreme inducement.

> *When anchor tenants line up to lease space, then the clout is with management. Far better lease terms are possible from a management standpoint.*

Assume a center has been planned for three major anchors and you have obtained Nordstrom and Robinson-May by offering rental incentives. Chances are, the third location can be leased without "giving away the store." The presence of two major anchor stores could be a strong draw for another major tenant who doesn't want to be left out of a premium location.

Shopping centers have become more than just places to sell merchandise. They have become community areas that have replaced the village green.

Courts have held that shopping centers cannot exclude persons who wish to obtain signatures for petitions or to hand out religious material as long as the activity doesn't impede commercial use.

Case Example

Union of Needletrades v. Superior Court (1997)56 C.A. 4th 996

A union was involved in a labor dispute with Guess. Guess had company stores in a number of malls. The union wanted to place pickets at the Guess stores. Taubman Company refused access because the union would not follow application procedures and would not accept the picket locations specified by mall management. The union sued claiming that they were denied free speech. The Superior Court refused to issue an injunction allowing the union to picket the stores and the Court of Appeals affirmed.

The court held that the malls were reasonable as to rules, time and place for picketing. The court pointed out that free speech does not mean that the union can impede commerce.

The court also pointed out that the plaintiff's intended picketing could lead to injury and damage which would affect the mall owner's insurance.

Note: This decision is not in conflict with the landmark case of Robins v. Pruneyard Shopping Center (1979) 23 C. 3d 899. In the Pruneyard case, Robins wanted to put a card table in a corner of a courtyard to obtain petition signatures. The court held that free speech must be protected, even at privately owned shopping centers. The court pointed out that the petitioning in this case was reasonably exercised.

Mega Malls

The four Ghermezian brothers built a mall in Edmonton, Canada, a city of 600,000 people. The mall, with 5.5 million square feet, was the largest in the world. The mall includes a 360-room hotel, 836 retail stores, a church, dozens of restaurants and an amusement park, all protected from the harsh Canadian winters. Besides strolling bands, tumblers, musicians and singers there is a hockey rink used by the Edmonton Oilers for practice, a full-sized Spanish Galleon floating in its own sea, a Disney-type aquarium with four 28-passenger submarines, a 142-foot high roller coaster with a triple loop, a waterpark with a 120-foot waterfall, indoor wave machine for surfing, powered waterskiing and a lot more.

Edmonton's population could never have supported such a mall but it has been fantastically successful. Per square foot sales figures are believed to be the highest for any North American mall. With parking for more than 30,000 cars and 250,000 visitors per day, the mall has been credited with a 70 percent increase in Edmonton tourism.

On the negative side, the Edmonton mall was also credited with disastrous results as to the Edmonton central shopping areas. The Ghermezian brothers believe that if a mall is built right it will dominate the market. They are correct as to Edmonton.

Malls with amusement features tend to detain people for many hours. The Edmonton mall can mean an entire day, including live evening theatrical attractions.

The Ghermezian brothers, along with U.S. associates, have built the huge Bloomington Fashion Mall of America near the Minneapolis airport and only minutes away from an existing regional mall. The Bloomington Fashion Mall of America has captured the market and is a vacation destination for hundreds of thousands of people. The mall includes a roller coaster, four-acre water park, over 800 stores, 100 restaurants and more. Like the Edmonton Mall, the U.S. mall is an international tourist destination. The drawing power extends to Europe and Asia.

Prior to the depression in commercial real estate in the early 1990s, there were a number of mega-malls in the initial planning stages. Now that the market has strengthened, old plans are being dusted off. Mega malls are tough competition for regional malls.

Mega-malls do NOT compete with neighborhood shopping centers, mini-malls, or even factory outlet malls because of different customer appeal.

Factory Outlet Centers

FACTORY OUTLET STORES *are malls featuring stores owned by manufacturers, distributors or others selling off-price merchandise.* Successful outlet malls carry name brand merchandise.

Examples of such outlets are the huge Ontario Mills store and the Cabazon Outlet stores (over 100) located within 50 miles of each other along Interstate 10 in Southern California.

The factory outlets that have failed have been primarily small outlets having 50 stores or less. The larger the number of stores, and the quality of the stores, the greater the volume per square foot.

Most of the large factory outlet centers are owned by a handful of Real Estate Investment Trusts (REITs) which employ their own management staffs.

Large Freestanding Retailers

Some retailers feel that their large retail stores don't need to be in close proximity to other retailers. As an example, a Home Depot or WALMART might locate on the outskirts of a shopping area to utilize a large but lower-cost site. Their major criteria would be excellent ingress and egress from a major street and being in close proximity to a significant population center. The building is built to the retailer's specifications and leased to them under a long-term net lease (not a percentage lease).

Even though such retailers can stand alone, they are still draws, and shopping centers and other free-standing stores will be attracted to the outlet which would then very shortly become the center of another shopping district.

Wholesale Operations

While **WHOLESALERS** *might consist of showrooms and some retail businesses, most wholesale locations contain office space, with the majority of the space warehouse related.*

Warehouses with large office areas are ideal for wholesalers.

Wholesale operators often have offices with windows overlooking warehouse operations. The ratio of office space to total wholesale area probably would be one to six. This could vary greatly depending upon the business.

Wholesale operations like to be in close proximity to other wholesalers of similar goods. As an example, the presence of one plumbing wholesaler would make another plumbing wholesaler consider a vacancy in the area.

Wholesale operators don't need prime locations. They need ingress and egress for trucks and proximity to major streets and highways. Also needed is security and a good fire suppression system. High ceilings allow for expansion where steel storage and second floor walkways are desirable.

TENANT SELECTION

Tenant Mix

The tenant mix becomes very important whenever a property has more than one tenant.

As previously stated, you want each tenant to help the other so that they can all be successful. You want this success even if the tenants are not on percentage leases.

Successful tenants pay rent on time, meet all lease terms, abide by property rules and are unlikely to move out.

The worst case of tenant selection we know of was a small eight-store complex with a center court running off a major foot-traffic area in a resort community. Two stores were on the main street with the other stores having access off the courtyard. A religious bookstore rented one of the corner stores. The other corner store was a "head shop" selling legal drug-related paraphernalia such as books on how to grow marijuana, tee shirts and posters. A gourmet coffee shop, an African antiquities store, a bicycle repair shop, beauty salon, clock repair store and an art gallery made up the remaining stores. The eclectic grouping provided minimal if any mutual support. After a few years, the only remaining occupant was the religious store. A high turnover rate among the other shops occurred despite bargain rents.

This small center could have rented to eight women's wear stores. This would make the center a must check location for pedestrian and vehicular shopping. Instead the owner's leasing philosophy was to rent to whomever came up with the rent first.

"First Come, First Served" should NOT be used for tenant selections.

Tenant Quality

When a person just starts in business the chance of failure is far greater than for relocating an existing business. The longer a business can exist the greater its chances of staying in business. If you have two similar prospective tenants, one new to the business and the other with an established clientele, the smart economic decision would be to select the existing business that wants to relocate.

Some types of new businesses have extremely high turnover rates. As an example, less than one half the new restaurants which open will still be in business in the same location 18 months later. An exception would be franchise operations. Certain franchisors study areas to select locations and therefore have a very low failure rate. As an example, it would be unusual for a McDonald's location to close for lack of business. Some franchises have high failure rates. Some franchisors are more interested in initial fees rather than in any long-term franchisee success.

In the 1970s, candle shops were in vogue. Candle shops kept opening even though few ever made money.

As a lessor, you should evaluate the economic viability of various businesses.

A number of major banks have made studies of various businesses and can provide figures as to the success of a business.

A temporary tenant renting a vacant location in a mall for a few months before Christmas might be a good economic decision when you have several vacancies. This type of tenant should otherwise be avoided. A three-month lease could cause you to lose the opportunity to rent to what could be a long-term tenant.

> *The depth of a tenant's pockets or the pockets of a lease guarantor is important in tenant selection.*

If a commercial tenant does not have much as to financial reserves, the tenant may not be able to last long enough to reach a break-even point, even though the business idea and operation should have been successful.

We know of one case where the business owners were starting a bakery. They were evicted before they even opened because all their money was spent on equipment and fixtures and nothing was left to pay for the last supplies needed or the rent.

> *The two major reasons why businesses fail are under-capitalization and lack of knowledge about the business.*

RENT SETTING

Determining Rents

> *There is NO simple rule for how much rent a commercial location is worth.*

Certainly a successful merchant who desires more space would pay more for an adjacent store than would other tenants. Similarly, competitors of a successful business would pay more than others to locate close to their competitor.

Location based on other stores is not the sole factor in determining rents. Parking, ease of ingress and egress, signage, etc. will all effect the desirability of a location.

Generally, smaller stores, such as 2,000 square feet, can command a higher per square foot rental than larger stores, such as 100,000 square feet.

In setting commercial rents you should consider what is available from other lessors as to similar desirable property. If a property bearing a high degree of similarity as to desirability has been vacant for 10 months, you can assume that the rent being asked is too high.

If there are no similarly desirable locations that are vacant you should look at rented property. You can assume that the average rental rate for similar property that is rented is too low or there would be some kind of vacancy factor.

When renewing leases, the prosperity of your tenant has a direct bearing on any rental increase.

If a tenant has a marginal operation, you should consider the effect of a vacancy before rents are raised. You might decide that in the long run you would be better off having the opportunity to seek a stronger tenant at a higher rent. Of course, your current vacancy factor, area vacancies and economic climate should all be considered.

Don't Be Unreasonable

A commercial property manager must realize that the success of both owner and manager depends upon the success of any tenant. You don't succeed if your tenants don't succeed.

As far as the tenant is concerned, an onerous lease can be onerous on the lessor and the lessee. Failing businesses mean vacancies, additional expenses and revenue which most likely will never be recouped.

In renegotiating leases, lessors and their agents will often try to "put the screws" to commercial tenants because they realize any change in location will have a negative effect on the tenants' businesses. Lessors and agents try for a win/lose negotiation where the landlord wins and tenants lose. This reasoning has validity for some highly profitable businesses. However, it can often lead to lose/lose results because the business fails and the lessor ends up with a vacancy.

Some locations, including small shopping centers, have developed a negative reputation in an attempt to maximize rents. A high turnover in tenants, with few lasting more than a year, can lead to difficulties in renting and the need to reduce rents to what would be regarded as below-market rents. In desperation, the lessor may accept marginal tenants not normally considered to fill the vacancies.

Bargain Rents

A vacancy can often mean a negative cash flow for an owner. Some owners don't have the resources to withstand an extended vacancy or vacancies. This can result in granting a bargain rent to solve immediate cash flow problems. Bargain rents create problems:

1. The owner takes an opportunity risk by tying up a property with a below-market rent, and loses the chance to rent the location at market rent to a future prospective tenant.

2. Other tenants will soon learn of the bargain rent and demand lower rents when their leases expire. They feel that the owner is worried that they'll vacate and will agree to the lower rent. They're probably right.

PARKING

Parking is an important item for commercial, office and industrial rentals. There are a number of problems as to parking.

Employees Taking Customer Spaces. In commercial and office leases, employees should have designated parking areas, usually in less desirable areas. The most desirable spaces should be for customers or clients. The property manager should notify tenants if an employee does not comply. Towing a vehicle away might solve the problem of a flagrant violator when contacting the offender fails.

Parking in Someone Else's Spot. When spaces are designated, such as for offices and some retail operations, a person is less likely to park in another's spot if that parking area is designated with a person's name rather than just a number or "reserved" sign.

An employee's feeling of self-worth is another advantage of assigning a parking space by name rather than number.

We all like to see our names in print. This helps employee morale and in turn keeps your tenants happy. This same idea can apply to residential parking.

Tenant Monopolization of Parking. Some tenants use more parking spaces than others. As an example, a real estate office may have 20 salespersons operating out of a 1,200 square foot office. At times the parking lot can be overflowing with salespersons' vehicles which creates a problem for real estate clients and customers to other businesses utilizing the same parking lot.

One solution would be to locate offsite parking for employees even if you have to pay for that parking. If just one tenant is the cause and you can't arrive at a solution, you could lose tenants and/or bargaining strength when other tenants come up for lease renewal.

You might have to consider NOT renewing the offending tenant's lease.

Excess Parking. Some properties have more parking or garage space than is required by the tenants. Excess parking can be rented out to others and offers a worthwhile addition to property income. If parking spaces are rented, consider either assigning spaces with names or special numbered stickers to determine if any unauthorized parking is taking place.

OVERBUILDING

> *Construction of commercial as well as office projects tends to be directly related to the availability of mortgage money for the projects.*

When money is available, developers scramble for their own projects with a number of them being planned at the same time.

The construction can take several years to move through the process from land acquisition, the approval, construction stages until the doors are ready to open. What frequently happens is that a great deal of similar space might become available for leasing within the same time frame. In such a situation, the law of supply and demand takes over and prospective tenants have great bargaining power for lower rents and lease concessions. Lower rents in turn will attract more prospective tenants to the area and eventually an equilibrium will be reached with the excess space being absorbed.

> *When the vacancy factor is reduced to a controllable point, rents will start to rise.*

COMMERCIAL LEASES

Commercial leases could be flat or gross leases, net leases, modified net leases or percentage leases.

Figure 6-1 is the first page of a multi-tenant gross lease. It would be applicable for commercial or industrial property. Figure 6-2 is the first page of a single-tenant net lease that could be applicable to commercial or industrial property.

You should be familiar with the lease types and clauses from the material in Chapters 3 and 4.

Office Property Management

With the growth of service and technical industries, the need for office space has increased dramatically over the past two decades.

Rents vary significantly based on location and the desirability of the space. Rents are usually expressed as a rent per square foot.

Office space is often rented with full janitorial services. Otherwise there could be a logistical nightmare with maintenance firms numbering in the hundreds working in one building. This could also present a security problem.

Figure 6-1

STANDARD INDUSTRIAL/COMMERCIAL MULTI-TENANT LEASE—GROSS
AMERICAN INDUSTRIAL REAL ESTATE ASSOCIATION

1. **1.**   **Basic Provisions ("Basic Provisions").**

1.1   Parties: This Lease ("Lease"), dated for reference purposes only, _____, 19 _____ , is made by and between_____ ("Lessor") and _____ ("Lessee"), (collectively the "Parties," or individually a "Party").

1.2(a) **Premises:** That certain portion of the Building, including all improvements therein or to be provided by Lessor under the terms of this Lease, commonly known by the street address of _____, located in the City of _____, County of _____, State of _____, with zip code _____, as outlined on Exhibit ___ attached hereto ("**Premises**"). The "**Building**" is that certain building containing the Premises and generally described as (describe briefly the nature of the Building):____ _____ _____

In addition to Lessee's rights to use and occupy the Premises as hereinafter specified, Lessee shall have non-exclusive rights to the Common Areas (as defined in Paragraph 2.7 below) as hereinafter specified, but shall not have any rights to the roof, exterior walls or utility raceways of the Building or to any other buildings in the Industrial Center. The Premises, the Building, the Common Areas, the land upon which they are located, along with all other buildings and improvements thereon, are herein collectively referred to as the "**Industrial Center.**" (Also see Paragraph 2.)

1.2(b) **Parking:** _____ unreserved vehicle parking spaces ("**Unreserved Parking Spaces**"); and _____ reserved vehicle parking spaces ("**Reserved Parking Spaces**"). (Also see Paragraph 2.6.)

1.3   **Term:** _____ years and _____ months ("**Original Term**") commencing _____ ("**Commencement Date**") and ending _____ ("**Expiration Date**"). (Also see Paragraph 3.)

1.4   **Early Possession:** _____("**Early Possession Date**"). (Also see Paragraphs 3.2 and 3.3.)

1.5   **Base Rent:** $_____ per month ("**Base Rent**"), payable on the_____ day of each month commencing _____. (Also see Paragraph 4.)

[ ] If this box is checked, this Lease provides for the Base Rent to be adjusted per Addendum _____, attached hereto.

1.6(a) **Base Rent Paid Upon Execution:** $_____ as Base Rent for the period _____.

1.6(b) **Lessee's Share of Common Area Operating Expenses:** _____ percent (%) ("**Lessee's Share**") as determined by [ ] prorata square footage of the Premises as compared to the total square footage of the Building or [ ] other criteria as described in Addendum ____.

1.7   **Security Deposit:** $_____ ("**Security Deposit**"). (Also see Paragraph 5.)

1.8   **Permitted Use:** _____ _____ ("**Permitted Use**") (Also see Paragraph 6.)

1.9   **Insuring Party.** Lessor is the "**Insuring Party.**" (Also see Paragraph 8.)

1.10(a) **Real Estate Brokers.** The following real estate broker(s) (collectively, the "**Brokers**") and brokerage relationships exist in this transaction and are consented to by the Parties (check applicable boxes):

[ ] _____ represents Lessor exclusively ("**Lessor's Broker**");

[ ] _____ represents Lessee exclusively ("**Lessee's Broker**"); or

[ ] _____ represents both Lessor and Lessee ("**Dual Agency**"). (Also see Paragraph 15.)

1.10(b) **Payment to Brokers.** Upon the execution of this Lease by both Parties, Lessor shall pay to said Broker(s) jointly, or in such separate shares as they may mutually designate in writing, a fee as set forth in a separate written agreement between Lessor and said Broker(s) (or in the event there is no separate written agreement between Lessor and said Broker(s), the sum of $_____) for brokerage services rendered by said Broker(s) in connection with this transaction.

1.11   **Guarantor.** The obligations of the Lessee under this Lease are to be guaranteed by_____ _____ ("**Guarantor**"). (Also see Paragraph 37.)

1.12   **Addenda and Exhibits.** Attached hereto is an Addendum or Addenda consisting of Paragraphs _____ through _____, and Exhibits _____ through _____, all of which constitute a part of this Lease.

2. Premises, Parking and Common Areas.

2.1   **Letting.** Lessor hereby leases to Lessee, and Lessee hereby leases from Lessor, the Premises, for the term, at the rental, and upon all of the terms, covenants and conditions set forth in this Lease. Unless otherwise provided herein, any statement of square footage set forth in this Lease, or that may have been used in calculating rental and/or Common Area Operating Expenses, is an approximation which Lessor and Lessee agree is reasonable and the rental and Lessee's Share (as defined in Paragraph 1.6(b)) based thereon is not subject to revision whether or not the actual square footage is more or less.

2.2   **Condition.** Lessor shall deliver the Premises to Lessee clean and free of debris on the Commencement Date and warrants to Lessee that the existing plumbing, electrical systems, fire sprinkler system, lighting, air conditioning and heating systems and loading doors, if any, in the Premises, other than those constructed by Lessee, shall be in good operating condition on the Commencement Date. If a non-compliance with said warranty exists as of the Commencement Date, Lessor shall, except as otherwise provided in this Lease, promptly after receipt of written notice from Lessee setting forth with specificity the nature and extent of such non-compliance, rectify same at Lessor's expense. If Lessee does not give Lessor written notice of a non-compliance with this warranty within thirty (30) days after the Commencement Date, correction of that non-compliance shall be the obligation of Lessee at Lessee's sole cost and expense.

2.3   **Compliance with Covenants, Restrictions and Building Code.** Lessor warrants that any improvements (other than those constructed by Lessee or at Lessee's direction) on or in the Premises which have been constructed or installed by Lessor or with Lessor's consent or at Lessor's direction shall comply with all applicable covenants or restrictions of record and applicable building codes, regulations and ordinances in effect on the Commencement Date. Lessor further warrants to Lessee that Lessor has no knowledge of any claim having been made by any governmental agency that a violation or violations of applicable building codes, regulations, or ordinances exist with regard to the Premises as of the Commencement Date. Said warranties shall not apply to any Alterations or Utility Installations (defined in Paragraph 7.3(a)) made or to be made by Lessee. If the Premises do not comply with said warranties, Lessor shall, except as otherwise provided in this Lease, promptly after receipt of written notice from Lessee given within six (6) months following the Commencement Date and setting forth with specificity the nature and extent of such non-compliance, take such action, at Lessor's expense, as may be reasonable or appropriate to rectify the non-compliance. Lessor makes no warranty that the Permitted Use in Paragraph 1.8 is permitted for the Premises under Applicable Laws (as defined in Paragraph 2.4).

2.4   **Acceptance of Premises.** Lessee hereby acknowledges: (a) that it has been advised by the Broker(s) to satisfy itself with respect to the condition of the Premises (including but not limited to the electrical and fire sprinkler systems, security, environmental aspects, seismic and earthquake requirements, and compliance with the Americans with Disabilities Act and applicable zoning, municipal, county, state and federal laws, ordinances and regulations and any covenants or restrictions of record (collectively, "**Applicable Laws**") and the present and future suitability of the Premises for Lessee's intended use; (b) that Lessee has made such investigation as it deems necessary with reference to such matters, is satisfied with reference thereto, and assumes all responsibility therefore as the same relate to Lessee's occupancy of the Premises and/or the terms of this Lease; and (c) that neither Lessor, nor any of Lessor's agents, has made any oral or written representations or warranties with respect to said matters other than as set forth in this Lease.

2.5   **Lessee as Prior Owner/Occupant.** The warranties made by Lessor in this Paragraph 2 shall be of no force or effect if immediately prior to the date set forth in Paragraph 1.1 Lessee was the owner or occupant of the Premises. In such event, Lessee shall, at Lessee's sole cost and expense, correct any non-compliance of the Premises with said warranties.

Initials: _____

MULTI-TENANT – GROSS   _____

Figure 6-2

AIR AMERICAN INDUSTRIAL REAL ESTATE ASSOCIATION

STANDARD INDUSTRIAL/COMMERCIAL SINGLE-TENANT LEASE – NET
(DO NOT USE THIS FORM FOR MULTI-TENANT BUILDINGS)

1.   **Basic Provisions ("Basic Provisions")**
      1.1   **Parties:** This Lease ("Lease"), dated for reference purposes only _____, _____, is made by and between _____
_____ **("Lessor")**
and _____
_____ **("Lessee")**,
(collectively the **"Parties,"** or individually a **"Party"**).
      1.2   **Premises:** That certain real property, including all improvements therein or to be provided by Lessor under the terms of this Lease, and commonly known as_____
located in the County of _____, State of _____,
and generally described as (describe briefly the nature of the property and, if applicable, the **"Project"**, if the property is located within a Project) _____
_____
_____
_____ **("Premises")**. (See also Paragraph 2)
      1.3   **Term:** _____ years and _____ months **("Original Term")** commencing _____
("Commencement Date") and ending _____ **("Expiration Date")**. (See also Paragraph 3)
      1.4   **Early Possession:** _____ **("Early Possession Date")**.
(See also Paragraphs 3.2 and 3.3)
      1.5   **Base Rent:** $_____ per month **("Base Rent")**, payable on the _____ day of each month commencing_____. (See also Paragraph 4)
☐ If this box is checked, there are provisions in this Lease for the Base Rent to be adjusted.
      1.6   **Base Rent Paid Upon Execution:** $_____
as Base Rent for the period _____.
      1.7   **Security Deposit:** $_____ **("Security Deposit")**. (See also Paragraph 5)
      1.8   **Agreed Use:** _____ (See also Paragraph 6)
      1.9   **Insuring Party.** Lessor is the **"Insuring Party"** unless otherwise stated herein. (See also Paragraph 8)
      1.10   **Real Estate Brokers:** (See also Paragraph 15)
            (a) **Representation:** The following real estate brokers (collectively, the **"Brokers"**) and brokerage relationships exist in this transaction (check applicable boxes):
☐ _____ represents Lessor exclusively **("Lessor's Broker")**;
☐ _____ represents Lessee exclusively **("Lessee's Broker")**; or
☐ _____ represents both Lessor and Lessee **("Dual Agency")**.
            (b) **Payment to Brokers:** Upon execution and delivery of this Lease by both Parties, Lessor shall pay to the Broker the fee agreed to in their separate written agreement (or if there is no such agreement, the sum of _____ % of the total Base Rent for the brokerage services rendered by said Broker).
      1.11   **Guarantor.** The obligations of the Lessee under this Lease are to be guaranteed by _____
_____ **("Guarantor")**. (See also Paragraph 37)
      1.12   **Addenda and Exhibits.** Attached hereto is an Addendum or Addenda consisting of Paragraphs _____ through _____ and Exhibits _____, all of which constitute a part of this Lease.

2.   **Premises.**
      2.1   **Letting.** Lessor hereby leases to Lessee, and Lessee hereby leases from Lessor, the Premises, for the term, at the rental, and upon all of the terms, covenants and conditions set forth in this Lease. Unless otherwise provided herein, any statement of size set forth in this Lease, or that may have been used in calculating rental, is an approximation which the Parties agree is reasonable and the rental based thereon is not subject to revision whether or not the actual size is more or less.
      2.2   **Condition.** Lessor shall deliver the Premises to Lessee broom clean and free of debris on the Commencement Date or the Early Possession Date, whichever first occurs **("Start Date")**, and, so long as the required service contracts described in Paragraph 7.1(b) below are obtained by Lessee within thirty (30) days following the Start Date, warrants that the existing electrical, plumbing, fire sprinkler, lighting, heating, ventilating and air conditioning systems **("HVAC")**, loading doors, if any, and all other such elements in the Premises, other than those constructed by Lessee, shall be in good operating condition on said date and that the structural elements of the roof, bearing walls and foundation of any buildings on the Premises (the **"Building"**) shall be free of material defects. If a non-compliance with said warranty exists as of the Start Date, Lessor shall, as Lessor's sole obligation with respect to such matter, except as otherwise provided in this Lease, promptly after receipt of written notice from Lessee setting forth with specificity the nature and extent of such non-compliance, rectify same at Lessor's expense. If, after the Start Date, Lessee does not give Lessor written notice of any non-compliance with this warranty within: (i) one year as to the surface of the roof and the structural portions of the roof, foundations and bearing walls, (ii) six (6) months as to the HVAC systems, (iii) thirty (30) days as to the remaining systems and other elements of the Building, correction of such non-compliance shall be the obligation of Lessee at Lessee's sole cost and expense.
      2.3   **Compliance.** Lessor warrants that the improvements on the Premises comply with all applicable laws, covenants or restrictions of record, building codes, regulations and ordinances **("Applicable Requirements")** in effect on the Start Date. Said warranty does not apply to the use to which Lessee will put the Premises or to any Alterations or Utility Installations (as defined in Paragraph 7.3(a)) made or to be made by Lessee. NOTE: Lessee is responsible for determining whether or not the zoning is appropriate for Lessee's intended use, and acknowledges that past uses of the Premises may no longer be allowed. If the Premises do not comply with said warranty, Lessor shall, except as otherwise provided, promptly after receipt of written notice from Lessee setting forth with specificity the nature and extent of such non-compliance, rectify the same at Lessor's expense. If Lessee does not give Lessor written notice of a non-compliance with this warranty within six (6) months following the Start Date, correction of that non-compliance shall be the obligation of Lessee at Lessee's sole cost and expense. If the Applicable Requirements are hereafter changed (as opposed to being in existence at the Start Date, which is addressed in Paragraph 6.2(e) below) so as to require during the term of this Lease the construction of an addition to or an alteration of the Building, the remediation of any Hazardous Substance, or the reinforcement or other physical modification of the Building **("Capital Expenditure")**, Lessor and Lessee shall allocate the cost of such work as follows:

PAGE 1   Initials _____ _____

FORM 204N-R-2/97

CATEGORIES OF OFFICE BUILDINGS

Office buildings are categorized by quality as well as by height.

Class A Office Buildings

CLASS A BUILDINGS *refers to newer, more desirable buildings.* Many glass towers fall into this Class A category. They tend to be architecturally distinctive. If you were to be asked to name the three most prestigious or desirable office buildings in your city, chances are that all three would fall into the Class A category.

> *Because of their desirability, Class A buildings command high rents for office space.*

Many image-conscious tenants would not consider locating in anything other than a Class A building.

Class B Office Buildings

CLASS B OFFICE BUILDINGS *are older, well maintained structures that have been out done by newer, more extravagant buildings.* Class B office buildings still provide desirable space. However, they cannot command the same rents as a Class A office space.

Class C Office Buildings

CLASS C OFFICE BUILDINGS *are usually older office buildings which are less desirable.* Class C office buildings are adequate but they tend to compete on price. When the General Services Administration asks for bids on government office space, Class C buildings usually bring out the low bidders.

> *Normally NOT in a prime location, Class C buildings do meet office use requirements.*

Class D Office Buildings

If you have watched old detective movies on television, the location of their office always seems to be in a **CLASS D BUILDING**. *These are the least desirable, seedy type buildings.*

Because Class D buildings offer the lowest rent, maintenance is often minimal. Lessors of nonresidential property have no statutory duties to maintain the property. The responsibilities for and level of maintenance would be specified in the lease.

Tenants in Class D buildings are there because they can't pay for Class A space and don't expect Class A maintenance. Class D buildings will probably be razed when the vacancy factor rises and income is not sufficient to maintain operational expenses.

Garden Office Buildings

A *GARDEN BUILDING* is a one-story building usually located in a suburban area.

Low-Rise Office Buildings

A *LOW-RISE BUILDING* would usually be from two to three stories high. It can have an elevator or be a walk-up. Some low-rise offices are located on the top floor of an older commercial building.

Mid-Rise Office Buildings

While the definition varies, we classify a *MID-RISE BUILDING* as from four to eight stories high. These buildings are usually located in small communities or at the periphery of high-rise structures.

High-Rise Office Buildings

While we classify a *HIGH-RISE STRUCTURE* as more than nine stories, there isn't any real standard as to height.

REPOSITIONING OFFICE BUILDINGS

What were once lower rent, less desirable structures have become highly desirable office locations because of features of the buildings or because of other tenants.

The Charm of History

In the 1950s and 1960s, some older buildings with open laced-iron elevator housings, rotundas and an abundance of marble were made modern by coverings of formica material. Frescos were painted over and these ancient buildings were turned into nondescript structures.

> *We have changed our attitudes from "New is better" to "Old is more desirable."*

Sound, older buildings which have retained their architectural distinction or have been restored to former elegance are now highly desirable structures. They are sought by firms that wish to convey an image of conservatism and solid trust. Law firms, accountants, investment consultants, insurance agencies and stockbrokers all have flocked to these structures. These tenants have driven up rents to match or exceed those of a new, Class A office structures.

Quite often tenants refurbish their offices with antique furniture, light fixtures and solid wood paneling to convey what they consider to be a desirable and prestigious image.

An old office structure in Milwaukee, Wisconsin, called the Mackie Building, once housed the Grain Exchange. The floor space was later used as a private athletic club before being closed off to gather dust for several decades. Turning back the clock over 100 years, the building was restored by the owners. This former exchange is now a focal point for society charity affairs and civic functions. It went from one swing ahead of a wrecking ball to a highly desirable location. The owners heeded the advice of management to the benefit of their profits.

Theme Buildings

> *Class C and D office buildings can command Class B rent if the demand for the particular space is there.*

Tenants will pay more to be in particular buildings because of other tenants. Therefore, a theme building can take itself out of competition with similar office space.

An example of such a building would be one which housed several wholesale jewelers yet had a great deal of vacant space. The management changed the name of the building to The Jewelry Exchange and actively sought tenants who were in various aspects of the jewelry business, such as jewelry settings, jewelry repair, antique jewelry, etc. The owners had an excellent security system installed and contracted for a guard service. They began renting space by offering free rent and very attractive lease terms. As the vacancy rate went down they were able to significantly increase rents and raise rents on lease renewals.

Tenants are happy because they are able to "feed off" each other due to their related businesses. In addition, buyers come to the building because of the concentration of wholesale jewelers. This is a win/win situation for both landlord and tenants.

Other theme buildings can be design centers as well as wholesale marts for shoes, women's wear, furnishings, etc.

TROPHY BUILDINGS

TROPHY BUILDINGS *are image structures*. They were built with pride of ownership in mind. Trump towers and the Pan Am Building are examples of trophy buildings.

Although usually not economically sound when built, as the return seldom justifies the expenses of construction, inflation has provided attractive returns to these structures over a period of time.

Trophy buildings incur high costs per square foot of rentable space because of central atriums as well as elaborate public and plaza areas. They are built to impress and provide a platform for company names.

Trophy buildings tend to bring a premium price when sold. During the 1970s and 1980s, Japanese investors were principal buyers of California trophy properties. They had bid up the price among themselves and purchased buildings based on the low cost the Japanese investors had to pay for borrowing in Japan. The investors often used Japanese stocks and Japanese real estate as collateral on their loans.

The collapse of the Japanese stock market coupled with a collapse in Japanese real estate prices led to a situation where Japanese owners suddenly had little if any equity in their U.S. buildings. To make matters worse, a U.S. recession and our savings and loan debacle led to a glut of empty office space.

Japanese lenders ended up owning these buildings and a need for cash led to the sale in a buyer's market. Many U.S. REITs bought up premier properties for prices in the 50 percent of reproduction cost range.

Property managers of trophy buildings have to play the hand they are dealt.

They have to provide a high level of maintenance expected by the owners, attract and keep quality tenants at relatively high rents. If the owners purchased the building at a bargain price from a lender, then the management could result in a respectable or even outstanding return for the owners.

The nation is once again experiencing a strengthening of the marketplace. The vacancy factor is materially decreasing. New office buildings are being planned, including several in the "trophy" category, although very few have actually broken ground.

THE INTELLIGENT BUILDING

Over the past few years we have been hearing a lot about *INTELLIGENT BUILDINGS that offer shared electronics for the tenants*. Some of these services, such as video conferencing capabilities, are attractive features that could influence tenants. However, some of the electronic features offered have become unnecessary because of lower cost technology available. Use of e-mail and low cost, high-powered computers has obviated the need for some of the shared facilities offered. As technology advances, intelligent buildings will still have a strong selling point in marketing space.

COMBINATION BUILDINGS

In central cities, office buildings often have commercial tenants on the first floor. Commercial tenants can pay much more per square foot than office tenants can pay for desirable space.

> *In high-rise office structures, the lower floors are the least desirable because they are noisier and lack views.*

Also, any lower floor windows which can be opened allow exposure to more polluted air than do the upper floors. Rents tend to increase with height.

Besides stores on the first level, **COMBINATION BUILDINGS** *might have restaurants and bars on the second level or at basement level, accessible by escalators and stairs.*

Some well known office towers have apartments. San Francisco has a number of office towers where several floors house executive type apartments. Trump Towers in New York and the infamous Watergate complex in Washington, D.C. fall into this category of combination buildings.

R & D FACILITIES MANAGEMENT

A **RESEARCH AND DEVELOPMENT (R&D) FACILITY** *would have offices for engineers, draftsmen, computers as well as a general administration function.* In addition there might be laboratories and/or a fabrication area for production of models and prototypes. There might also be test facilities on site. The makeup of an R & D facility would vary based upon the area of research and development involved.

R & D facilities are frequently in industrial-type parks or free standing buildings. They are often prestigious buildings with extensive grounds. On a per-square foot basis, not as many people work in an R & D facility as would work in a general office environment.

> *R & D differs from industrial and most office management in that R & D facilities frequently require an extremely high level of cleaning.*

SICK BUILDINGS

Tenants have complained of illnesses working in some office buildings. Quite often, in order to save energy, these buildings have sealed windows and air circulates through a ventilation system. Legionnaires disease is a worst case scenario. It is believed to be caused by bacteria in the cooling towers and/or ventilation system.

Far more common are chemical reactions. Many people are sensitive to chemicals used in building products and furniture. Fumes are emitted from synthetic carpets, woodchip partitions, and even paints. Some people have become seriously ill from working in a "sick building."

At the first indication of a problem, you should contact an HVAC (Heating, Ventilating and Air Conditioning) engineer who has had experience with sick buildings.

Remedies might include:

1. Cleaning of all duct work and water towers.
2. Modification of the ventilation system to provide fresh air rather than recirculation.
3. Windows changed so that they can be opened.
4. Removal and replacement of carpets, fabrics or chipboard products in the building that are believed to cause health problems. (Chemicals are used as binders in chipboard products.)

If a property develops a reputation of a sick building, you will have rental difficulties as well as possibly an effect on tenant retention. Competitors will be sure to let prospective tenants know of the problems with your building.

DEMOLITION OF SERVICEABLE OFFICE BUILDINGS

A number of profitable office structures in a good state of repair have been demolished. The reason for tearing down a sound structure is pure economics. Rising values have resulted in some buildings no longer bringing in an acceptable rate of return on the value of the property.

As an example, assume an office building was built on a site for a total cost of $3,000,000. Let us assume that the building could produce a net income of $300,000 for the owners. This 10 percent rate of return would make this building economically sound. However, assume greater demand caused the site value to increase to $30,000,000. If the owners wanted a seven percent return then the owner should expect a return of $2,100,000 just on land value plus a return on the value of the structure. But if all they were receiving was $300,000 it would mean the building exceeded its economic life. Even if almost new, such a building would be demolished to build a structure capable of providing the required return based on land value and building costs. Low-rise structures replaced by high-rise office buildings are perfect examples of what happens when land becomes too valuable for the structure. Property managers often recommend that owners replace their buildings.

VACANCY FACTOR

By Category

> *The office vacancy factor for an area is NOT uniform as to category of office buildings.*

As an example, an area might have a 20 percent vacancy factor in a depressed market. However, the vacancy factor for Class A office building could be 26 percent while the vacancy factor could be 12 percent for a Class C building.

The highest vacancy factors seem to be in Class A buildings during business recessionary periods. Office tenants will move upward in quality as they perceive their prosperity in periods of great economic growth.

NEW CONSTRUCTION

An ongoing problem is new competition for existing vacant space as new space becomes available in the marketplace. The absorption rate for new space is tied to the local economy. New space will mean an increased vacancy factor during a stagnant economic period unless marginal Class D office space is taken off the rental market.

> *As property managers, we try to anticipate the future demand for space.*

This is difficult to do. Not only will changes in the national and local economy affect the market but we are also affected by the plans of others. The marketplace is affected by the development of new space. Our perception of the marketplace will affect our strategy in negotiating leases as to the length of leases as well as lease terms.

We can be wrong as to the demand for space. Just a few years ago, Houston, Texas was loaded with "see-through" office towers (there weren't any tenants or partitions in the new glass towers). Experts predicted that it would take more than 20 years to absorb all this vacant space. The experts were wrong. An economic turn-around resulted in a demand for office space and the vacancies were filled in just a few years. No good economic models exist to anticipate the absorption rate of vacant space. We would like to incorporate every known fact into our planning, but it is still as much an art as it is a science.

COMPUTING SQUARE FOOTAGE

Office rents are quoted per square foot. For renting less than a full floor of office space, the price quoted would be for space actually rented. For an entire floor, the square footage rate is quoted which includes halls, etc. Rents for square footage may be expressed as a monthly or annual figure.

A number of methods are used in measuring square footage. When a prospective tenant provides a quote from another property, you want to make certain that the same method of measuring is being used. It's like one person using a ruler showing 11 inches to the foot while another person has a ruler with 13 inches to the foot.

The authors prefer to use what we regard as a realistic method of measuring. We use the **USABLE SQUARE FOOTAGE METHOD** *developed by the Building Owners and Managers Association*. We measure the square footage by diagramming the perimeter of the space. In arriving at the perimeter we measure:

1. The interior of the structure's exterior walls.
2. The exterior of interior corridor walls.
3. The center of partitions used in common with other tenants.

From the total square footage derived by simple geometry of length times width, we deduct areas for venting, elevators and stairwells located within our perimeter measurements.

> *To measure the square footage of entire floors, you would use the interior of all exterior walls and exclude ducts, stairwells and elevators.*

Because you are figuring in what will be interior hallways, you will have more rentable square footage than for a multi-tenant floor. However, the rent per square foot would be less per square foot when the tenant is to occupy an entire floor rather than just one office suite.

FIXTURING ALLOWANCE

Lessors often provide a *FIXTURING ALLOWANCE for the tenant. This allowance would be expressed in dollars.* Any special tenant requirements which exceed these authorized dollars would be the tenant's responsibility.

The property manager would probably want to specify the contractors to be used to prepare the space. A time period for work would be set and the lease would not begin until work has been completed. By limiting the work to contractors who will meet deadlines, the property manager avoids costly delays which is common with some contractors. As the party authorizing the work, the property manager has control over the work. If prospective tenants want changes, they should be made by change order and the cost agreed to in writing by the prospective tenants.

Some tenants want large, open spaces to hold cubbyhole work stations while other tenants prefer more traditional separate offices. Interior offices go to employees of lesser rank. Window offices go to managerial employees. High ranking executives would warrant corner offices. Although some office partitions may rise to the ceiling they are not load-bearing and can easily be removed.

Some fixturing expenses may go to noise reduction. Acoustical tile, partitions faced with sound absorbing materials, carpeting and sound baffles can all be used to reduce office noise in large areas.

KEEPING TENANTS HAPPY

Services which a tenant requires within a building can be a strong positive feature for office towers. Examples are restaurants, health clubs, quick-printing service, etc.

The health clubs are often used as a rental perk by offering a tenant several memberships as a part of the rental. While an executive would never consider excepting money, memberships for several executives might be acceptable. The health club benefits by the memberships while helping the landlord rent space.

One Los Angeles office building offers every employee a perk. The building owners have arranged with a health club in the area to provide half-price memberships all to the employees of their tenants. The club was happy to increase gross revenues and the employees who accepted the memberships feel that they received a bargain.

Similarly, offering some free parking space with the lease is a perk. Employers who make the lease decisions tend to get free parking while their employees pay to park.

A few large office complexes operate elegant executive restaurants at a loss. They provide gourmet quality cuisine at reasonable prices for designated executives of tenants and their guests. The rent is actually paying for the perk. An executive of a firm receiving such a perk would not want to relocate.

Some buildings use their roofs as helicopter pads. Others have turned the roof areas into gardens where workers who brown-bag their lunch can relax.

It helps to visit your tenants and talk to employees. You can plan your approach as to what advantages your property offers and possible further incentives to keep your tenants happy.

OFFICE LEASES

Although net leases can be used for office property, tenants generally prefer gross leases which detail their exact rental costs. Most office leases are gross leases.

In multi-tenant buildings, office leases should include a floor plan and specify space leased so that there are no disputes as to what space the tenant shall be entitled.

> *As an attachment to the lease, the lease should also include a copy of the Rules and Regulations for Tenants.*

If the lease involves improvements to the property, an attachment would indicate the lessor's responsibility for the improvements and that the tenant will pay for costs exceeding the lessor's allowance.

Figure 6-3, is the first two pages of a Gross Office Lease for a full-service office space. Most of the provisions of the lease were covered in Chapter 4. The lease form included here was developed by The American Industrial Real Estate Association.

Industrial Property Management

Industrial property includes manufacturing, fabrication and warehousing facilities.

Some industrial property is designed for specialized purposes while other space is modified for tenant needs similarly to office space modification.

LOCATIONAL NEEDS

Locational needs for industrial property are different than commercial property. Most commercial property users want high traffic locations while industrial property locations may be oriented as follows.

Supply Oriented. Locations close to the source of raw materials or close to component manufacturers would be supply oriented firms.

Market Oriented. A supplier located close to a prime user of the product would be market oriented. A machine shop which produces prototypes may want to locate close to a major customer in order to consult at various stages of preparation.

Transportation Oriented. A company fabricating large steel drums may want to locate close to a railroad line if they use rail transport, or be close to a major highway if they ship by truck. A fabricator of small costly items would probably want to locate close to an airport.

Labor Oriented. A company that wants to manufacture computer-related equipment and hire engineers and skilled fabricators would seek a silicon valley location. Where unskilled labor is needed, the supply and cost of such labor is an important location factor.

Figure 6-3

STANDARD OFFICE LEASE—GROSS
AMERICAN INDUSTRIAL REAL ESTATE ASSOCIATION

1. Basic Lease Provisions ("Basic Lease Provisions")

1.1 **Parties:** This Lease, dated, for reference purposes only, _____ 19_____
is made by and between _____
(herein called "Lessor") and _____
doing business under the name of _____ (herein called "Lessee").

1.2 **Premises:** Suite Number(s) _____ _____ floors, consisting of approximately _____ feet, more or less, as defined in paragraph 2 and as shown on Exhibit "A" hereto (the "Premises").

1.3 **Building:** Commonly described as being located at _____
in the City of _____
County of _____
State of _____, as more particularly described in Exhibit _____ hereto, and as defined in paragraph 2.

1.4 **Use:** _____

1.5 **Term:** _____, subject to paragraph 6.
_____ commencing _____ ("Commencement Date")
and ending _____ as defined in paragraph 3.

1.6 **Base Rent:** _____ per month, payable on the _____ day of each month,
per paragraph 4.1 _____

1.7 **Base Rent Increase:** On _____ the monthly Base Rent payable under
paragraph 1.6 above shall be adjusted as provided in paragraph 4.3 below.

1.8 **Rent Paid Upon Execution:** _____
for _____

1.9 **Security Deposit:** _____

1.10 **Lessee's Share of Operating Expense Increase:** _____% as defined in paragraph 4.2.

2. Premises, Parking and Common Areas.

2.1 **Premises:** The Premises are a portion of a building, herein sometimes referred to as the "Building" identified in paragraph 1.3 of the Basic Lease Provisions. "Building" shall include adjacent parking structures used in connection therewith. The Premises, the Building, the Common Areas, the land upon which the same are located, along with all other buildings and improvements thereon or thereunder, are herein collectively referred to as the "Office Building Project." Lessor hereby leases to Lessee and Lessee leases from Lessor for the term, at the rental, and upon all of the conditions set forth herein, the real property referred to in the Basic Lease Provisions, paragraph 1.2, as the "Premises," including rights to the Common Areas as hereinafter specified.

2.2 **Vehicle Parking:** So long as Lessee is not in default, and subject to the rules and regulations attached hereto, and as established by Lessor from time to time, Lessee shall be entitled to rent and use _____ parking spaces in the Office Building Project at the monthly rate applicable from time to time for monthly parking as set by Lessor and/or its licensee.

2.2.1 If Lessee commits, permits or allows any of the prohibited activities described in the Lease or the rules then in effect, then Lessor shall have the right, without notice, in addition to such other rights and remedies that it may have, to remove or tow away the vehicle involved and charge the cost to Lessee, which cost shall be immediately payable upon demand by Lessor.

2.2.2 The monthly parking rate per parking space will be $_____ per month at the commencement of the term of this Lease, and is subject to change upon five (5) days prior written notice to Lessee. Monthly parking fees shall be payable one month in advance prior to the first day of each calendar month.

2.3 **Common Areas—Definition.** The term "Common Areas" is defined as all areas and facilities outside the Premises and within the exterior boundary line of the Office Building Project that are provided and designated by the Lessor from time to time for the general non-exclusive use of Lessor, Lessee and of other lessees of the Office Building Project and their respective employees, suppliers, shippers, customers and invitees, including but not limited to common entrances, lobbies, corridors, stairways and stairwells, public restrooms, elevators, escalators, parking areas to the extent not otherwise prohibited by this Lease, loading and unloading areas, trash areas, roadways, sidewalks, walkways, parkways, ramps, driveways, landscaped areas and decorative walls.

2.4 **Common Areas—Rules and Regulations.** Lessee agrees to abide by and conform to the rules and regulations attached hereto as Exhibit B with respect to the Office Building Project and Common Areas, and to cause its employees, suppliers, shippers, customers, and invitees to so abide and conform. Lessor or such other person(s) as Lessor may appoint shall have the exclusive control and management of the Common Areas and shall have the right, from time to time, to modify, amend and enforce said rules and regulations. Lessor shall not be responsible to Lessee for the non-compliance with said rules and regulations by other lessees, their agents, employees and invitees of the Office Building Project.

2.5 **Common Areas—Changes.** Lessor shall have the right, in Lessor's sole discretion, from time to time:

(a) To make changes to the Building interior and exterior and Common Areas, including, without limitation, changes in the location, size, shape, number, and appearance thereof, including but not limited to the lobbies, windows, stairways, air shafts, elevators, escalators, restrooms, driveways, entrances, parking spaces, parking areas, loading and unloading areas, ingress, egress, direction of traffic, decorative walls, landscaped areas and walkways; provided, however, Lessor shall at all times provide the parking facilities required by applicable law;

(b) To close temporarily any of the Common Areas for maintenance purposes so long as reasonable access to the Premises remains available;

(c) To designate other land and improvements outside the boundaries of the Office Building Project to be a part of the Common Areas, provided that such other land and improvements have a reasonable and functional relationship to the Office Building Project;

(d) To add additional buildings and improvements to the Common Areas;

(e) To use the Common Areas while engaged in making additional improvements, repairs or alterations to the Office Building Project, or any portion thereof;

(f) To do and perform such other acts and make such other changes in, to or with respect to the Common Areas and Office Building Project as Lessor may, in the exercise of sound business judgment deem to be appropriate.

3. Term.

3.1 **Term.** The term and Commencement Date of this Lease shall be as specified in paragraph 1.5 of the Basic Lease Provisions.

3.2 **Delay in Possession.** Notwithstanding said Commencement Date, if for any reason Lessor cannot deliver possession of the Premises to Lessee on said date and subject to paragraph 3.2.2, Lessor shall not be subject to any liability therefor, nor shall such failure affect the validity of this Lease or the obligations of Lessee hereunder or extend the term hereof; but, in such case, Lessee shall not be obligated to pay rent or perform any other obligation of Lessee under the terms of this Lease, except as may be otherwise provided in this Lease, until possession of the Premises is tendered to Lessee, as hereinafter defined; provided, however, that if Lessor shall not have delivered possession of the Premises within sixty (60) days following said Commencement Date, as the same may be extended under the terms of a Work Letter executed by Lessor and Lessee, Lessee may, at Lessee's

Initials: _____

FULL SERVICE—GROSS

_____

PAGE 1 of 10 PAGES

198

option, by notice in writing to Lessor within ten (10) days thereafter, cancel this Lease, in which event the parties shall be discharged from all obligations hereunder; provided, however, that, as to Lessee's obligations, Lessee first reimburses Lessor for all costs incurred for Non-Standard Improvements and, as to Lessor's obligations, Lessor shall return any money previously deposited by Lessee (less any offsets due Lessor for Non-Standard Improvements); and provided further, that if such written notice by Lessee is not received by Lessor within said ten (10) day period, Lessee's right to cancel this Lease hereunder shall terminate and be of no further force or effect.

3.2.1 **Possession Tendered—Defined.** Possession of the Premises shall be deemed tendered to Lessee ("Tender of Possession") when (1) the improvements to be provided by Lessor under this Lease are substantially completed, (2) the Building utilities are ready for use in the Premises, (3) Lessee has reasonable access to the Premises, and (4) ten (10) days shall have expired following advance written notice to Lessee of the occurrence of the matters described in (1), (2) and (3), above of this paragraph 3.2.1.

3.2.2 **Delays Caused by Lessee.** There shall be no abatement of rent, and the sixty (60) day period following the Commencement Date before which Lessee's right to cancel this Lease accrues under paragraph 3.2, shall be deemed extended to the extent of any delays caused by acts or omissions of Lessee, Lessee's agents, employees and contractors.

3.3 **Early Possession.** If Lessee occupies the Premises prior to said Commencement Date, such occupancy shall be subject to all provisions of this Lease, such occupancy shall not change the termination date, and Lessee shall pay rent for such occupancy.

3.4 **Uncertain Commencement.** In the event commencement of the Lease term is defined as the completion of the improvements, Lessee and Lessor shall execute an amendment to this Lease establishing the date of Tender of Possession (as defined in paragraph 3.2.1) or the actual taking of possession by Lessee, whichever first occurs, as the Commencement Date.

4. Rent.

4.1 **Base Rent.** Subject to adjustment as hereinafter provided in paragraph 4.3, and except as may be otherwise expressly provided in this Lease, Lessee shall pay to Lessor the Base Rent for the Premises set forth in paragraph 1.6 of the Basic Lease Provisions, without offset or deduction. Lessee shall pay Lessor upon execution hereof the advance Base Rent described in paragraph 1.8 of the Basic Lease Provisions. Rent for any period during the term hereof which is for less than one month shall be prorated based upon the actual number of days of the calendar month involved. Rent shall be payable in lawful money of the United States to Lessor at the address stated herein or to such other persons or at such other places as Lessor may designate in writing.

4.2 **Operating Expense Increase.** Lessee shall pay to Lessor during the term hereof, in addition to the Base Rent, Lessee's Share, as hereinafter defined, of the amount by which all Operating Expenses, as hereinafter defined, for each Comparison Year exceeds the amount of all Operating Expenses for the Base Year, such excess being hereinafter referred to as the "Operating Expense Increase," in accordance with the following provisions:

(a) "Lessee's Share" is defined, for purposes of this Lease, as the percentage set forth in paragraph 1.10 of the Basic Lease Provisions, which percentage has been determined by dividing the approximate square footage of the Premises by the total approximate square footage of the rentable space contained in the Office Building Project. It is understood and agreed that the square footage figures set forth in the Basic Lease Provisions are approximations which Lessor and Lessee agree are reasonable and shall not be subject to revision except in connection with an actual change in the size of the Premises or a change in the space available for lease in the Office Building Project.

(b) "Base Year" is defined as the calendar year in which the Lease term commences.

(c) "Comparison Year" is defined as each calendar year during the term of this Lease subsequent to the Base Year; provided, however, Lessee shall have no obligation to pay a share of the Operating Expense Increase applicable to the first twelve (12) months of the Lease Term (other than such as are mandated by a governmental authority, as to which government mandated expenses Lessee shall pay Lessee's Share, notwithstanding they occur during the first twelve (12) months). Lessee's Share of the Operating Expense Increase for the first and last Comparison Years of the Lease Term shall be prorated according to that portion of such Comparison Year as to which Lessee is responsible for a share of such increase.

(d) "Operating Expenses" is defined, for purposes of this Lease, to include all costs, if any, incurred by Lessor in the exercise of its reasonable discretion, for:

(i) The operation, repair, maintenance, and replacement, in neat, clean, safe, good order and condition, of the Office Building Project, including but not limited to, the following:

(aa) The Common Areas, including their surfaces, coverings, decorative items, carpets, drapes and window coverings, and including parking areas, loading and unloading areas, trash areas, roadways, sidewalks, walkways, stairways, parkways, driveways, landscaped areas, striping, bumpers, irrigation systems, Common Area lighting facilities, building exteriors and roofs, fences and gates;

(bb) All heating, air conditioning, plumbing, electrical systems, life safety equipment, telecommunication and other equipment used in common by, or for the benefit of, lessees or occupants of the Office Building Project, including elevators and escalators, tenant directories, fire detection systems including sprinkler system maintenance and repair.

(ii) Trash disposal, janitorial and security services;

(iii) Any other service to be provided by Lessor that is elsewhere in this Lease stated to be an "Operating Expense";

(iv) The cost of the premiums for the liability and property insurance policies to be maintained by Lessor under paragraph 8 hereof;

(v) The amount of the real property taxes to be paid by Lessor under paragraph 10.1 hereof;

(vi) The cost of water, sewer, gas, electricity, and other publicly mandated services to the Office Building Project;

(vii) Labor, salaries and applicable fringe benefits and costs, materials, supplies and tools, used in maintaining and/or cleaning the Office Building Project and accounting and a management fee attributable to the operation of the Office Building Project;

(viii) Replacing and/or adding improvements mandated by any governmental agency and any repairs or removals necessitated thereby amortized over its useful life according to Federal income tax regulations or guidelines for depreciation thereof (including interest on the unamortized balance as is then reasonable in the judgment of Lessor's accountants);

(ix) Replacements of equipment or improvements that have a useful life for depreciation purposes according to Federal income tax guidelines of five (5) years or less, as amortized over such life.

(e) Operating Expenses shall not include the costs of replacements of equipment or improvements that have a useful life for Federal income tax purposes in excess of five (5) years unless it is of the type described in paragraph 4.2(d)(viii), in which case their cost shall be included as above provided.

(f) Operating Expenses shall not include any expenses paid by any lessee directly to third parties, or as to which Lessor is otherwise reimbursed by any third party, other tenant, or by insurance proceeds.

(g) Lessee's Share of Operating Expense Increase shall be payable by Lessee within ten (10) days after a reasonably detailed statement of actual expenses is presented to Lessee by Lessor. At Lessor's option, however, an amount may be estimated by Lessor from time to time in advance of Lessee's Share of the Operating Expense Increase for any Comparison Year, and the same shall be payable monthly or quarterly, as Lessor shall designate, during each Comparison Year of the Lease term, on the same day as the Base Rent is due hereunder. In the event that Lessee pays Lessor's estimate of Lessee's Share of Operating Expense Increase as aforesaid, Lessor shall deliver to Lessee within sixty (60) days after the expiration of each Comparison Year a reasonably detailed statement showing Lessee's Share of the actual Operating Expense Increase incurred during such year. If Lessee's payments under this paragraph 4.2(g) during said Comparison Year exceed Lessee's Share as indicated on said statement, Lessee shall be entitled to credit the amount of such overpayment against Lessee's Share of Operating Expense Increase next falling due. If Lessee's payments under this paragraph during said Comparison Year were less than Lessee's Share as indicated on said statement, Lessee shall pay to Lessor the amount of the deficiency within ten (10) days after delivery by Lessor to Lessee of said statement. Lessor and Lessee shall forthwith adjust between them by cash payment any balance determined to exist with respect to that portion of the last Comparison Year for which Lessee is responsible as to Operating Expense Increases, notwithstanding that the Lease term may have terminated before the end of such Comparison Year.

4.3 **Rent Increase.**

4.3.1 At the times set forth in paragraph 1.7 of the Basic Lease Provisions, the monthly Base Rent payable under paragraph 4.1 of this Lease shall be adjusted by the increase, if any, in the Consumer Price Index of the Bureau of Labor Statistics of the Department of Labor for All Urban Consumers, (1967=100), "All Items," for the city nearest the location of the Building, herein referred to as "C.P.I.," since the date of this Lease.

4.3.2 The monthly Base Rent payable pursuant to paragraph 4.3.1 shall be calculated as follows: the Base Rent payable for the first month of the term of this Lease, as set forth in paragraph 4.1 of this Lease, shall be multiplied by a fraction the numerator of which shall be the C.P.I. of the calendar month during which the adjustment is to take effect, and the denominator of which shall be the C.P.I. for the calendar month in which the original Lease term commences. The sum so calculated shall constitute the new monthly Base Rent hereunder, but, in no event, shall such new monthly Base Rent be less than the Base Rent payable for the month immediately preceding the date for the rent adjustment.

4.3.3 In the event the compilation and/or publication of the C.P.I. shall be transferred to any other governmental department or bureau or

Initials:_____

_____

Utility Oriented. Having low cost electricity might be an important locational factor to a firm requiring high power needs. A food processing firm might be interested in the quantity and quality of the water.

Quality of Life. Foot-loose industries do not have excessive problems with transportation or tapping into a particular labor pool. Location would be influenced by the quality of life offered to management. Quality of life factors would be:

1. **Climate.** The sunbelt might be a particular plus.

2. **Hobbies and Special Interests.** If a CEO is an avid skier, then Colorado, Idaho or Utah might be a desirable location for the firm.

3. **Schools.** The quality of education would be important for many executives who have children.

4. **Colleges and Universities.** A location close to a major college or university would appeal to many firms. College and university programs for families and executives themselves is important. Many firms work closely with colleges and universities by getting involved in doctoral programs and/or consulting with professors on research.

5. **Housing.** Quality and the cost of housing is important as to life style.

6. **The Arts.** Areas in which theaters, music and the arts are located attract many firms because of the contribution to quality of life.

7. **Crime.** A low crime rate is important in making a locational decision.

8. **Religion.** Executives in foot-loose industries will be influenced by religion. They want to be located near other people of similar beliefs. As an example, many Mormons have moved their facilities to Utah from other areas of the country.

7. **Locational Incentives.** Foot-loose industries would be interested in incentives offered by a community. Incentives would include low cost loans, low or no rent, a moratorium on property taxes, locally sponsored training program for employees, etc.

Many communities vie for industrial facilities which will employ local residents. These are usually communities having a high rate of unemployment. Often they will build a facility for the special needs of a user.

In leasing space to a foot-loose industry, a property manager might be competing against a community desperate to obtain the same tenant. In this case, the manager would have to stress locational advantages other than rental costs.

STRUCTURAL NEEDS

Historic Structures

When water was used to power factories, it was transferred from waterwheels to machines by belts, chains and shafts more readily done vertically than horizontally. Factories were multistory facilities during the industrial revolution. These structures were not efficient operations because of the cost of moving goods from floor-to-floor.

One-Story Factories

Manufacturers sought large sites for one-story factories to run a modern assembly line business. They moved toward suburban areas to obtain the necessary space.

Today, factory requirements include:

1. Water quantity for fire suppression systems and quality for processing application. Location to hydrants, quantity of water and water pressure are important for insurance purposes.
2. Adequate power as well as three-phase wiring is required for some applications.
3. Adequate ceiling height for movement of equipment, fork-lifts, truck operations, etc.
4. Overhead traveling cranes are important for moving heavy equipment or material.
5. Clear-span structures are desirable for ease in changing production lines and moving equipment.
6. Overhead doors provide easy ingress and egress of vehicles, equipment and material.
7. Loading docks are important for receiving and shipping. Some factories would want two sets of doors so that the arrival of material would not conflict with shipments.
8. Employee parking is an important consideration in maintaining a work force.
9. Industrial zoning is important as many communities have various zoning categories for particular uses.
10. Depending upon climate and the type of facility, heating and air conditioning as well as insulation could be significant factors.
11. While a problem as to leakage, underground tanks are nevertheless desirable for many industrial users.
12. Covered, secured and open storage areas are necessary for different industrial users. Besides the arrival of components and material, there may be a need to store goods prior to shipping.
13. Secure perimeter fencing could be important for many industrial users. Park security could be a leasing consideration if the factory is located within an industrial park.

SPECIAL USE STRUCTURES

SPECIAL USE STRUCTURES *are very limited as to use.* Although in one case a grain elevator complex was converted to apartments, generally such a complex has limited use.

Some special use structures, such as a cold storage or freeze storage facility, could easily be converted to another use such as general storage. However, such use would not take advantage of the structure's special features and should only be considered if a tenant cannot be found to use the structure "as is" or with the addition of any special features.

INDUSTRIAL PARKS

INDUSTRIAL PARKS *are subdivisions containing a number of free-standing buildings which house single-tenant or multi-tenant structures.* Large green areas encompass modern industrial parks which present an excellent image. Fountains, waterfalls or colorful plantings can be found at many industrial park entrances. There may be a security gate, although most parks are open with tenants responsible for their own security. Large lots are set aside for parking in the rear of the structures.

Some industrial parks are wholly owned by one individual or entity. Others are developed by investors who purchased one or more sites. Buildings within the park would have to conform with restrictive covenants as to setbacks, landscaping, height and possibly even architectural style.

WAREHOUSE SPACE

WAREHOUSES *are industrial related buildings even though no manufacturing or fabrication takes place on the property.*

Historically, warehouses were built near interconnecting transportation routes such as rail lines or sea ports. While major warehouse locations exist, the greater reliance on truck transportation allows warehouses to locate near any major highway.

> *A great many warehouses are in Nevada because there isn't any inventory tax.*

Warehouse space is marketed by the square foot. Height, size of doors, loading docks, fire suppression system, security system, and insurance rates where the warehouse is located are important factors to lessees.

EVALUATING A SITE

Evaluate the location and structure when you have an industrial property for lease. You should target specific types of users as well as particular users. You want to consider the favorable and negative features of your site and how to present them before making a general approach to a specific firm or through an Industrial publication.

PREPARING TO LEASE

The space should be clean and, where possible, well lighted before it is shown for marketing.

Any delay in preparation should be regarded as costly since waiting for a crew to remove debris from a vacated space would mean lost rent which could far exceed the cleanup cost.

INDUSTRIAL LEASES

Industrial leases vary significantly based on the type of property and services included as well as the length of the lease. Disclosures are often provided for industrial leases to protect the lessor from future lessee claims.

CHANGING USES

When vacancies are at a high level, property managers will seek tenants who are attracted by location and reasonable rent. As the vacancy factor is reduced, managers seek those tenants who are willing to pay much more for the space.

Managers of industrial property in Burbank and Santa Monica, California have been notifying tenants that their leases will not be renewed. They are repositioning there properties and go for "clean" firms. They are targeting post production entertainment companies and high-tech industries which can pay almost double for the square footage that small industrial shops could pay. (Property managers in other areas are actively seeking these tenants.) Former auto repair shops and machine shops are now renting for $1 and more per square foot. The art-oriented new tenants like the open trusses and skylights of industrial property.

There is a risk in chasing out small industrial users in that the new tenants tend to be in more volatile areas.

═══ CHAPTER 6 SUMMARY ═══

Commercial property is property involved in the buying and selling of goods.

The commercial space requirements for a community would be based upon population, number of households, discretionary purchasing power, demographics of the community and the drawing power of area businesses.

Commercial property might be located on pedestrian shopping streets, urban pedestrian malls, strip centers, mini-malls, neighborhood shopping centers, community shopping centers, regional shopping center, mega-malls, factory outlet centers, free-standing stores and would also include wholesale operations.

Tenant selection is very important in multi-tenant facilities. Tenants can contribute to each other's success if properly selected. Quality tenants will help reduce tenant turnover.

Rent setting for an area would not be based on comparables alone. Special needs of tenants, locational differences, etc., can affect rents.

A tenant's survivability can be affected if a landlord wants too high a rent. This can mean problems with rent collection, vacancies and additional costs related to renting.

Too low a rent would mean that later opportunities to obtain market rent may be lost. It could also result in other tenants wanting to negotiate rent reductions.

Parking needs create many problems in nonresidential leasing that must be addressed by management.

Since building nonresidential structures is related to the availability of loans, building and overbuilding tends to run in cycles.

You will notice that many of the clauses discussed in Chapter 4 are in the leases included in this Chapter.

Office buildings are categorized from Class A to Class D depending on quality and desirability. Office buildings may be one-story garden structures, low-rise, mid-rise or high-rise.

Some older office structures can be repositioned as to class by restoration or remodeling. Buildings can be more desirable to occupants because of the theme of the structure.

Intelligent buildings use shared state-of-the-art communication facilities such as teleconferencing.

Some buildings combine commercial, office and residential uses.

R & D facilities (Research and Development) include offices, laboratories and might also include fabrication facilities.

Sick buildings have problems such as bacteria (air conditioning ducts, etc.) and/or fume emissions from chemicals used in construction and/or decorating.

When a building has exceeded its economic life, due to increase in the value of the site, demolition and replacement should be considered.

The vacancy factor of an area would likely differ by class of office structure. When new space becomes available it must be absorbed by increased demand or other space will have to be taken off the market. Otherwise the vacancy rate will increase.

Square footage can be computed in various ways for rental purposes. Property managers should make clear how any square footage figures were arrived at.

Many office leases provide for a fixturing allowance for new tenants. Expenses beyond the allowance would be the tenant's responsibility.

Perks to management and employees make for happy tenants. Happy tenants are more likely to become long-term tenants.

Most office leases are gross leases. Leases often include a floor plan so that all parties fully understand what is being leased.

Locational needs for manufacturing properties is not based on traffic counts. Factors important are location in relation to supplies, market, transportation, labor supply, utility supply and the quality of life offered by the community.

Most industrial firms prefer a one-story plant for ease of movement of supplies and the finished product. Of concern as to facilities are the water quality, quantity and pressure for products and/or fire suppression, adequacy of electrical service for the tenant's needs, height of structure, overhead cranes, clear span, overhead doors, loading docks, parking, HVAC facilities, storage, underground tanks and the security of the structure and its perimeter.

Special use structures are very limited as to tenants.

Industrial parks have a number of free-standing structures and often attractive green areas.

Warehouse space is industrial related. The best warehouse locations relate to transportation. Personal property tax is also a consideration.

A property manager should evaluate a property to be leased as to who can use it and the specific strengths of the property for the user. A property manager could target specific industries and firms in marketing the property.

Industrial leases vary significantly based on the type of property, services included and length of the lease.

CLASS DISCUSSION TOPICS

1. What building in your area, if any, do you consider to be a trophy building? Why?
2. Are there any theme buildings in your area? What are they?
3. Identify a Class A, Class B, Class C and Class D office building in your community.
4. Provide local examples of strip centers.
5. Provide an example of a neighborhood shopping center, a community shopping center and a regional shopping center.
6. Give an example of a free-standing retail operation.
7. Give an example of what you consider a well managed shopping center. Why?
8. Give an example of a commercial, industrial or office property which you feel is not properly managed. Explain why.
9. Give an example of an area property that has an abnormally high tenant turnover rate. What do you suppose is the cause?
10. Give an example of a local commercial property having inadequate parking. If there are possible solutions, what are they?
11. Give an example of a local R & D facility.

CHAPTER 6 QUIZ

1. Which of the following would be of importance in determining the amount of commercial space required by a community?

    A. The number of households
    B. Discretionary purchasing power of residents
    C. The age breakdown of residents
    D. All of the above

2. An established shopping street that is restricted to foot traffic only would BEST describe:

    A. urban pedestrian mall
    B. strip center
    C. neighborhood shopping center
    D. mini-mall

3. A shopping center, having as its anchor tenant a single, large department store, would be a(n):

    A. neighborhood shopping center
    B. mega-mall
    C. community shopping center
    D. mini-mall

4. A symbiotic relationship would apply to:

    A. industrial sites
    B. selecting tenants who will benefit by each other
    C. free-standing single tenant structures
    D. the quality of life offered by a community

5. The best office building in a community would be:

    A. Class A
    B. Class B
    C. Class C
    D. Class D

6. A two or three-story office building, would be a:

    A. garden building
    B. low-rise
    C. mid-rise
    D. high-rise

7. A sick building would MOST LIKELY be the result of:

    A. a tenant going bankrupt
    B. having elderly tenants
    C. chemical fumes from construction products and/or furnishings
    D. desirability of the building

8. Demolition could be an economic decision for a sound building when:

    A. interest rates rise
    B. land values rise dramatically but rents do not
    C. the vacancy factor reaches five percent
    D. never

9. Office tenants WOULD GENERALLY have what kind of lease?

    A. Gross
    B. Net
    C. Percentage
    D. Percentage plus minimum

10. An industrial plant that locates next to its largest customer would be:

    A. supply oriented
    B. labor oriented
    C. utility oriented
    D. market oriented

Answers: 1. D; 2. A; 3. C; 4. B; 5. A; 6. B; 7. C; 8. B; 9. A; 10. D

Special Management Situations

KEY WORDS AND TERMS

Board of Directors
Clothing Optional
Condominium Association
Corporate Owned Farms
Docking Facilities
Elderly Housing
Farm/Ranch Management
Gentlemen Farms
Hotel/Motel Management
Independent Living
Institutional Management
Inventory Control
Lender Owned Farms
Life Care
Mediation
Medical Office Management

Mini Storage
Mobile Home Park Management
Nursing Facilities
Public Rooms
Recreational Vehicle Park Management
Residential Hotels
Resort Management
Section 8 Housing
Semi-Independent Living
Short-Term Residential
SRO
Storage Yard
Subsidized Housing
Time Share Management
Undivided Interest Developments

LEARNING OBJECTIVES

There are a number of property management situations which do not fall within what is ordinarily regarded as property management. These situations relate to type of property, use and type of ownership.

In this chapter you will gain an overall view, from a management perspective, of property management for specialized types of property and specialized uses.

Areas which will be covered include single-room occupancy, condominium association management, resort management, clothing optional properties, single-family dwellings, short-term residential properties, hotel/motel management, elderly housing projects, institutional management, subsidized housing, time share management, mobile home park management, recreational vehicle park management, farm and ranch management, managing docking facilities and the management of medical offices.

Single Room Occupancy (SROs)

SROs *refer to single room occupancy.* They are usually former transient hotels and motels that, because of a variety of factors, are either marginal or loss operations when rented on a daily basis.

Renting units by the month offers significant operational savings in housekeeping services as well as eliminating the need for full-time desk clerks. By changing from daily occupancy, the operation changes from a hotel/motel management plan and philosophy to a simple multi-unit rental unit.

> *SROs differ from residential hotels in that they do NOT offer the services a hotel does such as housekeeping, room service, 24-hour desk service, valet service, message service, etc.*

In many population centers there is a tremendous need for SRO units that consist of a single room and bath. They can be rented for significantly less than the normal bachelor (efficiency) or one-bedroom unit. The lower rent makes the units desirable for retirees, single working persons as well as persons receiving some sort of government assistance.

In large metropolitan areas you might find managers who specialize in SROs. They would likely present a management proposal to the owner of a large hotel or motel type property covering conversion to an SRO.

Property managers may team up with entrepreneurs who either buy or lease property for conversion to SROs with the property manager handling the conversion and operation. Because of the low prices that loss operations can be purchased or leased for, some property managers have elected to operate SROs as principals rather than as agents of others.

TENANT QUALIFYING

Because you are renting a single room does not mean that you should be less careful in tenant selection. Problem tenants can result in the exodus of desirable tenants. It can also result in damage to the property and long-term damage to the building's reputation.

Single room occupancy managers should be aware that these units often appear attractive to prostitutes, drug dealers, addicts and other criminal elements. Background credit and rental history is important and must be checked. A prospective tenant who wants immediate occupancy and offers several month's rent in advance is not necessarily superior to having a vacant unit.

SECURITY

Consideration must be given to security in changing a daily rental facility to an SRO. While the room locks and door chains might be adequate, exterior doors should, if possible, be locked with an electronic lock that can be released by individual tenants through a call system. In this way persons intent on mischief have two locks to go through.

In addition, a 24-hour security camera can be aimed at the entrance as well as any elevators. Service doors would likely already be set up for exit only with panic hardware. See Chapter 9 for a further discussion as to security.

OCCUPANCY

Because of the 1988 Amendment to the Civil Rights Act of 1968, it may NOT be possible to restrict occupancy to one person.

This could discriminate against married couples which would be familial status discrimination. (See Chapter 13.) However, because of the small size of the units, limiting occupancy to two persons would likely be upheld should it be challenged in the courts.

While hotels charge more for a double than a single, you should not charge more for two persons as it could be discriminatory based on familial status. You can of course charge more for large size rooms or different amenities such as a king size bed.

RENTAL PERIOD

Weekly rentals should generally be avoided as it will result in a greater turnover of tenants and higher vacancy and maintenance factors, which will likely result in lowering the net. In addition, weekly rentals will attract transients.

In property management, the more individuals you have to deal with increases the likelihood of encountering tenants who become serious problems.

LEASE

Renters in SROs should sign a lease, even if it is only a month-to-month tenancy, and pay some sort of property damage bond, even if it is only $50. Renters should also be asked to sign a copy of house rules and be given a copy. The rules may cover cooking in rooms, use of electric heaters, pets, noise, parking, etc.

UTILITIES

SROs are generally rented with all utilities. In most instances, the cost of rewiring would make separate utilities an uneconomic conversion.

They usually include heat and air conditioning, light, water and cable television. While telephones will likely be installed in the lobby, laundry room and perhaps other public areas, private telephones would be the tenants' responsibility. The existing telephone system utilizing a hotel or motel switchboard would not be used.

FURNISHINGS

SROs are generally rented fully furnished although some operations will allow a tenant to use his or her own furniture. This would likely lead to a longer term tenancy. A small refrigerator is usually added to the hotel/motel type furnishings.

While SROs generally prohibit hot plate use, some allow the tenants to use their own microwave ovens, if the electrical service will handle such use. Allowing microwaves will increase tenancy periods and avoids clandestine cooking in the rooms.

Some managers include the original televisions but will not replace or repair them. The set becomes the responsibility of the tenant and therefore reduces management's problems.

Most units include basic bedding, linens and towels with additional supplies being the responsibility of the tenant. However, units that do not supply bedding, linens and towels do not necessarily lose prospective tenants because of this practice.

HOUSEKEEPING

SROs should avoid housekeeping other than the lobby, elevators, hallways and public areas. The individual units should be the responsibility of the tenants. The only time units should be cleaned would be between tenancies. The units should always be rented in a clean and sanitary condition with fresh linens.

LAUNDRY ROOM

Usually space is available for a coin operated laundry room. The laundry room should be locked with entry only with tenant's keys or by a combination electric lock. Vending machines can be placed in the laundry room and/or in the lobby area.

Income from coin operated machines can be substantial in an SRO setting.

Therefore, proper maintenance of the equipment is important. Machines should either be on a maintenance contract or should be contracted for with an operator on a split-revenue basis.

RESTAURANTS/BARS

Property managers should avoid managing existing restaurants and/or bars.

The management problems and specialized nature of such operations usually result in disaster.

If feasible, the restaurant/bar operation should be leased out to an operator. Some motels that have converted to SROs have leased restaurant facilities at a very reasonable rent to moderately priced chain restaurant operators. The SRO owners find that the presence of a food service has aided in renting rooms.

PUBLIC ROOMS

In some cases, meeting and banquet rooms can be leased to the onsite restaurant operator. If this is not economically feasible, consideration should be given to convert the space to additional rental units. However, this is not always feasible due to the size of the meeting or banquet room and large windows. Some SROs use old banquet facilities as day rooms for their residents and even provide donuts and coffee on Sunday mornings.

There is a reason for promoting tenant socialization. Tenants who know each other, especially retired persons, are more likely to become permanent tenants.

Space that does not have any rental value and is otherwise not needed for operations should be converted to a storage facility. Air and heat ducts in this space should be closed.

55 AND OLDER

It is possible to restrict occupancy to persons 55 years of age and older. (See Chapter 13.) This will reduce crime and property damage as well as increase the average occupancy period for your tenants. You should analyze your market to determine if the area supports this restriction before you make a change.

A 100-unit, older motel or hotel that is occupied entirely by pensioners could provide relatively easy management, and provide a monthly gross income of $10,000 to $20,000 or more depending on the marketplace.

RESIDENT MANAGER

Most hotel and motel operations include either a large apartment unit for a resident manager of offices that can be converted to such use.

The **RESIDENT MANAGER** *would be responsible for enforcing house rules, taking rental applications, lease signing, supervision of housekeeping and maintenance, handling complaints and recommending or initiating eviction procedures.* In some cases the resident manager would actually collect the rents.

A resident manager who does the job well will usually insure a smooth operation. A careless resident manager who fails to meet his or her obligations can spell disaster for an SRO operation.

Condominium Management

Management of a condominium means dealing with the Board of Directors of the Homeowner's Association rather than an individual owner.

THE BOARD OF DIRECTORS

The **BOARD OF DIRECTORS** *of a Homeowner's Association is elected by the homeowners as their representatives.* The Board of Directors hires the property manager. Rather than dealing with an owner who is economically oriented, members of the association might have separate agendas, which might include the following.

Keep Fees Down. Such a director can drive a manager practically insane with constant questions about individual minor expenses. Often the director is a retired individual who has nothing else to do but be a self-appointed watchdog over expenses.

Keep It Beautiful. This director is very interested in the grounds and possesses a passion for gardening. They often insist on selecting the flowers, plants and colors to be used on the premises.

Be A Chief. Some directors strive to be important and are very impressed with themselves. Such a director can end up going over the head of the property manager in directing maintenance and grounds personnel.

An Obsession. Some people insist on having special plantings for their unit or other wishes and therefore run for office on the Board of Directors. It may even be an obsession with security or to have greater controls regarding children on the premises. Personal wishes should be considered as a part of the whole picture and not become a priority where they are not warranted.

Throw Them Out. Some directors run for office because they didn't like the decisions made by previous board members. In their clean-slate approach, they also may want to change the current property management which they cannot do if the firm has a solid contract. Such a director is politically motivated and may work hard to find a breach of the management contract. Management will be under great scrutiny.

The Time Waster. This type of director loves meetings at every opportunity. They enjoy lengthy meetings with a lot of talking where not much is really said nor accomplished.

The Nit-Picker. This director has a lot of time to worry about little things which the average person would ignore. Here is a person, probably a parliamentarian, who carries a copy of Roberts Rules of Order to every association meeting which requires the management to bone up on procedures. The nit-picker puts procedure before substance.

The Reasonable Director. Actually, there are few directors who are reasonable in every area and few who are unreasonable all of the time. Directors tend to have a combination of the traits listed and, like all of us, fall into varying shades of grey.

MANAGEMENT DUTIES

Management duties may include the following.

Supervision of Elections. The property manager would see that the election of the Board of Directors is held in accordance with the bylaws of the association.

Enforcement of CC&Rs. The enforcement that covenants, conditions and restrictions as well as rules and regulations must be uniform. Before a manager enforces a regulation not enforced in the past, the property manager should check with the Board of Directors for their views on enforcement. If a court determines a rule is unreasonable, the court will refuse to enforce it.

Recommendation As to Rule Changes. The property manager should notify the Board of Directors of any new rule or modification of a rule that may be necessary. The recommendation should be specific as to the language of the rule. If the board agrees, copies of the rule should be given to members to vote in accordance with the bylaws of the association. Some associations require only a simple majority to change rules and others require a two-thirds vote.

Preparation of the Annual Budget. In the preparation of the budget, the manager should consider past costs, inflation, necessary modifications to maintenance and any changes in improvements, taxes, insurance, etc. The budget should be submitted for Board approval.

Management of Insurance. The property manager would make certain that the insurance coverage was adequate but not excessive. Coverage would include replacement value for physical improvements from theft, vandalism, and damage from fire, smoke, and water, etc. It may also include earthquake and/or flood damage. Coverage should include high-limit liability insurance for members. The Board of Directors should be protected with a directors' liability policy. Workers Compensation coverage would be required for any employees.

Supervision of Maintenance. The property manager would be responsible for supervising all maintenance work and repairs.

Case Example

Portola Hills Community Association v. James (1992) 4 C.A. 4th 289

CC&Rs banned satellite dishes completely from the community. Jones installed a satellite dish that was not visible to other residents or to the public. The trial court found that the restriction was not reasonable so could not be enforced.

The Court of Appeals affirmed pointing out that under California Civil Code Section 1354, restrictions are enforceable unless unreasonable. Prohibiting a satellite dish that could not be observed by others does not serve any legitimate purpose of the association and was therefore unreasonable.

Case Example

Bernardo Villas Mgt. Corp. v. Black (1987) 190 C.A. 3d 153

A property manager sued the owner of a condominium unit to enjoin the owner from parking a new pickup truck in his carport and also to recover fines levied against the owner for violations of the CC&Rs. The CC&Rs prohibited the parking of trucks, campers, boats and recreational vehicles in the carports.

Both the trial court and the Court of Appeals ruled in favor of the owner. The court pointed out that California Civil Code Section 1354 holds that CC&Rs are enforceable unless they are unreasonable. Therefore, unreasonable restrictions would be unenforceable. The court pointed out that the presence of the truck in the carport was in no way offensive to a reasonable person. The truck was not used for commercial purposes. The court pointed out that the pickup trucks today are the equivalent of station wagons and convertibles. "One person's Bronco II is another person's Rolls Royce."

Note: This case points out the necessity of condo associations having reasonable covenants, conditions and restrictions. With the appeal, the association expended thousand of dollars to enforce a covenant which they should have realized was unreasonable.

Case Example

Franklin v. Marie Antoinette Condominium Owners Ass'n., Inc. (1993) 19 C.A. 4th 824

A property owner suffered damage to his unit because of a central plumbing leak. A jury determined that the association had been negligent in failing to maintain the plumbing system and had breached a contractual duty under the covenants, conditions and restrictions to maintain and repair the common areas.

The Court of Appeals reversed a finding in favor of the tenant because an exculpatory clause in the CC&Rs shielded the association from liability in the absence of gross negligence. While the tenant could enforce the association's duty to repair, the association was held not liable for the damages.

Case Example

Liebler v. Point Loma Tennis Club (1996) 40 C.A. 4th 1600

Liebler, an owner of a leased condominium unit, used the tennis courts. While Liebler never lived in the unit, the lease indicated that he was a co-tenant and shared the premises. The condo association had a rule that "The recreational facilities shall be used only by residents of PLTC and their guests." The rule goes on to specify that owners of rented units may not use the facilities. All nonresident owners were reminded, by letter, of this rule.

Liebler continued to use the courts and was fined by the association. Liebler then sued the association asking for an injunction against enforcement of the rule.

The Superior Court held the rule to be reasonable and that the association had authority to fine Liebler. The Court of Appeals affirmed and pointed out that CC&Rs are presumed to be reasonable when uniformly enforced. The Appellate Court pointed out that the rule was reasonable and was enforced against all owners.

Note: Liebler went to great lengths to have the appearance of being a resident. Basically, he wanted the use of recreational facilities but did not want to live on the premises.

Contracting for Services. Even if a condominium association has its own employees, there are still services which are best contracted for, such as swimming pool maintenance and exterior pest control.

Mediation. Personal problems between homeowners can develop into an ugly situation unless handled in a prompt and judicious manner. The property manager should not try to direct a solution but instead act with the help of both parties to reach an understanding. A manager can also ask a board member to mediate the dispute.

Mediation and arbitration can aid the property manager in his or her relations with the Board of Directors.

Attending Board Meetings. The property manager may help in preparing a meeting agenda and should attend all meetings to answer any questions and present plans for future work on the premises. In some cases, the property manager might take notes at the meeting and distribute copies to the members.

Many associations have committees for various aspects of the association. As an example, there could be committees for recreation, security, landscaping, etc.

Whenever possible, the property manager should be available to attend these committee meetings.

Security and Safety. The property manager should supervise and review security operations and safety procedures and make recommendations to the board as to any changes needed.

Collection of Assessments. While the assessments are set by the Board of Directors, the property manager is responsible for collecting assessments from the members.

Legal Action. Legal action to protect or enforce the interests of the association or to collect delinquent assessments should only be commenced after receiving Board of Director approval.

Accounting and Record-keeping. The property manager shall keep up-to-date accounts of all income and expenses as well as employee records, insurance files, maintenance schedules, etc. These records should be available to the Board of Directors and members. The property manager should never appear to be hiding anything from a member of the association.

Rentals and Sales. The rental or sale of units is not a property manager's responsibility. Some associations prefer that a property manager handle these areas rather than have a number of brokers showing properties within the complex.

The property manager is at an advantage over other agents when engaging in such brokerage activities because he or she has built up a relationship with the owners of the complex.

PERSONAL RELATIONSHIPS

A condominium association property manager is more likely to lose his or her client because of personal reasons rather than because of management errors. The following are some points to remember.

Treat Them As Owners. Treat every member of the condominium association as if he or she were a sole owner. Listen to their complaints and let them know what you will do about it.

Avoid Taking Sides. Cliques often form within the Board of Directors and/or association members. Remain neutral. Listen to everyone but say nothing negative about anyone.

Avoid Favoritism. Treat every member the same as to rules and regulations. Don't give preference because a person is a member of the Board of Directors. Don't allow a member to think that you owe your position to that person.

Don't Lie to Members. Never tell a member you will do something when you don't intend to do it.

Don't Hide Bad News. If there is an anticipated cost overrun, let the board know as soon as you have made that determination.

Always Complete Staff Work. Never present a problem to the Board of Directors without also presenting possible courses of action, your recommendations and why you think the recommended course of action is best.

People don't want to hear about problems without solutions.

Meet Deadlines. Don't give deadlines you can't meet just to please someone. Be realistic and then try to beat the deadline you have set.

Don't Underestimate Costs. People become angry when work exceeds an estimate. However, coming in under budget is like found money.

Ask for Advice. Although you should be the advisor and not the advisee as to most management matters, you can use the expertise of members and Board members in many areas. People like being asked for advice as to their areas of expertise.

As an example, while preparing specifications for a bid on a new pool heater you might ask a member who is a heating contractor to review your specifications.

Ask a person with gardening interests about changing plants for the common areas.

Know Their Names. Some condominium association property managers can address several hundred residents by name. Memory identification tricks can help you remember names such as repeating the name to yourself three times during introductions and associating the name with someone or something. Most people don't go to this much trouble, but a little effort can make a big difference in personal relations.

Return All Calls Promptly. People get angry when you don't return calls or appear to be hiding from them.

Stop Board Abuses Fast. If Board members begin directing employees or contractors this can lead to confusion and problems. You must inform the Board that you will do whatever they want as long as it is legal, but any directions to the staff must come from you.

Watch Out for Employees Working for Homeowners. Your employees must understand that they cannot do work inside owner's units for them on association-paid time. They must also understand that they are not to accept tips for performing their jobs because some owners will feel others were treated better.

Be Positive. Any problems associated with a planned action of the Board of Directors should be pointed out before they are approved by the Board of Directors. After they are passed is not the time to resist. Ask for clarification if you are uncertain as to what is actually desired. Carry out the Board's wishes with enthusiasm.

Know the Bylaws and CC&Rs. Understand the Board of Directors authority as well as your own.

> *Never exceed your authority, except in emergencies, without attempting to first notify the board.*

Understand the CC&Rs. You don't want members to know more than you do about your authority. Also understand the limitations imposed by the various statutes covering condominium associations.

COMPENSATION

Compensation for management is usually a set monthly fee per unit plus actual costs incurred. The association will also probably provide management with an office within the complex. Associations of 1,000 members or more may have a monthly management fee of $8.00 per unit, while a smaller association may charge a monthly fee of $15.00 per unit. One person might be able to handle several smaller associations located in the same proximity while a large association may require a full-time manager plus someone to handle secretarial and bookkeeping tasks.

Resort Area Management

Many property managers in resort areas will rent homes and condominium units by the month or by the **SEASON**, *which could be as long as six or seven months.*

The shorter the rental period, the higher the rent and management fee.

Some management companies charge fees from 25 percent to 33 1/3 percent of gross rent receipts plus cleaning expenses. These fees are justified by marketing expenses and the rents collected for the owners.

Property management companies in the Palm Springs area advertise using 800 numbers in Los Angeles, San Francisco, as well as Washington, Oregon, and Canadian newspapers. Inquiries are answered by sending photographs and information on available units and they conclude rentals by telephone using a credit card for the rental deposit.

These firms also obtain business from the referrals of other brokers, who don't handle rentals, by paying referral fees.

Rental firms located in resort areas are often specialty firms which handle these rentals only. However, some brokers have one or more agents designated to handle resort area rentals. Condominium association managers also compete for this business. In some condominium complexes, rental commissions are a significant portion of the property manager's income.

Clothing Optional

There are a number of clothing-optional apartment units located primarily in sun belt areas. Clothing optional units are not intended to appeal to perversion or voyeurism. These units are rented to nudists who are allowed to wear or not wear clothes in the common areas. Residents are often middle aged and believe strongly in the healthful aspects of sunshine. Also of concern is their physical fitness.

Nudists are willing to pay a premium for these units. Through friendships of other nudists, these clothing optional units often have waiting lists.

A clothing-optional unit should have privacy, such as an interior courtyard with a pool and other recreational facilities which can be reached by entering a solidly locked gated area. Resident managers of such units are generally also dedicated nudists. Besides the normal management duties, they might also serve as recreational director.

Single Family Dwellings

Management of a single-family dwelling is a specialized residential management area.

However, a large percentage of property management firms and real estate brokers handle some single-family dwellings.

OWNERS' GOALS

Owners hold some single-family dwellings as long-term investments. They expect both income and appreciation in value. A property manager can affect just one of these goals and that is income.

Single-family homes are often placed under property management because the owner is unable to sell the property at what he or she regards as a reasonable price. This owner wants or needs income from the property, usually to meet mortgage payments, until the property can be sold.

Some single-family homes are placed under management because the owners expect to re-occupy the homes at some later date. It may be due to a work-transfer out of the area or plans for future retirement. While the owner wants the income, he or she also wants the property maintained. Such an owner is usually more willing to agree to major expenditures. As an example, an owner who wants to sell a property would prefer to patch a leaky roof while an owner who hopes to retire in the house would agree to replace the roof.

Because single-family dwellings generally represent the highest per unit value of all residential housing, great care must be taken in tenant qualifications.

MAINTENANCE

In the case of property of lower value, the tenant is responsible for lawn maintenance and even minor repairs. However, the rent might include gardening services and sprinkler maintenance in some higher priced properties.

A pool should be maintained by a service company and the cost included in the rent. Pool maintenance by a tenant could result in black algae growth which is extremely difficult to control once if has gained a foothold. Improper chemical use can also result in pool stains.

Drive-by inspections on a regular basis are important if there is NO resident manager.

UTILITIES

All utilities except water should be paid by the tenant. You don't want a tenant to skimp on taking care of landscaping.

RENT PROBLEMS

When a tenant's rent is delinquent, or if an eviction notice has been sent out, you would want to drive by the property daily. You want to know when the property becomes vacant. A single-family property can be vandalized at the cost of tens of thousands of dollars in just a few days.

Furnished homes are particularly vulnerable to vandalism.

RENTERS

Who rents single-family homes? People who prefer to be homeowners rather than apartment dwellers. They might lack the down payment to buy, they might be new to the area and wish to rent before they buy, they might be waiting to have a house built or they may not know how long they will be in the area. In some case, hobbies and/or pets preclude apartment living for them.

Because of the high unit value, tenant qualification must be thorough.

MANAGEMENT FEES

Generally, management fees for single-family dwellings are much higher than for other types of residential property considering per unit and gross rents. This is necessary because of the problems involved in managing scattered single units.

Short-Term Residential Properties

Some efficiency and one-bedroom apartment developments are rented furnished for short-term use to business people who will have an extended stay in a community. Rentals are by the week or by the month. However, some corporations arrange to rent units on an annual basis.

These units are much larger than motel or hotel rooms and provide a far better quality of living for the tenants. The cost per night is less than a decent hotel room. In an area where decent hotel rooms might be $90 per night, an extended stay unit might rent for $400 per week.

A number of lodging chains have joined this lucrative market by building new facilities specifically to fulfill this need.

The rentals customarily include a small kitchen, bedroom, or bed area and a living area with a couch, chairs, work or dining table, etc. Daily housekeeping is usually included. Units might also include telephone answering machines. The management office should offer a copy machine, fax and computer modem.

Management problems and duties are similar to hotel and motel operations except that they do not include any food service. Some premises might include a leased restaurant.

Marketing of such property would include tourist guides such as AAA, providing information to a Chamber Of Commerce and contact with personnel, sales and engineering departments of major area employers.

Hotel/Motel Management

Hotels differ from motels as to services offered.

Hotels offer food service and usually include banquet and meeting facilities as well as luggage service to the rooms and room service.

Because of housekeeping, accounting and rental policies, hotel and motel operations require specialized knowledge and experience that few general property managers would possess.

A number of colleges and universities offer hotel/motel management programs. Generally these courses include supervision of food service, supervision of housekeeping, promotion of conventions, group sales, etc.

ELDERLY HOUSING PROJECTS

As post World War II baby boomers age, they will pass from the ranks of middle age to retirees and then to the category known as elderly.

The three basic categories of elderly housing are independent living, semi-independent living and nursing facilities. All three types of facilities encourage guests to bring their own furnishings.

INDEPENDENT LIVING

A number of independent living facilities include the following features.

Individual Units. Many elderly facilities feature luxurious apartments.

Common Areas. An Activity Director is usually on the premises along with an activity program which might include music recitals, bingo, shopping trips, morning coffee hour, religious services, bridge tournaments, craft classes, etc.

There may be a number of common areas so that residents have a choice as to activities.

Restaurant. Many facilities include food services for residents. To maintain reasonable costs some developments include, with the rent, a number of meals per month, such as 20 meals, additional meals would be paid for.

While it can be contracted out, many elderly facilities prefer to provide their own food service to insure nutritional quality and desirability of the meals served and to better meet the individual dietary needs of the residents.

SEMI-INDEPENDENT LIVING

These facilities might be interminglod with indopondent living facilities. Semi-independent living facilities might include the following.

Full-Meal Program. Individuals eat all meals in the restaurant on the premises.

Aide Service. An aide would stop by one or more times a day to check if the resident is taking his or her medication and assist with bathing if required. Each resident would have an emergency call button in their unit.

Housekeeping. Semi-independent living would likely include some level of housekeeping service.

NURSING FACILITIES

These facilities would be monitored by a nursing staff and could include ambulatory and non-ambulatory patients.

Generally, they have activity and food service centers separate from the independent and semi-independent care residents. Nursing facilities would not have locks on the doors. Some units use television monitors and personnel to check on residents. Some nursing facilities consist of one room while others may include a full apartment.

LIFE CARE FACILITIES

LIFE CARE FACILITIES *include independent living, semi-independent living and nursing facilities.* A number of major corporations have entered or are considering entering the life care market.

Some life care facilities required buyers to pay a large sum of money down such as $150,000 per person plus agree to pay a set fee per month which would not change. Because of competition, most life care facilities now offer to return all or most of the initial fee upon death or leaving the facility.

> *Life care provides complete medical facilities using medicare payments.*

THE PROPERTY MANAGER FOR ELDERLY HOUSING

> *Property management for elderly housing requires a property management, recreation, social service, food service and nursing background.*

One manager of an elderly housing unit mentioned that the closest she could equate her position was to the director of a summer camp with bookkeeping responsibilities. Actually, no one person will have all the skills needed. It requires a team effort.

SECURITY FOR THE ELDERLY

Security is a prime concern in elderly housing. Most projects have front desks manned 24 hours. Some have two electric entrance doors which can only be opened by front-desk personnel.

ALTERNATIVE ELDERLY HOUSING

Some apartments and condos offer special services for the elderly. However, they differ primarily in that occupancy is limited to residents 55 and older. The general quiet atmosphere is attractive to many senior citizens. These units consist of total independent living.

There are hotels that have become retirement hotels and rent month-to-month to senior citizens. They generally have food service and include meals as part of the rental fee. The restaurant can operate efficiently at a profit by offering these prepaid meals. Some retirement hotels offer very little as to activities while others offer a great deal. Quality can vary significantly. Some are former middle and low-line commercial hotels while others were once luxury hotels.

Some hotels with low occupancy have turned a number of lower floors into senior housing and use the more desirable upper floors for hotel rentals.

Institutional Management

The armed forces, other federal, state and local governmental agencies as well as charities, colleges and corporations own and operate housing facilities. Managers are generally employees of the appropriate entity. Management includes assigning units, inventory control (furniture where applicable) and maintenance functions. In some cases it also involves collecting rent or fees. Management might include food service or the responsibility to contract for food service.

Marketing of the housing would NOT be a general function of institutional property management.

Some institutional property management involves relatively short-term tenancies. In these case there would be much greater maintenance requirements. In most cases, housekeeping responsibilities would be involved.

Institutional management is more likely to involve a staff of employees rather than contract services. Bottom-line profits are not likely a consideration. However, a prime consideration would be the avoidance of problems reaching up beyond the property manager.

Subsidized Housing

SUBSIDIZED HOUSING *offers below market rent based on either government ownership or government benefits to the developer.* Access to subsidized housing is limited to low income individuals and families.

Some religious and nonprofit organizations also provide subsidized housing. The quantity of such housing is minimal compared to government-involved housing.

Subsidized rent payments are different than subsidized housing. Under various programs, including HUD's Section 8 Assistance program, the tenant's payment is augmented by the government. While the housing is not subsidized, the payment is.

The basis of subsidized housing if often the loan. A below-market rate loan allows an investor to obtain a fair return on his or her investment with a below-market rate rent. The loan is tied to a developer's agreement as to rent.

PROBLEMS OF SUBSIDIZED HOUSING

Subsidized housing creates problems for management, including the following:

Gangs and Crime. Subsidized housing often consist of one-parent households that exist with the financial assistance of the government. The mental state of "What's the use!" allows young people to join gangs for protection and self esteem. Gangs often dominate subsidized housing projects and crime can be rampant. Residents often live in fear. In Chicago and St. Louis, public housing high-rise apartments have been demolished because people were afraid to live in them.

Drug Addiction and Alcoholism. Public housing residents include a high percentage of drug addicts and alcoholics that result from a feeling of hopelessness. People feel trapped in a ghetto and seek the wrong type of relief. This exacerbates the crime problem.

Vandalism and Graffiti. Vandalism and graffiti tend to be the norm rather than the exception in some subsidized housing projects managed by governmental agencies. As units become vacant they are often stripped of plumbing fixtures and appliances.

Inadequate Budget. Property managers who work for government agencies have limited budgets and frequently play a losing "catch-up" game in trying to restore vandalized units, meet legitimate maintenance needs and provide some measure of security.

Impossible Policies. In some public housing projects, social agencies and not property managers determine eligibility to reside in the units. Families with histories of domestic abuse, alcoholism, criminal activities and children who have gang ties are admitted into the projects.

Property management in some housing projects lacks the power to evict problem tenants without bureaucratic approval.

Management Negativism. After battling public housing problems, managers who are public employees often take a "go with the flow" attitude. They give up in much the same way as many of their tenants. Managers see no benefit in agonizing over change without government support.

SOLUTIONS TO PROBLEMS IN PUBLIC HOUSING

Greater Management Authority. Many of the public housing problems would be solved if property managers had the authority to screen tenants, set rules and regulations and evict tenants who failed to follow these rules and regulations.

Where private owners received low interest loans to build low income housing, the problems associated with publicly owned housing are far less evident. Managers in such situations are empowered and use it to protect the property and the residents. We are beginning to see some public housing projects adopting a tough line on a no-drugs policy and holding parents liable for the actions of their children.

Welfare Reform. Welfare reform measures across the country are reducing the number of persons on welfare. Forcing people to work often gives them a feeling of worth where previously there was only despair.

The change in attitude can lead to a desire to be part of the solution rather than part of the problem.

Tenant Organizations. Some public housing projects have developed strong tenant organizations that watch out for the safety of the residents and meet regularly with property management personnel. They report criminal activities and even recommend eviction of problem tenants. Vandalism, graffiti and crime have decreased appreciably in some projects.

Privatization. Privatization of public housing projects has been proposed as a solution to many of the problems associated with this type of housing. Privatization with requirements as to rent limits would result in management incentives to protect the property and solve the problems that have plagued public housing. Decisions would be made by trained managers rather than social workers or bureaucrats.

Sell to Residents. In a few trial cases, public housing units have been sold to the residents with positive results. However, it has taken the units out of the inventory for future low income people.

Elimination of Public Housing. This proposal sounds harsh but actually has great merit. Under the Voucher and Section 8 systems, persons on public aid can rent anywhere. They are not restricted to what have become racial ghettos in many cities. If there is a housing need and sufficient public assistance in the form of vouchers, private developers will fulfill that need in a far more economical manner than could government (See *California Real Estate Economics* by Walt Huber. Educational Textbook Co. **www.textbooks.com**).

www.textbooks.com
(Educational Textbook Company)

Time Shares

A **TIME SHARE** *is a divided interest in a unit where a participating owner has exclusive use to the unit during a designated period of time.* The ownership could be in fee simple or it might be a leasehold interest for a designated number of years.

Time shares tend to be vacation-type units in vacation-type locations. This results in very intensive use of the unit as well as the common areas.

Typically, time shares are sold for 50 weeks a year allowing a two-week period in the "off season" for refurbishing the units.

MANAGEMENT DUTIES

Housekeeping. The property manager must supervise cleaning and preparation of a unit between occupants of that unit. Unlike hotel and motel housekeeping, the work is all scheduled for the same turnover day. Therefore, housekeeping requires a large crew of part-time workers or a cleaning contract to have these housekeeping duties completed.

Units are typically much larger than hotel or motel rooms and contain kitchens and sometimes multiple baths, so cleaning each unit is time consuming. Appliances need to be cleaned so that the unit is in pristine condition for the next occupant.

Inventory Control. Kitchen and decorator items tend to disappear when the unit is vacated. This happens because many units are rented or exchanged or owners have guests and sometimes items are broken and thrown out. At times decorator items may be exchanged for one of lesser value. Owners sometimes forget that they are only owners for one or two weeks of the year and exercise full ownership prerogatives.

> *Inventory checks are necessary, as whatever is NOT nailed down tends to get lost.*

If an item on the inventory list is missing, the previous occupant should be notified immediately and asked to return the item or pay for the value. Never accuse the person of theft. It might have been "inadvertently" packed with their belongings when they left.

New Occupants. Occupants should pick up keys at the management office. A key deposit should be obtained to insure their return. Security is compromised when keys are not returned.

A copy of the rules and any schedule of recreational or other activities should be given along with the keys to the unit. Because many time shares belong to time share trade organizations, rules should be available in German, Spanish, French and Japanese.

Maintenance of Buildings and Grounds. The time share manager would be responsible for maintenance of the buildings and grounds by either employees or contracted staff. Pride of ownership is important to time share owners so units must look like a luxury resort. This can be difficult because common areas are subject to intense use.

Recreation Director. Property management personnel are responsible for recreational activities at many time shares. They might schedule tours, golf tournaments, tennis tournaments, talent shows, theme parties, barbecues, etc.

The purpose is to have "happy campers." Owners will want to come back and not resent paying their monthly fees. In addition, when residents get to know each other, they develop friendships which help to make their stay enjoyable.

Collection of Fees. Time share owners pay a homeowner association fee to cover housekeeping maintenance, taxes, insurance and refurbishing of the units. This fee may be collected monthly or quarterly.

This is a problem with 100 units sold in 50 separate weekly increments since it means 5,000 owner statements and collections.

Rentals. Time share management may also provide a rental service for owners. Rental fees can be 25 percent to 33 1/3 percent of gross rent. A property damage bond is collected at the time of rental. This fee would be returned to the renter after the unit is vacated and inventory is taken. Some management offices will send out notices of other units available during "their week" to owners along with their statements or receipts. Friends often rent during the same week or weeks as the owners.

Another rental method is to notify owners of the same unit that the week prior or after their week is vacant. Owners can then double their vacation stay.

When there are many rentals available, advertising in newspaper classifieds using an 800 number can be effective in areas where many of the owners have permanent residences.

Other Duties. Budgeting and record keeping are similar to those duties of a condominium association manager.

Resales. Some property management offices list resales of units that they manage. Owners may be shocked to find that they must take a significant discount to sell their time shares. Resales of times shares regularly sell for 50 percent or even less than the original sale price.

Techniques used for renting a time share can be effectively used to sell units.

MANAGEMENT PROBLEM AREAS

Time share problem areas are similar to those associated with condominium management. Some of the problems become more intensified as to time shares.

Rules and Regulations. Times shares are vacation units and while some occupants do not go to extremes others do. Noise, drunkenness, the use of foul language, monopolizing recreational facilities, etc., are part of the everyday management problems. Calling the police is an option. However, managers should try to solve problems tactfully and without making the offender "lose face."

Collections. Some time share owners who have not finished paying for their units are often delinquent in making payments even though the association bylaws probably provide for late penalties. The lender, if there is one, will be reluctant to pay the fees or foreclose because of the questionable value of the unit. In some cases, lack of collections resulted in time shares not having sufficient funds to properly service the units. One desert time share development that has had many vacancies in the past few years is scheduled to have all the units sold at a tax sale.

You don't want to be a part of management if the development does NOT have sufficient monies to cover maintenance, insurance or taxes.

The rewards would be almost nothing and the aggravation and liability could be excessive.

Mobile Home Parks

***MOBILE HOME PARK MANAGEMENT** consists of leasing spaces for a tenant's mobile home, or manufactured home, which is a term the mobile home industry prefers.* Larger parks should have a resident manager.

In California, parks with 50 or more spaces must have a resident manager.

Besides renting space and collecting rents, management may sell utilities to the tenants and in some large parks cable television. Management is also responsible for maintenance of common areas which may include recreational facilities and a clubhouse as well as the enforcement of park rules.

MOBILE HOME RESIDENCY LAW

State statutes are important to managers of mobile home parks. The purpose of the statutes is to protect the rights of mobile home park owners as well as owners of mobile homes.

The protection offered mobile home owners under the Mobile Home Residency Laws is necessary because of the fact that mobile homes are really NOT mobile.

To move a mobile home will generally result in substantial damage to the unit as well as significant moving and relocation costs. The majority of mobile homes removed from parks are never again used as residences.

The following are requirements of the California Mobile Home Residency Law. A number of other states have similar requirements.

Lease Requirements. Every rental agreement must include:

1. The term of the tenancy and the rent.
2. The rules and regulations of the park.
3. A copy of the Mobile Home Residency Law (it may be an attachment).
4. A requirement that management maintain the improvements of common areas in good working condition.

   Due to an unforeseen breakdown, management has a reasonable period to repair. A reasonable period shall be as soon as possible in situations affecting health and safety but not to exceed 30 days except where demanding circumstances justify a delay.
5. A description of the physical improvements.
6. A listing of services to be provided and will continue to be offered for the term of the tenancy as well as any fees.
7. A provision allowing management to charge a reasonable fee for maintenance of the site where the mobile home is situated if the owner fails to maintain the site and unit in accordance with park rules. Before management can perform the maintenance, the owner must be given 14 days notice for compliance and the notice must state specific conditions to be corrected.
8. All other provisions of the space rental must be set forth.

Cancellation Rights. At the time the rental agreement is first offered to the owner, management gives the owner notice that the owner has 30 days to inspect the rental agreement and can void the agreement in writing within 72 hours of signing. If management fails to provide this cancellation information, the homeowner can void the agreement at his or her option upon discovering of this cancellation right.

Automatic Extensions. A lease cannot authorize automatic extensions or renewals at the sole option of either management or of the homeowner.

Exempt From Local Rent Control. The original rental agreement is exempt from local ordinances that establish maximum rents. If the rental agreement is not extended and no agreement over 12 months in duration is entered into, then the last month's rent shall be the base rent for application of local rent control.

Note: The original lease is exempt from rent control, but if the tenant does not extend or enter into a new lease, the last rent under the lease is the base rent for rent control.

Twelve-Month Lease Entitlement. The tenant can request up to a 12-month lease. The tenant is entitled to the same rent as offered by the lessor for a longer-term lease or being offered for a month-to-month lease.

Note: Tenants need NOT accept long-term leases offered by management.

Liability Insurance. Homeowners shall not be required to obtain liability insurance in order to use common areas.

Amendments to Park Rules. Amendments to rules require:

1. A written notice be provided to homeowners at least 10 days prior to a meeting setting forth changes.
2. A meeting with park homeowners for consultation between management and homeowners.
3. That rules may be changed with the consent or without the consent of homeowners upon written notice to the homeowners of not less than six months.

For regulations applicable to recreational facilities, the notice must be at least 60 days.

4. Rules enacted without consultation with homeowners are void and unenforceable.

Right of Entry. Mobile home park management has no right of entry to a mobile home without prior written consent of the owner. If such consent is given, it can be revoked in writing at any time. However, the park does have the right of entry upon the land for maintenance of utilities and park maintenance or if the homeowner fails to maintain the grounds. In the event of an emergency or when the resident has abandoned the mobile home, the park management may enter the mobile home.

Owner Disclosure. Upon the request of a resident, the park management must disclose the name, business address and business telephone number of the park owner.

Rent Increase Notice. Notices as to rent increases must be given at least 90 days prior to the increase.

Unauthorized Fees. Mobile home owners shall not be charged fees other than for rent, utilities and incidental charges for services actually rendered.

Homeowners should not be charged a fee for services rendered that are not listed in the rental agreement unless given a 60-day notice before such fee is imposed.

Pets. No fee may be charged because the homeowner has a pet unless the park provides special facilities or services for pets. The fee charged must be related to the cost of maintenance of the facilities or services and the number of pets kept in the park.

If new rules prohibit pets, the rule generally cannot be applied retroactively, however, a lost or deceased pet cannot be replaced with another pet by an owner.

Guests. A homeowner cannot be charged a fee for a guest who does not stay more than 20 consecutive days or more than 30 days in a calendar year.

No fee shall be charged if a senior homeowner shares a unit with a person giving live-in health or supportive service in accordance with a treatment plan prepared by a physician.

Family Size. Homeowner shall not be charged a fee based on the number of residents in the homeowner's immediate family. Immediate family means homeowner, spouse, parents, children, and grandchildren under the age of 18.

Utility Meter. When management provides submeter utility services, the billing must include meter readings. Management must also post the prevailing residential utility rate schedule of the serving utility. Utility fees must be stated separately on billings.

Security Deposits. Security deposits may be demanded only upon initial occupancy. (No additional security deposits can be demanded.)

For security deposits collected after January 1, 1989, the homeowner can request their return providing the homeowner has paid park rent and other charges within 5 days of due date over the 12 consecutive months prior to the request.

Termination of Tenancy. Management cannot terminate a tenancy or refuse to renew a tenancy except for the following reasons:

1. Failure of resident to comply with local ordinance or state law regarding mobile homes within a reasonable time after notification of violation.

2. Conduct which constitutes a substantial annoyance to other homeowners or residents.

3. Conviction for prostitution or a felony controlled substance offense anywhere within the park. However, the tenancy cannot be terminated if the person convicted of the offense has permanently vacated and does not subsequently reoccupy the mobile home.

4. Failure to comply with reasonable park rules within seven days after written notice of violation. No notice is required if the party has been given notice of the violation of the same rule on three or more occasions within a 12-month period.

5. Nonpayment of rent, utility or reasonable incidental charges. The park must give a three-day notice (after a five-day grace period). Payment during the three-day period will cure the deficiency. If the homeowner fails to cure the deficiency, a 60-day notice is required to terminate the tenancy.

The legal owner of the mobile home is entitled to notice of the default and can cure the deficiency within 30 days of mailing of the notice.

6. Condemnation of the park.

7. Change of use for the park. However, management must give 15 day's written notice of any appearance before a government body requesting permits or use change.

After all permits have been received, homeowners must be given six month's notice as to termination.

Note: A lease cannot be terminated because management wants the site for a person who has purchased a mobile home from the park owner.

Abandoned Mobile Homes. A park may post a notice of belief of abandonment on a mobile home that is unoccupied, rent has not been paid for 60 days and a reasonable person would believe it to be abandoned.

After 30 days from posting the notice the park may petition the court for a declaration of abandonment.

If the park management shows, by a preponderance of evidence that the home is abandoned and no party shows an interest in the mobile home, the court will enter a judgment of abandonment.

Management must enter and inventory the mobile home within 10 days of judgment of abandonment and post and mail a notice of intent to sell the abandoned mobile home and its contents. At any time prior to the sale any person having a right to possession may remove the mobile home from the premises after paying rents and other charges (including court charges).

Within 10 days of notice of sale, management may conduct a public sale of the mobile home and its contents. Management has the right to bid at the sale.

Any amount received over the amount that management is entitled to shall be paid to the county treasurer.

Advertising - For Sale. A homeowner has the right to post a for sale sign on the side of a mobile home facing the street (not to exceed 24 inches wide and 36 inches high).

Showing - For Sale. Management shall not prohibit agents from showing a unit that is for sale.

Transfer Fees. No transfer fees may be charged to heirs, joint tenants or personal representatives of a deceased owner or their agent.

The only charge management can impose on a purchase would be for a credit check.

Removal Upon Sale. Upon sale of a mobile home, management cannot require that the mobile home be removed from the park unless it is more than 25 years old or it is in a significant rundown condition. The management would have the burden of demonstrating that it is in a significantly rundown condition or in disrepair.

Prior Approval of Purchaser. Management may require prior approval of a mobile home purchaser when the mobile home is to remain in the park. Approval cannot be denied if the purchaser is financially able to pay park rent and charges unless, based on prior tenancies, management reasonably determines that the purchaser will not comply with park rules and regulations.

Within 15 days of receipt of information requested by the park from the prospective purchaser, the park shall notify the prospective purchaser in writing of acceptance or rejection.

Rejection for any reason other than credit or prior tenant problems could obligate the park to damages.

Any fees collected for a credit report must be credited to the purchaser's first month's rent. If the prospective purchaser is rejected, the credit fee must be refunded to the prospective purchaser.

Note: This differs from the nonrefundable credit fees allowed for apartment rentals.

New Rental Agreement. A purchaser of a mobile home must execute a rental agreement with the park. Failure to complete the rental agreement would subject the purchaser to an unlawful detainer action.

Age Requirement of Purchaser. Purchasers must meet the age requirement, if residency is limited to seniors, in accordance with the Fair Housing Amendments Act of 1988.

Nonwaiver of Rights. Lease agreements cannot require a purchaser or homeowner to waive any rights under the Mobile Home Residency Law.

Rights of Heirs to Sell. If the heirs or personal representatives of a deceased have paid rents and fees as they have accrued, they can sell the mobile home. Otherwise the park can insist on its removal. The heirs or representatives may also replace the mobile home with another mobile home prior to sale.

Lienholders' Right to Sell. Lienholders who foreclose can sell the mobile home if all of the rents and fees were paid as they accrued.

Sale of Park - Offer to Homeowners. The park owner shall notify the resident tenant organization, if they have formed an entity for the purpose of buying the park, at least 30 days but not more than one year prior to listing a park for sale or offering it for sale.

Managements Failure to Maintain. After 30-day prior notice by a homeowner, an action for failure to maintain physical improvements or reduction in service may be commenced by a homeowner. The prevailing party would be entitled to attorney fees.

If the failure or action of management was willful, the court may award compensating damages as well as $500 for each willful violation.

Failure to provide and maintain physical improvements would be considered a public nuisance.

Restraining Order. Management may obtain an injunction against a tenant for a violation of a reasonable rule or regulation.

Tenant Organization. Management cannot prohibit the organization of homeowner groups. Homeowner groups must be allowed to hold meetings in public areas within the park, such as a recreation hall.

COURT DETERMINATIONS

Courts have tended to side with the owners of mobile homes rather than park owners where fairness has been an issue.

Case Example

***Rancho Santa Paula Mobile Home Park Ltd v. Evans* (1994) 26 C.A. 4th 1139**

A mobile home park issued new rules requiring occupancy by a registered owner of the mobile home. This clause effectively prohibited subleasing. The Court of Appeals, in reversing the trial court, determined that the total ban on subleasing was unreasonable and therefore unenforceable.

CONDO - MOBILE HOME PARK

Some mobile home parks are owned by the homeowners. Each homeowner owns his or her site and the common areas are owned as tenants in common with the other owners.

In such a situation the property manager assumes a different management role. In effect the property manager is a condominium association manager (covered earlier in this chapter) but the condo units just happen to be mobile homes.

Some of these parks resulted from developer plans when the lots were sold as a condominium. Others were mobile home parks converted to condominiums by owners or purchased by mobile home owners who converted the park to condominiums.

Recreational Vehicle Parks

RECREATIONAL VEHICLES are motor homes, travel trailers, truck campers, camping trailers and other wheeled vehicles intended for recreational or camping use.

A number of states have laws for recreational vehicles similar to mobile home park legislation. The California Recreational Vehicle Park Occupancy Law covers elements of recreational park management.

CALIFORNIA RECREATIONAL VEHICLE PARK OCCUPANCY LAW

The law provides for the following:

Removal of Units. A defaulting owner's unit may be removed from the park after a 72-hour notice is served upon the unit owner. The owner can cure any violations during the 72-hour period.

If an occupant cannot move the vehicle because of physical incapacity or the vehicle is not motorized, the occupant shall have no less than seven days to move it from the park.

The park owner can have the unit taken by the police or sheriff to the nearest secured storage yard.

> *Reasonable care must be taken for the removal and the appropriate law enforcement agency must be notified of the removal.*

Termination of Tenancy. The owner shall not terminate a tenancy or refuse to renew a tenancy unless written notice is given. As to this notice:

1. It need not state the cause for termination if the tenant has resided in the park for less than nine months and a 30-day notice is given.

2. The cause of termination must be stated for tenants who have resided on the property for nine months or more. The causes that apply to termination of mobile home leases also apply to recreational vehicles.

3. The notice can be given by the tenant in accordance with park rules.

Recreational vehicle parks have a lien on the recreational vehicle and its contents for unpaid charges of a defaulting owner.

Farm/Ranch Management

Agricultural management is highly specialized.

While it involves maintenance and improvements to buildings and fences and may involve leasing as a lessor or lessee, management's duties tend to focus on the agricultural aspects. These duties would include soil management, economic decisions as to crops, labor management, equipment purchases or lease and maintenance and other farming activities.

CORPORATE OWNED FARMS/RANCHES

CORPORATE MANAGEMENT *deals with large farming or ranching activities.* It is likely to involve leased land as well as corporate owned land. Decisions as to management are primarily based on economics. The corporate owners are interested in the bottom line—profits. Corporate farm managers customarily have the education and training in both agriculture and accounting.

LENDER-OWNED FARMS

These are farms owned by lenders due to foreclosures. Generally, the lenders are interested in holding the farms only until they can be sold. However, they may wish to hold them until the market improves so they can recover their money.

While there now are far fewer farm foreclosures, problems still arise because of debt, weather, etc. that result in foreclosures.

Lenders who take back farms want the manager to protect the physical improvements and hopefully obtain some income. Since the lenders seldom want to take farming risks, they will generally lease the land one season at a time. Structures will either be boarded up or rented. The managers job would be in handling leases and seeing that the status quo is maintained.

GENTLEMEN FARMS

The owners of so-called **GENTLEMEN FARMS** *are seeking a home on a farm, a rural lifestyle and pride of ownership, but they do not wish to actually labor in the fields.*

The gentlemen farmer gains satisfaction by riding around his or her property and gazing at the land. Therefore, appearance is rated at least as high, and often higher than economics. Gentlemen farms can be orchards, ranches, or just general farming. Formerly, the great interest in California was in avocado groves but the current interest is in vineyards and wineries. In Kentucky, gentlemen farms are likely to be horse ranches.

While profit may be secondary to many gentlemen farmers, they want to be seeking a profit or the IRS will not allow the tax deductions which farmers can obtain.

Managers of foreclosed farms and gentlemen farms might handle farms of a number of owners while corporate property managers customarily handle farmers of just one owner.

Docking Facilities

Property management does not have to involve real property. Managing a marina requires the same management skills as managing commercial and residential properties.

If the marina includes a launch ramp, repair facilities, fuel services, shops and/or restaurants, they should generally be separately leased. The person who leases the repair facilities generally would also lease the fuel service and launch ramp. Generally, you would want a minimum rent plus a percentage on launching fees, fuel sold and repairs. If there is dry storage, the responsibility should logically fall to the on-site manager who would lease the boat slips.

Rent is usually based on size of the slip.

Utilities to slips can be and should be metered, especially if live-aboards are allowed or prevalent. Live-aboard slips can rent for significantly higher rents than slips which don't allow occupancy. Local zoning affects your right to allow live-aboards.

You will encounter some live aboard activity even though you may not allow it. Normally it is not worthwhile to make an issue of it unless there are complaints.

The biggest problem you will encounter in managing dock space is interpersonal.

Some owners will use their boats for constant parties. Loud music and raucous behavior can make life miserable for other boat owners. Therefore, restrictions as to noise and behavior must be strictly enforced. Owners cannot be allowed to throw bottles, cans and garbage into the water nor empty their sewage into the harbor.

Medical Offices (MDs)

Managing medical offices differs from other office management in both tenant selection and cleaning requirements.

Medical office rentals usually include cleaning services. The standard of cleaning required is normally much higher than for other office space.

Many MDs only want other MDs in the complex because much of their clientele is through referrals from other MDs. Leases frequently require that a stated percentage of the rental space (which is often 100 percent) will be rented to other Mds.

The most desirable medical buildings are those that are in close proximity to other medical buildings and hospitals.

Mini-Storage

Mini-storage facilities are usually the size of a garage or smaller and rent primarily by the month. The facility would be equipped with a light and possibly an interior electrical outlet with a water faucet on the outside of the structure. The units usually come equipped with a roll-up lockable door. A single restroom might be located in the office building on the premises.

Mini-storage facilities are used by individuals who just have too many possessions as well as businesses. Better facilities are usually fenced and have exterior lighting. These facilities are only open for use during designated hours. Normally, a fee is charged for after-hour use.

Unclaimed property can be sold to cover storage costs providing the statutory notices are complied with.

Storage Yards

STORAGE YARDS *are fenced and secured exterior storage areas.* Some grounds may have gravel while others may be paved. Space is rented for storing recreational vehicles, cars, trucks, boats and heavy equipment.

Management is almost identical to the management of mini-storage space. In fact many mini-storage facilities offer contiguous storage yards.

CHAPTER 7 SUMMARY

A number of property management situations present different problems and sometimes require special skills.

SROs are single-room occupancy units. They very often were former hotels and motels that have been converted for long-term residential use. SROs are really mini-apartments without kitchens and present the same management problems and considerations as apartment dwellings.

Condominium association management differs from other property management in that renting is not the primary purpose of management and the manager deals with a Board of Directors rather than an individual owner. A problem in management is that different members of the Board have different agendas. However, management must strive to carry out the wishes of the Board.

Resort-area management involves renting and managing homes and condominiums for monthly or seasonal tenants.

Clothing optional apartments appeal to nudists. They command premium rents and must be units offering privacy from outside viewing.

Single-family dwellings are often managed. They must be carefully watched as there is no resident manager.

Short-term residential properties are a cross between furnished apartments and motels/hotels. They are rented by the week or month, often for business purposes.

Elderly housing management is growing as our population is graying. The three types of elderly housing are:

1. Independent living.
2. Semi-independent living.
3. Nursing facilities.

Life care facilities are those where the resident is guaranteed that he or she will be taken care of even if nursing care is required.

Institutional management involves handling property management for governmental agencies, the military, colleges, charities and corporations. Managers are usually employees of the owning institution.

Subsidized housing is low income housing that is either government owned or housing where owners receive benefits to offer below-market interest rates. Public housing projects have been plagued by problems of crime, gangs, drug addition, alcoholism, vandalism and graffiti. Management has been hindered by inadequate budgets and responsibility without the authority to effectuate change.

Time shares are a divided interest in a unit where the time share owner owns a block of time (usually one week) in a specified unit. These projects are recreationally oriented and are subject to intensive use. The management is concerned with a number of unusual problems associated with a constant change of tenants. These include disappearance of personal property from units, violation of rules by tenants, necessity for weekly housekeeping for all units over a short span of time, recreational leader responsibilities, collection of fees from what would be thousands of owners, etc.

Mobile home park management involves leasing spaces. The manager must understand and comply with any applicable Mobile Home Residency Law which can govern just about every aspect of management.

Recreational vehicle park management is similar to mobile home park management except the stays are relatively short because the units can readily be relocated. The management is subject to the Recreational Vehicle Park Occupancy Law.

Farm/ranch management is very specialized in that it requires an expertise as to agriculture as well as property management knowledge. Properties likely to be managed are:

1. Corporate owned farms and ranches.
2. Lender owned property.
3. Gentlemen farms/ranches.

The goals of the various types of owners vary from lenders who are primarily interested in protecting the property, corporations which are interested primarily in profit and gentlemen farmers who want nice looking facilities as a prime objective.

Managers of docking facilities, such as marinas and yacht clubs, are involved in the rental of water space. Many of the skills required for managing other types of property, such as condominiums, are applicable to this type of management.

Medical office management differs from other office management in the degree of cleaning expected as well as tenant selection.

CLASS DISCUSSION TOPICS

1. Are there any hotel and motel units in your area that should convert to single-room occupancy? Why?

2. How many separate condominium projects do you estimate are within 10 miles of your location? What would you estimate the average number of units per development is? What do you think the average management fee per unit would be? What do you estimate are total management fees for a particular condominium association located within 10 miles of your location?

3. Do you know of any clothing optional apartments in your area? Which apartment complex in your area, if any, would be physically suited for a clothing optional operation?

4. Classify the larger elderly housing projects (government and privately owned) in your area as independent living, semi-independent living and nursing facilities.

5. Identify property in your area that would involve institutional management.

6. Identify subsidized housing projects in your area. Do they have problems? What are they?

7 Identify any time share projects in your area. What do you suppose would be the problems associated with those projects?

8. If you live or have lived in a mobile home park how would you rate management? Why?

CHAPTER 7 QUIZ

1. SRO stands for:

    A. selective residential opportunities

    B. single room occupancy

    C. subsidized residential occupancy

    D. semi resort operation

2. A property manager who was hired by a Board of Directors would MOST LIKELY be involved in:

    A. the management of single-family dwelling

    B. clothing optional management

    C. condominium association management

    D. medical office management

3. Hotel management differs from condominium management as to:

    A. housekeeping supervisory duties
    B. food service supervision
    C. both A and B
    D. neither A nor B

4. Housing where a resident has his or her own apartment without nursing, health services or food services would be BEST described as a(n):

    A. independent living facility
    B. semi-independent living facility
    C. nursing facility
    D. life care facility

5. Facilities for the elderly that provide all levels of care and charge a high entry fee are MOST LIKELY to be a(n):

    A. nursing home
    B. SRO
    C. independent living facility
    D. life care facility

6. Problems confronting publicly owned, low-income housing, include:

    A. vandalism and graffiti
    B. crime
    C. drug and alcohol abuse
    D. all of the above

7. Managers of government owned projects are hampered in their operation because:

    A. they often lack the ability to choose tenants and evict tenants
    B. of budgetary restraints
    C. of gang activity
    D. of all of the above

8. A fractionalized interest in a specific dwelling unit would BEST describe a:

    A. cooperative
    B. time share
    C. condominium
    D. mobile home lease

9. What type of owner would want his or her farm manager to place a greater emphasis on appearance than on financial return?

    A. Corporate owner

    B. Gentleman farmer

    C. Family farmer

    D. Lender-owner

10. Which of the following would be a duty of condominium association management?

    A. Management of insurance

    B. Supervision of maintenance

    C. Contracting for services

    D. All of the above

Answers: 1. B; 2. C; 3. C; 4. C; 5. A; 6. D; 7. D; 8. B; 9. B; 10. D

Liability and Risk Management

KEY WORDS AND TERMS

Binder
Boiler Insurance
Burglary and Theft Insurance
Business Interruption Insurance
Co-insurance Primary Policy
Comprehensive General Liability
Deductibles
Dram Shop Liability
Earthquake Insurance
Employee
Errors and Omissions Insurance
Extended Coverage Policy (Fire Insurance)
Fidelity Bonds
Flood Insurance
Government Seizure
Hazardous Waste
Homeowner Policy
Independent Contractor
Inland Marine Insurance
Innkeeper's Liability
Insurable Interest
Key Man Insurance
Leasehold Insurance

Liability Insurance
Libel
Medical Pay Coverage
Owners, Landlords and Tenants Liability
Partnership Insurance
Proximate Cause
Record Insurance
Rental Interruption Insurance
Replacement Cost
Respondeat Superior
Risk Management
Robbery Policies
Secondary Policy
Self-Insured
Slander
Standard Policy (Fire Insurance)
Strict Liability
Surety Bonds
Three D Policy
Umbrella Policy
Worker's Compensation Insurance

LEARNING OBJECTIVES

In this chapter you will learn about the liability as to personal injury and property loss that goes with property ownership and management as well as other risks that owners, tenants and managers are exposed to.

You will learn about evaluating risks and making decisions as to transferring risks to others using insurance. You will learn about the various types of insurance protection available.

Liability

Owners of property are liable for their own wrongful and negligent actions.

They can also be held liable for the actions of others. Besides actual wrongful acts, they can even be liable for failure to take action.

STRICT LIABILITY

STRICT LIABILITY *of an owner is liability for an injury to a person or damages to a property without being at fault.* The concept of strict liability would make an owner liable for an injury even though the owner was not negligent or acted in good faith.

The case of Becker v. IRM Corp. (1985) 38 C. 3d 454 held that a residential landlord had strict liability for latent property defects. In this case a recent purchaser of a rental property was held liable when a tenant fell against the shower door which was not tempered glass. The California Supreme Court held the landlord to be strictly liable and the fact that the landlord was not aware of the defect did not excuse his liability.

In a rare reversal, the California Supreme Court reversed the IRM decision in Peterson v. Superior Court (1995) 10 C. 4th 1185. The court held that the strict liability of landlords in the IRM case was a mistake.

California law now holds that proof of a landlord's negligence is required for a landlord to be liable for damages or injury. Other states generally follow similar reasoning.

INJURY AND PROPERTY DAMAGE

A person can be negligent without having any liability. To be held liable, an owner not only has to be negligent but the negligence must be the cause (proximate cause) of an injury or property damage.

A woman recently visited a tort's attorney. She had been the guest in the home of a wealthy charity fund raiser. A small shelf on the wall gave way and an antique Toby Mug fell from the shelf and shattered on her head. She wanted to know what she could expect to receive for damages. When asked the extent of her injuries, she replied that she wasn't injured at all. The falling mug didn't even cause any appreciable pain but she was mildly startled.

While there was negligence, since the shelf would not have fallen if it had been properly attached to the wall, there was no injury. The attorney informed the guest that owners are not liable for their negligence unless the negligence caused an injury.

Without an injury there can be NO recovery.

LIABILITY FOR EMPLOYEES AND AGENTS

Owners of property can be held liable for actions of their employees and agents within the scope of the employment or agency. The **ENGLISH DOCTRINE OF RESPONDEAT SUPERIOR** *is that a master is liable for the actions of his servants while carrying on duties for his or her master.*

Within the Scope of Employment

If an agent or employee had an accident during his or her off hours, the principal or employer would not be liable even if there was negligence. The negligence was not within the scope of the agency or employment. However, if the agent or employee put too much chlorine in the swimming pool causing several tenants to suffer eye injuries, the property owner would be liable. The negligence of the agent or employee occurred within the scope of employment or agency.

Slander and Libel

"Sticks and stones may break my bones but names will never hurt me" is not a true statement. Words, either written or oral, can result in monetary damages as well as damages to a person's reputation.

A published (written) false statement would be **LIBEL**, and could result in damages being awarded to an injured party. If the statement was merely careless or made based on a false belief, then damages would be limited to compensation for the resulting injury. If the false statement were intentionally made by one who knows it to be false, then punitive damages could be awarded that far exceed actual damages. Punitive damages are awarded to punish a wrongdoer for outrageous action.

SLANDER *would be verbal.* Assume in providing information about a former tenant the resident property manager told a prospective employer that "She's a hopeless alcoholic, her garbage was always overflowing with empty vodka bottles. She's also a tramp. She would bring a different boyfriend or customer home every night."

Assume the property manager had merely confused the person inquired about with another former tenant. It would nevertheless be slander. There would be property owner and property manager liability for the damages that resulted from the careless false statements. If the resident manager had a personal vendetta against the former tenant and made those statements with the knowledge that they were false, then the damages awarded could be punitive as well as compensatory.

> *Because of the danger of slanderous or libelous statements, some property management firms inform resident managers that they are never to discuss tenants and former tenants with anyone other than their supervisor.*

Some property management offices take the position that their records are privileged and will only be available to others upon a court order.

LIABILITY AS TO INDEPENDENT CONTRACTORS

As a general rule, persons are not liable for injuries or damages which result from the negligence of independent contractors. Independent contractors are hired to accomplish a task and are not under the direct supervision of the person who hired them. In property management, most service providers are independent contractors rather than employees. The Maehl v. O'Brien case is an exception to the general rule that there is no liability for torts of an independent contractor.

Case Example

Maehl v. O'Brien (1991) 231 C.A. 3rd 674

Plaintiff, who was an employee of an independent contractor, was injured in the felling of a tree on the defendant's property.

The court pointed out that while a property owner is not ordinarily liable for injuries caused by the negligence of an independent contractor, there is an exception to that rule. That exception being a contractor hired to perform dangerous work that is likely to cause physical harm. The owner was held liable for the injuries.

Note: In employing independent contractors, a property manager should insist that the independent contractor provide evidence of adequate liability insurance coverage.

LIABILITY FOR ACTIONS OF OTHER TENANTS

As expressed in the Portillo v. Aiossa case, an owner can be held liable for acts of a tenant, a tenant's pet, or a tenant's child if the property owner knew of the dangerous propensities of the tenant, pet or child and failed to take reasonable measures to protect others from the danger. The problem must have been foreseeable.

Case Example

Portillo v. Aiossa (1994) 27 C.A. 4th 1128

An owner leased a property to a tenant who operated a liquor store. The tenant kept a German Shepherd (guard dog) on the premises and posted a sign warning customers of the dog's mean disposition. (This was apparently to deter robberies.) A person delivering liquor to the property was seriously injured when the dog attacked him. He sued the landlord.

The trial court found that while the landlord did not have actual knowledge of the dog's disposition (the dog had previously bitten someone), he could have learned about it by a reasonable inspection of the premises. The trial court awarded the plaintiff $300,000. The landlord's defense that he had no actual knowledge was not enough. The landlord was held to a duty to reasonably inspect the premises. The landlord allowed a dangerous situation with the dog kept in an establishment open to the public.

Note: This case imposes a duty upon a landlord to make a reasonable inspection of the property. If the dog was not present during inspections by the owner then the owner would appear to have a defense against liability.

People sue in the direction of money. This is why landlords are often sued. Tenants may not have the resources or the insurance to satisfy a claim by an injured party.

LIABILITY OFF THE PREMISES

An owner generally does not have any liability outside the perimeter of his or her property.

CRIMINAL ACTIVITY

If you believe that criminal activity is being conducted at a property you manage, it is imperative that you make your thoughts known to the applicable law enforcement authorities. Be completely factual as to the reasons for your beliefs. However, do not share these beliefs with any other person, since, should you be wrong, you may have slandered your tenant which could lead to civil penalties.

If you knowingly allow criminal activity to take place at a property you manage as the owner's representative, you could subject an owner to forfeiture of his or her property and possibly monetary damages.

Case Example

Davis v. Gomez (1989) 207 C.A. 3rd 1401

A tenant began acting strangely. She talked to herself and seemed to be casting spells on others. Other tenants knew she had a gun in her apartment and complaints were made to the manager about her bizarre behavior. The tenant later shot and killed another tenant whose parents then sued the landlord for the wrongful death.

In ruling for the landlord the trial court pointed out that a landlord has no duty to check out the background of a prospective tenant. They also pointed out that a landlord was not in a position to evaluate her as a psychotic. While the landlord could have evicted the tenant, a wrongful eviction would subject the landlord to damages. In this case there was nothing foreseeable as to the murder as she had never before been violent. The landlord was held not to be liable.

Note: The Americans With Disabilities Act now applies to mental problems. If, in a similar situation today, a landlord evicted a tenant with this type of behavior, the landlord would probably be subject to significant penalties.

Case Example

Rosenbaum v. Security Pacific Corp. (1996) 43 C.A. 4th 1084

A tenant was afraid to park her car in her assigned garage space because of what she considered inadequate lighting. Because of the fear for her safety, she parked it on the street. One night, after parking her car on the street adjoining her apartment, she was robbed and shot in the head.

The Court of Appeals affirmed the trial court in determining that a landlord was not liable for criminal activity off the premises.

Note: The landlord could have been liable if the assault had taken place in the garage area and inadequate lighting was a contributing factor to the crime.

Case Example

Alcaraz v. Vece (1997) 14 C. 4th 1149

An apartment owner maintained an adjoining city property (10 foot strip off the road). A tenant was injured when he tripped over a depressed meter box in the lawn and fell.

The California Supreme Court held that since the landlord exercised control over the strip of land, the landlord had a duty of care as to the hazard which would be to warn tenants of the dangers.

Case Example

Southland Corp. v. Superior Court (1988) 203 C.A. 3rd 656

A customer was assaulted in a vacant lot adjacent to a 7-11 store. The lot was not controlled by the store but customers often parked there. The store's lease provided for nonexclusive use of the lot for extra parking. The 7-11 store did not discourage customers from parking on the lot.

The lot had become a hangout for youths. Store employees had called the police on several occasions to remove loiterers.

The court held that while a property owner or tenant is generally not liable for the condition of property it does not own, possess or control, the tenant in this case exercised sufficient control to charge them with a duty of care. If that duty was breached then the tenant could be liable for resulting damages.

Note: In this case the area was not properly lighted. Since the store used the lot, their duty of care could include lighting the lot.

As a property manager you should be aware that owners can be liable for property outside their premises if they assert control over it. If such is the case, you want to make certain that liability insurance coverage will cover owner liability for injuries occurring on this property.

Another exception as to owner liability off the premises is pointed out in the following case.

Case Example

McDaniel v. Sunset Manor Co. (1990) 220 C.A. 3rd 1

A landlord constructed over 1,200 feet of fencing around a large government subsidized housing project. One of the landlord's purposes in constructing the fence was apparently to protect the children since there was a creek adjacent to the property. There were over 300 children living in the project.

The fence frequently developed holes. Sometimes it took the landlord a week to get a hole repaired.

A two-year-old child crawled through a hole in the fence and was found in the creek. While her life was saved she suffered brain damage and became a quadriplegic.

The court held that by building the fence the landlord had a duty to maintain it. Negligence in construction or maintenance would result in liability for the landlord.

Note: The landlord had no duty to build the fence. Without a fence the landlord would not be liable for injuries on adjacent property. In this case, tenants would be lulled into complacency believing that their children were safe playing in a secured area.

Neither the landlord or a property manager is liable for his or her negligence that is not the proximate cause of an accident or loss. For instance, assume a property had a fire suppression system (sprinklers) that had mistakenly been turned off. Assume that an airplane crashed into the property and the explosion destroyed the property. If the negligence of the sprinkler system was not the cause of the loss or contributed to the loss, the property owner wouldn't be liable for injuries suffered by others. The negligence of the owner or his or her employees was not the proximate cause.

Case Example

Lew v. Superior Court (1993) 20 C.A. 4th 866

Lew was a landlord of an apartment building housing Section 8 tenants (subsidized low income). Illegal drug activity occurred on the premises. Neighbors sued asking for damages for emotional and mental distress caused by the illegal drug activity which occurred on the premises.

The Superior Court awarded a total of $218,325 in damages after determining that the owners knew or should have known of the illegal activity and should have used reasonable means to alleviate the activity.

The Court of Appeals affirmed the Superior Court decision. They pointed out that while the plaintiffs could have sought to abate the nuisance, they had a right to sue for damages.

Note: This should make landlords who rent to drug dealers think about their potential liability.

Case Example

U.S. v. 141st Street Corp. (1990) 911 F. 2d 870

A 41-unit apartment managed by the uncle of the owner was the center of a great deal of illegal drug activity. In fact, tenants in 24 of the apartments had been arrested for drug sales. Rents of $2,000 or more per month were charged for substandard apartments.

The police left messages with the President of the Corporation that held title to the property but calls were not returned. The President of the Corporation admitted visiting the property at least once a week but claimed to have no knowledge of any illegal activity.

The court in this case held that government seizure was proper since it was clear the landlord knew of the illegal activity.

Note: In this case, the amount of rent charged and collected would alert any landlord, even if they never visited the property, that it was being used for illegal activity.

A subsequent case (U.S. v. James Good [1993], 114 S. Ct. 492) held that prior to government seizure the owner must have prior notice or a hearing. Seizure without a chance to present a defense was held to violate the due process clause of the U.S. Constitution.

DRAM SHOP LIABILITY

Some states hold the property owner liable for injuries caused by premises serving liquor to minors or to other persons to the point of their intoxication or leading to intoxication. *These are **DEEP POCKET LAWS** which allow recovery against the owner of real property.* For premises selling liquor, as a lease provision, the tenant should be required to carry dram shop liability coverage protecting the lessor up to a stated limit.

HAZARDOUS WASTE

A term dreaded by owners and property managers is hazardous waste. The presence of hazardous waste could leave an owner in a maze of federal, state, county and city laws and ordinances.

Without going into detail as to various state and federal laws, the result is that an owner of property can be held liable for hazardous substances on the property which were caused by a tenant, former tenant or former owner of the property.

HAZARDOUS SUBSTANCES, as defined by the Environmental Protection Agency, include many hundreds of chemical compounds, and just about anything that is toxic and/or flammable.

Cost of cleanup can be substantial. In many cases, the cost can exceed the value of the property.

A property manager can protect the property owner against future liability by requiring the tenant to carry liability insurance that will indemnify the property owner for the cost of removal of hazardous substances. To substantiate the amount of or damage to a property, a qualified testing firm dealing in hazardous waste can test the soil and property prior to leasing and at the termination of tenancy. If this is not done, the tenant and/or the insurance carrier will likely claim that the problems were largely pre-existing.

Case Example

Los Angeles Chem. Co. v. Superior Court (1991) 226 C.A. 3rd 703

This case made it clear that a regulatory agency cannot enter private property without a search warrant to gather evidence that hazardous wastes are being improperly stored there.

Risk Management

There are many more risks than just owner liability and agent liability. There are also risks to property, and to income.

The term "risk management" does NOT mean living with risk, it means reducing risk to an acceptable level.

Insurance allows us to trade a certainty (premium cost) for an uncertainty (a loss). In other words, we put the burden of specified losses on an insurance carrier. Most people seek security in their lives and insurance is able to provide an insured with both mental and financial security.

Insurance will not protect an owner against all risks, such as government seizure of the property, however, it can protect owners against most common risks.

While a single loss that was not insured could be devastating to an individual who suffers that loss, the insurance company is like a gambling casino that takes in bets with the odds in their favor. From experience they are able to predict the percentage of premium dollars received that will have to be returned to policy holders to cover insured losses. Besides making money on the odds they set, they also are able to invest premium dollars received.

As a property manager you have a duty to your principal to advise protection against losses that can be insured against. Of course, you have a parallel duty to use your best efforts to make certain losses do not occur. While preventative measures reduce the likelihood of some types of losses, those preventative measures cannot eliminate the chance of loss.

Property managers usually develop a close working relationship with an insurance agent who understands the needs of the property manager and owners. They are helpful in pointing out areas of exposure and are often able to suggest ways to save money for property owners. A property manager can file a claim against an insurance agent who misrepresents a policy.

Case Example

Eddy v. Sharp **(1988) 199 C.A. 3d 858**

The plaintiff asked Sharp to provide insurance coverage similar to his present coverage. A cover letter with the policy said the policy covered all risks over eight of their listed exclusions. The cover letter did not mention that the policy did not cover damages for water backing up in drains. After a loss, the plaintiff discovered that the policy would not cover the loss.

The Court of Appeals held that an independent insurance agent is the agent of the insured and has both a fiduciary duty as well as a duty of due care. Sharp failed to accurately inform the plaintiff of the policy terms so a duty was breached.

Note: This case applies to independent agents only and not agents for a single insurer.

Insurance companies set conditions for payment of claims. One is that the carrier must be notified of a loss in a prompt manner. Another condition is that the insured will cooperate with the insurance company and truthfully answer questions as to a loss. Attempting to defraud the insurance company with inflated loss figures could absolve the carrier from paying the loss even though there was a real loss.

It is possible to obtain more than one insurance policy covering the same risk. When more than one insurance policy exists, the carriers pay the loss equally up to the limits of the lowest policy. The higher limit carrier(s) then pay up to their limits. An exception to the above are policies that state if they are primary or secondary. A secondary carrier has far less risk than a primary carrier since the secondary carrier only pays after the primary carrier has paid up to their insurable limit. An **UMBRELLA POLICY** *is a secondary policy which requires minimum primary coverage but pays losses in excess of that coverage up to the umbrella policy limit.*

SELF-INSURED

> *Some of our nation's largest corporations do NOT insure their property.*

They elect to be self-insurers. They realize that no single loss or even group of losses would have a significant negative effect on their financial well-being. Rather than pay insurance to a company that has high costs of selling and servicing policies, they can handle their claims at significant savings. Corporate property managers working for multi-billion dollar firms may be in a self-insured situation where risk management would consist of safety procedures to reduce the possibility of loss. However, this is not the situation in which most property managers find themselves.

IDENTIFYING AND ADMINISTERING RISKS

> *Risk management is a function of management.*

As a manager you must identify risks associated with a property, measure the risks, and then decide how to treat the risk. As an example, a meteorite destroying a property is one in a billion chance. Therefore, you might decide that protecting the property from such a calamity would not be in a best interest of the client. The risk of other happenings could be much greater. As a general rule, if you have any doubt either insure or obtain a written directive from the owner not to insure against the risk. **RISK ADMINISTRATION** *involves decisions as to insurance coverage, obtaining the coverage and reviewing the coverage because of changes in the economy.*

Some owners will want to keep insurance with their current agent who may have a family or social relationship with the owner.

You will want copies of all policies. You should analyze each policy as to adequacy and need.

The basic policies would be:

1. Fire and extended coverage (including vandalism).
2. Liability (including liability as to sprinkler systems).
3. Plate glass coverage.

4. Worker's compensation, if employees will be employees of the owners.
5. Flood and/or earthquake coverage.
6. Rental interruption insurance.
7. Bonding of employees.

In analyzing an owner's insurance coverage, you might realize there is an immediate need for additional protection.

BINDERS

BINDERS *provide temporary coverage until a policy can be issued.* Binders are generally for property and liability protection. You must have agreed with the agent of the insurer as to the coverage desired in order to obtain a binder.

While the binder can be a separate memorandum or in some cases a verbal statement, it is often provided in the application for an insurance policy. The binder is conditional coverage since the insurance company need not issue the policy. The insurance company instead could notify the applicant that a policy will not be issued and temporary coverage shall cease as of a specified date. Fire insurance binders are often issued prior to the payment of any premium.

If you find that you do NOT have required coverage, you should seek a binder protecting the property and property owner until a policy can be issued.

TYPES OF OWNER-INSURANCE POLICIES

You can insure against just about any loss. The likelihood of loss will, of course, affect the premium.

To insure, you must have an "insurable interest."

Otherwise a person could insure your property as to fire and a fire would mean they could collect. If this were possible, it is likely that the risk of your property burning down would be materially increased.

Properties that are not profitable for owners tend to be destroyed by fire more often than properties which show a profit. Arson is believed to be the cause of almost 50 percent of business fires. In addition, false and exaggerated claims for damages are often made. This has resulted in significantly higher insurance rates. These higher rates must be paid if you are not in a position to be a self-insurer.

Some of the insurance coverage you should consider for your clients, includes the following.

Fire Insurance

The Standard Policy. The ***STANDARD POLICY*** *of fire insurance is specified peril coverage.* It covers loss from:

1. fire;
2. lightning;
3. loss from removal of property from the above perils.

HOMEOWNER POLICIES *add liability coverage, as well as theft and vandalism, and contents to extended coverage policies. However, they are only available for homeowners residing on the premises.*

> *You want to make certain that casualty policies cover "replacement costs," NOT just "cash value."*

Cash value considers depreciation and, unless you were able to buy used, it would not be enough to replace an asset that was destroyed.

Burglary and theft protection is offered in many extended coverage owner policies. The coverage might also cover mysterious disappearance of property even though there is not evidence of a robbery or burglary. Policies that cover burglary might also cover damage to a property in the course of the burglary. Robbery policies would have a limit as to cash stolen.

Earthquake and Flood Coverage

> *Normal casualty insurance policies exclude earthquake and flood damage.*

There policies are separate coverage and can be added to other casualty loss coverage. They have high deductibles. As an example, earthquake coverage generally has at least a $10,000 deductible, so a $11,000 loss would only pay $1,000 in compensation.

Just because there has been no flood in recent years doesn't mean you should not consider flood insurance. At the very least, you should check a topographic map and study elevations and drain-off.

If you wish protection from mud slides, you might need additional coverage. Some flood policies cover mud pouring into a property but do not cover the property itself sliding away. This additional coverage is available.

Boiler Insurance

BOILER INSURANCE *protects an owner against losses associated with a boiler explosion.* Boiler explosions can destroy an entire structure with loss of life. Boilers seldom explode today. The reason can be largely attributed to boiler insurance. The insurers are experts in boiler maintenance and safety and make certain the boiler is properly maintained and is equipped with the proper operating safety valves.

Elevator Insurance

ELEVATOR INSURANCE *covers liability losses due to failure of elevator equipment.*

Liability Insurance

LIABILITY INSURANCE *covers a property owner's liability to other parties because of the condition of or operation of a property.*

> *Liability insurance does NOT automatically pay a person who was injured or whose property was damaged.*

The insurance carrier will only pay if the insured is legally liable for the loss. An insurance carrier may deny a claim of a third party, but if that third party brings a lawsuit against the Insured, the insurance carrier has a duty to defend the insured.

In some instances, an insurance carrier could be liable to an amount greater than the insurance coverage. As an example, assume an injured party agreed to settle his or her claim for the limits of the policy. Assume also the insurance company refused to settle and decided to let the court determine liability. Assume an award was in excess of the insurance coverage and the carrier paid up to the insurance limits leaving the insured liable for the remainder. The insured could sue his or her carrier for this overage. If a court determined that the carrier was unreasonable in failing to settle within the limits of the policy, a court could hold them liable for the amount of the judgment in excess of the insurance coverage.

Libel and slander is ordinarily not included in liability insurance coverage although it can be added. Generally, libel and slander coverage has a high deductible, such as $10,000.

There are a number of types of liability policies. The **OWNERS, LANDLORDS AND TENANTS LIABILITY (OLT)** *coverage pays for damage to property and/or persons caused by ownership, maintenance or use of the premises*. There are also Comprehensive General Liability (CGL) policies.

Medical Pay Coverage

MEDICAL PAY COVERAGE *covers actual medical expenses for persons injured on the premises without regard to who was at fault.* It is a "no fault" type policy. If a person trips over his or her own feet while on the property of the insured, medical expenses will be paid up to the limit set forth for medical pay. It is generally included as coverage in a liability or extended coverage policy of the owner.

Inland Marine Insurance

INLAND MARINE INSURANCE *is not insurance to cover your boat. Generally, it is a transportation related policy for personal property that can protect bailees of personal property in transit or in storage.* Inland insurance also provides floater policies for items of personal property and for loss of records such as accounts receivable. The coverage offered can be for named risks or cover all risks.

Management of warehouse facilities should consider inland marine coverage that protects the bailee for loss of the property. The owner of the property is not the party protected. However, if the insured is held liable for a loss the insurance carrier would indemnify the bailor.

Many buildings have works of art in their lobbies and public areas. They can be insured with an inland marine floater. Other items that are applicable to property management and can be covered by floater policies are signs, stain glass art windows and computer systems.

> *Ranch managers could even insure livestock with an inland marine policy.*

Rental Interruption Insurance

When a property is made unusable because of an insured loss, the insurance coverage will probably pay for the property loss. However, the owner has other losses. While mortgage payments must be made, the income stream from the property is interrupted by the casualty loss. **RENT INSURANCE** *gives the owner a cash flow to make up for the lost rent.* Mortgages do not excuse payments simply because the property was damaged or destroyed.

Fidelity Bonds

BONDING *is a process where an insurer agrees to pay for losses resulting from the dishonesty of an employee up to the amount of the bond.*

Insurers will check on the person to be bonded. If they refuse to bond the person then you should consider if you want that employee having access to client funds.

When a bonding company discovers employee dishonesty, the employer must discharge the employee unless the bonding company agrees to the continued employment. In some cases, payback arrangements are reached.

Fidelity bonds can be written for each individual employee or for a group of named individuals.

You should consider bonding persons having access to funds or property of others. Management contracts often require bonding.

Worker's Compensation Insurance

WORKER'S COMPENSATION INSURANCE *is required where any employees are involved.* It applies both to owners, who have employees, and property managers who employ others. It pays for injuries to employees when the injuries are work related. We are now seeing claims which go beyond what we formerly considered injuries. Persons who have had heart attacks have successfully claimed that their attacks were the result of stress on the job.

Additional Insurance Coverage

If there are vehicles used at the property for the property, they should be insured as to liability. Comprehensive insurance and collision coverage should also be considered.

For hotel and motel management, innkeeper liability coverage should be obtained. If the innkeeper is held liable for property loss of a guest, the innkeeper would be indemnified. The guest is not insured, just the innkeeper.

There are various packaged crime policies which cover burglary and robbery. A separate policy should be considered if the coverage is not provided in another policy. Some packaged policies also cover fidelity of staff. The **3D POLICY** *is a comprehensive policy that covers Dishonesty, Disappearance and Destruction.* It applies to personal property. It also covers forgery.

TYPES OF TENANT INSURANCE POLICIES

Some property managers are agents or employees of a tenant. They may work for large corporations or franchisors. These managers would have a different perspective on risk management. Coverage that they would be interested in would be:

Fire and Extended Coverage

This coverage would apply to tenant property improvements and personal property. Earthquake and/or flood coverage could be added to the fire coverage or it could be a separate policy.

Liability Coverage

The more money the insured has, the greater the liability coverage should be because more is at risk. After $1 million in coverage, additional millions are relatively inexpensive protection because the risk decreases to the insurance company. The tenant may wish to cover additional liability protection with a high limit umbrella liability policy. The cost of liability protection would relate to tenant use and operations as to the leased premises.

Medical Pay Coverage

As a matter of goodwill, most tenants want medical pay coverage for persons injured on the premises.

Inland Marine Coverage

Personal property of high value, such as decorative items and accounts receivable records, can be covered by these policies. To determine the necessity of such policies, evaluate the coverage provided by other policies. With computer records and disks at various locations, the risk of loss of records have been materially reduced.

Fidelity Bonds

Bonds for a tenant would more likely be a function of financial operations rather than property management. The same is true for workers compensation coverage. On the other hand, innkeeper liability coverage would more likely be of concern to property management.

Business Interruption Insurance

This protects the owner of a business as to earnings which could be lost if there was a period of time that the business was closed due to losses suffered by the premises. This coverage would significantly reduce the likelihood of a tenant defaulting on the lease after a casualty loss. Therefore, owners prefer that tenants have this coverage.

Extra Expense Coverage

Extra expenses deal with the unusual expenses resulting from a casualty loss. It might include the preparation of a temporary location, moving expense, equipment rentals, etc. These expenses would not be covered by business interruption insurance.

Leasehold Insurance

Because many leases provide for lessor cancellation rights when a property is destroyed, this policy protects the tenants lease value. Increased rents could give an advantageous long-term lease a significant value that would be lost if the lease were canceled.

Residential Tenant Coverage

Residents of apartments and rental homes can obtain the equivalent of a homeowner's policy except that there is no coverage for the structure.

Property managers who have insurance licenses have found that selling tenant's insurance can be a significant profit center for their business.

Because a tenant would have additional living expenses if a casualty loss made their rental uninhabitable, coverage for residential living expenses is available. This insurance covers the excess expenses caused by relocation. Rental value insurance is a little different in that it provides the rental required to lease similar property to that which was destroyed.

PROPERTY MANAGEMENT INSURANCE

Property managers must manage risk management for themselves as well as their clients.

Risk management would include fidelity bonding for employees, coverage for personal property including records, liability protection, etc. Coverage that a property manager might want in addition to coverage set forth for owners and tenants could include the following.

Errors and Omissions

This policy protects you against your goofs and defends you in resulting lawsuits. As an example, if your firm allowed an insurance policy to lapse and there was an uninsured casualty loss, you would likely be liable for the loss. An errors and omissions policy would protect you. Errors and omissions policies frequently have high deductibles, such as $10,000. These policies are expensive but are a necessary part of doing business.

Records Insurance

If not covered by other policies, the loss of client files, accounts receivable and payable as well as contracts could be devastating. While insurance is available, many firms use a scanner to copy paper records for their computer and download the material at another location.

Automobile Coverage

Any company vehicles should have high limit liability coverage. Collision and comprehensive policies should also be considered.

Since an employer can be liable for torts (a civil wrong or injury) of employees, a property management office would want copies of employee's automobile coverage showing high limit liability protection.

Key Man Insurance

A property management office may have one or more employees whose loss would have significant effect on the business. As an example, one person's family connections might be responsible for obtaining 40 percent of a firm's business. That person's death could have a significant effect on the business in that major clients could be lost. **KEY MAN INSURANCE** *allows you to have a term life or accidental death policy on that person's life with your firm as the beneficiary.* You have a beneficial interest in that person's life.

Partnership Insurance

> *If your property management business is a partnership, the death of one partner could be catastrophic to the business.*

While heirs of the deceased partner would have no right to conduct the business, they would be entitled to the value of the deceased partner's share of the business. A partner's death often requires the sale of a business to pay off the heirs of the deceased partner.

PARTNERSHIP INSURANCE *would involve policies of insurance of the life of each of the partners payable to surviving partners.* This would be coupled with an agreement that the proceeds of the policy are accepted for the interest of the deceased partner.

Surety Bonds

When contracting for major renovations or improvements, the property manager should consider a surety bond from the contractor. A **SURETY BOND** *guarantees the completion of the contract.* All to often, horror cases involve a contractor going bankrupt when only half the job has been completed. The usual results are that the job takes many more months and in some cases years to complete with the cost greatly exceeding the original contracted amount. Bonding companies generally require audited financial statements from the contractor before they will issue a bond. Generally, only large contractors can meet the requirements for surety bonding.

HOW MUCH INSURANCE?

A risk manager must decide on how much insurance to carry. The land is not going to be lost because of a fire so coverage that would include the land would be wasted insurance. You want your owners to be able to obtain protection at a reasonable cost. Additional protection must be weighed against the additional cost.

Deductibles

Deductible amounts for losses are really examples of risk sharing. The insured decides he or she is able to bear the risk up to a stated dollar amount.

Insurance companies like deductibles because the majority of casualty losses are small losses. Not having the paperwork of administering minor claims takes a significant burden off of the insurance companies and reduces costs. They offer lower rates as deductibles increase. As an example, an owner might wish to take a $5,000 risk that lowers a premium by a significant amount.

> *Deductibles simply make risk more manageable and should be considered in applicable situations.*

Lender Requirements

If a property is encumbered by a mortgage or trust deed, the encumbrance would likely provide that the lienholder be provided with a copy of the insurance coverage. It would also provide that failure to do so would entitle the lienholder to obtain necessary insurance coverage at the owner's expense. When the lender does this, the policy price is usually far more than the coverage would normally cost.

Lenders typically wish to see insurance policies that either cover an entire purchase price or their loan. Insurance in these amounts could be excessive or inadequate based on the property. As an example, replacement costs of an office building that was purchased at a time when rents were low and vacancies were high could be several times the purchase price. On the other hand, property where a great percent of value is in the land could have a loan far in excess of the cost to replace the structure. Therefore, a lender wanting insurance coverage to the loan amount would be asking you to throw away dollars buying excess coverage.

In many cases, by appraisal as to land and structure value, you can convince lenders to adopt a reasonable approach. If your loan requires replacement value insurance, you have legal basis for lower coverage and your attorney should be able to convince the lender without the commencement of a lawsuit. However, if the loan requires insurance to a set dollar amount or to the amount of the loan, then your only hope is to use reason to obtain agreement as to lower coverage.

80 Percent Coinsurance

Insurance referred to as 80 percent coinsurance is available for commercial property. Insurance is based on a cost per $1,000 of coverage. Because buildings are seldom totally destroyed, many owners wanted to carry only partial insurance and be self-insured for the balance. This was not in the best interests of insurance companies who wanted premium dollars for the likely portion of any casualty loss as well as for losses that are far less likely to occur. Therefore, insurance companies came up with 80 percent coinsurance requirements for commercial buildings.

Under **80 PERCENT COINSURANCE**, *an owner must carry insurance which covers 80 percent of the replacement cost to be fully reimbursed for any loss.* Even then the insurance would only pay up to the insured amount even if there was 100 percent loss.

Assume an insured only purchased insurance covering 40 percent of the loss and the policy included an 80 percent coinsurance clause. The insured would only be reimbursed for 50 percent of any loss incurred even if the loss was less than the amount of the policy. The reason for only 50 percent reimbursement is that the insured was only carrying 50 percent of the insurance that should have been carried (40 percent rather than 80 percent).

> *Proper risk management requires a property manager to review all insurance coverage as to adequacy, but special attention must be paid to 80 percent coinsurance situations.*

If you are handling insurance coverage for a building and you believe your coverage is less than 100 percent of replacement costs, you should have an owner's concurrence as to the coverage. While 80 percent may be an economical decision for commercial property, it is a decision as to risk that should involve the wishes of the owner.

═══ CHAPTER 8 SUMMARY ═══

Owners of property are liable for their own wrongful and negligent actions as well as for the actions of their agents and employees. For employee and agent liability, the wrongful or negligent act must have been within the scope of employment. The act also must have been the proximate cause of the injury suffered to persons or property.

An owner is also liable for slander (verbal false statement) and libel (published false statement) that injures another. Owners are not liable for injuries caused by their independent contractors unless the contractor was employed for a dangerous activity.

An owner could be held liable for an injury caused by a tenant, the tenant's child or tenant's pet if the landlord knew, or should have known, about the dangers presented and failed to warn or protect others in a reasonable manner.

Generally, an owner is not liable for injuries that occurred off the premises. An exception would be if the owner exercised control over the property where the injury occurred. Another exception would be where the owner attempted to secure a property with a fence but where the fence was faulty, allowing a child to leave the premises and be injured elsewhere.

Owners of property who allow criminal activity on their property could be subject to damages and government seizure of their property.

An owner can be liable for hazardous waste released or stored on the property even though the owner was not involved in bringing the hazardous waste onto his or her property.

Risk management involves bringing risk to an acceptable level. By trading a certainty for an uncertainty, insurance makes most risks manageable. However, not every risk is insurable.

Insurance agents who misrepresent a policy can be held liable for their misrepresentation. To collect on an insurance policy the insurance carrier must be promptly notified of a loss and the insured must cooperate with the insurance company.

Multiple policies of insurance can be issued for the same property and the carriers would equally bear the loss up to their policy limits. An exception would be secondary coverage which would only pay after the primary insurer had reached their policy limit.

Some large firms are self insured in that they feel that they have enough financial strength to not have to pay insurance premiums but instead settle claims themselves.

By a verbal or written binder, it is possible to obtain insurance protection prior to a policy being issued.

To obtain insurance, the insured must have an interest in property. This is known as an insurable interest.

Owner insurance policies include:

1. Fire insurance
2. Standard policy
3. Extended coverage policy
4. Earthquake insurance
5. Flood insurance
6. Boiler insurance
7. Liability insurance
8. Medical pay coverage

9. Inland marine insurance
10. Rental interruption insurance
11. Fidelity bonds
12. Worker compensation insurance
13. Innkeeper liability

Tenant insurance protection includes:

1. Fire insurance
2. Liability coverage
3. Medical pay coverage
4. Inland marine coverage
5. Business interruption insurance
6. Extra expense coverage
7. Leasehold insurance
8. Residential tenant policy

Property management companies may want to limit their exposure with:

1. Errors and omissions insurance
2. Records insurance
3. Automobile coverage
4. Key man insurance
5. Partnership insurance
6. Surety and fidelity bonds

Lower insurance rates can be obtained by deductibles. With a deductible, the insured pays the first part of the loss. The higher the deductible, the lower the premium.

Lenders generally want the loan covered by the insurance.

The 80 percent coinsurance requires the insured to insure at least 80 percent of the replacement cost in order to be fully covered (up to policy limits).

CLASS DISCUSSION TOPICS

1. Do you know of any real estate office that handles property management and also sells insurance? If so, what types of policies do they sell?

2. Discuss the types of insurance that would be desired by an owner of a major:

   a. apartment complex
   b. shopping center
   c. industrial park

3. Discuss ownership risks that cannot be managed by insurance.

4. Are you protected by errors and omissions coverage? If so, who pays for the coverage? What is the deductible amount?

5. Identify areas where an owner would be interested in earthquake, floor or mud slide protection.

6. Do you have a personal umbrella liability policy? Why?

7. Is anyone in your office bonded? If yes, then why? If no, should anyone be bonded?

CHAPTER 8 QUIZ

1. Ownership of what type of property would make an owner strictly liable for injury to a tenant?

    A. Residential property
    B. Commercial property
    C. Industrial property
    D. None of the above

2. Slander which damages a person would be described as a (an):

    A. intentional written statement that is false
    B. unintentionally false written statement
    C. true statement which damages a person's reputation
    D. false verbal statement

3. An owner's liability as to acts of a tenant would be based on:

    A. foreseeability
    B. agency law
    C. strict liability
    D. an insurable interest

4. Obtaining insurance protection prior to the issuance of a policy would be known as a (an):

    A. option
    B. binder
    C. bond
    D. right of first refusal

5. The standard policy of fire insurance protects an owner for all EXCEPT:

    A. fire loss

    B. lightning damage

    C. hail damage

    D. loss suffered in removal of property that suffered a fire

6. Inland marine coverage would be applicable for:

    A. a bailee as to stored property

    B. insuring an expensive painting

    C. both A and B

    D. neither A nor B

7. Fidelity bonds provide protection against:

    A. employees leaving for other employment

    B. employee theft

    C. inflation because of the rising interest rates

    D. mysterious disappearance

8. Who is required to provide workers compensation insurance?

    A. Firms having in excess of 10 employees

    B. Firms having in excess of five employees

    C. Firms having in excess of one employee

    D. Firms having any employees

9. A property manager accidently rented the same property to two separate tenants. The manager's protection, in this case, would be provided by:

    A. homeowner's insurance

    B. errors and omissions coverage

    C. leasehold insurance

    D. innkeeper liability

10. A property manager is considering awarding a $300,000 contract for renovation of a commercial building. The protection the property manager would be interested in would be:

    A. a fidelity bond

    B. a surety bond

    C. worker's compensation coverage

    D. errors and omissions coverage

Answers: 1. D; 2. D; 3. A; 4. B; 5. C; 6. C; 7. B; 8. D; 9. B; 10. B

Chapter 9

Security and Safety

KEY WORDS AND TERMS

Armed Guards
Carbon Monoxide Detectors
Closed Circuit Alarms
Covert Cameras
Deadbolt
Dual Units
Electronic Gates
Electronic Security Alarm
Emergency Lighting
Emergency Oxygen
Emergency Telephones
Employee Name Tags
Employment Checks
Fire Extinguishers
Fire Doors
Foreseeability of Harm
Guard Gates
Guard Dogs
Guard Patrols
Hasps
Infrared Beams
Inherently Dangerous Areas

Latch Bolt
Microwave Fields
Mortised Lock
Motion Sensor Lighting
Occupancy Rules
Open Circuit Alarms
Overt Cameras
Proactive Guard Patrol
Reactive Guard Patrol
Security Committees
Smoke Detectors
Solid Core Doors
Sound Sensors
Speed Bumps
Spot Detectors
Sprinkler Systems
Strike Plate
Tailgating
Television Cameras
Ultrasonic Alarms
Vibration Detectors

LEARNING OBJECTIVES

In this chapter you will learn about the importance of security in property management. You will also learn about various security options available to you. Upon completion of this chapter, you should be able to make intelligent choices as to types of security measures which would be applicable for a particular property.

You will also learn about the safety requirements of the Occupational Safety and Health Act and how it applies to property management.

Security: An Overview

SECURITY DEFINED

Security is more than just feeling secure. It is the knowledge that persons and property have a right to that feeling.

SECURITY OBLIGATIONS

As a property manager you have moral and in some cases legal obligations to take reasonable measures to protect your tenants, their guests and the personal property of your tenants and their guests.

Foreseeability of Harm

A landlord's duty to take security precautions relates to the foreseeability of loss or injury.

Case Example

Ann M. v. Pacific Shopping Center (1993) 6 C.A. 4th 666

An employee of a tenant in a shopping center was raped inside the store during business hours. She claimed that the shopping center had not provided adequate security. The Court of Appeals as well as the California Supreme Court upheld the trial court's verdict in favor of the landlord.

The court pointed out that "a high degree of foreseeability is required to order or find that a landlord's duty of care includes hiring security guards." In the absence of similar incidents of violent crime, there was no degree of foreseeability.

Note: If there had been prior violent crimes on the premises, the court seems to conclude that they could have found for the plaintiff.

The case of Lisa P. v. Bingham came to a different conclusion based on prior crimes.

Case Example

Lisa P. v. Bingham (1996) 43 C.A. 4th 372

A robber took store receipts and then forced two women into a back room of a store in a shopping center. He hit one and raped the other woman. Prior to this crime the shopping center had three robberies but no rapes. The owner of the shopping center and the property manager were sued for failing to provide protective measures.

The Superior Court, in granting summary judgment for the defendant, held that a high degree of foreseeability of criminal activity is required to hold a landlord to a duty to have security guards.

The Court of Appeals reversed the Superior Court and held that violent criminal activity on the premises (robberies) would place a duty on the landlord to hire security guards.

Note: The court placed prior criminal acts as the criteria for security guards rather than foreseeability.

This case could place property managers in a quandary as to the degree of criminal activity that would necessitate hiring security guards as well as what property it would apply to. Many properties certainly could not economically justify security guards, but economics was not given as a criteria. However, it is unlikely that the owner or manager of six-store mini-mall would be held to a duty of hiring security guards because the anchor tenant, a 7-11 store, had two robberies.

Harm could be foreseeable when the condition of the building does not provide reasonable security. Examples of problems that could result in lessor liability include:

1. unlighted or poorly lighted entry ways and paths;
2. the presence of shrubbery around an entryway that provides a convenient hiding place;
3. broken locks on apartment entrances or locks that can be easily opened with a credit card;
4. security doors that are left unlocked

Some areas within a building or types of buildings present a greater foreseeability of loss to property and persons as in the case of Shoron P. v. Armon Ltd.

Advertising Security

Never advertise a property as being safe or secure. It could be considered a warranty as to security. An owner could be held liable for a tenants loss of property and/or

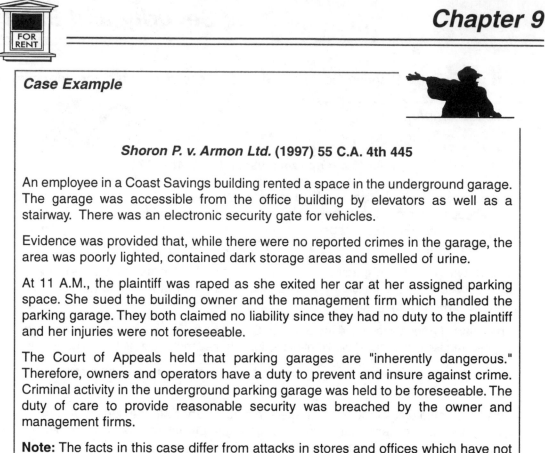

Case Example

Shoron P. v. Armon Ltd. (1997) 55 C.A. 4th 445

An employee in a Coast Savings building rented a space in the underground garage. The garage was accessible from the office building by elevators as well as a stairway. There was an electronic security gate for vehicles.

Evidence was provided that, while there were no reported crimes in the garage, the area was poorly lighted, contained dark storage areas and smelled of urine.

At 11 A.M., the plaintiff was raped as she exited her car at her assigned parking space. She sued the building owner and the management firm which handled the parking garage. They both claimed no liability since they had no duty to the plaintiff and her injuries were not foreseeable.

The Court of Appeals held that parking garages are "inherently dangerous." Therefore, owners and operators have a duty to prevent and insure against crime. Criminal activity in the underground parking garage was held to be foreseeable. The duty of care to provide reasonable security was breached by the owner and management firms.

Note: The facts in this case differ from attacks in stores and offices which have not been held to be inherently dangerous.

The duty of owners and managers applies to tenants and guests but not to others as in the case of Waters v. Housing Authority.

physical and emotional injuries if the property was represented to the tenant as being safe in order to rent the premises.

Security Disclosure

A lessor who knows about more than the ordinary security problems in the property, complex or neighborhood should make a prospective tenant aware of the risk.

Although a property manager probably would not have to tell a prospective tenant that one of the tenants had a car broken into and lost a car radio several months before, a series of crimes may subject the property manager to disclosure.

When in doubt as to what to disclose, disclose.

Case Example

Waters v. Housing Authority (1987) 505 NE 2d 922

This New York case involved a rape victim who was dragged into a building by her assailant. Neither the victim nor the assailant were residents of the building. The victim alleged that there were no locks on the exterior doors to the building and that the vestibule areas was poorly lighted.

The court held that while a landlord has a duty to offer reasonable protection for the safety of residents and guests, the owner has no duty as to general members of the public. The court pointed out that extending the duty of property owners would not result in safer streets.

Note: If the plaintiff had been a tenant in the building, a different decision would have been likely.

Case Example

Olar v. Schroit (1984) 155 C.A. 3d 861

A woman was assaulted in a condominium complex where she was renting a unit. At the time of rental, the owner of the unit told her that the property was safe, and that security precautions to protect the occupants had been taken by the condominium association. She claimed in her suit that security was lax and that adequate precautions for her safety had not been taken.

The court held that when representations as to security are made to induce a tenant to rent, then there is a duty to maintain security. They also held that misrepresentations by an owner or property association as to security could subject them to liability if represented security could have prevented the loss or injury.

Security and Safety

Security and safety are interrelated. Many methods of obtaining security also help to ensure safety of residents and employees.

Security has become a matter of prime concern for property managers. Managers of large properties are frequently using security consultants to identify areas of security concerns and suggest methods to deal with these matters.

Property managers should seek help from local police departments. Many police departments will perform a security survey at no cost and make security recommendations. Fire departments will conduct a fire safety inspection. A safety engineer can check a property as to dangerous conditions and recommend safety procedures, equipment and changes. Injuries to personnel will increase your worker's compensation contribution while injuries to tenants will increase insurance costs.

The best risk management is really risk prevention.

Perfect security is impossible to obtain because whatever we design or work to protect, someone else can find a way to defeat it if they're willing to put in the effort and take the risk. However, thieves, vandals and persons who wish to assault others are like most people in that when they have a choice between an easy target and a difficult target, they will choose the easy one. Therefore, you want any property that you manage to present as many problems as possible to those intent on wrongdoing and pose less risk for owners and occupants of those properties.

You will see that there are numerous ways to increase security as to both persons and property. We can provide greater security through many methods. Actually, security planning involves a combination of methods.

If there is a breach of our security, evidenced by loss or damage to property or injury to persons, we should use our efforts to remedy the situation that caused the problem. Keep in mind that courts could determine that a future problem was foreseeable based on past experiences on the property.

LIGHTING

Persons intent on wrongdoing tend to be extremely surreptitious. They don't want to advertise their presence or intent.

Exterior Lighting. Forget about saving pennies with 15 watt bulbs. You want entryways, parking and garage areas and walkways well lighted. Ornamental, 12-volt systems look great for knee-high path lighting and keeping costs down but they don't do much for security. The same holds true for some multi-colored lighting. The tinted lights materially reduce the candlepower for any lighted area. For parking and outside storage areas, consider high-intensity mercury or sodium vapor lamps which are set high enough to give daylight conditions to a wide area. Enough lighting should be used to avoid areas of dark shadows. Exterior lights can be on clock systems. But if so, the clocks should be reset on a monthly basis to adjust for changes in sunrise-sunset times. Many properties use photo electric cells which automatically turn lighting systems on at dusk and off again at sunrise.

Motion Sensor Lighting. Flood lights that are on a motion sensor tuned to a high degree of sensitivity and set for at least four minutes can be a deterrent to criminal activity in parking areas as well as along walls and fences. While small animals might cause the lights to come on, it is better to risk scaring a raccoon if you also scare off a thief.

A benefit of motion sensor lighting is the savings in electricity and in the comfort your tenants will experience.

Motion sensor lights should be set to go on in darkness when a person is within a certain number of feet or yards from the light. Therefore you should consider having detectors installed which are not a part of the sensor lights.

Entryways and Halls. Entryways and hallways in apartments and office structures should be well lighted. Fixtures should be of a type that it would be difficult to remove or loosen a bulb. Light switches should not be placed in public areas so that criminals cannot easily control the environment.

At times, dangerous conditions are the direct cause of tenants. They find it easier to replace a light bulb in their apartment with one from the hallway or entryway than going out and purchasing them. You can solve this problem, cut costs and make the property safer by using fluorescent lighting in the public areas of the building. Fluorescent tubes don't fit most household fixtures so the problem of theft would be almost nil.

Emergency Lighting. Emergency lights are battery operated and are kept charged by being hard-wired to the buildings electrical service. When the electricity goes off the emergency lights go on. Such lights are a safety feature for vestibules, public hallways, public restrooms, storage areas, laundry rooms, indoor parking areas and enclosed malls. These lights also serve as a security measure where thieves may turn off the electricity.

Locked Circuit Breakers. Circuit breakers that are located in locked rooms or cabinets act as a deterrent to muggers who look for well-labeled breaker systems to cut off exterior or hall lighting.

LANDSCAPING

Proper landscaping along pathways and entryways can reduce crime.

Avoid large bushes close to entryways and walkways. A pair of six foot Arbor Vita flanking an entryway may look impressive but it can be deadly for your tenants and/or their guests. As a rule of thumb, allow at least 20 feet of grass, flowers or very low ground cover along both sides of walkways and entryways.

Large trees and shrubs allowing a hiding place for someone should be removed along with low tree branches within 30 feet of entryways, pathways and parking areas. Areas around the perimeter walls and fences of the property should be relatively clear so that persons walking in the areas can have unobstructed vision for quite a distance. Any objects such as a tree which could be used to scale a fence or climb on top of a structure or enter the property should be removed.

FENCES AND WALLS

Fences do more than make good neighbors. They discourage intrusions.

While a healthy young person can scale a six foot wall, he or she prefers not to. In today's world where most people get in their car to travel one block, criminals will do the same. They want to get as close to the area of planned criminal activity as possible and get away just as easily. Fences and walls make entry and exit activity more difficult.

Lawn furniture that is left too close to walls aids in the exit of the wrongdoer. Heavy or anchored tables can't be used as ladders.

Chain-link fencing topped with barbed wire is an excellent deterrent for exterior storage areas as well as perimeter fencing for warehouse or industrial areas. The gate should also have barbed wire topping to deter entry. Gates on chain-link fences should be secured in at least two places or the gate can be twisted to allow a person to squirm through. Chain-link security fencing should be combined with a lighting system flooding an unobstructed ground's area. Having to scale a fence with barbed wire to cross a well-lighted open area is not an inviting environment for criminal activity.

DOORS

Composition. Exterior and apartment doors should be either solid core wood or metal clad doors. Hollow core doors simply have a light wood framework covered with thin plywood or masonite sheeting. Hollow core doors can be easily smashed in while solid core doors will resist forced entry.

Metal-clad solid core doors provide the greatest resistance to forced entry.

Peepholes. Apartment doors should be equipped with a peephole viewer. The small, wide angle lens allows the viewing of visitors before opening the door.

Security Chain. Apartment doors should also be equipped with a quality security chain. The chain should be anchored into the wood or metal door frame with at least one-inch screws or longer depending upon the thickness of the door.

Even the best of security chains is limited by the thickness of the door. Short screws won't resist determined kicks to the door.

Sliding glass doors should be equipped with an inside pin through the metal frame and the door so if the lock is forced, the doors cannot be opened. Holes for the pin can be placed so the glass door can be pin-locked while open only an inch or so for ventilation.

Hinges. Hinges should be installed on the inside of doors. As basic as this may seem, there are constant cases where entry was gained by removing the pins and lifting the door off its hinges.

LOCKS

Skeleton Key Entry. Although difficult to realize, many burglars carry a common skeleton key. Many interior locks, especially older buildings, and some exterior locks can be opened with this key. Skeleton keys can be purchased at most hardware, variety stores and lock shops.

Locks which use skeleton keys only keep honest people out.

To anyone with wrong intentions these locks allow an easy entry. Such locks should be replaced.

Burglar Pry Bars. Simple pry bars are available at any hardware store. They are the tool of choice for most burglars. The burglar can rip the wood from around the door lock with a pry bar and gain entry. One lock placed at the top and one at the bottom of a door can make the jobs of thieves more difficult because they can't use the door itself as leverage to break the lock or loosen the lock.

While quality locks can be picked by professionals if given enough time, most burglars are not professionals and operate with a smash-and-grab technique so they are in and out and away in just a few minutes.

The quicker the burglary, the less the chance of being caught.

Key in-the-Knob Locks. Most residential locks and some used for commercial property are of the key in-the-knob variety. The knobs are not recommended because the locks can be quickly pried off leaving the latch bolt exposed for easy removal. Some combination locks have a dead bolt immediately above the key/knob type of lock. Again, ripping off the knob may allow access to the latch bolt as well as the dead bolt above it. One solution is to add an auxiliary dead bolt about six inches above the existing lock.

Mortised Locks. Until the last few years most locks were mortised into the center edge of the door leaving very little wood around the lock. This placement created a weakening of the door which left the strongest lock worthless when forced with a bar. Mortise locks also commonly used a cylinder held in place by a single set screw. A well equipped burglar could quickly twist the cylinder out of the lock to gain entry.

Beveled Bolts. Thirty years ago, locks had a bolt where the function was more to keep the door closed than to keep intruders out. The latch bolt with a curved or beveled surface could easily be pushed open with a credit card by first running a screwdriver to pull the jamb strip loose. A metal plate driven into the jamb will deter this type of entry. Sophisticated burglars use a curved tool to work around this metal plate.

Strike Plate. The strike plate may also be a weak point on a door. The strike plate should be held in place by screws at least four inches long which go through the jamb into the studs around the door jamb. Some strike plates are heavier and extra long which requires additional screws. Staggered holes can reduce the chances of the jamb splitting when the door is kicked.

Jamb and Casing. One-piece steel jambs and casings will prevent pry bars from entering the edge of a door. The door will still be vulnerable to severe kicking and very few locks and/or doors can hold against a half dozen vigorous kicks from an athletic 200 pound individual.

Better Locks. As previously stated, more tumblers and sophisticated spacing and depth can make locks more difficult to pick.

Some latch bolts have little bevels as an anti-shimming measure. However, there are ways to get around such deterrents. Burglars can use a bar to push a door over toward the hinges so that the bolt clears the strike plate to open the door. This can be accomplished with most doors and if the door opening is just a quarter inch too wide for the door, the latch bolt may barely catch the strike plate. Forced entry is quite easy.

Today, better locks are now equipped with longer bolt throws with straight shafts which cannot be pushed open by a credit card or other tools. However, for most locks the latch bolt throw is seldom over five-eighths of an inch so that the bolt isn't much more than one-quarter inch into the strike plate.

Some new locks use a magnetic key. A series of magnets imbedded in the key interface with the lock. These locks are excellent because they are very difficult to pick.

Similar to the magnetic key lock are card locks. Push-button coded locks don't require a key and can defy most criminals.

Dead bolts. *DEAD BOLTS consist of a square face and long throw and cannot be pried open with a credit card or thin metal screwdriver.* The beveled-faced bolt is a latch bolt. Although usually installed on the interior, dead bolts can also be keyed for oxterior entry. A reinforced cylinder guard should be used with a keyed dead bolt. The guard is a heavy steel plate which surrounds the cylinder so it can't be twisted out or otherwise tampered with. The guard plate is held in place by screws from the inside of the door which go through an inside plate and into but not through the exterior guard plate. The door is "sandwiched" between these two steel plates which hold the locking mechanism and resists prying.

These dead bolts are excellent security locks. Using a lock mechanism with numerous tumblers can make picking the lock difficult.

While it may seem easy, in the movies the use of a tension tool in one hand and a pick in the other against a multi-tumbler lock is a talent few burglars possess.

A double cylinder dead bolt that requires a key to open both sides is available on the market. This dead bolt is for use in a door having a small window. A burglar who breaks the window still can't reach in and turn the dead bolt. We strongly recommend that you do not use a double cylinder dead bolt. A person who can't locate the door key or is too nervous to use it may end up trapped in an emergency situation. You may also expose yourself to a liability situation.

This type of dead bolt violates fire ordinances in some areas of the country.

Cylinder upgrading should be considered if locks are being picked. Cylinders can be changed without replacing the entire dead bolt assembly. Your local locksmith can assist you in any upgrade decisions.

Dead bolts mounted on the surface of interior doors are easy to install. These dead bolts are quite effective if the screws are long enough to penetrate solid wood. Pine is a relatively soft wood. You would want hardwoods as the preferred surface for holding dead bolt screws.

Garage-Type Doors. Garage and warehouse doors should be secured by side bolts and bottom bolts.

Padlocks. The short blow of a hammer or a good bolt cutter will make short work of all but the best padlocks. A thin metal strip can be inserted along the shank in many padlocks to release the lock mechanism.

Padlocks with very short shanks are more difficult to open with a hammer. They also prevent any large bar from being inserted to pry the lock open.

In some better padlocks, the key is really a flat piece of metal with magnets inserted which are keyed to a portion of the lock casing.

Hasps. Padlocks, although often used, are easily bypassed by burglars who twist off cheap hasps with a bar. The weakest link is often the hasp. Quality hasps securely fastened should be used in combination with a quality padlock.

WINDOWS

Protection Against Breakage. Breaking a window is an easy way to gain entry if a burglar is not concerned about making noise. The only protection against this are metal window grills or bars, metal security curtains or having a window which won't break. Lexan, a plexiglass like plastic, is clear and can't be broken with an ordinary hammer. This type of window should be considered for lower windows.

Another solution for lower level windows is the use of glass block windows. The lower windows of some commercial buildings have often simply been bricked over. Windows with wire reinforcement can be broken but will still resist forcible entry.

There is a safety problem in block windows or installing bars or grills. An emergency exit has been blocked. Check with your local building and fire departments before blocking off windows or installing bars. Your actions could be a code violation and you could be held liable for injuries that relate to your action.

Latches. Normal window latches won't protect a doublehung or glide-by window unit from a pry bar. Drilling a hole through the sash and the window casing overlap and inserting a 3/8th inch bolt through the hole provides better security. There are also metal clamps available in hardware stores for light-weight aluminum window casings. For sliding glass doors, burglars will use a bar to either break the locking mechanism or to lift the door out of its track. Here again, you can drill holes through the metal track and window casing to place a pin or heavy nail.

Glass Cutting. If time is not a factor, but noise is, the thief will cut the glass if it is accessible. This gives easy access to reach the latch to open the door or window.

> *Signs and/or labels indicating the property is protected by electronic security even though NO such security exists will deter an unsophisticated criminal.*

Metal tape around the edges of windows of some buildings appears to be wired for electronic security even though they are not actually wired. Dummy security systems are intended to deter criminals.

Never let a tenant think you have a security system when you don't. This would be the same as warranting the security and could expose you to legal liability.

ELECTRONIC GATES

Some industrial parks as well as condominium and apartment projects can limit access by use of walls, fences and gates.

ELECTRONIC GATES *are unmanned gates that swing back or glide open on a track.* To enter, a resident or employee will use an opener in his or her car, an electronic card or punch in a combination at the gate. An electronic eye usually opens an exit gate. Some exits are left open and instead use a one-way barrier that would destroy tires of any vehicle that used the exit for entry purposes. (Note: this exit allows entry by pedestrians.)

Radio channels, cards and code keys can be changed to increase security. Management must keep track of openers and cards and would want to change codes when either is reported lost or stolen. There is a problem when codes are changed because some users fail to get the information and become frustrated trying to open the gate.

The wooden bar electronic gate is not recommended. All too frequently, a frustrated user will get out of his or her car and will take the end of the wooden bar and, using it like a lever, pull it open causing the board or mechanism to break.

> *Police, fire and ambulance services must be given openers or codes for emergency use.*

Service personnel can create a problem in that they must be given access. The system becomes less secure as more persons have the codes or openers. Service contractors and employees of service contractors are believed to be the cause of the majority of break-ins within a number of gated residential communities. If true it can be understandable considering the wealth of many persons living in some of the gated communities and the fact that some service providers, such as gardening services, pay minimum wages.

Electronic gates must provide for guests and visitors. Some use a telephone so that a tenant can be contacted and the gate may then be remotely opened.

Speed bumps within gated communities slow traffic. Besides being a safety feature, it is also a security feature in that slow moving vehicles are more likely to be noticed.

Speed bumps should be painted with yellow reflective paint as well as warning signs posted to avoid liability for a speed bump induced accident.

A problem with some electronic gates is that an unauthorized car may be able to "tailgate" another vehicle and thus gain entry. A gate that is opened for vehicles can also be opened for foot traffic. A video camera installation coupled with the electronic gate is a better crime deterrent.

GUARD GATE SERVICES

Considering vacations, it takes five employees, full time, to man a 24-hour guard gate with just one person. If there is also to be a roving patrol such as used at many retirement communities and large condominium projects, then five additional employees would be required. This is with a one-person patrol. If more than one gate is to be manned, add five more employees for each gate. Add to salaries social security contributions, workers compensation, unemployment insurance and time-and-a-half work requirements and any benefit's package. You can see that security is not a small matter when guard gates are to be manned. In addition to labor costs there are also equipment and maintenance costs.

Some large developments want special uniforms for their guards. While the blue blazer, gray slacks and white shirt with tie look is cultivated by some, others want the pre World War II image with campaign hat and boots. Distinctive looks are sought to make the residents feel important. The problem with the image is it can be costly. One 26-home enclave in the Palm Springs area has a 24-hour manned gate which results in over $2,000 per month in homeowner fees without a clubhouse, golf course or gardening being involved in the cost.

Some multiple-gated communities only operate one gate from 10 P.M. until 6 A.M. and leave other gates locked. This offers significant savings in manning gates. Other developments have resorted to electronic sliding gates.

GUARD SERVICES

Security guards have their origin from "Watch and Ward" groups in old England prior to the development of police forces. Citizens took turns rotating their time patrolling neighborhoods at night.

Founded in 1855, the first paid security service was Pinkerton, which was formed with the realization that public policing could NOT meet all security needs.

Guard services control access as well as prevent or detect unauthorized activities and break-ins.

Some security services will use undercover operators. As an example, one condominium management company had an undercover agent join the gardening staff and shortly thereafter determined who was breaking into condominiums in the gate-guarded community.

Security companies conduct background checks on employees that property managers are considering hiring. Although the fact that a person might previously have been guilty of a theft does not mean that person will steal again, the recidivism rate of criminal activity usually indicates that a person is likely to do so again.

With a few exceptions, most property management firms probably do NOT possess the expertise needed to hire, train and supervise an employee guard service.

Therefore, most guard services are contracted for. After specifications are developed, property management firms would go out for competitive bids. Security consultants can help develop guard service specifications and can provide contract supervisory services to make certain that problems don't develop and the security provided is what is being paid for.

Some guard services simply consist of a drive-through. Others check doors and conduct more drive-by checks. Basically, the service providers will give you what you are willing to pay for.

Armed guards pose a risk to tenants and others. They can also create a liability nightmare. Most guard employees or guard services that are contracted for by property management firms are unarmed. Weapons are generally not required, although armed response would be appropriate when responding to an alarm.

Guards can summon authorities with radios and cellular telephones when needed. Your security guards should contact local police to report any suspicion of possible criminal activity on the premises.

At apartment complexes, your security personnel should notify the proper authority when there is evidence of spousal abuse, child abuse or abuse of the elderly. Report only the facts. If information was received by others, report it as such and give names of witnesses.

Security personnel should keep logs of all suspicious observations, things out of the ordinary as well as any action reported to other authorities.

GUARD PATROLS

Guard patrols are proactive or reactive. A **PROACTIVE PATROL** *protects or discourages criminal activity by following slow-moving vehicles, checking persons who don't seem to fit the area, etc., and residents who may be acting in a suspicious manner.* **REACTIVE PATROLS** *answer alarms and calls by neighbors and generally act in the capacity of an after-the-fact patrol.* They try to identify and/or catch a perpetrator.

Good proactive patrolling uses random routes and random times which makes it difficult for criminals to plan avoiding detection by the patrols.

Some guard patrols are equipped with infrared scopes for night vision allowing intruders to be easily spotted.

GUARD DOGS

Fenced facilities such as mini-warehouses, storage yards and some industrial complexes might wish to consider guard dogs. They do deter criminals. When the fur rises on the dog's back or neck and teeth are bared, even the most fearless criminal will make a hasty retreat.

Guard dogs must be secured when gates are open to tenants and guests. You should also post signs warning the public and intruders about the dogs. A person should be on duty to respond to agitated dogs.

You will have a liability problem if the dogs get loose. Another liability problem is if children gain access to the guard-dog area and are injured. The doctrine of attractive nuisance would probably apply in this case since dogs do attract small children. It makes no difference that the children are trespassing and that they could read the warning signs.

Concrete should be poured deep enough along fence lines so that the dogs can't dig under the chain link fence.

A number of guard dog companies can supply you with trained dogs. Some owners simply purchase the meanest looking dogs at the pound without regard to their training. This could be dangerous in that a dog could kill rather than only hold at bay an intruder.

ELECTRONIC SECURITY ALARMS

Alarms are not a recent innovation. The first burglar alarm company was founded in 1858.

Entry Alarms

Motion detectors, pressure sensitive plates and wiring windows and doors so that opening them breaks or closes a circuit are just some of the electronic means of detecting an entry into a property.

When a circuit is opened or broken, there may be a time delay which allows a person to punch in a code or use a devise to cancel an alarm. Often people forget or get flustered and an alarm is set off accidently.

There are open circuit and closed-circuit alarms. An **OPEN-CIRCUIT ALARM** *goes off when a circuit closes.* A circuit is completed and the alarm goes off when a window is opened.

An open-circuit alarm will NOT function if a wire is cut.

A **CLOSED-CIRCUIT ALARM** *has continuous low voltage current running through the circuit and the alarm goes off when that circuit is broken.* Cutting a wire will set off the alarm. A closed-circuit alarm goes off if the current of electricity is accidentally interrupted or turned off and creates a false alarm. Operating the system by battery and wiring the storage battery to a charger will solve this problem.

A closed-circuit alarm system is the preferred security alarm system.

Vibration alarms are also available which will detect sawing or breaking through a wall.

Electronic intrusion devices are used by individual home owners and condominium owners. Other users are mini warehouses, office buildings and industrial parks.

Alarm Specifications. You should use an independent security consultant to determine if you need a system and if so what kind. The consultant will develop required specifications before you put the installation and maintenance of the system out for bids.

Any bid should include multi-year service or have options for service renewal. Otherwise, the installer will have a "lock-in" as to future maintenance services because it is their system. The firm that sold the system could otherwise bargain from a position of strength and significantly increase maintenance fees.

Sounding the Alarm. Formerly, many systems were wired to sound alarms at local police stations. Police were devoting too much time to false alarms. Now, most alarms are wired by telephone directly to central alarm services.

When an alarm goes off, the service will telephone the installation site. A password must be given when the telephone is answered at the site. If not the service will respond, often with armed guards. The service will coordinate their response with local police.

Unsophisticated burglars will probably be frightened off when a loud piercing alarm goes off. Based on the location, a more sophisticated burglar realizes that they have several minutes to work safely.

Alarms can consist of sounds and lights suddenly flooding the premises or flashing on and off. It is very disturbing to intruders.

Alarms that blare continuously disturb the neighborhood. Many alarms are equipped with an automatic shut-off after five or ten minutes. In big cities, false alarms may be so frequent that people regard them as a nuisance and tend to ignore them. In smaller communities, neighbors are more apt to check on an alarm going off.

Interior Alarms

Pressure Plates. Besides alarms connected to windows and doors, alarms can be connected to pressure plates placed under carpeting or mats.

Sound Sensors. *SOUND SENSORS really consist of a microphone and an amplifier.* The alarm goes off when any irregular noise exceeds the alarm's setting. Some systems have a silent alarm which goes off at a central listening station. Some systems operate so that the central station can tune in to the property and listen.

Ultrasonic Alarms. *ULTRASONIC ALARMS use a low frequency sound wave which reverberates in all directions.* Inanimate objects send back a signal. A moving intruder would set off a change in a signal and set off the alarm. Unfortunately, air disturbances, noise and electrical interference can set off false alarms. Temperature and humidity will effect the range of these detectors.

Microwave Fields. Microwave fields are used by other motion detectors. A disturbance in the field will set off the alarm. Microwaves penetrate material other than metal so motion in another room or unit might set off an alarm. False alarms can occur from "cross-talk" when microwave fields overlap. So more isn't always better than less. Another problem is that fluorescent lighting is sometimes picked up by microwave detectors and read as a motion due to radiated ionization. Water moving through plastic drains may also be read as motion.

Infrared Beams. *INFRARED BEAMS are those beams visible with infrared glasses that we see in all the spy movies.* If a beam is interfered with, an alarm goes off. The advantage of these units is that they can cover long distances and can be used outdoors. When used outdoors, they should be set up high enough so that small animals don't set them off.

Spot Detectors. A spot detector is a single-location detector which is set off by touching a particular metal object.

Vibration Detectors. Vibration detectors can be fined tuned to sense a glass cutter or a person tip toeing across a floor. They are subject to false alarms from truck traffic, sonic booms and sometimes just the sound of an air conditioner kicking in.

Dual Units. *DUAL UNITS combine two sensor technologies which require both sensors to indicate that there is an intruder before the alarm goes off.* This unit can be an advantage because it practically eliminates false alarms. However, if one part of the alarm is inoperative the unit is useless. Some new units are equipped now to send an alarm even though one sensor may be inoperative.

Any alarm is worthless it if isn't turned on. It can be turned on automatically by a clock or manually. If the alarm system is manually operated, a person must be delegated that responsibility and supervised.

Alarm Box

The alarm itself should have no external wires that can be cut. The alarm box should be incapable of being disabled with ordinary tools.

TELEVISION CAMERAS

Security cameras placed in lobbies, hallways, elevators, storage areas, laundry rooms, etc. can act as a deterrent to crime. Don't hide the fact that security cameras are on the premises. You should consider placing signs to point out this fact. Some vandalism of the cameras may occur but at the same time you may end up with photos of the vandals themselves.

Mock Cameras. Some stores used mock cameras to deter shoplifting. Although a good deterrent, property management should not use mock cameras because they could give tenants a false sense of security on the premises and as to their actions as tenants. If you use both real and mock cameras then advise the tenants and guests that the premises are not totally covered by cameras to record their movements.

Monitoring. While security cameras in large apartment complexes and office buildings may be monitored by guard response, most cameras simply provide 24-hour taped coverage which can later be viewed should a crime occur. Cameras can act as a deterrent but all tenants can hope for are photographs of any criminal activity. Tapes should be stored for at least 48 hours before being reused.

Cameras can reduce the probability of crime and vandalism inside and outside the premises.

Covert Cameras. Most cameras are overt installations being used as a crime deterrent. A covert or hidden camera can be installed if you find it necessary to try and catch the perpetrator or perpetrators where a series of thefts have occurred. Installing hidden cameras is especially important if there is a suspicion that the problem may involve a management employee or employees. Covert equipment, which can be rented, is usually compact in size so that it can be easily concealed using just a small camera lens opening.

Indoor and Outdoor Cameras. Camera units are available for use either indoors or outdoors. However, keep in mind that any camera is useless unless the viewing areas are well lighted.

Maintenance. Solid state cameras perform the best with minimum maintenance although maintenance contracts can be arranged. Guard service employees or management employees can learn to reload the cameras. The cameras can be stationary or set to sweep a viewing area. Cameras are available to record in black and white but most use color tapes.

Use of Tapes. Tapes can be viewed at high or slow speed as well as viewing per frame. Most tapes record dates and times so the time of an incident can be checked quickly.

Sensors activate some cameras so that they only turn on due to motion. This makes tapes easy to monitor.

> *Like other elements of security, cameras are only part of a total program.*

BOMB SEARCH

> *If you receive a telephone call as to a bomb, immediately notify the authorities and evacuate the premises.*

You want the occupants to be moved at least 100 yards from the property because flying debris can injure over a wide area. Leave any search to professionals. Similar action would be prudent if you had reason to suspect that a package on the premises contained a bomb.

Some tenants may generate a degree of hate which could result in a bomb scare. This type of tenant can include birth control centers, governmental offices and some political and religious groups. Strange packages at any location involving these types of tenants should be treated seriously.

RENT COLLECTION SECURITY

Not too many years ago rent collectors used to come to each door to collect the month's rent. These rent collectors carried a lot of money to cash social security and welfare checks. Many lower-income tenants without checking accounts would have to buy money orders to send their rent in the mail. So, since tenants didn't have to pay a fee to cash a check with the rent collector, many of them waited for that knock on the door.

Security is a problem in the inner city where most of these rent collectors worked. Carrying a lot of cash even when accompanied by a guard is an invitation for disaster. Solutions would include the following.

Resident Manager

Managers can instead insist that rents be paid by money orders or checks. In other words, no cash! The method also solves another problem of concern about the honesty of the resident manager.

Mail Only (Checks and Money Orders). Any problems are spotted quickly when tenants are required to mail their rent to a central office. However it this data is not relayed to the resident manager, he or she can be delayed in working to correct problems as to late payments and bad checks.

Cash At Office Only. Some property management offices accept cash put into a slot in a safe placed next to an employee who hands out rent receipts but has no access to the safe. However, this practice could endanger the employee.

The authors recommend that whatever property is managed, that all tenants pay by check or money order.

We suggest that checks and money order be mailed to one address. Upon receipt, all checks should be stamped "For Deposit Only" immediately. After mail delivery or pickups, rents should always be deposited as soon as possible and not left on the premises. A metered self-addressed envelope can be enclosed with rent statements to ease the mailing process for tenants.

SHOWING UNITS

A number of reported cases involved assaults on female resident managers and leasing agents while showing vacant units.

As a security measure, a property manager should know the person's name and ask for identification prior to a showing. This is just using common sense. All the manager has to say is, "Our owner's require that we see a driver's license or other photo identification of a prospective renter before we show a unit." A serious prospect will not object.

EMERGENCY TELEPHONES

The installation of emergency telephones should be considered for large developments. Some large retirement communities have installed emergency telephones which connect to a gate house so that a guard may be notified in case of trouble.

EMERGENCY OXYGEN UNITS

Some elderly housing communities have placed emergency oxygen units in public areas such as recreation buildings and pool areas.

EMPLOYEE BACKGROUND CHECKS

A number of firms will check the backgrounds of prospective employees. Background checks are particularly important where security personnel are involved. Thefts are often traced to employees who were charged with safeguarding the very items taken. You don't want to be the person who hires the fox to guard the hen house.

STAFF SUPERVISION

Condominium associations that hire their own employees are able to more closely supervise the maintenance and grounds staff. Additionally, employees know each other and know the homeowners or tenants. Also employment may be long-term compared to employees of contractors. Intruders are more likely to be caught in a condominium environment than in individual homes where services are separately contracted for by each owner.

EMPLOYEE NAME TAGS

Employee name tags, including gardening staff, help the tenants identify individuals and think of them by name rather than just an employee. Claims have been made that name tags reduce employee theft. For instance, tenants would probably remember by name which employees were in an area where a theft occurred.

OCCUPANCY RULES

Residential units should have occupational safety rules. They might include:

1. Prohibit storing flammable liquids in garages and storage areas.
2. Prohibit small children using the pool or pool area without supervision.
3. Prohibit children using any hot spa or sauna.
4. Prohibit the use of bicycles and roller skates on pathways or halls.
5. No glass containers in pool area.
6. No alcohol in the sauna or hot spa.
7. Hours of pool use.
8. Closing and locking of garage doors.

SECURITY COMMITTEES

Many property managers encourage tenants to form security groups. The tenants voice recommendations to the property management and to each other as to security matters. Where residential developments are involved, tenants are encouraged to be aware of strangers and inquire why they are in the area and to write down license numbers of suspicious vehicles.

Tenant meetings help them to know their neighbors by name and they are more likely to show concern about the security of their neighbors' property and/or personal well-being.

VACANT UNITS

Vacant apartment units and vacant homes are often vandalized. In some instances, the cost or repairs due to vandalism can exceed the value of the property. In some cold-climate areas, if the electricity is cut off the plumbing can freeze which can result in water damage as well as extensive plumbing and fixture repairs.

If the property will be vacant for some time, you would want to have the valves turned off at each plumbing fixture or the water shut off to the property (unless it is needed for landscaping). Also heat must be maintained in the building, or plumbing must be drained and antifreeze placed in all drains so the traps don't break. The preferred method to drain the plumbing is to use an air compressor to be certain that all water is blown from the lines.

Boarding up the premises might be a wise choice if the property is going to be vacant for some time and other neighboring properties have been vandalized. Alternatives to boarding up property are:

1. A house sitter who would have use of the property until it is rented or used.
2. Pay a neighbor to check the property daily.
3. Installation of alarm systems.

An owner can be subject to liability if a vacant property can be accessed even if it involves a case of trespassing.

The **ATTRACTIVE NUISANCE DOCTRINE** *is that an owner can be found liable if his or her property has a condition likely to attract small children and the property poses dangers for children.* As an example, a vacant house could be expected to attract children. If a child were able to enter the house, the owner could be liable for dangerous conditions in the house should they result in injury to the child. If a child fell through a hole in the floor, then the owner could be liable. Cases have held property owners liable for the suffocation of children crawling inside old refrigerators abandoned on the property.

Vacant units can become homes to vagrants, drug addicts and youth gangs. Their presence will increase crime at neighboring properties. Managers want to keep out such occupants and want to know about any forced entries of properties so they can contact authorities as soon as possible.

FIRE EXTINGUISHERS

Fire extinguishers should be placed in public areas of commercial, office and residential structures.

Extinguishers enclosed in "break glass" containers reduce theft but do not eliminate it entirely.

Fire extinguishers will often disappear within days of replacement in some government subsidized housing projects. Drug addicts and alcoholics look at the units as found money because they can be sold on the street for a few dollars. Fire codes may require replacement. A locked "break glass" container use to be a deterrent but now the glass and extinguisher will need to be replaced.

You should have a service contract for any fire extinguishers used at your properties. The contractor ensures that all fire extinguishers are fully charged.

FIRE DOORS

Fire doors should be self-closing and are never to be locked, chained closed or blocked. Fire requires oxygen to burn. Fire doors limit the spread of fire, slow its advance and/or allow the fire to burn itself out due to lack of oxygen.

Fire exit doors should be equipped with panic hardware for easy opening. Fire doors can be secured from outside entry by simply not having an exterior lock or hardware.

One-way fire exits should have alarms and the door should clearly indicate that opening the door will set off an alarm.

The alarm isn't really for fire alert as much as it is for security.

Without the alarm, entrances that you don't want used will be opened by tenants and even propped open allowing others to enter the premises. Another danger is that someone with lawful access to the building will open the door for others to enter.

FIRE SUPPRESSION

Sprinklers are fire suppression systems.

Most residential properties lack sufficient water supply and pressure for an effective sprinkler system.

The two types of sprinkler heads are a metal plug which melts at relatively low temperature allowing the sprinklers to turn on, and a glass bulb filled with liquid which expands to break the glass setting off the sprinklers when subjected to heat.

Sprinklers should be connected to an alarm water flow in the system that would set off an alarm at the fire station or private security system.

SMOKE DETECTORS

Smoke detectors should be hardwired rather than battery operated.

This can reduce the likelihood of an inoperative unit and also their disappearance. Batteries can become disconnected or simply wear out.

Smoke alarms can easily be tested by lighting a length of cotton rope and holding the smoking rope under the detector.

CARBON MONOXIDE DETECTORS

Where garages are built within the same structure as residential units, you should consider carbon dioxide detectors. Actually, it would be a good idea to have detectors in every unit since a heating unit that is not working properly can result in dangerous carbon monoxide levels. These detectors are now quite economically priced at about $25. Tenants should sign for detectors which are provided for them. This small dollar expenditure by management shows tenants that you are concerned about their safety.

INJURIES ON PREMISES

You should immediately call for medical assistance if persons are injured on the premises or take them for medical help if they are ambulatory.

Direct pressure should be applied to control any bleeding. Where breathing has stopped, CPR should be used if you have someone trained in CPR. Don't move injured parties if they cannot move by themselves. Get names and handwritten statements from any witnesses after the injured parties have been taken care of.

SAFETY RULES

You should establish and enforce applicable safety rules for employees. They might include use of leather gloves while pruning, use of goggles and a face filter while operating edgers and blowers as well as precautions as to use and storage of flammable material.

OSHA (OCCUPATIONAL SAFETY AND HEALTH ACT)

While originally targeted at hazardous waste, OSHA has been expanded so as to be a matter of some concern to property managers. OSHA applies to interstate commerce, however, very loose interpretations as to what interstate commerce really is has included property management as part of this definition.

One category covered by the act is personal protection, and OSHA has developed standards of safety and health for personal protection. In some cases the standards seem ludicrous, such as the written requirements as to the placement of toilet paper in bathroom stalls and about 20 pages on ladder safety.

An employer who hires seven or more employees must keep records and file reports with OSHA.

Records must also be kept at the work site. These records include work related injuries and illnesses.

OSHA covers the maintenance of structures which includes personal protective devices. As an example, goggles must be worn while using certain lawn maintenance equipment.

An OSHA inspection that reveals a broken hammer handle which has been taped could result in a significant fine.

Many firms do a self-audit of safety procedures and equipment to avoid any problems. Other firms have independent consultants audit operations for safety violations. OSHA inspectors are like any other people. Some act with reason and do not make an issue of a minor infraction while other inspectors tend to go by the book.

OSHA has a number of free documents covering various types of activities. You can write for information at: U.S. Department of Labor, OSHA Publications, P.O. Box 37535, Washington, D.C. 20013-7535. OSHA's FAX is 1-900-555-3400 ($1.50/minute).

www.osha.gov
(Occupational Safety and Health Act - OSHA)

OSHA requires a posting of a log on illnesses and injuries. (See Figure 9-1.)

STATE OSHA

A number of states, such as California, have also passed Occupational Safety Hazards Acts (CAL OSHA in California).

California provides free on-site technical assistance to help identify and correct safety and/or health hazards. This service is confidential and information will not be made available to OSHA enforcement offices.

Figure 9-1

U.S. Department of Labor

For Calendar Year 19 _____   Page _____ of ____

Company Name

Establishment Name

Establishment Address

Form Approved

Extent of and Outcome of INJURY						Type, Extent of, and Outcome of ILLNESS								
Fatalities	Nonfatal Injuries					Type of Illness							Fatalities	Nonfatal Illnesses				
Injury Related	Injuries With Lost Workdays				Injuries Without Lost Workdays	CHECK Only One Column for Each Illness *(See other side of form for terminations or permanent transfers.)*							Illness Related	Illnesses With Lost Workdays				Illnesses Without Lost Workdays
Enter DATE of death.	Enter a CHECK if injury involves days away from work, or days of restricted work activity, or both.	Enter a CHECK if injury involves days away from work.	Enter number of DAYS away from work.	Enter number of DAYS of restricted work activity.	Enter a CHECK if no entry was made in columns 1 or 2 but the injury is recordable as defined above.	Occupational skin diseases or disorders	Dust diseases of the lungs	Respiratory conditions due to toxic agents	Poisoning (systemic effects of toxic materials)	Disorders due to physical agents	Disorders associated with repeated trauma	All other occupational illnesses	Enter DATE of death.	Enter a CHECK if illness involves days away from work, or days of restricted work activity, or both.	Enter a CHECK if illness involves days away from work.	Enter number of DAYS away from work.	Enter number of DAYS of restricted work activity.	Enter a CHECK if no entry was made in columns 8 or 9.
Mo./day/yr.													Mo./day/yr.					
(1)	(2)	(3)	(4)	(5)	(6)	(a)	(b)	(c)	(d)	(e)	(f)	(g)	(8)	(9)	(10)	(11)	(12)	(13)
												(7)						

Certification of Annual Summary Totals By _____ Title _____ Date _____

OSHA No. 200

POST ONLY THIS PORTION OF THE LAST PAGE NO LATER THAN FEBRUARY 1.

CHAPTER 9 SUMMARY

Security is a prime concern of property management. Security involves taking reasonable measures to protect tenants and their property and guests.

Although the lessor has moral duties, legal duties are either set forth in statute or by courts. Courts are concerned with the foreseeability of loss or injury in determining if a landlord or manager has a duty.

The many ways in which owners and managers can fulfill their security duties include:

1. Lighting. Wrongdoers prefer darkness as a cloak for their activities. Lighting involves entryways, parking areas, hallways and other common areas, and may consist of various types of lights based on need. Emergency lighting should be storage-battery operated.

2. Landscaping. Allowing a clear view and few places to hide for climbing into units increases safety.

3. Fences and Walls. They restrict entry and criminals prefer to get in and out of property quickly and with ease.

4. Doors. Solid core doors or metal clad doors resist forced entry.

5. Peepholes. Having a view of a person at the door makes it more difficult to gain entry to an occupied unit.

6. Security Chain. A quality security chain well anchored into the door and jamb will resist forced entry.

7. Locks. Quality locks resist picking and forced entry. Knob key locks and mortised locks are not much of a deterrent to forced entry. Dead bolts are far better security locks. They should be used with a good strike plate and a solid jamb.

8. Windows. Break resistant windows resist forced entry. Pins between sliding window units are far better than normal window locks. Pins can also be used for sliding glass doors.

9. Electronic Gates. Electronic gates limit access, but don't protect against access at other points of the premises or crimes by persons who have been given access.

10. Guard Gates. Guard gates are expensive to maintain because of personnel costs.

11. Guard Services. Guard providers will give you whatever services you wish to pay for. You should consider a security consultant to determine specifications for guard services.

12. Guard Dogs. Dogs should only be used in a secured vacated area. They must be secured when tenants are in the area.

13. Electronic Security Alarms. Alarms can be interior or exterior and be connected to intrusion detection devices attached to windows or doors, pressure plates, motion detectors, sounds, heat sensors, etc. The may be connected directly to a police department location, but are most likely connected to a central alarm company office.

14. Television Cameras. Cameras can be a deterrent to criminal activities. For proper use, the area must be well lighted. Tapes can be viewed to determine the identities of any wrongdoers.

15. Bombs. Bomb threats must be taken seriously. Certain tenants such as birth control centers and government offices are more likely to be the subject of threats and/or actual bombs.

16. Rent Collection. By accepting only checks and money orders the danger to property management personnel is greatly reduced.

17. Security in Showing Units. As a safety measure, an employee showing a unit should first request photo identification from a prospective tenant.

18. Emergency Telephones. Emergency telephones connected to guard gates can help to promptly report any emergencies.

19. Emergency Oxygen. Elderly housing developments might have oxygen available in public areas for emergency use.

20. Employment Screening. You reduce the probability of future crimes by checking the backgrounds of job applicants.

21. Staff Supervision. Tight supervision reduces staff crimes.

22. Employee Name Tags. Employees who are known by name among tenants and other staff are more likely to be identified for wrongful activity if any. This works as a crime deterrent.

23. Occupancy Rules. Rules can reduce both accidents and crime.

24. Security Committees. Involving tenants in security matters results in proactive tenant actions as well as the likelihood of catching any wrongdoer after the facts.

25. Vacant Units. Vacant units must be protected against vandalism, illegal occupancy, and the elements.

26. Fire Extinguishers. Fire extinguishers should not only be available on the premises but also be operable. A maintenance contract should be considered to keep them in working order.

27. Fire Doors. Fire doors should never be locked. The doors should also be self-closing. Panic hardware and alarms should be installed on exterior doors.

28. Fire Suppression Systems. Sprinklers should have an alarm attached to the water supply (flow alarm) which is connected to a central system or fire department.

29. Smoke and Carbon Monoxide Detectors. These detectors are for safety of the tenants.

═══ CLASS DISCUSSION TOPICS ═══

1. Estimate the total guard costs at a multi-gated project or facility in your area.

2. What type of security should be considered for a high-rise apartment building?

3. What type of security should be considered for a large shopping mall?

4. What type of security should be considered for a large mobile home park?

5. What properties in your area have poor lighting in the parking areas?

6. What properties in your area have what you consider to be good security? Why?

═══ CHAPTER 9 QUIZ ═══

1. In ascertaining a landlord's duty to provide for security, determinant(s) of that duty would be:

    A. cost of the property
    B. foreseeability of harm
    C. prior criminal activity on the premises
    D. both B and C

2. You could be liable to a tenant who was the victim of a crime if you advertised an apartment as being:

    A. behind security gates
    B. managed by a security conscious firm
    C. safe
    D. patrolled by security guards

3. Which of the following would help to provide for security of the tenants?

    A. A well lighted parking area
    B. The absence of high bushes and trees around entryways
    C. Emergency lighting in halls and entrances
    D. All of the above

4. The best break-in resistant doors would be:
   - A. hollow core
   - B. solid core
   - C. those having peepholes
   - D. interior doors

5. The most secure door lock would be:
   - A. one with the fewest tumblers
   - B. mortised into the door
   - C. one with a knob key
   - D. a dead bolt

6. The more difficult padlocks to force open have:
   - A. long shanks
   - B. hasps
   - C. short shanks
   - D. tumblers

7. Ways to prevent lower windows from being entered include:
   - A. replacing glass with glass block
   - B. replacing glass with Lexan
   - C. window bars
   - D. all of the above

8. The LEAST desirable electronic gate employs:
   - A. a radio controlled opener
   - B. a sliding gate
   - C. a gate which swings open from the center
   - D. a wooden bar that drops

9. A proactive guard patrol would:
   - A. question persons who appear out of place
   - B. respond quickly to alarms
   - C. investigate crimes
   - D. all of the above

10. Alarms can be activated by:
   - A. breaking or opening a circuit
   - B. movement
   - C. vibration
   - D. any of the above

Answers: 1. D; 2. C; 3. D; 4. B; 5. D; 6. C; 7. D; 8. C; 9. A; 10. D

Maintenance and Energy Conservation

KEY WORDS AND TERMS

Aluminum Wiring
Automatic Damper Control
Blanket Wrap
Blown Insulation
Built-up Roofs
Caulking
Contract Specifications
Double Glazed Windows
Duct Work
E Value
Energy Conservation
Exterminator
Florescent Lights
Foam Roofs
Force Account
Graffiti
Heating and Air Conditioning Engineers
Improvements
Insulation
Insulation Paint
Maintenance

Maintenance Records
Name Tags
Patch-and-Hope Repairs
Pigeons
Pressure Washing
Preventative Maintenance
Priority of Repairs
R Value
Rebond Pad
Roof Pitch
Solar Heat
Solar Lights
Standardization
Temporary Help Services
Ten-day Week
Tile Roofs
Venting
Water Conservation
Weatherstripping

LEARNING OBJECTIVES

In this chapter you will learn about maintenance, property improvements and energy conservation.

You will understand the basis of making decisions as to the use of employees or contract providers for maintenance work, the importance of privatizing maintenance tasks, setting specifications and striving for standardization. You will also appreciate scheduling work by need rather than by calendar days.

You will gain an overview of the specific maintenance problems which a property manager can expect to encounter as well as the corrective measures that are likely to be appropriate.

You will understand the importance of the difference between repairs and improvements.

You will gain the insight to make a preliminary energy audit of a property and recommend how energy and water can be conserved.

Your Maintenance Program

MAINTENANCE *is the upkeep of property.* It involves cleaning, repairing and servicing of a property to obtain the use benefits needed at the present time and in the future.

> *The best form of maintenance, ideally, would be preventative maintenance.*

Changing filters, belts, oiling bearings, painting, etc., can reduce breakdowns or more costly maintenance or repair.

Problems will occur no matter how good your preventative maintenance program is. Things that can break will break at some time. Repair or replacement then becomes necessary.

Some maintenance programs deteriorate to the point of "putting out fires" or repairing what has broken resulting in preventative maintenance taking a back seat. If this is the case, long-term economies could be realized by increasing the staff so that part of the work schedules can be spent on preventative maintenance duties.

Keeping some sort of records such as ledgers, stickers or tags could provide a method for checking the preventative maintenance schedule on vehicles and equipment. Tags could be attached to serviced indoor equipment, including a date and signature of the employee performing the task.

Preventative maintenance schedules could be documented in a computer as a reminder of both work performed and checking on work completed.

EMPLOYEE VERSUS CONTRACT SERVICES

For many years, battles raged within the General Services Administration of the Federal Government as to using force account or contracts for maintenance services. **FORCE ACCOUNT** *refers to the use of employees versus contract services.*

On the side of force account were government personnel services whose basic existence and size directly related to the number of employees. Property managers preferred the use of contract services because their budgets couldn't be met by using employees. Weighing the use of employees on a federal government pay scale with full health benefits, sick days, vacations and retirement made the use of contract labor significantly less expensive in the long run.

A similar situation exists with large unionized corporations. The pay scales and benefits of employees results in their use being more costly than those of contractors. Contractors either provide no health services, or minimum health services, minimum vacation time, and no retirement. When there is a health plan, the employee often must contribute a portion (often one-half) of the health benefit costs. Wage scales usually begin at minimum wage level and don't graduate much beyond this point. By using contract labor, the federal government saved in the neighborhood of 30 percent to 45 percent which still left a profit for contractors.

Large nonunion building management firms can match the savings possible for cleaning and servicing large office buildings. Work done by employees can mean greater control but can also mean a heavy supervisory burden.

> *The authors have had extensive experience with both contract and employee services and strongly recommend contract cleaning services.*

Advantages include locking in costs and avoiding little problems so that management can focus on the big issues. There are paperwork advantages that contract labor has over employees. The Social Security contributions, workers compensation, unemployment coverage, liability protection and tax withholding are taken care of by the contractor. While you still pay these costs, they are included in the contract price.

We realize that our view is not universal within the property management field. Some property management companies have their own cleaning firms that are actually profit centers for the companies.

The authors prefer that services such as cleaning and landscaping be contracted for and minor repairs be handled by the owner's qualified employees. Being able to direct minor jobs is important for tenant satisfaction.

YOUR OWN MAINTENANCE COMPANY

Some management companies totally own maintenance companies that deal in minor repairs and maintenance work. Reasons for controlling a maintenance firm used at a number of properties are:

1. You can achieve better utilization of resources. As an example, a development may only need a handyperson 25 percent of the time for a few months, but 100 percent of the time the rest of the year. The units, however, may be paying a full-time person for a 40-hour week even though the only work done might be "busy" work. Work done by a contractor could mean big savings to an owner in such cases.

2. By controlling maintenance, you are the one who determines what is to be handled first as to a priority or an emergency.

3. Saving Costs. Using handypersons to change washers, install new valves in toilets, repair sprinkler systems, replace electrical outlets, etc., can mean significant savings to the owners rather than contracting for work to be done.

4. Your own maintenance company can be a separate profit center because you can save an owner money while still making a reasonable return on the company.

Controlling your own company that is performing the majority of maintenance and cleaning work should not be a problem as long as the owners understand that the firm is yours, what and how the work is priced and that the owner has given written permission to use your firm.

> *Use of your firm's maintenance organization should NOT be a requirement of management.*

You have a duty to recommend to owners that employees be used rather than your company if the properties can support a full-time staff and owner-employees offer advantages over your contracting services.

Where feasible, you should obtain competitive bids for significant repairs before deciding to use your maintenance company so as to avoid the appearance of a conflict of interest. Failing to do so would be a disservice to the owners.

Bids will not be competitive unless there is a meeting of the minds between you and the contractors as to the work to be performed and materials to be used. As an example, a new commode can be purchased for under $50 to $300. There are many types of commodes which affect operation, maintenance and initial cost.

Various management associations have developed sample specifications to aid in contracting.

PRIORITY OF REPAIRS

While some resident managers might prioritize repairs by who is making the most demands, repairs should be prioritized by importance if several tasks are to be assigned to one employee or an independent contractor.

Special circumstances sometimes affect the order in which tasks are performed. However, we recommend the prioritization shown in the chart on the next page.

STANDARDIZATION

Your managed properties were probably built by different contractors during different periods. Brands and quality of appliances, fixtures and hardware will vary. Repairs are not always possible because parts are no longer available. At times, replacement of an item makes more sense than trying to repair it.

For replacement, many property management firms use standardized items such as faucets and locks, using good quality items that will require less repair.

> *The "Standardization" of items makes them easy to repair by employee maintenance personnel having a supply of parts.*

DEVELOPING CONTRACTOR RELATIONS

You want to develop a core of dependable contractors who will do good work at the time they say they will perform the job and whose work is competitively priced.

> *Property management should NOT regard price alone in determining maintenance and repair contracts. Reliability is every bit as important.*

Recommended Priority of Repair

Critical (Do It Now or Sooner!)

1. Broken pipes or flooding.
2. No heat and the interior temperature is below 60.
3. No air conditioning and the interior temperature is over 85.
4. No water.
5. No electricity.
6. A "sparking" electrical outlet or appliance.

Priority Number 1

1. Garage door will not open and tenant's car is inside.
2. It is raining and there is a significant leak in the roof.
3. Inoperable commode in a one-bath unit.
4. No hot water.
5. No air conditioning and building temperatures are from 80 to 85.
6. No heat when interior temperature is from 60 to 65.
7. Any problem which involves safety.
8. Receipt of a health or fire code violation.
9. Inoperable stove or refrigerator.
10. Inoperable locks.
11. Work that must be performed before a unit can be rented.

Priority Number 2

1. Broken windows.
2. Other heating and cooling problems.
3. Minor roof leaks.
4. Presence of insects and/or rodents.
5. Inoperable commode in unit with more than one bath.

Priority Number 3

1. Gurgling commode.
2. Leaky faucet.
3. Cracked windows.
4. Drafts around doors or windows.
5. Inoperable electrical outlet or lighting fixture.
6. Moisture problem such as mold on interior walls.
7. Inoperable dishwasher.

Priority Number 4

1. Cracked or broken tiles.
2. Cracked walkways.
3. Broken or cracked drywall.

These lists are not intended to be all-inclusive but rather to give you an idea of the type of repairs which should take precedence as to their degree of importance.

You can build an excellent relationship by giving most of your work to just a few contractors. You can and should expect preferential treatment by contractors as to work timeliness, priority emergency responses and callbacks due to the volume of work you provide.

PATCH-AND-HOPE REPAIRS

You won't be able to always properly repair or replace an item or a system. There could be a delay in obtaining replacement items or parts. This may result in a "patch-and-hope that it will hold" operation. Patch-and-hope work can actually end up more expensive than if the job had been done right the first time. The owners should be notified of any patch-and-hold job as to what you are doing and why. The owners could otherwise become agitated when they find out they are paying twice for the same repair. Explain that it is a "stop gap" effort to avoid losing tenants.

Of course any repairs that are not critical should be delayed until they can be performed properly. You should explain to the tenants the reason for any delay in repairs.

THE 10-DAY WEEK

Maintenance Schedules tend to get in a rut when tied to calendar dates.

As an example, mowing the lawn once a week might be scheduled and performed regardless of the need. While lawns might require cutting regularly because of greater growth during the summer months, other times of the year this task could be performed every 8 days, 10 days or even 12 days depending upon the need. This can free valuable manpower for other maintenance duties and could even lower staff requirements.

In using an extended week, when lawn care becomes due on a weekend or holiday, move the whole calendar forward to the next work day.

The same can be done for office cleaning tasks which could vary based on need. For instance, floor maintenance should be more frequent during rainey periods than during dry periods.

Pool maintenance may need to be performed daily during warm periods and intensive use. The maintenance could be reduced to two or three times a week during colder periods and reduced usage.

Managers who are flexible can reschedule work around need rather than becoming slaves to the calendar. However, this method may not be practical for contract services.

MAINTENANCE RECORDS

Property managers, including on-site managers, must keep records of all maintenance requests and complaints.

The problem should be logged in as to when work was requested, what has or is being done to alleviate the problem, when the work was completed and by whom. If a purchase order was written up then the order number must be assigned so it can be tracked.

The person who reported a problem or made a complaint should be notified as soon as possible as to how and when the problem will be resolved. In some cases, nothing can be done. As an example, resident managers receive complaints from tenants that furnaces or air conditioners are too loud when checks will reveal that the units are well maintained and operate properly with no excess noise, loose bearings or slipping belts. You want to be concerned about problems. However, some people imagine problems or try to find fault with things. It's unfortunate, but all you can do in such situations is to reassure the tenants that what they view as a problem is really normal.

IDENTIFY YOUR MAINTENANCE PERSONNEL

Employee maintenance personnel should be uniformly dressed to make their presence evident to tenants.

They should wear a prominent name tag so it is clear to the tenants who did what. When tenants identify maintenance personnel by name, the personnel become individual people and tenant/maintenance personnel relations tend to improve. When tenants know personnel by name, they tend to become more understanding and tolerant of problems. As an example a tenant may be angry and say,

"That repairman you sent over must be a complete ninny. Ten minutes after he left it wasn't working."

Instead, the tenant might say,

"Could you send Ralph back. I don't think we solved the problem."

While this may sound over simplified, we have found that knowing names does change attitudes.

Some personnel of management firms are given personal cards to hand out to tenants when needed. They can tell tenants, "Call me if you have a problem again." Tenants are more likely to be satisfied if they feel that they have a good relationship with your personnel.

STAFFING

Professional organizations and the General Service Administration have developed staffing requirements for cleaning services based on the types of properties and the level and frequency of cleaning desired. These staffing requirements are only guides. Special circumstances as well as climactic conditions can alter the staffing requirements.

Other maintenance staffing is affected by the age of the property, quality of construction, climactic conditions, common areas, etc.

Specific Maintenance Tasks

ROOFS (New)

If you are replacing asphalt shingle roofs, the labor to install the shingles will exceed the cost of the shingles. It is false economy to buy low cost shingles. Overlapping heavyweight roofing paper should be used under the roof. Asphalt shingles, wood shingles and tile can be used on a pitched roof with a 4-inch or greater pitch. This means that for each 12 inches horizontally, the drop vertically should be at least 4 inches. By using a level and a ruler, you can quickly determine pitch.

Roofers will recommend that the first roof be removed when replacing an asphalt shingle roof. However, a second asphalt shingle roof can be installed directly over the original shingles by using at least 1 1/2 inch galvanized nails. We have applied many second roofs over existing roofs without significant problems.

Foam roofs, built-up roofs and rubber roofs can be used on flat or slightly pitched roofs. Rubber roofing is quite expensive but it provides an excellent roof.

The most widely used built-up roofs may come with a 15-year or 20-year guarantee.

These roofs consist of three sandwiched layers of roofing paper between applied hot-mopped tar. A gravel surface is then applied to reduce running tar and to provide a surface to walk on.

Foam roofs normally require an application of reflective and protective paint every two years or they will show deterioration. It can be an excellent roof if applied properly.

Tile roofs seldom have to be replaced.

The only damage might be objects falling on the roof, improperly walking on the roof or tile being blown away by strong winds.

Tile roofs normally can be expensive. The cost might be 200 percent greater than the cost of a built-up roof. Tile roofs are also heavy. Replacing singles with tiles would require engineering work to determine what if any additional roof supports would be required to support the weight of the tile roof.

Tile roofs can be of clay or concrete tile. Concrete tile is less expensive. Some concrete tiles are significantly lighter than other tiles but still heavier than shingles.

Tile roofs require at least a 4/12 pitch. They might be used in remodeling a structure that is being repositioned in the marketplace to obtain higher rents.

Flat roof buildings are frequently remodeled with a fake mansard style roof facade. The edge of the building might have 10 to 12 feet of tile roof at a 6/12 to 10/12 pitch. It is a relatively low cost remodeling effort and can change the appearance of the building.

ROOFS (Repairs)

A roof leak is often not related to where the leak appears to be. Water will follow a rafter or joist and drip through the ceiling, sometimes as far as 20 feet from where the roof leaks.

You can often determine likely spots for future leaks by visually checking a roof as well as where the current leak starts.

On built-up roofs there may be cracks in the roofing around vents, the ridge line or internal valleys in the roof. Long, straight cracks parallel to the eaves where sheets of roof paper overlap usually are the site of many leaks. Repairs are relatively simple by using roofing plastic repair material that is applied with a four inch scraper. (There are mastics that can be applied when the roof is wet). Simply brush the loose gravel off a strip on both sides of the crack and trowel on about a six inch wide swath of mastic. This also works for cracks around vents and chimneys.

If you can't locate the source of the leak, but there are areas where a portion of the pitched roof meets a flat portion, then apply mastic along the juncture. This will probably solve the problem. The same can be done around chimneys and where the roof meets any vertical wall. Apply roof cement when in doubt. It is better to patch 10 areas and find three leaks than it is to patch five areas and only locate two of three leaks.

Asphalt shingle roofs leaks can be repaired by using a caulking gun and tubes of roofing cement. Use the best mastic you can buy. Get under the edges of the shingles, around vents and chimneys with the caulking gun. The source of leaks on shingled roofs are normally less obvious than on built-up roofs. New shingles can be inserted using plenty of mastic where there are damaged or missing shingles.

While you will probably not be making roof repairs yourself, if you understand problems with leaks and roof repairs then you can supervise the work and train resident managers.

If roof repairs become a regular event, you should probably consider a new roof to preserve the structure.

PLUMBING

Because of the sheer volume of business a property manager can offer a plumbing firm, significant savings in costs can be realized by entering into a negotiated contract. The contract might specify a price per call including one-half hour of service and an hourly rate thereafter. Fixed prices might be negotiated for replacement of various sizes of water heaters (both gas and electric).

Contracts can also be negotiated for any drain cleaning services, septic system services, etc. Each owner benefits from the quantity provided by negotiating for many properties.

Minor plumbing work can be performed by general maintenance personnel.

FURNACES AND AIR CONDITIONERS

Consider a contract provider for annual services for checking oil and grease, gas levels, belts, bearings, etc. Your contracted cost per unit should be reasonable when it involves a large number of similar units. Servicing can significantly reduce expensive repairs and emergency service calls.

You should also consider negotiating for a price per call contract similar to the plumbing contract previously discussed.

Figure 10-1 is a Service Agreement for Maintenance of Heating, Ventilating and Air Conditioning. Where HVAC is a tenant responsibility, such a contract would likely be required as a lease provision.

Figure 10-1

AIR **AMERICAN INDUSTRIAL REAL ESTATE ASSOCIATION**

STANDARD FORM SERVICE AGREEMENT

[THE USE OF THIS FORM IS DEEMED TO BE IN COMPLIANCE WITH THE HVAC REQUIREMENTS OF LEASE PARAGRAPH 7.1(b)]

HEATING, VENTILATING, AND AIR CONDITIONING

_____ ("Contractor")
agrees to maintain and service certain heating, ventilating, and air conditioning equipment located at _____

for _____ ("Lessee").

This Agreement shall include the maintenance and service of the following equipment:

Description of Equipment	Make	Model	Serial No.
_____	_____	_____	_____
_____	_____	_____	_____
_____	_____	_____	_____
_____	_____	_____	_____
_____	_____	_____	_____
_____	_____	_____	_____
_____	_____	_____	_____

Said service and maintenance shall include the following:

☐ **A. Fans and Blowers**
1. Lubricate all moving parts as required.
2. Adjust tension on all belt drives and align when necessary.

☐ **B. Filters**
1. Clean or replace every ___ days with _____

☐ **C. Motors and Motor Controls**
1. Clean, oil, and/or grease.
2. Check for overload under full operation.
3. Check contractors and clean as necessary.
4. Check time clock for proper setting.
5. Check and adjust operation of all electric or pneumatic controls.

☐ **D. Gas Furnaces**
1. Check combustion.
2. Check and clean pilot.
3. Check fan limit control.
4. Check pilot safety device.
5. Check automatic gas valve.

☐ **E. Boilers**
1. Check combustion.
2. Check and clean pilot.
3. Check fan limit control.
4. Check pilot safety device.
5. Check low water cut off.
6. Check automatic water feeder.
7. Check water strainer.
8. Check pressure regulator.
9. Check relief valve.
10. Drain and recharge expansion tank.
11. Blow down boiler and controls.
12. Check automatic gas valve.
13. Check boiler control settings.
14. Check steam valves and traps.
15. Adjust controls as required.

☐ **F. Dampers (Automatic or Manual)**
1. Check and adjust for correct operation.
2. Check all linkage and adjust where necessary.
3. Check fire damper for fusible links.

☐ **G. Compressors**
1. Lubricate all bearings as required.
2. Check oil level and pressure.
3. Check head pressure. (Adjust if required)
4. Check suction pressure. (Adjust if required)
5. Check head bolts and anchor bolts. (Adjust if required)
6. Check refrigerant charge.
7. Test for leaks.
8. Check rotation.
9. Align and tighten belts.
10. Check amperage and voltage.

☐ **H. Evaporate Condenser, Cooling Tower and Air Washers**
1. Lubricate all motors and pumps and fan bearings.
2. Check pump packing. (Adjust or replace when required)
3. Check coil. (Scale or dirt)
4. Check spray nozzles. (Clean and adjust when required)
5. Check water strainer. (Clean when required)
6. Check pump strainer. (Clean when required)
7. Check float control. (Adjust when required)
8. Check drip pan and rain connections.
9. Check drive belts. (Align and adjust when required)
10. Check rotation of fan.
11. Check bleeder line. (Adjust when required)
12. Check water valve setting.
13. Adjust automatic controls.
14. Drain and flush sump pan.

☐ **I. Air Cooled Condensers**
1. Lubricate all motors and fan bearings as required.
2. Check pump packing.
3. Check coils. (Scale and dirt)
4. Check air intake screen. (Clean when required)
5. Check drip pan and drain connections.
6. Check drive belts. (Align and adjust when required)
7. Check rotation of fan.
8. Adjust automatic controls.

Page 1 of 2

FORM AA-8701

☐ **J. Controls-Electric and/or Pneumatic**
   1. Check thermostat contacts.
   2. Check starter contacts.
   3. Check damper motors.
   4. Air controls-drain water.
   5. Clean air compressor intake.
   6. Check air compressor oil.
   7. Check air compressor motor.
   8. Lubricate air compressor motor.
   9. Spot check stats for calibration.

☐ **K. Fin Coils (Water, Steam or Refrigerant)**
   1. Check for leaks.
   2. Check strainers.
   3. Check coil face for dirt.

☐ **L. Pad Type Evaporative Coolers**
   1. Oil and adjust all motors, bearings and drives as required.
   2. Adjust water distribution over pads.
   3. Check pads for dirt, looseness, sagging or disintegration.
   4. Flush sump and check for leaks.
   5. Adjust float.
   6. Oil and check pump and motor.

☐ **M. 1. Check Water Treatment Control**

☐ **N. Boiler Water Treatment**
   1. Take water analysis and make recommendations.

Maintenance, and service inspection will occur no less than quarterly and Contractor agrees to provide quarterly maintenance inspection reports, in writing, to both Lessee at the building address shown below and also to Lessee's Lessor _____

located at_____.

ADDITIONAL TERMS AND CONDITIONS

1. Lessee to receive 10% discount on repair parts.
2. Lessee to receive _____ % discount on labor.
3. Any alterations, additions, adjustments or repairs made by others, unless authorized or agreed upon by Contractor, will be cause to terminate this Agreement.
4. Repairs necessitated by fire, floods, acts of God, abuse or the improper use of equipment listed will be the sole responsibility of Lessee and are not covered by this Agreement.
5. This Agreement does not cover any work or changes which might at some future date be required by government regulations, or insurance company requirements.
6. While this Agreement covers all functional components of the air conditioning system, it does not cover ductwork, structural supports or other sheet metal components which may deteriorate due to corrosion or rust.
7. NEITHER PARTY to this Agreement shall hold the other responsible for any indirect or consequential damage of a commercial nature such as, but not limited to, loss of revenue or loss of use of any equipment or facilities.
8. Contractor's maximum liability based upon any claim or cause of action shall not exceed the yearly contract price of this Agreement.
9. Payment for this Agreement will be net upon receipt of invoice. Contractor reserves the right to discontinue service any time payments have not been made as agreed.
10. This Agreement may be terminated by either party upon 30 days written notice. A refund for the remaining contract period will be made on a prorata basis, with deduction for work already completed.
11. Lessee shall receive Priority Service.

BILLING ADDRESS

The address for the billing of Lessee shall be: _____

_____

CONTRACT PRICE

The price for this service contract shall be $ _____ per year, payable _____.

TERM

The initial term of this contract shall be from _____ to _____.

CANCELLATION

In the event that this agreement is canceled or terminated, Contractor agrees to provide written notice of said cancellation or termination to Lessor at the address listed above.

Dated: _____   _____
                                       CONTRACTOR

Dated: _____   _____
                                       LESSEE

NOTE: These forms are often modified to meet changing requirements of law and needs of the industry. Always write or call to make sure you are utilizing the most current form: AMERICAN INDUSTRIAL REAL ESTATE ASSOCIATION, 700 So. Flower St., Suite 600, Los Angeles, CA 90017. (213) 687-8777.

Page 2 of 2
STANDARD FORM SERVICE AGREEMENT

                              FORM AA-8701

PAINT

When one of the authors actively engaged in property management, he required the same brand of off white color paint be used for all residential units. By using quality paint, a maintenance worker could touch up a unit between tenants in less than one hour. A little spackle was applied to picture holes and allowed to dry before painting.

For exterior trim, six basic colors of paint were used. Touch up was easy and repainting never required more than one coat.

Consider if the entire building needs repainting or just the trim before going ahead with exterior painting. It is often just the eaves that need to be painted. By using matching paint, the trim can be repainted without doing the entire exterior.

Often, just one or two sides of a building require repainting. With matching colors, you don't have to repaint the whole building.

> *Owners are thrilled when you save them money. This is the type of savings they'll tell their friends about.*

To match existing paint, you can cut a chip from the wood trim and take it to any major paint store. A machine will compute the color formula to match your chip close enough to the original color. If you use the new paint, paint an entire wall or trim on one side. Don't paint just one small area or the matched paint might be obvious to the naked eye and appear to be a patched up job.

Do not use latex paint to paint decks. Latex paint peels on decking within a year from exposure to the elements. You can match latex colors with a semi-transparent or solid color oil base paint made for decks.

Spray painting is fast but it can create liability problems. Contractors should be able to verify that they carry high limit liability protection. Dark color cars parked half a block away during a spray painting job may develop a speckled appearance from just a gentle breeze.

CARPETING

The way to save on carpeting is not by using an inexpensive pad. Even good carpeting will wear out fast from a cheap pad. The pad should be at least 9/16th of an inch in thickness and made up of recycled foam chunks (rebond) rather than a pad uniform in color and texture. Rebond pads hold up well and don't mat down like cheaper pads.

Where you can save on carpeting is by obtaining a competitive price on installed, per square yard carpeting based on quality and pad.

The contract would indicate yardage you used in the prior year and while you're not obligated, if you do buy carpeting, you agree to purchase it from the contractor at the agreed installed price per square yard.

Your contract could include both residential and commercial carpeting prices and would probably be negotiated rather than given to a low bidder. You want to negotiate with a firm you have worked with before and were satisfied with the promptness and quality of work.

If you had used 5,000 yards of carpeting per year at an average price of $18 per yard installed, that amounts to $90,000 worth of business. For that much business you can expect a firm to sharpen their pencils. At $90,000, cutting the cost by $3 per yard would mean a savings of $15,000 and, in the above situation, this price cut may be conservative.

While you may enter such a contract for just one owner's property, you could do so for multiple owners. The more business you can provide, the better the price break.

If you can guarantee a minimum number of yards of carpeting then even greater savings are possible.

We suggest that colors be limited and carpet scraps be stored for future repair purposes. A light neutral Berber carpet with a tight pattern wears well. It doesn't matt down and show traffic patterns and it cleans well. The disadvantage of Berber carpeting is that if a loop is pulled, it can unravel like a run in a nylon stocking. This requires extensive repair work. There are dozens of brands of carpeting with each firm producing a number of grades. The minimum FHA specifications are of a low quality carpeting which you would not want to use in a rental property. The carpet just would not hold up.

When evaluating carpeting, experts will look at the backing.

When the lines of threads are tight and close together on the jute backing, this means it is a denser, better quality carpet. By checking the underside of a very cheap carpeting and expensive carpeting you'll soon realize the difference in carpet quality. Your carpet dealer will be your best instructor. Because the dealer will want your continued business, he or she will instruct and guide you as to carpet types and quality for your properties.

AIR FILTERS

Dirty air filters reduce the flow of air, increase cooling and heating costs and place unnecessary strain on air conditioning and heating systems.

Tenants have been known to remove filters when air flow decreases. This results in dirt, otherwise trapped in the filter, to flow into the rental space. Dirty streaks form across ceilings and around heating and cooling vents. This results in the need to repaint between tenants. Because removal of a filter is difficult to substantiate, the property damage bond may not cover the cost. The tenant will claim normal wear and tear.

Because air filters are relatively inexpensive and easy to install, many lessors install new filters at the beginning of tenancies and replace the filters on a regular basis.

New metal filters are available that can be washed. Some property managers who have used them have indicated to us that the washing time of the metal filters is more costly than simple replacement with fiber glass filters.

In some properties, such as laboratories, cleanliness is of extreme importance. You may use electronic filters to electrically charge particles in the air and trap them. These filters require a regular maintenance schedule.

PRESSURE WASHING

Walkways in malls and shopping centers can get filthy over a short period of time with stains, wads of gum, etc.

Pressure washing and/or steam cleaning can be used on walkways, patios, garage floors, concrete driveways and parking areas. It is a quick way to remove dirt. Most stains can also be removed or be significantly reduced with available detergents on the market that can be used with the pressure washer.

Pressure washing can also be used to clean exterior walls and remove algae-type growth from walls in areas with high moisture and humidity.

Professional pressure washers charge by the job or a per/hour rate. Some management firms own their own pressure washers or have purchased them for owners of large properties.

GRAFFITI

Gang slogans, messages and obscenities spray-painted on walls will affect an area economically. Many people are intimidated by areas of heavy graffiti.

One large department store has one of its service personnel go around the exterior of the building at 7 a.m. every morning and roller-paint over any art displays from the night before. After many months, the graffiti has almost ceased because the perpetrators have realized what is happening.

Painted buildings are best touched up with latex based paint. However, for brick and stone structures, pressure washing, solvents, and even sandblasting may be necessary to obliterate graffiti. Once gone from brick or stone, there are a number of treatments which can be applied to act as a sealer and/or make paint difficult to adhere, allowing pressure washing to quickly remove the graffiti.

EXTERMINATORS

Although some tenants will bring roaches, earwigs, ants, etc., into your building because of poor housekeeping, even the most immaculate tenant can't eliminate this problem.

For apartment units, we recommend negotiating a price per unit for monthly extermination service.

When you're negotiating for 1,000 units you will find that exterminators will develop very sharp pencils. Don't use employees to do extermination work because of liability problems.

PIGEONS

Managers of commercial and office properties often encounter serious problems involving pigeons. They create a mess and are believed to be responsible for the spread of disease. Many properties have more than one person employed on a full time basis just to clean sidewalks and benches in plaza areas.

The most effective way to eliminate the pigeons is to cut off their source of food.

Pigeons disappear when people stop feeding them. While you have no control over off-site feeding, you can stop tenants, employees and guests from doing so on your property.

Some commercial firms claim that they can rid your property of pigeons. The schemes include:

1. Cutouts or Plastic Owls and Snakes. These scare the pigeons for a short time, however, they soon realize they're no threat.

2. Ultra-high Frequency Sounds. The effect does not seem to be permanent.

3. Recordings of Distress. Recordings of pigeons in distress or pain are a short-term remedy.

4. Gooey Substances. Sticky substances spread on ledges works for awhile but soon collects dirt which cakes the substances and the pigeons return.

5. Bed of Nails. Plastic strips with protruding plastic nails (about 3" x 4" in length) can be attached to ledges to take away the roosting site. While they are effective, they must be applied to every possible roosting area. Even then, you may only find that the pigeons have moved to the next building and still mess your walkways, etc.

6. Raptors. Hawks moving into an area will cause the pigeons to decrease significantly. Check with your Department of Natural Resources or Fish and Game Commission. Making your property more inviting to raptors could have a negative effect. One property manager who managed to attract raptors to his office building received many complaints from horrified tenants witnessing hawks tearing apart pigeons on the ledges of their office windows.

7. Traps. State and local officials might approve the use of traps to catch the pigeons. If you release the pigeons rather than destroy them, they will likely migrate back to your property.

8. Poison. **Never use poison**. Dead pigeons cause public relations problems. Also, you could pass the poison on to a protected species such as raptors. In addition, you can expose yourself to great liability even if you received approvals to use poison.

We are not aware of any magic bullet for pigeon control. Your state Department of Fish and Game might have some suggestions based on your situation.

GULLS, DUCKS AND GEESE

Like pigeons, these birds cause problems to property owners. A beautiful landscaped garden and pond can become an eyesore that no one will come near.

Some golf courses have resorted to controlled shooting to try to keep the numbers in check. *ROCKET NETS can catch whole flocks for relocation purposes and have been effective with geese.* You must check with your Department of Fish and Game before dealing with migratory waterfowl. Local ordinances may prohibit shooting them or the use of poison. In Las Vegas, one golf course is using a specially trained sheep dog to chase ducks and geese away from the greens.

CLEANING

Depending upon the size and type of cleaning, you can use contract services or employees. You want to set up specifications of the jobs to be done so that personnel and supervisory personnel know what is expected of them.

By attending trade shows, you will discover equipment and products that can make the cleaning jobs more efficient as well as provide labor savings.

TEMPORARY CLEAN-UP WORK

A relatively low-cost clean-up method is to use a temporary service when you need unskilled labor to do simple jobs around your property. These services cover withholding, worker's compensation, unemployment insurance and carry liability coverage. Hiring temporary service is often quicker than trying to bring in a contractor.

Your local services most likely have people with their own tools who are qualified to perform some trade tasks.

NEVER hire the jobless who congregate in the early morning hours at the local 7-11 store or other locations as you could create a worker's compensation problem should any hired worker be injured.

In addition, you might find that you're hiring someone with physical or emotional problems or drug or alcohol dependency.

ALUMINUM WIRING

Aluminum wiring was used from the 1960s into the early 1970s because it was cheaper than copper.

The price of copper was relatively high because of the Vietnam War. Aluminum wiring tends to oxidize where it meets copper wire or a brass electrical fixture connection. A gap develops and electricity can jump the gap and can result in a serious fire hazard.

By removing electrical wall plates, you can usually determine if you have aluminum wiring (a silver grey wire). An electrical contractor or engineer should be contacted if any corrective measures are needed. It could be just cleaning connections or it could mean rewiring.

Improvements

DEFINITION

IMPROVEMENTS *are additions to property.* Improvements are more than just repairs because you are giving the property something that was not there before.

An improvement could be an air conditioner which the building did not have. However, replacing an air conditioning compressor unit and cooling fan assembly are only repairs.

> *A property owner would prefer that your monthly statement show work performed as a repair rather than as an improvement.*

Repairs can be totally written off as an expense in the year the work was performed. An improvement must be added to the owner's cost base and only a small portion written off on the improvement each year. There are gray areas as to what are repairs or improvements. Don't be dishonest. In such situations, your billings should reflect whether you regard the work performed as maintaining a status or giving the property something it never had.

ECONOMIC AND UNECONOMIC IMPROVEMENTS

> *An over improvement is NOT economic.*

In determining the economics of an improvement, consider the effect the improvement has on the net. As an example, assume you want to add a tennis court at a 12-unit apartment building site. Assume the construction costs will be $60,000 and the estimated annual maintenance will be $2,400. Assume that the tennis court can allow you to raise rents $20 per unit per month.

The mathematics of this improvement are:

12 x $20   = $240.00 per month additional income
12 x $240 = $2,880.00 increase in annual gross income

$2,880.00
- 2,400.00 annual maintenance
   $480.00 annual net income

$480 ÷ $60,000 = .008

The investment would provide 8 tenths of one percent return on income. No investor would consider this acceptable. Nevertheless, the investment might be made by an owner who wanted pride of ownership and/or use of the courts.

However, assume a hot spa and sauna could be added for $8,000 which would allow rents to be raised by $20 per month for each unit. Assume estimated maintenance costs at $1,800 per year.

Using these figures

$20 x 12 = $240 per month rent increase
$240 x 12 = $2,880 per year rent increase

$2,880.00
-1,800.00 maintenance
$1,080.00 net revenue gain

$1,080 ÷ $8,000 = 13.5

A 13.5% return on investment would make this improvement appear economically viable.

An uneconomic investment based on present mathematics might nevertheless be economically sound if it keeps vacancies down in a marketplace where an oversupply of units is anticipated. Another factor is if tenants are less likely to move, additional maintenance and vacancy periods are reduced.

The owner of a 15-unit, garden-style office complex recently spent $25,000 on improved landscaping that included a fountain, bird feeders, picnic tables, etc. in an interior courtyard. Although the tenants were on multi-year leases with no chance of rent increases, the owner's sole purpose for the improvements was tenant retention when the leases expired. The owner of this office complex wanted a unique feature that would keep the tenants and their employees happy.

When an area is undergoing a positive change, such as a gentrification of a rundown neighborhood, improvements to bring a property up to par with neighboring properties would normally be an economic decision as to income and increase in value. When the neighborhood is declining, improvements are unlikely to be economically sound.

Curb-appeal improvements, such as new facades or landscaping, don't affect the rental space but it will affect the rental. Improvements such as these increase interest in the property by prospective renters, and give the tenants a sense of pride which can reduce tenant turnover.

Mechanic's Liens

Unpaid contractors, subcontractors and material providers can place a lien against property for which they supplied goods or services if they have not been paid. This is called a **MECHANIC'S LIEN.** In many states, unlicensed contractors cannot file a mechanic's lien.

If a tenant has authorized work on the premises, you want to make certain that the contractor cannot go against the property. You would record and post a **NOTICE OF NONRESPONSIBILITY** *on the premises to protect against this type of problem. The notice would state that the owner is not responsible for any work on the premises.* This notice must be both recorded and posted within a statutory period of having knowledge of any work that has begun. Failure to do so could subject the owner to liabilities for the work, even though the owner was not the person who authorized it.

> *As the property manager, your failure to protect the owner could subject you to liability.*

The contractor could foreclose on the property to satisfy the judgment if it were not paid.

In shopping centers where stores are being fixtured and/or remodeled by tenants, you will often see notices of nonresponsibility posted on the plywood covering the storefront.

Where ground leases or other leases require the tenants to construct improvements, the owner would generally not be protected by a notice of nonresponsibility.

> *In many states prior to filing a lien, a contractor must serve a preliminary notice on the prime contractor, the lender and the owner.*

In representing the owner, if you receive such a notice from a subcontractor then you would want to make certain that the subcontractor is paid. You could pay direct or as part payment for the work, give the prime contractor a check payable to the subcontractor who had filed a preliminary notice.

The filing period of a lien differs by state. Filing a notice of completion may shorten the lien period.

A bill does not have to be paid just because the contractor threatens to file a lien. If the lien is filed, you can get it removed by posting a bond. You can then have the court decide as to the rights involved.

Mechanic's liens seldom become a problem on small repair jobs. They do become problems on large dollar repairs or improvements where subcontractors are involved.

Even though contractors may fail to file a lien, it does not mean that they aren't entitled to be paid. The debt remains even though the lien rights are lost. To enforce the debt, the contractor would have to sue on the debt, obtain a judgment and then go against the debtor's property.

Energy Conservation

From a strictly economic sense, the reduction of energy costs to property owners is a benefit as it increases the bottom-line return on an investment.

An additional benefit and ethical consideration is that the use of less energy produces cleaner air and the saving of non-renewable resources for the future. Savings in energy and water consumption is earth-friendly activity that all of us should embrace.

Saving on water is becoming more important as our clean water sources are depleted and our need for water increases.

HEATING AND AIR CONDITIONING ENGINEERS

A heating and air conditioning engineer can evaluate your building and make energy-saving recommendations.

Older air conditioning and heating units are less efficient than newer units today. An engineer can evaluate usage and tell you how long it should take to recover the initial costs of installing a new unit so that an economic decision can be made.

The engineer can also recommend economic modifications of existing systems and energy conservation methods for your particular property. Your local gas and electric companies may provide this evaluation as a free service.

GOING TO INDIVIDUAL UNITS

Landlords who pay for central air and heat provide no incentive for tenants to conserve energy. Tenants who pay for these services become cost conscious.

Heating and air conditioning engineers can evaluate your building as to the cost of changing a central system to individual systems for each unit. You will have to figure in any rent adjustments where needed if the tenants are to bear these costs. You can also determine how long it will take to recapture your investment in the individual systems. Sometimes conversion is too costly to make economic sense.

AUTOMATIC DAMPER CONTROL

An automatic damper control on a furnace keeps the flue open while the burners are on and closes it when the burners go off. Furnace generated heat which would otherwise escape the building through the flue is instead trapped within the building to provide additional heat.

ELECTRIC USE CONTROLS

Lower electric rates are possible in many areas. This is possible if you agree to have the electric company install a unit which allows the provider to turn off the air conditioning unit for up to 15 minutes if an overload is threatened within the service. The savings makes sense because this service only affects the air conditioner for relatively short periods of time. Check your local electric utility provider as to the availability of this type of plan.

WATER HEATERS

You will want to use an energy efficient water heater if it is to be replaced rather than just shopping for the lowest priced unit. Savings can quickly add up for a slightly higher priced unit. If your using a gas water heater, you will want one with an electronic ignition rather than one where the pilot light is constantly burning up gas.

All water heaters should be wrapped with an insulation blanket.

LIGHTS

Have you ever seen yard lights turned on in the middle of the day? By operating lights on a single photo electric cell or a timer you can avoid this problem. A timer should be checked every few weeks to adjust for the change in times of sunrise and sunset and readjusted after any power outage.

More light for less energy is possible by using exterior mercury or sodium vapor lighting.

In common areas, fluorescent lights use considerably less power for the desired level of lighting. The fluorescent tubes produce less light as they get older. Therefore, some managers change them once a year. They claim that following this procedure also avoids flickering tubes and costly trips replacing one tube at a time. This is a time consuming problem in office buildings with thousands of fluorescent lights.

FIREPLACES

Fireplaces work because the air traveling over the chimney draws air out of the building. However, what makes for a cheery blaze can be an expensive waste of energy. Unless the flue is closed, cool or hot air will be drawn from the building. In most modern buildings fireplaces are equipped with a metal lever to close off the chimney opening. Fireplaces in older buildings lack this feature.

Many old Victorian homes with multiple fireplaces have been converted to highly desirable office units. As a manager of such property you want to be certain that the fireplaces are inoperable by blocking off the flues or that glass doors are installed so the air vents can be closed when the fireplace is not in use.

SOLAR HEAT

Solar heaters act as heat collectors drawing heat from the sun and transferring it to a water source. Solar heaters are not likely to be cost effective for heating a structure. However, in some areas of the country they have become quite cost effective in heating water, particularly swimming pools.

Early solar collectors made of plastic soon deteriorated in the sunlight which caused leaks in the system. Products have improved today and prices have also come down. Past installations of solar units were often done at exorbitant prices.

You should evaluate the cost effectiveness of using solar heating for swimming pools because using this system alone is not adequate. You will need a back-up gas heater when the weather cools and the sun does not shine for several days. You will also need a gas heater to back up any solar heating system to reach desired temperatures for use with a spa.

Talk to owners and managers who use particular solar systems about any savings and/or problems.

SOLAR LIGHTS

Solar powered lights use a solar battery to receive power from the sun. The lights can then be set to go on at dusk using a photo electric cell. Lighting is limited to the size of the solar collector. Although not sufficient for security purposes, they can be used to light driveways and for landscaping effects. Solar powered lighting is normally used for limited illumination in non-critical areas where the cost would be excessive for electrical wiring.

WATER CONSERVATION

If the owners supply water to the units, as manager you should be interested in water conservation methods. Low volume adapters placed on kitchen faucets and showers reduce water usage. These are especially important if owners supply hot water.

Water tanks on older commodes can be fitted with one or two bricks to reduce the use of water. You would then want to check that the commode works properly. Of course, if this method now requires two flushes, it defeats the purpose.

In summer, more water may be used on greenery than is used inside homes. This is a significant area where water savings are possible.

If you don't have an on-site maintenance service, you should sign on with a sprinkler service who will check regularly and adjust and repair the system as needed.

Clocks on automatic sprinkler systems should be adjusted according to the time of year. In warm weather, sprinklers should be on every day. In severe heat, during the evening or early morning hours. Watering can be cut to every second or third day during cold periods. Use also depends upon if you're watering lawns or flower beds, which may require different sprinkler heads and more or less time.

Resident managers or maintenance personnel may find in winter that the sprinklers need only be on 20 to 25 percent of the time that they need to be on during the summer months. Setting sprinkling time is not a real science; the best method is to cut back in the water until the grass begins to look dry and then increase the watering time.

New lawns or rehabilitating neglected lawns requires setting the sprinkler system to several times per day, each for short periods to keep the ground moist but not washing away the seeding. Evening hours are the best when water pressure is high, such as 11 P.M. to 3 A.M. You would want your resident manager or maintenance personnel to make a visual inspection daily for trouble spots and broken sprinkler heads or lines. They should inspect each clock station approximately every two weeks.

Repairing sprinkler systems is very low-tech work and it only takes PVC cement, a stock of PVC fittings, a few extra pieces of tubing and sprinkler heads to handle most repairs. Should training be required, most home improvement companies regularly conduct classes in the installation and repair of sprinkler systems.

> *Resident managers should be on the alert to shut off sprinkler systems when the grounds are saturated by rain.*

VENTING

Dead air space above the ceiling becomes super heated from the sun on the roof. Even with relatively good insulation and passive venting, this hot, dead air space adds to cooling costs.

> *Wind-powered, rotating turbine-style vents are a low cost way to solve the problem.*

The wind-powered vent expels hot air and forces outside air in through other roof or eave vents. Wind-powered vents help but they don't let in much air compared to power vents.

POWER VENTS *are large power fans that push air out of the building and can be mounted on the roof or gable end.* They can be purchased for approximately $100.

Included with the power vent is a thermostat which allows the fan to turn on when attic space reaches the setting on the thermostat (such as 80 degrees) and turn off when the temperature falls below the setting. One problem with power vents is that in desert communities the fans tend to run 24 hours per day for months on end because of the desert heat. Burned out bearings after two years of constant operation are not uncommon. However, replacement is a half-hour job which is well worth the savings. Most of these fans mounted on sloped or gabled surfaces can be installed within one to two hours. They use no more current than a 16 inch or 20 inch house fan so the benefits are significant compared to the cost.

INSULATION

Insulation is measured by **R VALUE (RESISTANCE VALUE).** *The higher the R Value, the better the insulation.* You should use R Value to evaluate insulation material.

Ceiling

If the building has a roof with a pitch and the rooms have flat ceilings then there is dead air space between the ceiling and roof. There should be an access panel to this dead air or attic space. The panel might be in a closet or in an attached garage. To check ceiling insulation is simple with access to this space.

Today, if you have less than 8 inches of insulation, consider adding to make it between 12 inches and 18 inches in the ceiling area. Insulation is light so it will not cause a weight problem for the ceiling drywall unless there is a significant roof leak.

> *The additional insulation will probably be cost-effective in energy savings within three years.*

It is relatively inexpensive in material and labor costs to blow in loose insulation. We feel that this method is the better way to go for flat surfaces rather than using batts of insulation. Batt insulation tacked into place works best for sloped surfaces such as between rafters inside a building.

Any insulation improvements will save the owner money as well as the tenants if they are paying their own heating and cooling bills. Besides justifying a rent increase, lower costs will make the tenant less likely to move.

Insulation can also be placed in a hanging or dropped ceiling. However, the dead air space created between the dropped ceiling and the roof should be vented.

Where you have a flat or pitched roof with vaulted ceiling and high heating and cooling costs, you might want to consider installing a foam roof. Foam roofs contribute to insulation. Foam roofs should be regularly treated with a special paint that helps to reflect light and prevent the foam from deteriorating.

Another option for a flat roof building is to install two-inch styrofoam planks to the ceiling and apply a plaster-like coating for a finished appearance.

Walls

> *Place your hand on the inside of an exterior wall and on an interior wall. If you feel little difference in the temperature then the insulation is probably adequate.*

If the exterior wall feels hot when temperatures soar or cold when the thermometer drops, the insulation may be inadequate or might be nonexistent.

One solution is to apply styrofoam sheets with mastic to the interior of the exterior walls and then finish the surface with a troweled or sprayed treatment. If new aluminum or vinyl siding is planned, styrofoam sheathing can be added.

Insulation was not used in the exterior walls of many old frame structures. You can easily determine if this is the case by removing an electrical plate and checking around the box. To blow in insulation or insert foam insulation, you can cut access holes through either the interior or exterior walls.

The blown insulation often settles so that the upper few inches of the wall ends up with little if any insulation which can be a problem.

> *In the past, foam insulation forced into exterior wall cavities caused toxic fumes, creating an allergic reaction in many people.*

Before you decide to insulate, consult with a heating and cooling engineer as to cost effectiveness based on cost recovery through energy savings, as well as the most effective method and materials to use.

Caulking and Weatherstripping

> *Savings in heating and cooling costs can be achieved by using tubes of caulking, that cost about a dollar each.*

Check the caulking around windows and doors and where the exterior wall and foundation meet. Another area to check is where the top of the wall meets the soffit. Caulking should be done in areas where it has deteriorated or is missing.

Any exterior painting contracts should include caulking.

Drafts around windows and doors normally indicates a need for better weatherstripping. Your maintenance personnel should be familiar with the best type to use of the various brands on the market.

A snugly fitting threshold with a raised vinyl insert is one of the easiest solutions to a draft coming in from under a door.

Windows

Consider double or triple glazed window units that provide extra insulation when windows are to be replaced during remodeling.

Storm window units are available that are really add-on exterior glazed units. They are usually double-hung or sliding units installed easily on the exterior of existing windows. The are relatively inexpensive. Some are aluminum frames with built in plastic moldings for a tight fit over an exterior wall.

In the sunbelt, many people believe that single glazed windows are adequate, but heat can go both ways. Old, single-glazed windows allow a lot of heat to enter which raises air conditioning costs in many warm parts of the country.

Reflective tinted windows can also reduce the heat of the sun but also reduce the light entering the building. Again check with a heating and cooling engineer before attempting to change any windows.

Basement Walls

Frost lines in cold climates can be four feet or more into the ground. Concrete block or poured concrete walls do not provide much insulation.

The easiest way to insulate the interior walls of a basement is to apply two inch thick styrofoam which is available in 4 foot by 8 foot panels. Mastic can be used to apply the styrofoam directly to the basement walls. Plaster can be troweled onto the styrofoam surface for a finished appearance.

Basement Windows

While regular windows are often double glazed, basement windows are usually single glazed. This can create heat loss in cold areas. Two solutions are storm window kits, or clear plastic exterior shields which leave dead air space outside the basement windows. These weather shields are readily available.

Insulation Paint

A new Radiance paint is available in the United States. It has a low E-Value, which means it reflects heat. This paint is applied to interior surfaces. Developers claim that it radiates 40 percent of the heat back into the room in winter and blocks heat from entering in the summer. Energy savings of up to 30 percent have been reported with this paint. If your local paint dealers are not familiar with this product, they can contact ChemRex, Inc., 889 Valley Park Drive, Shakopee, MN 55379 or call (800) 766-6776.

www.radiance comfort.com
(ChemRex, Inc.)

Consider a special reflective paint for flat roofs. Dark colored roofing can be hot because dark colors, such as black, absorb heat whereas the reflective roof paint is relatively cool and could be cost effective.

This principal of dark colors absorbing heat and light colors reflecting heat can be applied when you decide to re-roof with asphalt shingles. In cold areas of the country, where heating costs are greater than cooling costs, a dark colored roofing would be beneficial. If cooling costs are your primary concern then you would probably be interested in re-roofing with white shingles.

Duct Work

Dirty ducts slow the passage of air through a structure. For efficient heating and cooling, air ducts should be cleaned with frequency that would vary according to location.

Ducts that carry hot or cold air as well as hot and chilled water pipes should be wrapped with insulation to minimize loss or gain in temperature through heat transfer.

COMPUTERIZED BUILDINGS

Over 30 years ago, Honeywell developed a program where computers determined how heating and air conditioning should be operated inside a building. For instance, assume an office building is vacant from 7p.m. until 7a.m. the following morning and that at 7 p.m. the temperature outside is 80 degrees with an expected low of 79 degrees. At what temperature should the interior of the building reach during the unoccupied hours for the air conditioner to cool the building down to 75 degrees by 7a.m. the following morning? If this were to be determined by guessing, a great deal of energy probably would be wasted allowing the cooling system to run unregulated during the evening hours.

A computerized building system can calculate the most energy efficient operation considering exterior temperatures and the direction and speed of the wind. Basically, the computer relays to the operating engineer or the controls directly how the system should be operated to obtain the required temperatures during the work day using the least amount of energy.

This concept first surfaced in the early 1960s when energy was cheap and computers were expensive, so it took many years to adopt. Even now, few buildings are making full use of available technology.

CHAPTER 10 SUMMARY

While preventative maintenance should be the main focus, breakdowns will occur which require repairs and/or replacements.

Economic factors as well as management requirements play a part in decisions about what maintenance, if any, shall be performed by employees or contract services. Some management firms have their own separate maintenance companies. These firms avoid a conflict of interest by fully informing owners as to how they charge for the work. The property owners in turn must give informed permission to use these maintenance firms.

By developing work specifications, you can get truly competitive bids with bidders conducting their bidding on a level playing field.

Standardizing replacement hardware makes future repairs less costly.

Repairs should be prioritized so that minor jobs are not performed first while major problems are placed on a waiting list. Repairs should not be "first come first served."

The property manager should develop a core group of responsible contractors who can be counted on to do a proper job. Price alone is not enough. Reliability and service are also of great importance.

In scheduling work as needed rather than performing work by the calendar, you might be able to free personnel for other tasks.

Maintenance records are important to track work and identify problems.

Maintenance personnel should wear identifying uniforms and name tags for tenants to recognize and build up a relationship with your personnel.

Staffing requirements will vary as to the particular property and management needs.

Specific maintenance tasks include:

    1. Roofs. Repair or replacement may be necessary. Pitch and the load-bearing capabilities of the roof would determine the type of roof replacement.

2. Roof leaks can often be visually identified. If not, areas to check are around vents and chimneys, where the flat area meets the pitched area or where the roof meets a wall.

3. Plumbing. A property manager may want to negotiate with a plumbing firm to contract on a per-call basis to include one-half hour of labor plus an hourly rate thereafter.

4. Furnace and Air Conditioning. An annual service contract as well as a per-call contract should be considered.

5. Paint. Limiting the colors makes touch-up jobs easy. Exterior paint jobs can be limited to only those sides that require paint or just the trim or part of the trim.

6. Carpeting. A quality pad is important to the life of the carpet. Try standardizing and contracting for quality carpet at a price per square yard to include labor and material. This arrangement can apply to multiple properties.

7. Air Filters. Management should be in charge of replacement to make certain the job has been done. Clean filters reduce wear on equipment and interior painting needs.

8. Pressure Washing. Sidewalks, patios, garage floors, driveways and parking areas and walls should be cleaned periodically.

9. Graffiti. Graffiti should be removed as soon as it appears. Pressure washing, painting or even sandblasting may be required for removal.

10. Exterminators. Exterminating jobs should be contracted for as to price per unit to ensure savings.

11. Pigeons. Pigeons create problems for office buildings and require frequent cleanups. Prohibiting the feeding of pigeons by tenants will help alleviate the problem.

12. Gulls, Ducks and Geese. They also create problems such as cleaning. Contact your state Department of Fish and Game for control possibilities.

13. Temporary Clean-Up Work. Consider using a temporary-help service for special jobs. The cost is usually less and the work is often done faster than if contracted for.

Improvements involve providing something new that was not there before. The owner must write off costs over the life of the improvements while repairs are expensed out during the year in which the repairs were made.

Economic decisions about improvements include the return on the investment in increased revenue, the effect on vacancy rate and future revenues.

A mechanic has a right to file a mechanic's lien after a preliminary notice. After filing a notice of completion the period for the mechanic to file a lien is set.

If a tenant authorizes work to be done, the property manager would want a notice of nonresponsibility recorded and posted so that the property does not become subject to a lien.

Energy conservation is important to reduce costs and help preserve our environment. Heating and air conditioning engineers can recommend cost savings. Individual heating and cooling units give tenants an incentive to save energy.

Automatic damper controls reduce the loss of heat through the flue. Some electric companies give reduced rates if you agree to have your air conditioning units equipped with a shut-off unit to allow your electric provider to turn off your air conditioner for brief periods should a threatened overload occur.

Consider one of the new more energy-efficient water heaters when replacement is needed. Existing water heaters should be wrapped with an insulation blanket.

Outside lighting should be connected to timers or photo electric cells. Florescent lights are less costly to operate.

Fireplaces draw hot and cold air from the building when left open.

Solar heat may be cost effective for swimming pools. Solar lights can be used for lighting landscapes.

Water conservation is possible by using low flow adapters on faucets and showers, the use of low water requirement commodes, use of bricks in commode tanks, checking sprinkler systems.

Venting dead air space reduces the heat build-up. Passive vents, air turbine or wind power vents, are available as well as the preferred fan-operated power vents.

Additional insulation can be installed in both ceilings and walls to conserve energy. Caulking and weatherstripping will also reduce energy needs. Double glazed windows provide better insulation than single glazed windows.

Styrofoam insulation can be applied with mastic to basement walls and weather shields can be place around basement windows.

Radiance paint is purported to radiate heat back into a building and prevent heat from entering during hot summer months. Reflective paint on a roof can reduce heat absorption. Light color shingles also reduce heat absorption.

Dirty ducts impede air flow. Ducts should be cleaned periodically and wrapped with insulation if used for hot or cold air.

Computerized systems installed in a building determine how heating and cooling systems should be operated.

Chapter 10

══════ CLASS DISCUSSION TOPICS ══════

1. Give examples, if any, of buildings which you feel are not properly maintained. What could be the reasons for the maintenance problems?

2. Do you know of any property management company in your area which has an affiliate maintenance company? If yes, why do you suppose they have their own maintenance firm?

3. Make a list of 10 possible repairs. How would you prioritize them?

4. Give examples, if known, of repairs handled by resident managers.

5. Which buildings or properties in your area do you know of that have problems with pigeons or waterfowl?

6. Give examples of properties in your area where conservation of electricity or water does not appear to be a priority.

══════ CHAPTER 10 QUIZ ══════

1. Which of the following repairs should be given the highest priority?

    A. Dripping faucet
    B. An inoperable commode
    C. An electrical outlet that does not work
    D. A broken bath tile

2. A roof with a one inch pitch every 12 inches needs new roofing. You would NOT use:

    A. a built-up roof
    B. tile
    C. rubber roofing
    D. foam roofing

3. The location of a roof leak is not evident. Areas to consider as to likely spots would be:

    A. around vents
    B. around the chimney
    C. where the roof meets a wall or parapet
    D. all of the above

4. To reduce summer air conditioning costs, the best color for roof shingles would be:

    A. white
    B. black
    C. brown
    D. green

5. Dirty air filters:

  A. reduce cooling and heating effectiveness
  B. cause additional wear on equipment
  C. both A and B
  D. neither A nor B

6. Pigeons can be completely eliminated as a problem by:

  A. using recordings of wounded birds
  B. placing plastic owls on the property
  C. placing plastic snakes on window ledges
  D. none of the above

7. The advantages in using temporary service workers rather than a contractor for unskilled labor jobs would be:

  A. speed in getting the job done
  B. a likely lower cost
  C. both A and B
  D. neither A nor B

8. From an owner's point of view, the difference between improvements and repairs would be:

  A. repairs are more costly
  B. improvements must be written off over the life of the improvement
  C. repairs can be shown as an expense in the year of the repair
  D. both B and C

9. An insulated blanket would likely be used to cover a(n):

  A. water heater
  B. air filter
  C. sprinkler system
  D. solar collector

10. The purpose of placing bricks in a commode tank would be to:

  A. soften the water
  B. reduce the use of water
  C. prevent the tank from cracking
  D. increase the water pressure

Answers: 1. B; 2. B; 3. D; 4. A; 5. C; 6. D; 7. C; 8. D; 9. A; 10. B.

Records and Controls

KEY WORDS AND TERMS

1099
Ad Register
Annual Statement
Audits
Beneficiary Ledger
Broker Funds
Cash Ledger
Columnar Records
Commingling
Comparative Operating Statement
Computer Management Software
Employee Files
Eviction Register
Good Funds
Inactive Files
Inspection Report
Insurance Register
Interpleader Action
Interest Bearing Trust Account
Inventory File

Journal
Lease Files
Monthly Statement
Mortgage File
Move-Outs Owing
Occupancy Factor
Offset of Trust Funds
Operating Budget
Operational Costs and Expenses
Pass-Through Funds
Payroll Records
Percentage Lease Verification
Purchase Orders
Reconciliation of Trust Account
Rent Rolls
Telephone Records
Trust Account
Trust Fund Account
Utility Files
Vendor Files

LEARNING OBJECTIVES

In this chapter you will learn about records that must be kept and records that should be kept.

Records that must be kept include trust account records. Many records are not mandatory but are used to communicate to owners and to plan ahead. Trends and changes can indicate problems or improvements. Records which indicate these can be the basis for improving operations.

You will learn that data can be assembled in many valuable formats and that by use of a computer, it becomes a practical task as well.

Your duty to your client, laws and good business practices require records that not only show operational results and what is happening but they can also be used as a planning tool for the future. Records by themselves are not enough, they must also be used or they are merely history.

Trust Fund Accounting

Property management involves the receipt of funds such as rents, security deposits and money received for a particular service or disbursement.

*Money that is not the funds of the property manager, or is not yet the funds of the property manager but are being held for some purpose or future disbursement, would be considered **TRUST FUNDS**.*

Funds received on behalf of a principal or others would be trust funds. **NON-TRUST FUNDS** would be broker-owned funds.

Trust funds do not have to be cash. They could be a personal note, or a note secured by a trust deed or even a pink slip to a car given as a deposit (these would be trust assets). The property owner must be informed of the nature of any deposit not in the form of cash, check or money order.

DEPOSITS RECEIVED BY PROPERTY MANAGER

A property manager who receives funds of others may properly do the following:

Trust Account. Funds can be placed in the property manager's trust account. The deadline is the end of the third business day following the receipt of the funds.

Service Provider. The property manager may pay the funds to a service provider such as a credit agency or for a repair bill if authorized to do so. (The checks received might be made out to the service provider.)

Principal. If the principal is entitled to the funds, they can be given directly to the principal. Payment to the principal could create a problem if the deposit has to be returned to the person who made it because the principal fails to perform some condition or the funds were otherwise subject to some condition or required performance that fails to occur.

CHECKS HELD UNCASHED

A property manager may hold a lease deposit check and other deposits uncashed if the tenant or prospective tenant has instructed the property manager not to cash the checks until something happens such as the lessor agreeing to the lease. The property owner must be informed when tenant payments are held uncashed.

Upon satisfaction of any condition placed by the person depositing the funds, the funds must be placed in the property manager's trust account or must otherwise be disbursed.

FUNDS RECEIVED BY EMPLOYEES/AGENTS

Funds received by employees or agents of the property manager must be either turned over to the broker or deposited directly into the broker's trust account if the person receiving the funds is authorized to do so.

THE TRUST ACCOUNT

> *The broker's (property manager) trust account must be a non-interest bearing demand account (checking account).*

It should be in a financial institution insured by the Federal Deposit Insurance Corporation (FDIC).

The account must clearly indicate that it is a trust account held by the broker as a trustee. Otherwise, broker bankruptcy, death or creditor judgements could tie up and possibly reach assets which were intended to be held in trust for others.

INTEREST BEARING TRUST ACCOUNTS

Interest bearing trust accounts are not commonly maintained by property managers but they are possible. As an example, an industrial lease for a long-term, such as ten years, might have a $20,000 security deposit. If this were the case, the person depositing these funds might want the funds to be in an interest bearing account as the interest over the lease period could be considerable.

The owner of the funds, who would be the lessee, could request the funds be placed in an interest bearing account in a bank, savings bank, credit union or industrial loan company providing the account is insured by the Federal Deposit Insurance Corporation.

In order to deposit funds in an interest-bearing account, the following criteria should be met for the account.

Name of Broker. The account must be in the name of the broker as trustee.

Insurance. All of the funds must be covered by insurance. (Deposits over the FDIC insurance limit might have to be placed in several accounts.)

Separation. The account must not only be separate from any broker funds, it should also be kept separate from trust funds held for others (this requires a separate trust fund for each such account). This relieves the broker of responsibility for determining interest allocations among a number of holders covering various time periods.

Disclosure. The broker must disclose to the person from whom the funds were received and the beneficiary of the funds:

1. the nature of the account;
2. how interest will be calculated and paid;
3. whether service charges will be paid to the depository and by whom;
4. possible notice requirements or penalties for withdrawal.

Broker May Not Benefit. Interest earned on funds may not benefit the broker or any person licensed to the broker (directly or indirectly).

DISBURSEMENTS FROM TRUST ACCOUNT

Withdrawals can generally be made from trust funds by a broker or by a salesperson or broker (under a written contract with the designated broker) who have been specifically authorized in writing to make withdrawals.

An unlicensed employee of a broker can also be authorized to make withdrawals. However, the unlicensed employee should be covered by a fidelity bond that is at least equal to the amount of the trust funds that the employee would have access to at any time.

Your state law will govern trust fund handling. California law is typical of state requirements. The California Code of Regulations 2834 covers trust fund withdrawals.

(a) Withdrawals may be made from a trust fund account of an individual broker only upon the signature of the broker or one or more of the following persons if specifically authorized in writing by the broker:

(1) a salesperson licensed to the broker.

(2) a person licensed as a broker who has entered into a written agreement pursuant to Section 2726 with the broker.

(3) an unlicensed employee of the broker with fidelity bond coverage at least equal to the maximum amount of the trust funds to which the employee has access at any time.

(b) Withdrawals may be made from the trust fund account of a corporate broker only upon the signature of:

(1) an officer through whom the corporation is licensed pursuant to Section 10158 or 10211 of the Code; or

(2) one of the persons enumerated in paragraph (1), (2) or (3) of subdivision (a) above, provided that specific authorization in writing is given by the officer through whom the corporation is licensed and that the officer is an authorized signatory of the trust fund account.

(c) An arrangement under which a person enumerated in paragraph (1), (2) or (3) of subdivision (a) above is authorized to make withdrawals from a trust fund account of a broker shall not relieve an individual broker, nor the broker-officer of a corporate broker licensee, from responsibility or liability as provided by law in handling trust funds in the broker's custody.

COMMINGLING TRUST FUNDS

COMMINGLING is the prohibited practice of mixing broker or general account funds *with trust funds.* Commingling could also be holding cash or checks uncashed without approval of the parties involved. Commingling is generally grounds for suspension or revocation of a real estate license.

Section 10176 of the California Business and Professions Code provides for revocation or suspension of a real estate license because of commingling.

 www.leginfo.ca.gov/.html/bpc_table_of_contents.html
(California Business and Professions Code)

Grounds for Revocation or Suspension

10176. The commissioner may, upon his own motion, and shall, upon the verified complaint in writing of any person, investigate the actions of any person engaged in the business or acting in the capacity of a real estate licensee within this state, and he may temporarily suspend or permanently revoke a real estate license at any time where the licensee, while a real estate licensee, in performing or attempting to perform any of the acts within the scope of this chapter has been guilty of any of the following:

(e) Commingling with his own money or property the money or other property of others which is received and held by him.

Article 8 of the National Association of Realtors® (NAR) Code of Ethics states:

"Realtors shall keep in a special account in an appropriate financial institution, separated from their own funds monies coming into their possession in trust for other persons, such as escrows, trust funds, client monies, and other like items."

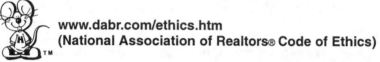

www.dabr.com/ethics.htm
(National Association of Realtors® Code of Ethics)

In California, it is considered commingling for a broker to fail to deposit designated trust funds into his or her trust account within 3 business days following receipt.

BROKER FUNDS IN TRUST ACCOUNT

> *Brokers can keep a small amount of broker funds (according to state law) in the trust account.*

The reason for allowing brokers to keep some of their own money in the account is to avoid any bank charges creating a shortage in the account. (Some brokers have the bank charges for their trust accounts charged against their general account.)

Based on state law, a broker may also keep earned commissions in his or her trust account for a designated time period, such as 30 days.

RETURN OF TRUST FUNDS

If a lease or other transaction cannot be completed for reasons other than the default of the person depositing the funds, unexpended funds must be returned to the person making the deposit.

A shortage in the trust account could result if a deposit is returned before the deposit check has cleared and the deposit check fails to clear. This problem can be avoided by a contract which clearly indicates that any check deposited must clear before any funds will be returned.

Once a deposit has cleared a bank, it is considered **GOOD FUNDS**. Good funds also include cashier checks. A broker should not return a deposit or write a check to a service provider unless the check is written on good funds.

CONFLICTING CLAIMS ON TRUST FUNDS

Should both owner and tenant make a claim to funds held by the broker, the broker should NOT turn the disputed funds over to either party.

If the broker turned over funds to one party without approval of the other party and a court later determined that the party receiving the funds was not entitled to them, the broker could be liable if the party receiving the funds were unwilling or unable to return those funds.

If the parties are unable to reach an agreement on disposition of trust funds, the broker could commence an **INTERPLEADER ACTION**, *which is a legal proceeding where the stakeholder (broker) deposits the funds with the court and ask the court to distribute the monies to the rightful claimant.*

An "interpleader action" forces the parties to plead their case in court which can be an expensive process for both parties.

Frequently the legal expense is not justified by the dollars involved. The broker should recommend that the parties reach an agreement or compromise. Some purchase contracts call for mandatory arbitration of disputes involving entitlement to trust funds.

OFFSET OF TRUST FUNDS

Trust money held by a broker CANNOT be used to offset claims that the broker may have against the party depositing the funds or the broker's principal.

As an example, suppose a prospective tenant placed a deposit with a lease application. Suppose the lease application was not accepted and the prospective tenant was entitled to the return of the deposit. Even though the prospective tenant may owe the property manager money because of another transaction, the property manager must return the funds in full and may not use such funds to offset the debt.

A salesperson with access to trust monies cannot take trust funds out of the account because the broker, owner, or tenant owes the salesperson a debt. The money remains trust money until the funds are disbursed.

TRUST FUND RECORDS

Brokers should keep a record of all trust funds received including uncashed checks held. This record (including computer records) must set forth in chronological order the following information in columnar form.

Date. Date the trust funds are received.

Source. From whom trust funds were received.

Amount. Amount received.

Date Deposited. With respect to funds deposited in an account, date of said deposit.

Disbursement Data. With respect to trust funds previously deposited to an account, check number and date of related disbursement.

Pass-Through Funds. With respect to trust funds not deposited in an account, identify other depository and the date that the funds were forwarded. (If the funds pass through the broker's hands, even though the check or note is made out to another party, they are still considered to be trust funds.)

Daily Balance. Daily balance of said account. (Trust accounts should be balanced daily and reconciled with the bank account at least once a month.)

A separate record must be kept for each beneficiary or transaction that sets forth information sufficient to identify the transaction and the parties to the transaction, and also include the information required above.

While computer records may be kept rather than using forms, a backup disk is a safety factor that should be considered. There are a number of excellent software programs available for trust account record keeping.

Most states do not require that records be kept on particular forms, but we have included the following forms which have been prepared by the California Association of Realtors.

Figure 11-1. Columnar Record of All Trust Funds Received and Paid Out. CAR TF11-1

Figure 11-2. Separate Record For Each Beneficiary or Transaction. CAR TF11-4

Figure 11-3. Record of All Trust Funds Received - Not Placed In Broker's Trust Account. CAR TF11-2

RECONCILIATION OF TRUST ACCOUNT

The trust account should be reconciled at least once a month with the record of all trust funds received and disbursed (this applies to separate beneficiary records).

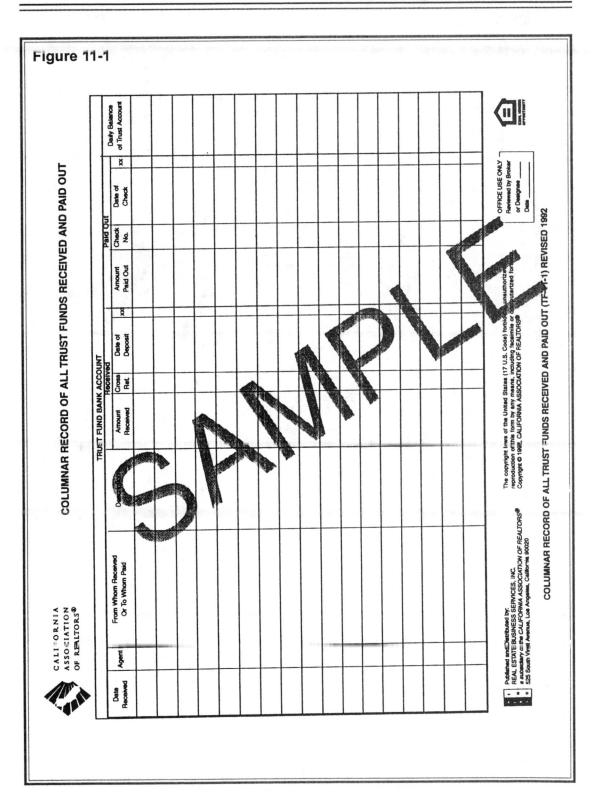

Figure 11-1

COLUMNAR RECORD OF ALL TRUST FUNDS RECEIVED AND PAID OUT

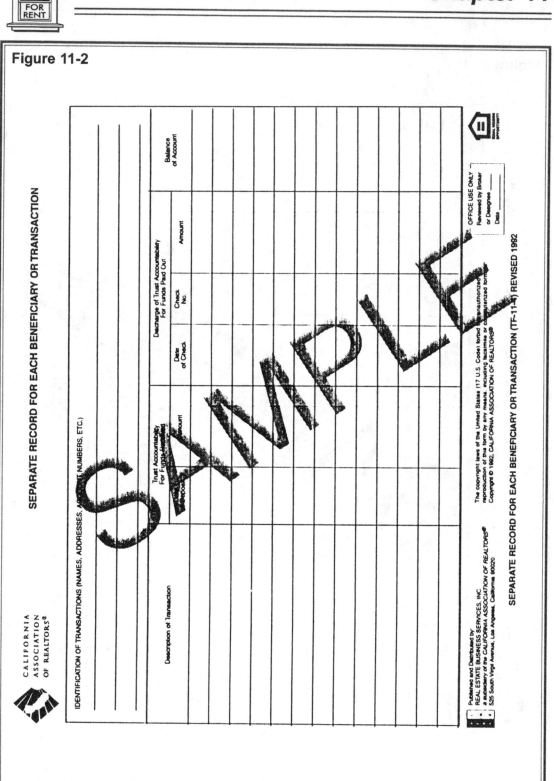

Figure 11-2

Figure 11-3

A record of the reconciliation should be maintained. This record must identify the:

1. **Identification of Account.** Bank account name and number;

2. **Date.** Date of the reconciliation;

3. **Beneficiaries.** Account number or name of the principals or beneficiaries or transactions;

4. **Broker Liability.** The trust fund liability of the broker to each of the principals, beneficiaries or transactions.

RETENTION OF TRUST RECORDS

A real estate broker must maintain trust records (as well as other records relating to a transaction) for a statutory period, such as three years.

The retention period shall run from the date of closing of the transaction.

After notice, the records shall be made available for examination, inspection and copying by the Department of Real Estate, and be subject to audit without notice.

DRE AUDITS

Your state Department of Real Estate views a shortage in a trust account and an unauthorized use of funds as very serious violations of the law. Because of the importance of safeguarding funds of others, there is a continuous program of examination of broker's records. Audits may result in disciplinary action if the trust fund is not in balance or if dangerous handling procedures are discovered. Criminal violations may be referred to the appropriate district attorney for possible criminal prosecution.

Owner Reports

MONTHLY STATEMENT

The monthly statement to an owner should show gross revenues and expenses paid. Expenses should be broken down by category so that an owner can see what has happened during the prior month. Figures for both income and expenses from a prior year for the same month can be included.

The check and monthly statement should be mailed so that they will be received by the owner on or about the same date each month. Some property managers beat their contractual obligation date for their monthly accounting.

If a check accompanying a monthly statement will appear to an owner to be surprisingly large or small, then the statement should include a notation explaining the difference.

ANNUAL STATEMENTS

The **ANNUAL STATEMENT** *is more than just a compilation of monthly statements for an owner's account to use in preparing taxes. It can also be a management tool to keep business, better owner/management relations and to use to upgrade the property.*

Some property managers like to meet with the owners to give them the annual statement. It provides an opportunity to strengthen owner/manager relations. It puts a face and adds a personality to letters and telephone calls. An owner who knows and likes a property manager is less likely to get angry at management because of a single problem.

Multiple Owner Properties

When an owner has multiple properties there should be separate statements for each property as well as a combined statement.

Comparative Operating Statement

A comparative operating statement can show the past year and prior year figures. A benefit of such a statement is that it points out the problems and the strengths relating to the property and/or the economy. It is easy to understand and quickly explain where the differences are that relate to changes in the bottom line.

Expenses should be broken down into categories that can be clearly understood. If the property manager receives calls from owners as to what something means, it is an indication that the annual statement needs clarification.

Occupancy Factor

Some management firms include an occupancy factor in their annual statement. They will also indicate the occupancy rates for the prior year or prior years. It shows changes and helps to explain bottom line changes.

Average Rents

Some annual statements show average rent for the year to per unit or per square foot. The average rent is shown on prior years and the percentage change is noted.

Balance In Account

The annual statement should show the balance in the account as well as deposits held in trust, such as security deposits, with an explanation such as why fixed costs or variable costs have risen or decreased. An annual report might point out that while the occupancy rate declined 1.7 percent from the prior year, the area occupancy rate for similar property has declined by 2.4 percent. This is not "spin control" it is explaining the "why?" of changes. Owners want to know "why?"

> *Everything but the "notes" on an annual report can be computer generated.*

Addendums

As an addendum to the annual report, you should include an inspection report. The inspection report should be a detailed form with comments. Future significant expenses should be noted. When owners are informed of work required a year or more ahead of actual expenses, they except the expenses more readily. The inspection report could indicate that a patched roof may require full replacement within the next three years.

Some property managers like to include estimated expenses and income for the coming year (operating budget). They will try to be realistic which means not overly conservative or optimistic. They will also include a paragraph as to how the annual statement related to the prior year estimates and reasons for deviation.

Some management firms like to provide an insurance summary showing amount and type of insurance coverage for each property as well as the name of the carrier.

The summary would footnote any changes made in insurance coverage and why.

> *The annual statement is an excellent communication tool if used properly.*

The owner's 1099 statement should be included with the annual statement if applicable.

Management Records and Controls

LEASE FILES

Lease files would have the original lease signed by the tenant. Computer files would show lease termination dates, dates for extensions or exercise of options as well as lease clauses or reference to a standard form if one were used. By use of a scanner, the entire lease can be available for computer viewing. The file would include a subfile of expiration dates.

PERCENTAGE LEASE VERIFICATION

While percentage leases generally require that tenants use a totalizing cash register (a register that can not be turned back), some tenants will find ways to avoid paying the required percentage on every sale.

Some lessors use the service of companies like Willmark. These firms are investigation companies that will run periodic checks. While larger retailers will seldom "play games", some smaller retailers will use every opportunity to avoid reporting sales. A checker will often arrive just at closing time and select a small item and take it to the store owner. The checker will have exact change including tax. The checker, who will be in a hurry will indicate this fact and will leave with the merchandise before the sale can be rung up. If the sale is not shown as one of the last sales of that day or the first of the following day, the owner has pocketed the money.

Larger firms seldom fail to report because, should an employee realize what is happening, the employee would be in a bargaining position to name his or her own employment terms.

INSURANCE REGISTER

The **INSURANCE REGISTER** *should indicate the insurance coverage on every property managed, the name of the carrier and policy due dates.* The policy due dates should also be flagged on a computer tickler file to make certain that coverage does not lapse on a property. It is not excuse to claim "They never billed me" when you have an uninsured loss.

Insurance coverage should be reviewed for every property managed upon taking over management duties and on an annual basis thereafter.

> *Some firms do an insurance review at the time the annual statement is prepared.*

MORTGAGE FILE

The **MORTGAGE FILE** *would show mortgage payments to be made, to who, the amounts and due date.*

RENT ROLLS

The rent rolls of all tenants, the rent they pay as well as due dates can be broken down by individual properties.

The rolls should show when tenants paid rent, any checks given that failed to clear, late changes assessed against the tenants and any rental arrearage.

With computer programs, the property manager can check on all tenants or tenants as to a particular property and can retrieve data on current rent status. The rent rolls would also show dates for scheduled rent increases.

EVICTION REGISTER

Some firms having a great many residential units track evictions using a separate register which shows when notices were sent and dates for unlawful detainer actions.

MOVE-OUTS WHO OWE

Some tenants will move out either owing rent or whose property damage bond was insufficient to cover damaged or missing property. A file should be kept on these persons and indicate your efforts to collect amounts due and accounts sent to collection services or attorneys.

Quick action should be taken to collect from "move-outs." While some of these accounts will be legally or practically uncollectible, others will be paid willingly but often over a protracted period of time.

Your initial collection effort should be letters and/or telephone calls. Collection agencies and attorneys may charge up to 50 percent of a claim, depending upon the amount. While no one likes to give up 50 percent, receiving 50 percent is better than receiving nothing.

When you can't locate a past renter, consider using a "skip tracer." These persons and firms have broad computer based access to locate the missing person. Once the person is located, you can use an attorney or collection agency to collect your past due account.

> *You have a duty to your owner to make a reasonable effort to collect all rents and damages due the owner.*

INVENTORY FILE

An inventory file should be maintained by property as to equipment, furnishings and appliances that are owned by the property owner.

VENDOR FILES

Vendor files would include approved vendors to be used by resident managers. It would include vendor history.

UTILITY FILES

Utility files would show dates for utility payments and payments made.

PAYROLL RECORDS

Payroll records must be sufficient for preparation of annual W-2 forms for employees showing income and deductions.

Records must show federal and state tax withholding as well as employee and employer social security contributions. Separate records must be kept for your payments to the government.

Computer systems will compute and prepare checks for employees as well as for tax and social security payments.

Workers compensation and unemployment compensation payments will also have to be scheduled and appropriate checks sent.

PURCHASE ORDERS FILES

Purchase order numbers should be assigned to purchases of material or services above a particular figure, such as $50. The purchase order should be tracked as to receipt of goods or completion of service. There are computer systems to aid in preparation of and tracking purchase orders.

INACTIVE FILES

Files should be maintained after management ceases for a minimum of three years.

Your Own Records and Controls

OPERATION COSTS AND EXPENSES

Besides maintaining records for owners, you want records for your own management use. They can be monthly or just annual. They would show your firm's income by category and expense by category.

By using a spread sheet format showing prior years, significant changes become readily apparent.

Besides just profit and loss, you probably would want records as to occupancy factors for all the properties you manage. You would also want records as to the type of property and annual percentage changes in rents for the same properties from the prior year by type of property.

Records could include the number of units and/or square feet under management as well as figures from prior years. You can prepare a realistic budget from all this information.

Quarterly reports showing budgeted and actual figures can help you in realizing areas that need to be addressed as well as to make changes in your operating budget.

MANAGEMENT OFFICE INSURANCE FILE

Besides keeping records of owner property insurance, you must make certain you keep records of your own property insurance covering office equipment, maintenance equipment, vehicles as well as liability coverage. Your insurance might also include bonding of employees.

> *Do NOT rely on others to make certain that you are covered. Use your computer to track coverage.*

You should also make certain that any employee using his or her own vehicle for company related business has adequate liability coverage. The employee can request coverage information be supplied to your firm by the employee's carrier.

AD REGISTER

Keeping track of what is being advertised is very important for a number of reasons.

1. **Owners.** You can show owners what you are doing to rent their space.

2. **Agents.** Agents will know what is being advertised so that they can be prepared to answer inquiries.

3. **Management Evaluation.** By evaluating ads and cost of ads for individual properties, a property manager can evaluate the economic effectiveness of the ad, the advertising media and the management contract.

TELEPHONE AND WALK-IN RECORDS

Records of telephone calls and walk-ins as to rentals should be maintained. When the caller is asking about a particular property, the person answering the telephone should find out if the party is calling from a rental sign or an ad. The same should apply to walk-ins.

Records should also be kept as to rental showings that result from telephone calls. From these records a great deal can be learned.

1. **Ad Response.** The effectiveness can be gauged by knowing the number of calls resulting from an ad. A property manager is likely to find that ads in a particular price range, area or emphasizing particular features are more effective then others.

2. **Is the Ad On Target?** If an ad brings many calls but few showings of the rental space, it would indicate that the ad is not giving the reader a true impression of the property.

The same would be true for a property that has been shown many times but has not been rented.

3. **Are the Agents Properly Trained?** If some agents are having a high percentage of telephone calls resulting in showings and have good sales while other agents have a very low percentage of calls resulting in showings, it would indicate that the less successful agent needs help with his or her telephone techniques.

EMPLOYEE FILE

You should keep an employee file that would include employees' employment applications (if any), and any pre-employment check that was performed.

The file should include employee reviews. The file should indicate employee wages and include a copy of any employment contract signed by the employee.

If a complaint has been received as to an employee's work related activities, the complaint should be included in the file and what investigation or disposition was made as to the complaint.

An employee file could be important to you in case of a lawsuit for wrongful termination or for a claim that you failed to adequately check on an employee's background or failed in a duty of supervision.

AUDIT

If you do not personally handle bookkeeping tasks, you should either perform your own audit or hire someone from outside the firm to perform one. In addition to an annual audit, it would be money well spent to have an accountant spend at least one full day going over records, deposits and disbursements at least once per quarter.

It is not a matter of your trust as to your employees, it is a mater of your agency duty to protect funds of others. You would be remiss in this obligation not to make certain that all funds are properly accounted for. It is a good business practice.

Computer Management Software

There are a number of firms that offer computer management software programs. Most of the programs are for DOS computers.

We have included information on just a few of the available programs. You will likely be able to evaluate programs at real estate trade conventions or by writing software firms. Most firms offer demonstration disks so that you can see what the program is capable of performing.

Realty Automation, 11365 Eastshore Drive, Hayden Lake, ID 83835; 1-800-653-8428.

Realty Automation offers residential and commercial software which can be used for:

1. Single-family and multi-family residentials,
2. Commercial office buildings,
3. Commercial strip centers and shopping malls,
4. Mini-storage or self service storage facilities,
5. Condominium or owner associations,
6. Marinas, warehouses, airports, etc.

All of the above are included in the basic software package. It is an easy-to-use program and the company offers a 60-day money-back guarantee.

The system requires a 486DX or better personal computer with 8 megabytes of Ram. It is Windows 95/98 or Windows 3.1 compatible.

 www.fullhousesoftware.com
(Realty Automation)

Features of the program include:

1. Complete accounting (Cash or Accrual),
2. Complete tenant (or member) tracking,
3. Manual or automatic check-writing capabilities,
4. Extensive report generating capabilities.

Spectrum Software, 43430 East Florida Avenue, F295, Hemet, CA 92544; 1-800-366-9840.

Spectrum offers a modestly priced ($175) program known as Unit Boss 3.0 which can handle 160 separate properties with an unlimited number of units. Functions include six different income and 19 expense accounts. Month-to-month and year-to-year income/expense statement can be displayed or printed as can year-to-date and end-of-year statements. The program allows for a record of all properties, properties of a single owner, specific properties and a specific vendor or tenant. Other features include:

1. Basic property data,
2. Tenant lists,
3. Ex-tenant lists,
4. Rent raises due,
5. Mail labels for tenants and owners,
6. Printing of rent receipts,
7. Displays/prints management contract data,
8. Owner's names, addresses and telephone numbers,
9. Tenant data sheets,
10. Eviction status,
11. List of vacant units,
12. Late payers,
13. End of lease dates,
14. Company names, addresses and telephone numbers can be printed on every report.

Realty Software, P. O. Box 4285, Park City, UT 84060.

Realty Software's Property Management Plus program, which sells for as low as $150, is applicable to residential and commercial management. Among other functions of the software it provides:

1. Expense details by date, owner, building and category with over 200 categories;
2. Graph income and expenses for visual analysis. It can graph any utility such as electricity by unit or by building;
3. Ledger showing income and expenses between two dates for a building or an owner. It can be used for trust accounts;
4. Operating statements showing security deposits and owner funds. Figures can be month-to-date and year-to-date cash flows before and after taxes;
5. Tenant information by name and building;
6. Late rent reports showing delinquencies and it automatically calculates late fees for all lease types;
7. Vacancies;
8. Expiration report to rent increase or lease renewals;
9. Rent statements.

www.loki.com/~tech
(Realty Software)

A maintenance option of the program can:

1. Track all requests for active or completed maintenance;
2. Prioritize maintenance;
3. Print work orders.

A management option of the program provides:

1. Owner/building information files;
2. Calculates management fees;
3. Prepares checks for owners;
4. Prepares 1099 forms;
5. Prepares owner balance reports on demand;
6. Lists owner and properties alphabetically;
7. Balance sheets for one property one-owner or all properties.

CMS Inc., 311 B Maple Avenue, Vienna, VA 22180; 1-800-397-1400.

CMS offers Promas Landmaster Property Management software. The software is priced from $300 to $1,995 depending upon the number of rental units covered and if it is to be used with DOS or Windows. Pricing includes initial support services. The software will provide:

1. Owner profiles;
2. Unit profiles;
3. Tenant profiles;
4. Cross reference features;
5. Notes;
6. Event reminders;
7. Receivables;
8. Tenant history;
9. Receipt history;
10. Scheduled receivables;
11. Rent;
12. Late fees;
13. Receipts;
14. Tenant receipts;
15. Payables;
16. Invoices;
17. Invoice history;
18. Scheduled payments;
19. Check writing;

20. General ledger:

   a. General ledger history;
   b. Bank account history;
   c. Deposit receipts;
   d. Reconciled bank accounts.

21. Maintenance;
22. Work orders;
23. Owner statements;
24. Scheduled statements;
25. Letters and notices.

AMS Advanced Management Systems, P.O. Box 20760, Charleston, South Carolina; 1-800-366-5152.

AMS offers Resort Management Systems software designed to meet the special needs of firms handling resort rentals. The system helps you determine which units are available and their features for your reservations. It provides arrival and departure lists, owner statements, and commonly used reports including income projection.

www.ams-rms.com
(Advanced Management Systems)

Versions are available for multiple work stations. Installation and training in using this system is also available. A one work station system is available for approximately $995.

CHAPTER 11 SUMMARY

Funds of others or for some later disbursement that come into the control of the property manager are trust funds until disbursed. When trust money is received, it can be placed in a trust account, paid to a service provider if that was its purpose or given to the principal if the principal is entitled to the funds.

The broker's trust account should be a non-interest-bearing demand deposit (checking) account in an FDIC insured institution. The account must be clearly titled as to trust purposes. Funds from multiple beneficiaries can be in the same account.

If the depositor of funds requests, funds received can be placed in an interest-bearing account with interest benefiting the owner of the funds. Interest-bearing accounts should not mix funds of more than one owner.

Funds can be withdrawn from the trust account by the broker, a salesperson or broker licensed with the broker or an unlicensed bonded person. However, any party other than the broker should not have authority for withdrawal of funds.

A broker may not commingle personal funds with trust funds but may keep a small amount of his or her own funds in the trust account.

If two or more persons claim an interest in trust funds, the broker should commence an interpleader action. Trust funds cannot be used to offset other claims owed to the broker. Records must be kept for trust funds showing the date money was received, from who, the amount, the date deposited and disbursement data. A record must be kept of payments made directly to service providers or returned uncashed.

Trust accounts should be reconciled monthly.

Owners should receive a monthly statement as well as an annual operating statement. The statement might compare income, expenses, etc. by category with the prior year or years. Owners like to know changes in rents and occupancy factors.

The annual statement might include an inspection report, operating budget, insurance summary and the owner's 1099.

Additional records that will aid management, include:

1. Lease files;
2. Insurance register;
3. Mortgage file;
4. Rent rolls;
5. Eviction register;
6. Move-outs owing funds;
7. Inventory files;
8. Vendor files;
9. Utility files;
10. Payroll records;
11. Purchase order files;
12. Inactive files.

A property management firm would also want records of its operations for budgeting and to consider operational adjustments. Records would include:

1. Profit and loss statements;
2. Management office insurance files;
3. Ad register;
4. Telephone records;
5. Employee files;
6. Audit reports.

Most record-keeping can be handled utilizing readily available computer software which is available from a number of firms.

CLASS DISCUSSION TOPICS

1. If you are working in a general real estate or broker's office, does your broker use computer software for record keeping? If so:

  a. Which software programs are used
  b. Which reports or files are kept

2. Before computers, how do you suppose large property management firms kept track of their accounts and prepared reports?

3. If you were an owner with property being managed, what information would you want from your property manager and when would you want it?

4. What problems can you envision in administering 80 leases for a single owner where the leases were negotiated with different attorneys?

5. How should insurance agents be chosen for owner property and when should you evaluate policy costs?

6. Does your firm keep employee files? Ask your broker what is kept in the files and why.

CHAPTER 11 QUIZ

1. A property manager may hold a check received as a rental deposit uncashed:

  A. if the manager does not think the prospective tenant's rent application will be approved
  B. until the lease has been signed and the rent is actually due
  C. if the prospective tenant requests it be held until lessor agrees to the tenancy
  D. at his or her own discretion

2. Which of the following constitutes commingling of trust funds?

  A. A property manager who leaves $1 of his own money in the trust account
  B. A trust account containing funds belonging to several different owners
  C. A trust account that is interest-bearing
  D. Trust money deposited in a broker's personal account

3. A broker's trust account was not designated as a trust account. Claims of third parties for the trust monies would result from:

    A. creditor judgments against the broker

    B. bankruptcy of the broker

    C. death of the broker

    D. all of the above

4. Beneficial information that an owner would desire with an annual statement would include:

    A. information as to occupancy rates

    B. comparison of expenses and income with prior years

    C. both A and B

    D. neither A nor B

5. A skip tracer would be used to:

    A. collect bad checks

    B. locate former tenants

    C. reproduce lost documents

    D. copy computer programs

6. Payroll records would include:

    A. income

    B. social security deductions

    C. income tax deductions

    D. all of the above

7. Keeping telephone records would allow a property manager to evaluate:

    A. responses to an ad

    B. effectiveness of an ad

    C. effectiveness of an agent

    D. all of the above

8. An employee file should include:

    A. employees' applications

    B. employees' employment contract

    C. employees' evaluations

    D. all of the above

9. A broker audit of his or her firm's bookkeeping:

   A. is required by law
   B. indicates the broker does not trust his or her employees
   C. is good business practice
   D. is a waste of money

10. Computer software is capable of:

   A. producing graphs of income and expenses
   B. automatically calculating late fees
   C. preparing and tracking work orders
   D. all of the above

Answers: 1. C; 2. D; 3. D; 4. C; 5. B; 6. D; 7. D; 8. D; 9. C; 10.D

Chapter 12

Promotion and Advertising

KEY WORDS AND TERMS

Advance Fee Rental Agencies
Billboards
Bird Dogs
Bulletins
Business Cards
Car Signs
Chambers of Commerce
Classified Ads
Code Violations
Daily Newspapers
Display Ads
Evictions
Fee Splitting
For Lease Sign
Foreign Language Papers
Internet
Junior Posters
Logos

Movie Screen Ads
Name Tags
Newspaper Columns
Personal Promotion
Personnel Office
Press Releases
Public Transit Ads
Radio
Referral Fees
Referrals
Rental Magazines
Speculators
Standard Billboards
Talking Signs
Telephone Solicitation
Throwaway Papers
Yellow Pages

LEARNING OBJECTIVES

In this chapter you will learn how to enhance your firm as well as personal image to help you in obtaining management contracts.

You will also learn of many sources you can use to locate management opportunities. You will see that there are many ways to locate owners who need your services.

One of the most important tasks of management is to fill space with tenants. If you fail to do this, you fail as a manager. You will learn many ways to locate tenants who can use your space.

Promoting Your Firm

When you promote the name and image of your firm to the general public or to specific groups, your greatest benefit is likely to be the effect of the promotion on owner attitudes or perception of your firm.

A positive image will increase your business.

Prospective tenants don't buy "name brands." They are not likely to rent because of your name recognition and your accomplishments. They rent because they desire benefits of a particular property.

Your firm name and image can be reflected in a positive light in a number of ways.

MEETING OWNERS

You should attempt to meet people who can help you in your business. These would be owners of investment property as well as people who have business and/or social relationships with property owners.

Membership in Property Owners Groups

By being an active member or leader in your local chapters of property owner's groups (See Chapter 1), you will get to meet owners of property. By making presentations to the group on areas of management and showing a common and knowledgeable interest, you can build up a rapport that can lead to significant management contracts.

Public Speaking

Most service organizations, such as Rotary Clubs, are constantly looking for speakers. If you develop a presentation on an area or areas of interest to most business people, the organizations will be happy to have you as a speaker. As an example, a subject you could speak on, "O.K.! We have a new tax law — but what does it mean?" With that example you could cover the changes in the law in general and tie in examples as they relate to your property management business.

Accountants are a good group to speak to because they can influence clients into seeking professional management.

Teaching

Teaching a class or seminar at a local community college will enhance your professional image. If you teach a real estate class, such as real estate practices, your students will likely be real estate agents who could refer business your way.

If you teach a class in property management, your class will likely consist of both real estate agents and property owners. You will have an opportunity to sell yourself to owners because you're the "expert."

Religion

Being active in a religious group serves to show others that you are a moral person and this can lead to business.

Organization Membership

Taking an active roll in service organizations such as Rotary and Kiwanis and Lodges such as the Masonic order will give you a wide group of acquaintances who will likely view you in a positive light.

PRESS RELEASES

Press releases can sell your firm as a "can do" professional management firm. Press releases could herald accomplishments such as the following.

New Management. Being chosen to manage a significant property or development.

Professional Achievements. The fact that the property manager or an employee received professional designations should be announced with a press release.

Major New Tenant. The fact that your firm has negotiated a lease with a major local or national tenant is newsworthy and reflects favorably on your firm.

Achievements of Individuals. The fact that a property manager has received an award from your firm will reflect well on that individual and your firm when dealing with third parties. As an example, the fact that an agent has leased 1,000,000 square feet of commercial space in one year would be a remarkable and newsworthy achievement.

Project Leasing. Leasing a major project, such as a new shopping center, warehouse complex or industrial park, could lead to a number of press releases. Promoting events such as "Leasing Ahead of Schedule," "50% Leased in Only 50 Days," "100% Lease," "First Lease Finalized."

New Employee. If you hire a new property manager, a press release covering the new employee's prior work history and education and family data would be in order. It should also cover the duties of the new employee.

This type of press release makes new hires feel good about themselves and it also informs those who know the new hires that they will be working in property management for your firm.

Promotions. When an employee receives a promotion or change in job title, this information could be used in an effective press release.

Change in Office Location. Opening an office for the first time, a change in office location, or opening another office can be the subject of a press release.

PERSONAL PROMOTION

Individual managers within your firm can help your firm and themselves with personal promotion.

Business Cards. A distinctive business card with the name of your firm and clear indication that your firm is in the property management business will help spread the name of your firm. The card should also have the agent's photograph, name, telephone/fax numbers, etc., to benefit the agent.

Name Tags. Name tags with your firm name and logo help identify the agents employed with your firm. The name tags should be readable from a distance of about six feet.

Car Signs. Car signs with the name of your firm and the agent's name are beneficial to the firm and the agent because of the exposure possible.

NEWSPAPER COLUMNS

By writing a column for a local newspaper such as "Tenant vs. Landlord," which covers tenant and landlord rights and obligations as well as interesting legal cases in the management area, will serve to enhance your professional status in the community.

If you're a significant advertiser in the newspaper and if you are willing to provide the column at no charge to the paper, your request will likely be accepted.

It is important that the column bear your photograph and that it be well written. Consider using a professional writer to prepare the column.

PROFESSIONAL JOURNALS

Writing articles for professional journals will help your reputation within the property management profession. It can lead to referral management or consulting work.

PROFESSIONAL ASSOCIATIONS

Active participation and leadership positions within professional associations of property managers will enhance the professional reputation of your firm.

> *Gaining professional designations within the association you are active in will increase your personal reputation as well as that of your firm.*

MANAGEMENT SIGNS

Discreet signs or plaques placed on quality properties that are managed by your firm will help your image. Some firms place these plaques in the elevators where they are likely to be read, while others place them at the entryway to the building. The signs might also indicate that your firm should be contacted for leasing information or give the location of the management office.

LEASED SIGNS

While signs indicating property is for rent or lease are effective tenant promotional tools, the fact that it has been leased can help you as to promoting your firm to owners of other properties.

A "Leased" banner over a "For Lease" sign is much the same as a "Sold" banner is over a "For Sale" sign. It indicates success, and people like to deal with winners.

LOGO IDENTIFICATION

A *LOGO is a special or unique design applicable to your firm.* You want to have your logo on all of your signs, business cards, stationery and in your advertisements. With a well developed logo, persons interested in investment property will recognize and relate your logo with your firm's name. There are commercial artists who specialize in logos.

The logo should be tied to a color so that you always see the logo with a particular color. This enhances logo identification.

YELLOW PAGES

A yellow page ad under Real Estate Property Management will bring in inquiries as to management and rentals. Many larger management firms use display ads in the yellow pages.

To the reader, a larger ad relates to a larger management firm, although this is not necessarily the case.

> *You should consider more than a bare minimum yellow page ad.*

INSTITUTIONAL ADVERTISING

> *Institutional advertising sells your name rather than a product.*

A yellow page ad is institutional advertising as would be an ad in a program book for a charitable event.

These ads merely note your presence in the marketplace and sell your firm based on what you do.

While most ads placed by a property management firm will be to lease property, some ads will be institutional in nature.

Sources for Obtaining Management

> *The basis of property management is to have property to manage. Without management contracts there can be NO property manager.*

Obtaining new contracts is a continuing necessity as contracts will be lost for many reasons. As an example, when a shopping center or large apartment complex is sold to a REIT, management will be lost since REITs manage their own property.

There are many sources to use to obtain property management as well as leads to management opportunities. Most property managers use a combination of sources or programs to obtain management. Some management firms have an on-going promotional program to obtain management and follow carefully thought out plans.

We endorse planning. We feel that just as a property should have a management plan, so should the property manager have his or her plan to maintain and increase inventory to manage.

REFERRALS FROM OWNERS

Owners, who are your clients, are an excellent source of business. If they are pleased with the work you do for them, they generally are willing to refer you to other owners they know. If an owner contacts you from a personal referral, you know that owner has been half sold by the referral source. You also know that it is unlikely that you are competing with other firms for the management.

There is much more to do than wait for referrals to come to you. By discussing your needs with owners, you can get information about other owners. You can make the initial contact. A good time to ask owners for help is at a face-to-face meeting, such as when you have gone over an annual statement or have brought an owner good news such as an advantageous lease. When an owner is pleased with your services, the owner is likely to be very willing to tell you about other owners who they feel could use your management skills.

REFERRAL FEES FOR MANAGEMENT

Generally, brokers can pay referral fees for property management to other brokers. This can provide a huge source of referrals since most real estate offices do not handle property management but will handle the sale of properties that may need professional management.

By letting other brokers know about your organization and what you do as well as the benefits to the office making the referral can result in your services being half sold to referral clients before you've ever met them.

Some offices use open houses and Christmas parties to invite real estate agents to their offices and to sell them on the benefits you offer to owners and to referring agents.

> *Brokers who have the greatest chance to provide you with management opportunities are brokers who specialize in investment property.*

Some property managers will actually recommend other property managers. This would be the case when a property manager is specializing in an area or type of property and the referral firm does not manage property in that geographical area or as to that type of property. Referrals in such cases are likely to be mutual.

BIRD DOGS

BIRD DOG *is not a derogatory term. It refers to a person who points you toward opportunities.* A mother who keeps her eye out for a future daughter-in-law for her son would be a bird dog.

In property management bird dogs should look for management opportunities and tenants. The best bird dogs are relatives or friends who want you to be successful.

Bird dogs need reassurances that you appreciated their help even if it didn't lead to success. Sooner or later they will come across opportunities which can be of help to you.

NEIGHBORS

Owners of income property adjacent to property that you manage can often be convinced, by logic, that you should also manage their property.

The economics of scale start with resident managers. One resident manager or management office could be shared by adjacent similar properties. If there are maintenance staffs or contracts, the costs could likely be reduced because of the advantage of having side-by-side work sites. Advertising costs could also be shared. While both owners would have to agree, expanding management to a contiguous property or properties makes economic sense.

GETTING OWNERS TO BUY

When a rental property comes on the market for sale and it is located adjacent or close to a similar property you manage, you could have an opportunity to gain another management opportunity.

By providing your owner with purchase information and the benefits of owning an adjacent property, you can at times earn a sales commission as well as obtain another property to manage.

If your owner is not interested in purchasing, you should point out to the listing agent that you would like to show a prospective buyer the economics possible with joint management.

PROPERTY SALES

Sales of income property, as reported through local MLS services or press releases, can mean a new owner and often new management. New owners will often be very interested in a management proposal.

BANKS

Banks and other lending institutions have an inventory of properties from foreclosures. Some lenders have huge property inventories while others have just the occasional properties. Sometimes the lenders only wish to protect the property from vandalism while other times active management is required.

You should begin lender contacts with your present bank and find out about their needs and how they are handling them. You should also contact other lenders. Some management firms specialize in relatively short-term management of foreclosed properties.

In addition to foreclosures, banks often gain control of property through their trust departments. Since trust departments prefer to deal with securities rather than real estate, they will generally sell the real estate, but management is necessary until the properties can be disposed of.

While you want a lender's management business, the lender likely desires your business. Property management firms have large trust accounts containing rental and security deposits as well as rents received but not yet disbursed. Lenders like the idea of having a large account for which they need not pay any interest.

> *The size of your trust account will dictate the leverage you have in dealing with a lender.*

VACANT PROPERTY

Vacant property or property having a high vacancy rate will likely have an unhappy owner and are often ripe for management. County records will make it fairly easy to determine ownership. If an owner resides outside of the area, your chances for obtaining management will increase dramatically.

One property manager, in obtaining management for vacant single tenant properties, asks for a management contract with the provision that no management fees shall be owed until the property has been leased. If not leased within a designated period of time (from three to six months), the owner can cancel the management contract without obligation. If the property has been vacant for a long period of time, such as over one year, the owner would view this approach as a no-lose situation.

PROBLEM PROPERTY

Sometimes it is relatively easy to obtain management of problem property, but you must determine if you want the management on a case-by-case basis.

Code Violations

Code violations as to health, safety and building codes are a matter of public record. Code violations often indicate problems. The problems could relate to poor management and/or financial problems of the owner. An owner plagued with problems, especially if he or she lives outside the area, can be ripe for management.

Evictions

The records of unlawful detainer actions are indicative of problems. Sometimes they relate to poor tenant qualifying.

Where the tenant owes many months rent it is indicative of poor management.

Substandard housing might also result in renting to tenants who are more likely to default.

Tax Delinquent Properties

When an owner of income property does not pay his or her taxes when due, it indicates a financial problem. While the problem could stem from other reasons, it could be management related, which professional management could solve.

Poor Maintenance

If you see an income property which is poorly maintained with poor or nonexistent landscaping, broken screens, etc., the problem could be management related. You should contact the owner about your services.

NEWSPAPER ADS

Classified ads are not going to read "I need a property manager," but they can indicate the need for management.

Rental Ads

Rental ads that seem to appear in the newspaper forever either indicates a great many vacancies or the inability to fill a vacancy, both of which indicate a need for management.

Rental ads offering significant concessions as to free rent or otherwise indicate a desperate owner are clues to management needs.

Ads for Trade

When an owner wants to trade an income property, it usually means that the owner is not happy with his or her situation. Such an owner could be a likely management prospect if you can show the owner a different vision of the benefits of ownership with professional management.

For Sale by Owner

For Sale by Owner ads often contain clues as to the need for professional management. "100% Occupancy" could mean that the owner is not realizing rental potential. "Raisable Rents" means that the owner realizes rents are too low but isn't doing anything about it.

Words indicating desperation, such as "Submit All Offers" or "Must Sell," indicate a problem.

A good approach to use for this situation as well, as some of the other situations noted, would be to offer to prepare an analysis of the property showing the income that can reasonably be obtained over expenses. Ask the owner, "If you could remove yourself from management problems and maximize your income, would you be interested in retaining ownership?"

REAL ESTATE INVESTORS

REAL ESTATE INVESTORS *buy property primarily for income and/or value appreciation.* They expect a relatively long holding period. Discussion with brokers in your area should likely reveal major players.

Investors are usually willing to talk to anyone. The fact that they are open to ideas is what has led them to success. Offering to evaluate a property they own or are considering buying and preparing a management plan for them will give you an opportunity to prove you are a professional. It is an offer hard to turn down.

Many property management firms will start a management relationship with an investor on a single property. It is likely to be the investor's biggest headache. The firm's performance on one problem property can lead to not only handling all of the investor's property but a close relationship that includes evaluation of purchase opportunities.

DEVELOPERS

Developers of investment properties may be developing for particular buyers or with the intention of selling. Many developers develop for their own property portfolios. They keep what they develop and consequently must either become involved in management or use a professional manager.

Building permits issued will help you in locating developers. Since proper property management really begins with the planning, it is never too early to contact a developer.

Developers are generally willing to schedule an appointment. You want to show the benefits you can offer to the developer. A similar approach would be used with an investor.

SPECULATORS

SPECULATORS *differ from investors in that they buy, try to enhance value and sell.* With the change in capital gains, speculators now want to hold properties for at least 18 months to take advantage of the 20 percent capital gain's rate.

Speculators are active players in the real estate market. Many property managers work closely with speculators and consult with them as to property changes to enhance value and likely rents that are possible. In return they expect and get the property management. They are often able to retain management when the property is sold to new owners.

> *Local brokers dealing in investment properties can give you the names of many speculators active in your market area.*

FANNIE MAE

The Federal National Mortgage Association (Fannie Mae) will designate brokers to handle the renovation of their properties. The services are short-term and do not include leasing. If you are interested in handling this work, contact a Fannie Mae office near you.

WHEN THERE IS A MANAGER

You will contact some owners who appear to be in need of professional property management only to find that the owner has a management contract with another firm.

The property problems that you perceived might not be the result of management deficiencies but rather owner limitations.

> *Do NOT criticize the property management firm handling the property.*

Without knowledge of all the facts, you do not know if you could do a better job. We strongly recommend that you leave your name, or card, if a face-to-face meeting and end the conversation. If you have mentioned any reason why the owner needs management, we suggest, "I am quite sure that_____ has the situation under control." While stealing accounts might be alright for garbage haulers, it should not play a part in property management.

> *We regard property management as a profession and those engaged in it should act as professionals.*

However, if an owner who has a property management firm contacts you, there is nothing wrong with showing the owner what you can do. However, do not denigrate the work or ability of the current property management.

CONSULTING CONTRACTS

Some owners want your services and are willing to pay for them, but they do not wish to give up property management.

As an example, some Real Estate Investment Trusts will hire consultants to evaluate a property for management or evaluate an ongoing management operation of a large property or complex.

Contacts will be initiated by the property owner based upon the reputation of the property manager being hired.

Beware of the owners who want your services but have NO intention of paying for them.

Some owners will take advantage of property managers by asking the manager to evaluate a property and prepare a management plan so that they can be considered for management.

If you have reason to believe that the owner does not intend to give management, no matter how good a plan you prepare, you might consider contracting for this work. Ask the owner to agree to a fixed fee for this effort with the provision that it will be waived if you receive a management contract.

LEASING

Many management companies will also take exclusive listings to lease nonresidential property.

Such agency agreements do not provide full management services. Nevertheless, these agreements are worthwhile because they offer an opportunity for property managers and the firm to significantly increase earnings.

Many property management firms take these listings because working closely with an owner can result in an excellent owner-agent relationship. After an owner realizes what you can do for them, it is often just a short step to obtaining a management contract for the property that was leased and other properties that he or she owns.

Figure 12-1 is the first page of an Exclusive Agency Agreement For Leasing, which was prepared by the American Industrial Real Estate Association.

Figure 12-1

STANDARD OWNER-AGENCY AGREEMENT
FOR SALE OR LEASE OF REAL PROPERTY
(Non-Residential)
AMERICAN INDUSTRIAL REAL ESTATE ASSOCIATION

1. BASIC PROVISIONS ("BASIC PROVISIONS").

1.1 **Parties:** This Owner-Agency Agreement (**"Agreement"**), dated for reference purposes only _____ , 19 ____ , is made by and between _____ , whose address is _____ , telephone number (_____) _____ , Fax No. (_____) _____ , (**"Owner"**), and _____ , whose address is _____ , telephone number (_____) _____ , Fax No. (_____) _____ , (**"Agent"**).

1.2 **Property/Premises:** The real property, or a portion thereof, which is the subject of this Agreement is commonly known by the street address of _____ located in the City of _____ , County of _____ , State of _____ , and generally described as (describe briefly the nature of the property): _____

(**"Property"**). (See also Paragraph 3).

1.3 **Term of Agreement:** The term of this Agreement shall commence on _____ and expire at 5:00 p.m. on _____ , except as it may be extended (**"Term"**). (See also paragraph 4)

1.4 **Transaction:** The nature of the transaction concerning the Property for which Agent is employed (**"Transaction"**) is (check the appropriate box(es)):

(a) ☐ A sale for the following sale price and terms: _____

and other additional standard terms reasonably similar to those contained in the "STANDARD OFFER, AGREEMENT AND ESCROW INSTRUCTIONS FOR THE PURCHASE OF REAL ESTATE" published by the American Industrial Real Estate Association (**"AIR"**), or for such other price and terms agreeable to Owner;

(b) ☐ A lease or other tenancy for the following rent and terms: _____

and other additional standard terms reasonably similar to those contained in the appropriate AIR lease form or for such other rent and terms agreeable to Owner.

2. EXCLUSIVE EMPLOYMENT AND RIGHTS.

2.1 Owner hereby employs Agent as Owner's sole and exclusive agent to represent Owner in the Transaction and to find buyers or lessees/tenants (**"lessees"**), as the case may be, for the Property. Agent shall use reasonably diligent efforts to find such buyers or lessees. All negotiations and discussions for a Transaction shall be conducted by Agent on behalf of Owner. Owner shall promptly disclose and refer to Agent all written or oral inquiries or contacts received by Owner from any source regarding a possible Transaction.

2.2 Owner authorizes Agent to:

(a) Place advertising signs on the Property;

(b) Place a lockbox on the Property if vacant;

(c) Accept deposits from potential buyers or lessees; and

(d) Distribute information regarding the Property to participants in THE MULTIPLE (**"MULTIPLE"**) of the AIR and/or any other appropriate local commercial multiple listing service, to other brokers, and to potential buyers or lessees of the Property. Owner shall identify as "confidential" any information provided to Agent that Owner considers confidential and does not want disclosed. All other information provided by Owner may be disclosed as Agent may deem appropriate or necessary. After consummation of a Transaction, Agent may publicize the terms of such Transaction.

2.3 Agent shall comply with the Rules of Professional Conduct of the AIR, if a member or if not, the Rules of Professional Conduct of the Society of Industrial and Office Realtors, and shall submit the Property to the MULTIPLE. Agent shall cooperate with participants in the MULTIPLE and may, at Agent's election, cooperate with other real estate brokers (collectively **"Cooperating Broker"**). A Cooperating Broker may, as a third-party beneficiary hereof, enforce the terms of this Agreement against Owner or Agent.

2.4 If the Transaction is a sale and Agent finds a prospective buyer for the Property, or if the Transaction is a lease and Agent finds a prospective lessee for the Property, Owner hereby authorizes Agent also to represent and act as the agent for such buyer or lessee (and Owner consents to such dual agency. If a Cooperating Broker finds such a buyer or lessee, then Agent shall act as agent for Owner only, the Cooperating Broker shall act as agent for the buyer or lessee only, and the Cooperating Broker shall not be Owner's agent, even though the Cooperating Broker may share in the commission paid by Owner to Agent. A Cooperating Broker shall not be an agent or subagent of Owner or Agent.

2.5 Owner agrees that Agent may, during the ordinary and normal course of marketing the Property, respond to inquiries on the Property by showing and providing information on the Property, as well as on other competing properties, to prospective buyers and lessees and that such activities may result in the payment of a commission to Agent by a third party.

3. PROPERTY.

3.1 The term "Property" shall include all of the following which are currently located on the Property and owned by Owner: permanent improvements, electrical distribution systems (power panels, buss ducting, conduits, disconnects, lighting fixtures, etc.), telephone distribution systems (lines, jacks and connections), space heaters, air conditioning equipment, air lines, carpets, window coverings, wall coverings, partitions, doors, suspended ceilings, built-ins such as cabinets, and _____

(if there are no additional items write "NONE"). If the Transaction is a sale, the term "Property" shall additionally include, to the extent owned by Owner, oil and mineral rights, leases and other agreements which will continue in effect after Owner's transfer of title to the Property.

Initials ____

Initials ____

FORM OA-1-6/97

Promoting Space

PROMOTING SPACE *refers to getting the message out to prospective tenants that you have space available for lease.* In other words it deals with "advertising."

If you are not successful in finding tenants then you will have failed as a manager because without tenants you are looking after an empty shell.

FEE SPLITTING

Just as you can cooperate with other brokers in obtaining property management you can cooperate with others by your willingness to split leasing fees with firms that have a tenant for your space.

This cooperation should go both ways. Prospective tenants with whom you are working can be rented space controlled by another management firm if space that you control does not meet the tenant's needs.

Just because you might compete vigorously to get management accounts does not mean that you shouldn't cooperate with others.

Cooperation is in the best interests of your owners and your refusal to do so could raise questions as to ethics, and could be a breach of fiduciary duties.

ADVANCE FEE RENTAL AGENCIES

There are rental agencies that charge prospective renters a fee for a list of available rentals. People who pay these advance fees are usually very serious about renting.

If there are advance fee rental agencies active in your area, you should provide them with weekly updated lists of your available rentals. It is a no-cost method of spreading the word about your rentals.

USE OTHER TENANTS

An excellent way to fill vacancies is to inquire of other tenants if they have any friends (in the case of residential vacancies) or firms that they do business with and would like to have in the property.

In cases of residential rentals, a tenant who has close friends living in the property is less likely to move out than are other tenants.

Firms like to have other firms which they do business with close at hand to enhance communications. All firms benefit by this arrangement.

"FOR LEASE" SIGNS

Signs and banners proclaiming space or units available for rent or lease are the most cost effective advertising available.

In very desirable, high-trafficked areas, many managers are able to use property signs as their only source for tenants.

You can also obtain institutional benefits from signs that include your firm name and logo.

For maximum effectiveness you want large letters and good contrast for your signs. The most effective contrasting colors would be yellow and black.

Your sign may capitalize the first letter of each word but the rest of the sign should be lower-case lettering. Avoid stylized fancy lettering as it is difficult to read. Also keep sign wordage to a minimum for quick comprehension.

If your property has something special like "Pets Allowed" or "Health Club," these feature can be added using a strip sign attached to the "For Lease" sign.

TALKING SIGNS

Talking signs simply indicate that an interested party can get greater information by dialing their radio to a particular frequency. The signs do not talk but low frequency radio waves do.

These signs can be FM or AM. AM models have a slightly longer range but are still under 300 feet. The transmitters are in the building and use continuous tapes broadcasting a message. Installation simply requires that they be plugged in. Machines are available for under $200 each through radio supply and real estate supply vendors.

The signs give a 24-hour message which could include the size of available rentals, when they can be shown, rental rates, property damage bonds, pet restrictions or allowed pets, special amenities included, parking information, etc. Talking signs can be a pre-sale tool in that, after hearing the message, anyone who views a unit or space available has probably found what meets their needs. For an apartment building, the message could be:

"We have two large two-bedroom units with hardwood floors and two full baths. There is a formal dining area that could be used as a study. Appliances, two parking spaces and a storage locker are included in the monthly rent of $680. A security deposit of $500 is required. Small pets are permissible with prior approval of management. You can view the units by stopping at Unit 1A weekdays from 9 A.M. to 3 P.M. or weekends from 10 A.M. to 2 P.M."

Some brokers who use talking signs use a locally recognized voice for the message.

FLAGS, BALLOONS AND THE OPEN HOUSE

When a unit with vacancies is on a well travelled street, simply placing an "Open House" sign with a few balloons or flags outside will bring in traffic. This works best on Saturdays and Sundays from the hours of 11a.m to around 3p.m.

With more vacancies, or a location on a side street, open houses can be tied in with newspaper ads.

THE INTERNET

The Internet can be an effective and low cost tool to rent all kinds of property. You can include photographs as well as detailed rental information. An "800" number will increase the volume of contacts that you receive from your website.

PERSONNEL OFFICES

Large employers in your area will probably have new and transferred employees relocating to your area.

By talking with personnel managers you should be able to work out a mutually beneficial arrangement. Knowing the names of employees moving to the area gives you the opportunity to contact them and find out their needs prior to actually meeting with them.

CHAMBERS OF COMMERCE

Chambers of Commerce receive area inquiries in a constant stream. They will supply you with the names and addresses of persons and firms interested in or who are moving to the area.

You can mail out information on your rentals including an "800" number for them to call for further information. If you have one, you may also want to include your Internet address.

BILLBOARDS

Billboards can be effectively used to promote new, large rental developments where the owners wish to stabilize the property quickly. Billboards are expensive. They fall into different categories.

Bus Stop Displays. Bus stop displays are usually about 3 feet by 6 feet and are limited by their size as to the message.

Junior Posters. Junior posters are also known as 8-sheet displays. They have a 5 foot x 11 foot viewing area.

Standard Billboards. Standard billboards are 12 feet x 25 feet in size.

Bulletins. These are the large highway billboards. They are 14 feet x 48 feet. A bulletin in a well trafficked area could cost $3,000 to $5,000 per month and this is without special effects.

PUBLIC TRANSIT ADS

Ads are sold on the inside and outside of buses. While the outside ads are traveling billboards, the inside ads are studied by many transit passengers simply because there is nothing else to do.

> *These ads can be effective for low-range and mid-range rentals that emphasize transit convenience and price.*

CLASSIFIED ADS

People looking for rentals do check the local newspapers. Classified ads are effective for what they are supposed to do. They don't rent but they bring inquiries about rentals.

> *Ads should indicate area, size (number of bedrooms) and monthly rent.*

If there are unusually positive features, like a garage or pets allowed, this should be included.

The heading should be the strongest feature or a combination of features such as:

West Hollywood - $600
Bring Your Dog
4BR - West L.A.

Ads should be evaluated for effect and changed on a regular basis as new ads tend to be more attractive to persons who have been checking the classifieds for some time.

Newspapers offer lower rates for classified ads that run for longer periods of time. We feel this is a false economy. The greatest effect is when the ad first appears. People seeking rentals check the classifieds for new rentals. We believe that an ad should run for no more than three days. The ad should then be rewritten for a later insertion.

The best days to advertise are generally on the highest circulation days, which are normally weekends, since this is when many people search for rentals.

The best time to advertise is at the first of the month when 30-day notices are often given out. Even if nothing is available, you can advertise what will be available at the end of the month. Being able to avoid a break in rent production is good management.

DISPLAY ADS

DISPLAY ADS *are block ads.* They are costly and should be reserved for advertising a large number of properties to rent or for a large nonresidential property. They are good for initial leasing of new units.

If you use models in the display ad photographs, be careful that the photos do not raise the question of discrimination. As a rule of thumb when you use models in your photographs, try for 20 percent to 25 percent minority representation.

SELECTION OF NEWSPAPERS

The media choices you make are important as ads for particular properties will be more effective in particular papers.

Daily Newspapers

Chances are your daily newspaper is the newspaper with the greatest number of classified rental ads for the type of property and area in which you are advertising.

Your area may be served by a local daily newspaper such as the Orange County Register and an area daily such as the Los Angeles Times. Because of the huge circulation area for the Los Angeles Times, advertising rates are significantly higher. Since most persons renting come from a 20 miles' area, the Orange County Register would likely be more cost effective to advertise a rental in Orange County than the Los Angeles Times.

Weekly Throwaway Papers

Throw-away papers give you the opportunity to target a smaller area. An advantage of the throwaways is that many lower income households today do not subscribe to newspapers on a regular basis and these free papers are readily available.

The ads are usually mixed so that the reader must search for what they are looking for. These throwaways are effective for rentals and should be utilized where applicable. You can use classified as well as display advertising at a relatively low cost.

Foreign Language Papers

Foreign language papers can target readers who are interested in what you have to lease.

As an example, in advertising a commercial location or residential unit in an area having a significant Korean presence, you might consider using a Korean language newspaper in addition to other advertising.

A location for a small fast food or donut shop in a mini-mall might be advertised in a Vietnamese newspaper as well as other media.

> *When advertising, you must be careful to avoid illegal steering.*

If you only advertise property in the Korean newspaper for renting property in the Korean neighborhood, you could be suspected of steering. Advertise property located in other areas in the same newspaper to avoid any hint of your discriminating in advertising.

Special Interest Papers

There are a wide variety of English language papers that target national origin groups, religious groups as well as racial groups.

Gay-orientated publications can be productive for upscale area residential rentals and unusual rentals such as lofts. Because many of the readers are in business for themselves, they are also a good media for advertising commercial space.

RENTAL MAGAZINES

When you have a number of residential units available and your property has good curb appeal, you should consider rental magazines which, like home sale magazines, are available free in newspaper racks in most areas of the country. Rental magazines are usually monthly pictorial magazines and are quite effective in reaching people relocating to the area.

MOVIE SCREEN ADS

Movie theaters advertise on screen before the feature films. An ad in a local theater featuring rentals in the area can be effective if the screen advertising indicates that brochures are available in the lobby that provide additional information. Otherwise viewers will forget who the advertiser was for the rental that appeared interesting.

RADIO

Radio stations can supply you with a great deal of information as to the demographics of their listeners. The information includes age, education, income, etc.

With this information you can target rental audiences to the group or groups likely to be renters. As an example, a station having a great many educated, affluent young listeners would probably include many who were interested in one-bedroom units with pool and health club facilities in a desirable location.

Ad times are 15 seconds, 30 seconds or one minute. Your local radio station can help prepare your radio ads. Morning or afternoon "drive time" is usually the most expensive.

TELEVISION ADS

Television advertising is generally expensive but many communities now have classified advertising cable channels that project your ads. Some of the channels allow you to include a voice override. These cable classifieds appear to be an effective way to promote residential rentals. We don't think that they will be effective advertising for commercial, office or industrial space.

TELEPHONE SOLICITATIONS

Many leasing agents who handle nonresidential property will analyze who can use the property and then start calling using the yellow pages of their local telephone book. It is tedious, but one or two successes per month can produce above-average income, depending upon the rent.

NEIGHBORHOOD WALK-AROUND

Some agents who have available vacant commercial, industrial or office space will walk the areas talking to other tenants about the available space. A side benefit of this procedure is that an agent discovers the needs of renters in the area for other properties which the agent may have available.

FURTHER AD HELP

If you want assistance in the actual composition of ad copy and greater insight into the use of advertising media, we suggest two books published by Real Estate Education Company. *The Big Book of Real Estate Ads* and *Power Real Estate Advertising,* by William and Bradley Pivar.

CHAPTER 12 SUMMARY

There are a number of ways to promote your firm and personal image.

Meeting people who can help you, which would include:

1. membership in property owner groups;
2. public speaking before groups such as Rotary;
3. teaching real estate related classes at your local community college;
4. being active in religious organizations;
5. belonging to service organizations and/or lodges.

Press releases can positively portray you and/or your firm. Press releases could cover:

1. new management contracts;
2. professional achievements of you or employees;
3. a major new tenant for a property;
4. achievements of individual agents within the firm;
5. the leasing activity of a major new project;
6. a new property manager in your firm;
7. promotion of a property manager;
8. a change in office location, new office or opening of a satellite office.

Personal promotion of an individual would include:

1. business cards;
2. name signs;
3. car signs.

Writing a newspaper column will help your image with the general public.

Writing an article for a professional journal or active participation within a professional organization will enhance your image within the profession.

Management signs on quality properties will show the presence of your firm. Strip "Leased" signs over "For Lease" signs indicate the success of your firm.

Use of a logo on all your firm's signs and ads tends to increase the market presence of your firm in the minds of the public as well as within the profession.

Many persons will view the size of a yellow page ad with the firm's importance within the marketplace.

Institutional advertising are ads for your firm that do not sell a particular property.

There are many sources for obtaining management as well as leads to management opportunities.

Referrals from owners are a quality source because contacts will be half sold before you talk with them.

By paying referral fees you gain management opportunities from the contacts of other brokers.

Bird dogs are people who like you and are concerned with your success. A bird dog will keep his or her eyes peeled for opportunities of management or leasing.

Owners of properties contiguous to properties you manage are a natural for management because of savings possible in managing contiguous properties.

When property comes available for sale adjacent to a property you manage, you should point out to your owner the management economies possible if he or she would purchase the property.

New owners of income property should be contacted as to management.

Lending institutions require management for their foreclosures and trust inventories of real estate.

A property that has been vacant for long periods of time or has a high vacancy factor will likely have an unhappy owner who could be ripe for management.

Problem properties are often those where obtaining management might be relatively easy, but you must decide if you want to manage them.

Problem properties include:

1. properties having outstanding code violations;
2. properties having a high number of evictions;
3. properties where the owners are delinquent in taxes;
4. poorly managed property evidenced by the physical condition of the premises.

Newspaper advertising can hint as to an owner's need for management. Advertising hints may include:

1. continuously running rental ads;
2. ads indicating an owner wants to trade income property for something else;
3. an owner's For Sale ad that indicates the owner is extremely motivated to sell.

Real estate investors, developers and speculators are all excellent sources for management opportunities.

Fannie Mae is a source of contracts to manage and renovate (usually single-family homes) until they can be sold.

If an owner indicates he or she already has a property manager, don't pursue management unless instigated to do so by the owner.

Consulting contracts involve advice without action. Leasing contracts involve leasing activity without management. However, many successful leases have led to management.

You market your vacant property by seeking tenants. There are many ways to locate persons and firms that can use your space. They include:

1. referrals from other brokers wishing to cooperate and share in the leasing commission;

2. providing advance fee rental agents with the information to residential vacancies;

3. canvassing tenants to see if their friends or firms they deal with would like to live or occupy space close to the tenants.

4. "For Lease" signs are the most cost effective way to find tenants;

5. talking signs give a radio message about the property;

6. weekend open houses for residential vacancies are effective on high-traffic streets;

7. the internet is a low-cost method to spread information about your inventory of vacancies;

8. major area personnel offices can give you information as to new hires and job transfers;

9. Chambers of Commerce can supply information as to firms and persons interested in relocating in your area;

10. billboards can be used for large leasing projects. They include:
    a. bus stop displays;
    b. junior posters;
    c. standard billboards;
    d. bulletins;

11. public transit ads can be outside the bus or inside placards;

12. people do check classified ads so most property management offices use the classified columns as part of their marketing plan;

13. display ads. These are block ads and are fairly costly;

14. rental magazines cover residential projects;

15. there are a selection of newspapers which include:
    a. daily newspapers;
    b. weekly throwaway papers;
    c. foreign language papers;
    d. special interest papers;

16. movie screens can be used for area residential rental ads;
17. radio ads can be used for property likely to appeal to the demographics of a station's listeners;
18. while television ads are expensive, there are cable television stations that run a classified channel which can be an effective residential rental medium.
19. telephone solicitations targeted at firms who can use particular nonresidential space are very effective;
20. you may discover persons who are interested in nonresidential vacancy space by knocking on doors in the area.

CLASS DISCUSSION TOPICS

1. How does promotion of a property management firm differ from promotion of a general real estate brokerage firm?

2. Which property management sources are also sources for sale listings?

3. Can you think of any other sources for property management?

4. How does your office promote a sale listing? How does this differ from promoting a lease?

5. Identify a nonresidential property in your area that has been vacant for a long period of time. How would you promote this particular space?

CHAPTER 12 QUIZ

1. You can personally promote yourself by all of the following EXCEPT:
   A. business cards
   B. name tags
   C. car signs
   D. fee splitting

2. A logo refers to a(n):
   A. geographical location
   B. identifying design
   C. operational plan
   D. estimated operating budget

3. Which of the following ads would be an institutional ad?
   A. An ad that simply gives the firm name and the words "Property Management"
   B. A letter to an owner requesting property management
   C. A classified "For Rent" ad for an apartment
   D. A "For Lease" sign on a commercial building

4. The term "bird dog" refers to a(n):

    A. illegal practice

    B. problem property

    C. teaser contract offer

    D. person who watches for opportunities for you

5. Indications of a problem property include:

    A. code violations

    B. frequent evictions

    C. poor maintenance

    D. all of the above

6. Speculators differ from investors in that speculators:

    A. buy with cash

    B. expect to have a shorter holding period

    C. buy more expensive property

    D. only buy raw land

7. When you discover that a prospect you have contacted for management already has a management firm, the professional approach would be to:

    A. ask when the contract expires

    B. agree to cut the price

    C. thank the owner and end the discussion

    D. sign a contract that does not take effect until the other contract expires

8. Which of the following contracts include partial management duties?

    A. An exclusive right to lease

    B. A management consulting contract

    C. An offer to purchase

    D. Both A and B

9. Advance fee rental agencies:

    A. charge a fee to prospective tenants

    B. charge owners to advertise their properties

    C. provide prospective tenants with lists of vacancies

    D. both A and C

10. The most cost effective method of advertising to fill a vacancy would be a(n):

    A. television advertising

    B. radio advertising

    C. "For Rent" sign

    D. classified advertising

Answers: 1. D; 2. B; 3. A; 4. D; 5. D; 6. B; 7. C; 8. D; 9. D; 10. C

Fair Housing and Ethics

KEY WORDS AND TERMS

Americans With Disabilities Act
Blockbusting
Civil Rights Act of 1866
Civil Rights Act of 1964
Civil Rights Act of 1968
Civil Rights Act of 1870
Equal Credit Opportunity Act
Equal Housing Opportunity
Equal Housing Opportunity Poster
Executive Order 11603
Fair Housing
Fair Housing Amendment Act

Familial Status
Fourteenth Amendment
Jones v. Mayer
Mental Handicap
Physical Handicap
Readily Achievable
Redlining
Reverse Caregiver Law
Steering

LEARNING OBJECTIVES

You will learn about the various civil rights laws and, in particular, their applicability to property management.

In particular, you will learn about the Civil Rights Laws of 1866, 1870, 1964 and 1968 including the 1988 Fair Housing Amendment Act. You will also understand the importance of the Americans With Disabilities Act and the Equal Credit Opportunity Act.

You will gain an appreciation for ethics as good business and the ability to analyze a situation from an ethical viewpoint.

Fair Housing (Federal)

Fair housing does NOT mean equal housing.

People are not equal in their energy, productivity or as to income and savings. Equal housing would not be fair because it could reward sloth rather than accomplishments. Fair housing refers to equal housing opportunity. The right of all persons to live where they wish to live, subject only to economics, without artificial barriers being placed before them.

There are a number of federal as well as state laws and court decisions which provide for fair housing. Property managers must realize that fair housing is the law of our land and that discriminatory practices will not be tolerated by the courts, the public or by their profession.

THE CIVIL RIGHTS ACT OF 1866

This act, passed shortly after the Civil War, actually predated the 14th Amendment to the Constitution. The act provides that "all citizens of the United States shall have the same right in every state and territory as is enjoyed by white citizens thereof to inherit, purchase, lease, sell, hold and convey real and personal property."

The act had not been enforced by the courts until 1968 when, in the case of Jones v. Mayer, the U.S. Supreme Court held that the Civil Rights Act of 1866 could be enforced by a private citizen. Until that time, it had become a forgotten relic which courts had refused to enforce because of some very narrow interpretations.

What is important as to the Civil Rights Act of 1866 is:

Application. It applies to race only.

Property. It applies to both real and personal property.

No Exceptions. Since there are no exceptions to this act it serves to wipe out exceptions set forth in some later acts.

Violations. Violations of the act could result in a judgment for compensatory and even punitive damages. The court could also order an injunction to make a person cease from discriminatory activities. Continuance would place that party in contempt of court.

14TH AMENDMENT

The *14TH AMENDMENT provides that no state can abridge the privileges of citizens or deprive them of property without due process.* It also provides for the equal protection of all persons under the law. It is a broad civil rights act which implicitly provides for fair housing.

CIVIL RIGHTS ACT OF 1870

This law was really just the reiteration of the 1866 law. It was passed since Congress was worried that courts might later claim that the 14th Amendment superceded the Civil Rights Act of 1866.

EXECUTIVE ORDER 11603

This 1962 order, issued by President John F. Kennedy, prohibited discrimination in housing where there was federal involvement, such as loan programs or federal grants.

CIVIL RIGHTS ACT OF 1964

This act simply made law what was set forth in the prior executive order. The application of this act was still very limited.

CIVIL RIGHTS ACT OF 1968

This is our Fair Housing Act.

It prohibits housing discrimination based upon race, color, national origin and religion. In 1974, coverage was extended to sex and the 1988 amendment extended coverage to handicapped as well as for familial status.

Exemptions

There are four exemptions to the Civil Rights Act of 1968. However, these are not exempt by the Civil Rights act of 1866.

1. Nonprofit housing owned or leased by religious groups may limit sale or lease to members of their group as long as membership in the religion is not discriminatory.

2. Private clubs can discriminate in the sale or lease of housing if they limit the sale or lease to members and it is for non-commercial purposes.

3. Owner occupants, who do not use agents, may discriminate for one-to-four residential units providing no discriminatory advertising is used.

4. Persons who own three or less single-family rental homes are exempt if they do not use an agent, do not use discriminatory advertising and are not in the rental business.

Prohibitions

1. Agents cannot discriminate as to owners, buyers, lessors or lessees.

2. It is illegal to claim a property is unavailable when it is actually available.

3. Directing prospective buyers or tenants towards or away from property based on race, color, etc., is illegal. This is known as "steering."

4. Refusal to loan within an area is known as "redlining" and is an illegal practice.

5. Inducing panic selling by representing that minority groups entering the area will lead to crime or reduced values is illegal. This is known as "blockbusting."

6. Discriminatory advertising is prohibited (this was covered in more detail in Chapter 12).

7. Different lease terms based upon race, color, etc., would be illegal. A lessor, seller or lender cannot hold a party to different qualifications because that party is a member of a protected group.

8. An owner or manager cannot take retaliatory action against a tenant because of a just complaint as to property condition or violation of statute.

9. Agents may not discriminate by refusing access to multiple listing services.

From the National Fair Housing Advocate November 1996:

Orthodox Jews cannot break an electrical circuit on the Sabbath as it constitutes working on the Sabbath. A New York apartment complex installed electronic locks on the entryway. Orthodox Jews had to wait until another nonorthodox tenant opened the door in order to gain access. The plaintiffs asked the management company to go back to manual locks.

In reversing the decision of a trial court that the landlord had acted in a discriminatory manner, the court on appeal indicated that the fact that an act creates a burden on some individuals does not make the action discriminatory. It was obvious that electric locks were installed for the sole purpose of deterring crime. There was no allegation that the act had discriminatory intent. The court held that the inconvenience placed on some could not be deemed discriminatory (Seigel v. Blair Hall).

Note: This case points out that innocent acts can be deemed discriminatory by others and could require you to defend your actions.

From the National Fair Housing Advocate October 1996:

A discrimination case against a Florida mobile home park was settled for $81,250.

A Hispanic couple alleged that they were discouraged from applying to rent lot space at the park. They had reached an agreement to purchase a mobile home in the park and when the resident manager met the couple, they were told they would not like living in the park. They nevertheless applied for a lot and their application was rejected.

The park did not require a minimum income level. They required only good credit and one financial reference. The park management, however, required the Hispanic couple to submit three credit references, three personal references and identify three bank accounts in their names. The couple met all of these additional requirements but were still rejected.

The park owners claimed that the reason the couple was rejected was that it was a seniors-only complex and the Hispanic couple were not over 55. However, the owner of the mobile home that they wished to buy was only 52 years of age at the time her application to rent was approved.

A young white, non-Hispanic tester was told of several available lots and no age restriction was mentioned. A young Hispanic tester was told that he would not be able to rent because he was too young.

After the court ordered the owners of the park to submit income and net worth information to support a punitive damage claim, the park settled. (Pina v. Mutchnik No. 94-6084 [S.D. Fla]).

From the National Fair Housing Advocate October 1996:

A white woman won a settlement from the owners of a rental house in Lincoln, Nebraska.

She applied for an apartment with her black boyfriend. Her daughter would also be living with them. The rental application was denied because the references were deemed inadequate, the boyfriends' income was not considered sufficient if anything happened to her and the landlord wanted no more than two persons in the unit.

The apartment in question was later rented and occupied by five people (a couple, their children and a grandchild). This cast doubt on the real reason why the rental application was refused.

From the National Fair Housing Advocate September 1997:

A Minnesota mother of three was awarded $490,000 by a jury based on discrimination. She charged that her landlord discriminated based upon race, sex and disability. (continued)

She was awarded $153,000 for racial discrimination, $105,000 for emotional distress, $60,000 in punitive damages and $18,000 for out-of-pocket expenses.

The lawsuit alleged that the landlord treated African-American tenants differently than white tenants. She referred to African Americans as "You people" and let herself into apartments without notice or knocking. She also allegedly refused to schedule maintenance for African-American tenants.

It was also alleged one of the landlords chased the tenant's daughters with a stick and called a daughter a "crazy nigger." Witnesses claimed she had chased an African-American boy with a hammer after he rode his bike on her lawn and had called him a "nigger."

The plaintiff, who has a mental disability, claimed one of the landlord called her "crazy", "goofy", "cockeyed" and "idiot."

The husband of the landlord allegedly told the plaintiff that "girls could be short on the rent" and that he became sexually aggressive and intimidating.

There were numerous other complaints in this case. The award, when given, was the largest housing award to a single-family since the Fair Housing Act was passed in 1968.

Note: Discrimination applies to all aspects of dealing with tenants, not just refusal to rent and rental terms.

1988 FAIR HOUSING AMENDMENT ACT

This act extended the coverage afforded by the 1968 act to handicapped as well as familial status.

Handicapped

HANDICAPPED *includes both physical and mental handicaps*. Physical handicaps affect a life function. Hearing, sight and mobility would be covered. While drug addiction is not considered a protected category under handicaps, alcoholism AIDS, cancer, etc., are protected.

Important points for property managers are:

1. A lessor cannot refuse a handicapped tenant who has a seeing eye dog or other support animals even if the lessor otherwise has a no pets policy. Security deposits cannot be increased over what others are charged because of the seeing eye dog or support animal.

2. A tenant may modify his or her unit and common areas at the tenant's expense so that they can enjoy the premises as would a non-handicapped tenant. No additional security deposit may be charged because of the modifications although the tenant may have to agree to restore the premises at the end of the tenancy if a non-handicapped tenant would not wish the modifications. The tenant need not restore modifications to common areas.

3. The owner must make reasonable accommodations to rules and policies to allow the handicapped tenant to enjoy his or her unit. This could include a designated parking space close to the unit.

4. A landlord need not rent to a handicapped tenant whose presence would pose a health or safety danger to other tenants. Example would be a highly contagious disease or mental disorder that results in violent behavior toward others.

From the National Fair Housing Advocate October 1996:

A HUD administrative law judge approved a $13,000 settlement based on a claim of racial and disability discrimination.

The resident manager of an apartment complex refused to allow an elderly black couple to move from a second story unit to a ground floor unit. The complex had no elevator and the couple complained of poor health and had difficulty using the stairs. The manager told the couple that no units were available.

After the couple wrote the management company about their requests to move to the first floor, the management company notified them that their lease would not be renewed and that they would have to vacate upon its termination.

A HUD investigation revealed that a ground floor unit was available at the time the couple made their requests and that white disabled tenants were transferred to the first floor without written request. HUD alleged that the property management firm was not able to explain why white tenants were transferred to other apartments regularly but the black couple was told that units were not available. The management company claimed that they did not intentionally discriminate.

From the National Fair Housing Advocate November 1996:

A $60,000 settlement was reached in a lawsuit against a California Homeowner's Association. It was alleged that a condominium association refused to allow a woman in a wheelchair the right to make reasonable modifications to her rental unit to accommodate her physical disability.

She wished to build a ramp for access to her unit. The association denied her the request to build a ramp. She paid rent to the owner of the unit for three months without being able to use it. She then installed a temporary ramp. She was ordered by the association to remove it since "ramps displace landscape."

In addition to the refusal to allow a ramp, the condominium association complex was not accessible to the handicapped in other ways. Some walkways were too narrow for wheelchairs and there were no ramps at the clubhouse, denying wheelchair access.

In addition to the monetary award, the settlement required the property be inspected for accessibility, establish procedures for dealing with accessibility requests and the members of the association were required to attend training in fair housing.

From the National Fair Housing Advocate November 1996:

The owners and managers of a Maryland apartment complex settled a disability discrimination lawsuit by agreeing to furnish the plaintiff with an apartment for life (lifetime value estimated at $340,000 plus pay $160,000 in compensatory damages).

The plaintiff, who is deaf, blind and has Usher's Syndrome wished to rent a unit. He made it clear that he was able to live independently and even offered to pay a full year's rent in advance. The agent refused the offer stating that the complex did not have facilities for the handicapped and recommended a nearby complex.

The federal lawsuit alleged intentional discrimination because of the plaintiff's disability and steering him to alternate housing (both fair housing violations).

From the National Fair Housing Advocate December 1997/January 1998:

A disabled person wished to purchase a unit modified for a handicapped person. He asked the association to make accommodations to the rules prohibiting a home business. Since he had been unable to work outside his home since the late 1980s, he wished to meet clients in his home.

The board of directors told him that two-thirds of the residents had to agree to grant the exception. There were two votes, both of which resulted in disapproval. The unit was not purchased by him. He purchased another unit elsewhere that required expensive modifications for his handicapped use.

The Fair Housing Council of Greater Washington filed a complaint resulting in a $180,000 settlement. It was noted that a disabled person's need to work at home should have been accommodated if it did not interfere with the quiet enjoyment of other owners.

From the National Fair Housing Advocate November 1996:

A San Jose woman settled a discrimination lawsuit for $126,000. She was confined to a wheelchair and her only access was using the apartment elevator. The elevator was frequently out of order forcing her husband to take her up and down the stairs if she wanted to leave the apartment.

The defendants were repeatedly notified of the condition of the elevator and their solution allegedly was to have her call a maintenance man to help her up and down the stairs.

Note: Apparently failure to properly maintain the premises can be discriminatory if it unreasonably denies handicapped access.

From the National Fair Housing Advocate November 1996:

An appellate court in New York determined that a co-op must make reasonable alterations of common areas to accommodate handicapped residents.

The co-op had a policy that no co-op funds could be spent installing wheelchair ramps or other accommodations for handicapped residents.

The court ruled that the refusal violated federal law.

From the National Fair Housing Advocate November 1996:

Owners and managers of a California apartment complex agreed to a $100,000 settlement of a claim that they discriminated against a tenant with a mental disability.

The apartment manager told a tenant she could not keep her dog since they had a no-pet policy. The tenant's doctor wrote a letter to the owners and managers that the tenant needed the companion dog to help in controlling her mental disability. Attempts to mediate the problem failed and the tenant was served with an eviction notice. The tenant's suit resulted in the settlement.

Note: The 1988 amendment to the Fair Housing Act adds mental disability as well as physical disability to the protected group. The law allows support animals. The only defense the apartment complex could raise is that a "companion dog" is not a support animal. The landlord and manager decided to settle rather than risk an adverse court decision coupled with the cost of litigation.

This case indicates a manager should seek legal counsel before evicting a tenant with a pet if it is claimed that a pet serves a necessary purpose for a handicapped person.

A similar case reported in the February 1997 National Fair Housing Advocate involved a man who had several stress related disabilities. One of the few sources of relief was his cat. His mental health counselor wrote to the management that the cat was a necessary service animal. The complex began eviction proceedings. The HUD administrative law judge awarded the man $5,569 and a penalty to HUD of $5,000.

Familial Status

FAMILIAL *relates to family*. Important aspects of the amendment as it relates to familial status are:

1. A lessor cannot discriminate because there are children under the age of 18 living with the parent (parent, guardian or custodian).

2. A lessor cannot discriminate because a person is pregnant or in the process of gaining custody.

3. Exemptions that apply to familial status would be housing occupied by at least one person age 55 or older when at least 80 of the units have persons 55 or older (formerly this exemption required that the units have facilities which are special to the needs of older persons but this limitation has been removed).

Several states such as California have **REVERSE CAREGIVER LAWS**. *They allow persons who do not meet the age restrictions for senior housing to move in if they are providing needed care for someone who lives in the complex.* The person need not have medical training.

Non-seniors claiming to be providing needed assistance to a person in a senior community could likely reside as a permanent guest, if state law or state court decisions allowed caregivers in senior housing.

> *Asking the marital status of prospective tenants could be dangerous if the tenants later claim that the refusal to rent to them was based on their marital status.*

While state courts differ, the California Supreme Court has held that lessors may not refuse to rent to unmarried couples even though the lessors' religious beliefs were that they were aiding in sin if they allowed the couples to cohabit in the lessors' dwellings. The U.S. Supreme Court is likely to rule in this matter. Freedom of religion in this case is colliding with the basic rights of tenants.

From the National Fair Housing Advocate September 1997:

An Ohio landlord settled a familial status lawsuit by paying $100,000, agreeing to attend fair housing training along with his employees and to apologize to a family for not allowing them to move into a building he had designated adult only.

The landlord in this case had wrongfully designated some buildings for adults and some for families. At the time the family applied, the only vacancies were in adult buildings and the family was denied a rental in a family building.

Case Example

College Area Renters and Landlords Association v. City of San Diego (1996)
42 C.A. 4th 543

The city of San Diego passed a municipal ordinance regulating the number of persons who could occupy a residence in a college area. Occupancy was based on square footage, parking and other listed criteria.

The Court of Appeals determined the ordinance was unconstitutional in that it applied only to renters. Owner occupants can have huge families without regulations.

Therefore, the ordinance discriminated against one category of occupants, so it violates the equal protection principles of the Constitution.

Note: However, a landlord can reasonably limit occupancy.

Case Example

PFAFF v. U.S. Dept. of Housing and Urban Development (1996) 88 F. 3d 739

Owners told their rental agent that occupancy of a 1,200 square foot two bedroom home would be limited to four persons because of its small size and lack of a basement or backyard. A rental application had been received from a family of five. The rental applicants then filed a complaint with HUD based on discrimination as to family status. An administrative law judge awarded $4,212.61 in compensatory damages, $20,000 for emotional distress and $8,000 in civil penalties.

The U.S. Court of Appeals reversed the administrative law judge's decision. The Appellate Court pointed out that landlords do not have to prove a compelling business reason for limiting occupancy since HUD has not set occupancy guidelines. The court held that occupancy of four was not unreasonable to protect the property. Since HUD has in the past used a two-person per bedroom rule of thumb, four persons should be presumed to be reasonable.

Note: The Appellate Court was strongly critical of HUD for going after the property owner when they had no guidelines.

From the National Fair Housing Advocate October 1996:

The Fair Housing Council of Orange County settled a racial and family status lawsuit for $775,000 against Clark Biggers, the owner of four apartment complexes in Southern California.

FHC alleged that Biggers discriminated against minorities and families with children. Families complained that they were either charged higher rents or were denied apartments at Bigger's complexes.

The Los Angeles Times felt that the FHC got "the short end of the settlement because an attorney for the FHC received $645,000 of the $775,000 settlement."

Note: A settlement does not mean admittance of guilt. Defendants often find it is cheaper to settle than to fight, even when they dispute the merit of the allegations.

ADVERTISING

Discriminatory advertising is prohibited by the Civil Rights Act of 1968.

Advertising that a property is close to a minority area or with a minority connotation such as "only two blocks from Martin Luther King High School" could be discriminatory. Mentioning a preference such as "females preferred" in an ad would be discriminatory even though expressed as a preference not an absolute.

HUD discourages use of specific words in advertising that indicate discrimination. Words included are, black, white, colored, Catholic, Protestant, Jew, Chicano, restricted, etc.

Selective use of advertising media, such as advertising a property in a minority area in papers only aimed at that minority group, could be discriminatory (steering).

There has been a great deal of confusion as to what could or could not be advertised. Some "experts" claimed that it was discriminatory to advertise a view as it might offend the blind.

On January 9, 1995, HUD supplied a memo to its staff as to guidelines for discrimination investigation. The memo covered several points:

1. **Race, color and national origin.** Terms such as "master bedroom," "rare find" or "desirable neighborhood" were allowable. There had been concern that "master" was masculine and sexually discriminatory as well as being a term common to slavery.

2. **Religion.** Statements such as "apartment complex with chapel" or "kosher meals available" does not show preference for persons who might use these facilities.

3. **Sex.** "Master bedroom," "mother-in-law suite" and "bachelor apartment" are permissible. Many state organizations had been advising members that these terms were discriminatory.

4. **Handicap.** Reference to "view," "walk-up," "walk-in closets," etc. do not violate the act nor does "jogging trails" or "walk to bus stop." It is also acceptable to advertise "non-smoking" or "sober" as these are prohibited activities. You cannot advertise "no alcoholics" or "non-smokers " as these refer to groups of people.

5. **Familial Status.** Advertisements using terms such as "2 BR," "cozy," "family room," "no bicycles allowed" and "quiet streets" are allowed but limiting age or sex of children is not allowed.

Advertising for singles or even a preference for adults would be discriminating.

Despite the HUD memorandum, there are still many unanswered questions as to what HUD will or will not allow. A complicating factor is that words have different meanings in different areas of the country, as well as among different ethnic groups. Several state organizations have come up with guidelines as to acceptable, caution and not acceptable language.

Figure 13-1 is a list prepared by the Oregon Newspaper Publishers Association.

ENFORCEMENT OF THE CIVIL RIGHTS ACT OF 1968 (as amended)

Remedies include:

1. HUD initiation of complaints on its own authority.
2. Individuals can file complaints with HUD.
3. Individuals can commence legal action.
4. Remedies:

The court could award:

a. Actual damages;
b. Punitive damages;
c. Court costs and attorney fees;
d. The court could issue an injunction.

Equal Housing Opportunity Poster

Failure of a leasing agent to prominently post the Equal Housing Opportunity Poster (Figure 13-2) will shift the burden of proof as to discriminatory practices from the person claiming discrimination to the agent. This can be an extremely difficult task.

Figure 13-1

Discriminatory and Nondiscriminatory
Advertising Language

Not Acceptable

able-bodied	impaired, no	responsible
adult living	Indian	retarded, no
adult community	Irish	shrine
adults only	integrated	stable
African	Jewish	white
agile	landlord (description of)	white only
alcoholics, no	Latino	
Asian	married	
bachelor	mature couple	
bachelor pad	mature individual	
blacks, no	mature person(s)	
blind, no	membership approval	
board approval	required	
required	mentally	
Catholic	handicapped, no	
Caucasian	mentally ill, no	
Chicano	Mexican-American	
Chinese	Mormon Temple	

Caution

active	gays, no	physically fit
children, no	gender	Polish
church(es), near	gentlemen's farm	Puerto Rican
colored	golden-agers only	quiet tenants
close to	grandma's house	responsible
couple	handyman's dream	retarded, no
country club, near	healthy only	season worker, no
couples only	Hispanic	single person
desirable	lesbians, no	singles only

neighborhood
crippled, no
domestic's quarters
deaf, no
drinkers, no
employed, must be
empty nestors
ethnic references
exclusive
executive
female roommate
fisherman's retreat
female(s) only

male roommate
must comply with
mosque
nationality
newlyweds
nondrinkers
non-smokers
no play area
older person(s)
one child
one person
Oriental
physically fit

smokers, no
SSI, no
stable
synagogue, near
temple, near
tenant (description of)
unemployed, no

Acceptable

apartment
bus, near
credit check
required
den
drinking, no
drugs, no
drug users, no
Equal Housing
Opportunity
family, great for
family room
fixer-up
neighborhood
hobby farm
male(s) only
man (men) only
mature
mother-in-law
nanny's room
near
neighborhood
name

no student(s)
number of bedrooms
number of persons
number of sleeping
areas
nursery
nursing home
play area
prestigious
privacy
private
private driveway
private entrance
private property
private setting
public transport, near
quality
restricted
retired
retirees
school district
school name
secluded

Section 8, no
secure
senior(s)
senior citizen(s)
senior discount
senior housing
sex or gender
single woman, man
smoking, no
square feet
sophisticated
students
townhouse
traditional style
tranquil setting
two people
verifiable income
view with
view of
walking distance of
within
woman (women)

Figure 13-2

U.S.. Department of Housing and Urban Development

**EQUAL HOUSING
OPPORTUNITY**

**We Do Business in Accordance With the Federal Fair
Housing Law**
(The Fair Housing Amendments Act of 1988)

It is Illegal to Discriminate Against Any Person Because of Race, Color, Religion, Sex, Handicap, Familial Status, or National Origin

- In the sale or rental of housing or residential lots

- In advertising the sale or rental of housing

- In the financing of housing

- In the provision of real estate brokerage services

- In the appraisal of housing

- Blockbusting is also illegal

Anyone who feels he or she has been discriminated against may file a complaint of housing discrimination:

    1-800-424-8590 (Toll Free)
    1-800-424-8529 (TDD)

U.S. Department of Housing and Urban Development
Assistant Secretary for Fair Housing and Equal Opportunity
Washington, D.C. 20410

Previous editions are obsolete   form HUD-928.1 (3-89)

From the National Fair Housing Advocate January 1997:

A 20-year-old man and his 19 year old wife were not allowed to fill out a rental application because they were both under the age of 21 and the apartment complex had a 21 and over policy. The age to contract is 18. It was alleged that the age policy was discriminatory and illegal. The apartment complex settled the matter for $5,200.

From the National Fair Housing Advocate March 1997:

Glendale Federal and the management company they used had to pay $440,000 to settle a discrimination case based on race, national origin and family status.

After foreclosure, Glendale Federal hired a management company that terminated the tenancies so that the building could be renovated. The building was in a white neighborhood close to the U.C. Santa Barbara campus.

It was alleged that evictions were not necessary as the work contemplated could be performed without dislocating the tenant. It was alleged that the evictions had a disparate impact on Hispanics and families with children. The allegations were that Glendale wished to replace the Hispanic tenants and families with children with college students without children.

Note: It used to be considered good management if the character of a building could be changed resulting in higher rents. Now, you must be concerned with who will be replaced and are they members of a protected group. The management company could have simply raised rents which would have provided vacancies.

From the National Fair Housing Advocate November 1997:

A California landlord agreed to a $7,500 settlement of a federal lawsuit alleging discrimination based on family status.

The plaintiff inquired as to a rental. When the landlord found out about two young sons, the landlord indicated that he did not want to rent to a family with children because the property was on a steep hill. A tester then inquired about the rental and the owner again stated that children would not be appropriate because of the steep slope and the fact that there was a creek running through the backyard that presented a safety hazard. The tester told the owner she did not think her children would be in danger. Upon later contact with the owner, the owner told the tester the property had been rented to persons without children.

Note: This case seems to say "Don't be your brother's keeper."

AMERICANS WITH DISABILITIES ACT

This act protects those with physical and mental disabilities. It requires owners, operators, lessees and managers of commercial facilities to make their facilities accessible to the extent that is readily achievable. The reasonableness of providing access would be based on the difficulty of achieving access and the expense involved considering the total property value and the financial ability of the person responsible.

> *The Americans with Disabilities Act makes it discriminatory to deny equal enjoyment of goods, services, facilities and accommodations in an existing place of public accommodation (nonresidential).*

This would include stores, offices and service providers.

To comply with the act, a leasing office might have to:

1. provide handicap parking close to an office;
2. ramp the curb or steps;
3. lower a front counter for wheelchair access;
4. move furniture to provide wheelchair access;
5. add a paper cup dispenser by a water fountain;
6. install grab bars in washrooms;
7. any other reasonably achievable action that will allow full use and enjoyment of facilities by the handicapped.

> *An owner can charge more for sale or lease of handicapped accessible facilities.*

Enforcement

The Americans with Disabilities Act can be enforced by:

1. an action by a citizen;
2. an action by the U. S. Attorney.

Penalties

Penalties for violations are severe:

1. $50,000 for first discriminatory act;
2. $100,000 for each additional act;
3. Damages (compensatory);
4. Attorney fees.

EQUAL CREDIT OPPORTUNITY ACT

The importance of this act as to property managers relates to qualifications of prospective renters.

Property managers may not ask applicants questions as to childbearing intentions.

Applicants CANNOT be refused because of race, color, religion, national origin, sex, marital status, age or because the source of income is public assistance.

Case Example

Gilligan v. Jamco Development Corp. **(1997) 108 F. 3d 246**

This case involved a family who contacted a property manager about a vacancy. They indicated that their source of income was Aid To Families With Dependent Children (AFDC). The property manager refused to allow them to inspect units or to apply for a rental because they were on AFDC. The property manager never inquired about the amount of income the plaintiff's received nor did the manager inform them of the rent. A fair housing tester then contacted the property manager. The tester told the property manager she received welfare income. The tester was informed that Verduga Gardens was not a "Welfare Building." This tester was immediately followed by a second tester who indicated that he was working. The second was shown an apartment.

The U.S. Court of Appeals held that discrimination applied to the application process and that AFDC did not make the plaintiff ineligible. Refusal to accept a rental application was discriminatory.

Note: This case points out the need to understand that all rental applicants must be treated equally.

Can a property manager refuse to rent to a person who can be expected to lose assistance in the future? Unless the law is changed, the answer appears to be "No."

Fair Housing (State)

The reason that states have fair housing laws is primarily because the state legislation preceded the federal laws. As an example, California passed the Unruh Act which prohibits any business from discriminatory practice. This was interpreted to include real estate agents and property owners.

The Unruh Act provides for actual damages plus $250 for each offense.

California later passed a comprehensive fair housing act (California Fair Employment and Housing Act) which is commonly known as the Rumford Act. The only exceptions to this act was a person renting a room in their own housing unit as well as nonprofit religious, charitable and fraternal organizations. These exceptions were not applicable to the Unruh Act or the 1866 federal act.

California's Rumford Act provides that an owner or manager could be required to rent another available unit to the person discriminated against and be subject to a $10,000 civil penalty.

Many discrimination cases are brought under state law rather than federal law because of generally lower costs for litigation.

Most states also provide that discriminatory actions of a real estate licensee shall be grounds for disciplinary action which could include revocation of license.

Fair Housing Partnership Agreement (FHPA)

The National Association of Realtors (NAR) entered in a Fair Housing Partnership with the Department of Housing and Urban Devlelopment (HUD). The Partnership focuses on identifying and eradicating housing discrimination. Because those issues and the priorities differ from community to community, NAR and HUD did not develop a specifc model for local partnerships. Local NAR associations and HUD field offices are encouraged to develop local partnerships based on the following principles of the national partnership:

1. Sharing responsibility for the achievement of fair housing, identifying fair housing issues and concerns,

2. Developing measurable strategies and actions to address identified issues and concerns,

3. Evaluating the process of actions taken, and

4. Determining future strategies and actions based on that evaluation.

Ethics

Ethics is simply doing what is right.

If a wrong was committed ethics would dictate that the wrong be corrected.

The problems that arise is "What is right?" Some persons analyze actions from their own viewpoint. We have grown beyond the "If it's right for General Motors, it's right for America" way of thinking. We have gone beyond absolute self interest as justification of actions. However, beyond is actually back in a historical perspective. We are coming to realize that ethics isn't that difficult to understand.

Ethics is the application of the oldest rule for distinguishing right from wrong—The Golden Rule.

If we wouldn't want to be treated in a particular manner, we cannot ethically justify treating others in that manner.

Placing interest of a client first is not incompatible with ethics. It is in the best interests of owners to treat employees, contractors and tenants in a fair manner. Actually, if you were to take advantage of others it would be detrimental to you over the long haul.

Good ethics is good business.

Ethics differs from the law. Ethics is what is right. The law sets minimum standards of behavior. The law, however, could be unethical, such as early laws mandating racial segregation.

The following management situations and suggestions will help you in understanding the ethical considerations of property management.

Situation 1

Your firm, which manages Crayton Towers, has just merged with a competing firm that manages the adjacent and identical Winston Towers. Both of these high-rise apartment buildings have a 10 percent vacancy factor. You intend to establish just one rental offered for both buildings. You feel that this would be more efficient and that costs could be reduced. The Winston Towers contract calls for the reimbursement of advertising costs, an agent rental bonus, and a slightly higher management fee than the Crayton Tower contract. The Crayton Tower contract has no charge for rentals.

What, if any, are the ethical problems involved?

Analysis

With the difference in costs and commissions, you are bound to have problems as to perception of wrongdoing. At the very least, the owner of Winston Towers should know how you will be allocating advertising costs since one office will be handling all advertising calls and walk-ins. However, this in itself would not be enough. Because the Winston Towers' contract is more lucrative, the owner of Cranston Towers could feel that Winston Towers would be getting preference as to rentals. Even if you did not intend to give preference, your on-site leasing agent would be influenced by the bonus offer for Winston Towers' rentals.

There are two ways you could be fair to both owners. One way would be to continue two separate management arrangements with separate leasing offices. The other way would be to combine the offices but negotiate identical contracts so that it would not be in the best interest of the property manager or the leasing agent to prefer one building over the other when leasing.

Situation 2

You are managing agent for a free standing single tenant office structure. The building is in a racially integrated middle class neighborhood. The property has been vacant for over one year because of a high office vacancy factor in the area coupled with insufficient off-street parking. The out-of-state owner is desperate for a tenant because of high mortgage payments.

Another agent has procured a prospective tenant for the structure. It is the "Hitler Society of America," a new Anglo-Saxon hate organization. They have been endowed by a wealthy benefactor who has agreed to a ten-year lease with one year's rent in advance. The benefactor has also agreed to sign as a guarantor on the lease. The Hitler Society of America wishes to use the structure as a national headquarters which will handle its publications and training of cadre for the various state organizations that will be established.

While the group's activities are obnoxious, checking with the State Attorney General, the FBI and local law enforcement officials indicates that as of now the group has managed to remain inside the law.

What should you do?

Analysis

This situation could be ethically decided two ways.

If you believed that the first amendment rights of free speech are so important that they must be protected at all costs, then you could ethically lease the property.

However, you should fully disclose to the owner the nature of the tenant's activity before leasing. You should also check with your insurance carrier to ascertain if the carrier will continue to insure the structure based on the tenant. To not do so could be negligence on your part. If after full disclosure the owner wished the leasing to go forward, you could then ethically execute the lease.

On the other hand, if you felt that leasing to this tenant would be the equivalent of yelling "Fire" in a crowded theater, then you would feel that free speech should not be paramount in this situation. Because you are an agent, you would have to tell the owner about the tenant and you could ethically recommend that the prospective tenant be rejected. If the owner wished to rent anyway, you could ask to be relieved of management.

If you signed the lease and kept management, your actions would be unethical because you believed them to be dangerous to the community without any overriding principal such as free speech.

This case illustrates that ethical decisions are NOT always black and white.

They are influenced by your own application of the golden rule, not what someone else says.

Situation 3

You are managing a spectacular 4,200 square foot ocean front home that was built for the view. It sits atop of a 300 foot cliff that drops vertically only 75 feet from the patio. There is no fence by the cliff as the owners did not want to obstruct their view.

You feel you will have no trouble renting the home even though the rent is $10,000 per month and, in fact, the first persons to view it placed a rental deposit. They are a family with three children ages two, four and six. You warned them of the dangers as to small children because of the cliff. You also told them about the small child who was killed falling off the cliff at the home next door. However, the parents love the view and indicate that they will make certain that their children do not get too close to the cliff. Checking their application reveals that the prospective tenants are well qualified.

Analysis

If you truly believe that the children are in danger, you should do all in your power to prevent the family from renting the property. You could ask the parents to sign a waiver of liability in the hopes that it would make them reconsider renting.

The 1988 Amendment to the Civil Rights Act of 1968 prohibits you from refusing to rent to a family because of the age or presence of children. However, law is not the same as ethics. Ethics is the way things should be. Law on the other hand sets legal limits to behavior. You could ethically violate the law in refusing the tenants but legally you would be liable and subject to legal sanctions.

Situation 4

A tenant in a building having many small children has been criminally charged with child molestation. He denies the charge and is out on bail. Other tenants have asked you to evict the tenant.

Analysis

The tenant has not violated lease provisions and should not be considered guilty until proven so. The tenant should only be given notice to leave if you now were aware of something prior to his rental that, had you known, you would have refused the rental. As an example, if you now find out that the tenant had a previous conviction for child molestation, then you could be acting in an ethical manner in giving the tenant notice to vacate.

═══ CHAPTER 13 SUMMARY ═══

The Civil Rights Act of 1866 provided that every citizen shall have the same rights as white citizens to purchase and lease real as well as personal property. There were no exceptions to the act. The Civil Rights Act of 1870 simply reiterated the 1866 Act. The act was not enforced by the courts until 1968 when the Supreme Court held in Jones v. Mayer that the act could be enforced by a private citizen.

The 14th Amendment to the Constitution is a broad statement of civil rights that implies fair housing.

In 1962, President John F. Kennedy issued Executive Order 11603 which bans discrimination in housing having federal involvement. The Civil Rights Act of 1964 made this executive order into law.

The Civil Rights Act of 1968 is also known as our Fair Housing Law. It prohibits discrimination in housing based on race, color, national origin and religion. It was amended to cover sex, handicapped and familial status. The act provides that:

1. agents cannot discriminate;
2. it is illegal to claim a unit is unavailable when it is available;
3. it is illegal to steer prospective tenants based on race, etc.;
4. refusal to loan within a designated area is illegal redlining;
5. blockbusting, the inducement of panic selling, is illegal;
6. discriminatory advertising is illegal;

7. lease terms that differ based on race, etc., are illegal;
8. retaliatory action against a tenant exercising legal rights would be an illegal practice;
9. agents may not discriminate by refusal of multiple listing access.

The 1988 Fair Housing Amendment Act protects persons with mental and physical handicaps as well as to familial status. An owner cannot refuse to rent because of a seeing eye dog or support animal. Tenants may modify units to provide handicap access. Lessors cannot discriminate because there are children under the age of 18 or because the lessee is pregnant. Qualified senior housing (55 or older) is exempt.

The Americans With Disabilities Act requires places of public accommodation to provide that handicap access is readily achievable.

Ethics is simply doing what is right. It differs from law which sets a minimum standard. Ethics goes beyond the law to the way things should be. However, ethical action could be illegal and legal action could be unethical. The golden rule is the best test for determining if a course of action is ethical.

CLASS DISCUSSION TOPICS

1. A property manager has recommended a real estate attorney to many of her clients. When the attorney does personal business for the property manager, the attorney's bills seem extremely low and sometimes the attorney even forgets to bill the property manager. Is there a problem?

2. A tenant moved out owing rent. When you entered the property, you noticed an old vase was left on a shelf along with a great deal of junk. You recognize the vase as having great value and a check with a dealer indicates it is worth in excess of $5,000. What should you do?

3. Most of the paint you buy is from Roger's Paint Store. They give excellent service and their prices are competitive. Roger's Paint Store is owned by your best friend. Is there a problem?

4. You receive two applications for the same apartment. The agent taking the second application did not know of the first application so the prospective tenant was not told that an application had been received.

The first application as taken from a caucasian tenant and the second was taken from an African American. Both tenants qualify for the rental. What should you do?

5. You receive a check for $1,500 plus a letter of apology from a tenant who moved out of a rental 17 years ago owing back rent. The property was sold 15 years ago and you are unable to locate the former owner although you used a skip tracer. What should you do?

6. A property manager called the INS to report an illegal alien. The illegal had lived in the unit for nine months but was now behind in rent. Did the manager do anything wrong?

CHAPTER 13 QUIZ

1. The Civil Rights Act that applied only to race was the Civil Rights Act of:

    A. 1866
    B. 1964
    C. 1968
    D. 1988

2. Directing a prospective tenant away from a property because you did not feel that they would be comfortable there based on the race of the current residents would be:

    A. blockbusting
    B. steering
    C. redlining
    D. legal

3. Which of the following would NOT be a member of a protected group under the 1988 Fair Housing Amendment Act?

    A. A blind person
    B. A person with AIDS
    C. A drug addict
    D. An alcoholic

4. A tenant has a seeing eye dog. The lessor can:

    A. charge an increased rent because of the pet
    B. increase the security deposit to cover possible damage by the dog
    C. refuse to rent to the person if there is a no-pet policy that is uniformly
       enforced
    D. do none of the above

5. An exception to the prohibition against discrimination as to familial status would be:

    A. children under the age of 18
    B. a prospective tenant who is pregnant
    C. housing for the elderly
    D. an unmarried mother

6. Which of the following advertising language would be acceptable?

    A. "Mother-In-law suite"
    B. "Walk-up"
    C. "Family room"
    D. All of the above

7. A property management office installed a wheelchair ramp. They also installed grab bars in their washrooms. They did this to comply with:

    A. the Unruh Act
    B. Americans With Disabilities Act
    C. Executive Order 11603
    D. Fair Housing Amendment Act of 1988

8. A property manager, in qualifying a tenant, can refuse a tenant for all EXCEPT:

    A. poor credit history
    B. problems with prior landlords
    C. no verifiable source of income
    D. income from public assistance programs

9. A property management office failed to display an equal housing opportunity poster. The result would be:

    A. revocation of the broker's license
    B. a $1,000 fine
    C. a $10,000 fine
    D. shifting of the burden of proof if discrimination is claimed

10. The best test to determine if an action is ethical would be to consider the:

    A. cost
    B. legality
    C. golden rule
    D. benefits

Answers: 1. A; 2. B; 3. C; 4. D; 5. C; 6. B; 7. B; 8. D; 9. D; 10. C

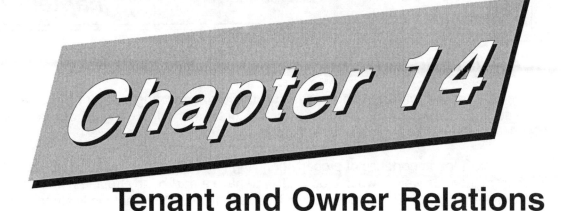

Tenant and Owner Relations

KEY WORDS AND TERMS

Change In Terms
Confidentiality
Constructive Eviction
Eleven Month Year
Eviction
Fair and Honest Dealing
Fiduciary Duty
Full Disclosure
Honesty
Leases in Spanish
Low Balling
Loyalty
Mitigation of Damages

Obedience
Physical Eviction
Quit or Cure
Quit or Pay Rent
Reasonable Care and Skill
Retaliatory Eviction
Seizure of property
Surrender
Tenant Complaints
Tenant Repair Rights
Unlawful Detainer
Waiting List
Waste

LEARNING OBJECTIVES

In this chapter you will learn about the importance of educating a tenant about lease clauses and occupancy rules. You should also understand the dangers of renting to friends or relatives or having a romantic entanglement with a tenant.

You will learn the importance of properly handling tenant complaints and what you can learn from them as well as what to do when you have a particularly troublesome tenant. You will learn how to deal with the death of a tenant when the death is likely to affect the continuance of the tenancy.

How to handle tenant waiting lists without getting into trouble will be covered as well as the tenant's right to make repairs and deduct the cost from rent.

You will learn about "waste" and your rights when a tenant commits waste.

Other areas that you will become acquainted with are dealing with extended tenant absences, changing the terms of a tenancy, tenants who fail to take possession, surrender of the lease and the avoidance of surprise charges.

You will learn how to handle tenant procrastination as to paying rent and the eviction process. Related constructive eviction, retaliatory eviction, physical eviction and property seizure is included.

You will learn when you should pay a tenant to leave and how you would mitigate damages when a tenant vacates prior to lease expiration.

You will learn of the necessity of proper owner/manager communications and the fiduciary duties a manager has to an owner.

You will learn why being over optimistic about income or underestimating costs is not good management policy.

You will learn the dangers of romantic relations with tenants.

In dealing with homeowners association members you will learn to be courteous and neutral as to internal politics.

You will appreciate the necessity to avoid any violation of the law or to aid an owner in any such violation.

While the owner may be your principal, you will realize that the owner also has obligations to you as the property manager and that you have the right to enforce these obligations.

Tenant Relations

TENANT EDUCATION

As previously stated, tenants should fully understand the lease provisions as well as the property rules and regulations at the time the lease is signed. You can do this by going through the lease paragraph by paragraph. You can do the same with the occupancy rules and regulations. A great many of the tenant problems that occur could have been prevented by carefully explaining what was expected of the tenants.

> *In California and several other states, if a lease is negotiated in Spanish then a Spanish translation must be provided to the tenant.*

Spanish translations of commonly used residential leases are readily available. For other tenants who do not speak English, you should arrange to have someone present when the lease is signed who can explain the lease and occupancy rules. This is the time to avoid future problems.

State law generally requires that tenants in multi-family apartments be given the name and address of the person to whom notices and demands are to be sent and who is responsible for management of the property.

RENTING TO FRIENDS AND RELATIVES

> *Your relationship with tenants should be on a business basis.*

While you should be friendly and fair, you do not want a situation to develop where there could be any perception or misunderstanding as to the fact that your loyalties lie with your principal, the owner of the property that you manage.

People close to you make terrible tenants. They tend to feel they are special and expect special treatment and relaxed occupancy rules. When your aunt buys a poodle, do you give her notice? If Uncle Charley promised to have the rent to you on Thursday and didn't, do you give him a three-day notice?

What do you do when a rental qualifying check on cousin Albert revealed that he qualified for the annual tenant from hell award according to a prior landlord? Not only was he antagonistic to management, but he argued with other tenants, sued two of them and the property manager.

These questions are raised to show you the position you could place yourself in when renting to relatives or close friends.

In addition, if you gave the person any inducement to rent, such as free rent, it could appear to be a breach of your fiduciary duty of loyalty to the owner. At the very least, when renting to a relative or close friend you should inform the owner prior to the rental and give the owner all rental details and how you qualified the tenant.

ROMANTIC ENTANGLEMENTS

Don't get involved with a tenant or rent to anyone you are involved with.

Enforce this prohibition with employees in your office. To start with, you could put yourself in a position of having divided loyalties. Should the relationship sour, you also have a good chance of losing a tenant.

A property manager related to us how he rented an apartment he managed to a girl friend. When the girl friend failed to pay the rent on time and he called her about it, she told him "Do you think your wife would like to know about our relationship?" Although that ended the relationship, he ended up paying the rent for over two years.

TENANT COMPLAINTS

You should keep a record of every tenant complaint.

Using your computer you can relate complaints by tenant, time period and type of problem. This ability can help you in a number of ways. It can indicate maintenance deficiencies, personnel problems, service contract problems and problems relating to the tenant.

It is not enough that you record the complaint. When the action was taken and by whom is also important. You don't want a tenant to have to make a second call as to why nothing was done. It indicates a disgruntled tenant.

If the tenant was not told what action will be taken as to a complaint at the time it was received, the tenant should be notified as soon as possible thereafter about what action has or will be taken by whom and, if not yet solved, when.

Tenants should never be led to believe that their complaint has fallen on deaf ears. Similarly, tenants should never be led to believe that you will doing something when you will not. As an example, suppose a tenant complains that the automatic sprinkler system wakes him up and he wants the sprinklers set to run during the daytime rather than at night. Assume you run them at night because of better water pressure and to avoid interference with the gardeners and use of walkways by the tenants. If you are not going to make any correction based on this tenant's complaint, you should explain this to the tenant and give truthful reasons.

Some property managers take an easy way out and lie. They might say the water district requires them to run sprinklers at night. A lie such as this puts the blame on someone else and the property manager comes off as being on the side of the tenant. The problem with lies is they tend to be forgotten by the teller who will come up with a different story at a later date. Another problem is the person might want to carry it one more step and call the water department and discover the lie.

It is NOT enough to be technically honest with answers, you should be scrupulously honest when servicing tenant complaints and all other aspects of tenant relations.

LET THE TENANT GO

Some people do not have the temperament to live in close quarters with others in an apartment building. They may be constantly complaining to management about noise such as another tenant flushing a toilet in the middle of the night. They might also harangue other tenants about what they perceive as significant problems. You will find such tenants and you will swear that their purpose in life is to make you miserable. A "tenant from hell" could result in the loss of other tenants, so something has to be done.

Eviction may not be an option since the tenant's actions might needle others but might not be sufficient cause for eviction. If you start an eviction action, this tenant might be able to successfully defeat your action by claiming retaliatory eviction and you could even end up paying damages.

A first step would be to talk to the tenant. From our experience, talking seems to be ineffective because of the selective listening of such a tenant. We have let such tenants out of their leases and in one case we actually paid the moving costs to arrive at our solution.

Unfortunately, tenant qualification seldom reveals such a tenant. We have found that they might be renting after having been an owner for many years. We have also found, in a few instances, that quarrelsome tenants had recently had an upheaval in their lives such as the death of a spouse. While their personal tragedies are unfortunate, they cannot be given carte blanche to disrupt the lives of others.

DEATH OF A TENANT

The death of a wage earner, in the case of a residential tenant, or the death of a business owner, in the case of a commercial rental, could result in future rent collection difficulties. Some problems can be avoided in a tactful manner but it is very difficult to do so.

One property manager always sends flowers and a kind note in such a case. About 10 days after the funeral she makes an appointment to see the spouse or survivor and lets the party know that she is willing to help. As to residential property she offers to release the tenant from the lease and help them find a less expensive rental if rent will be a problem. For commercial property, she offers to suggest business brokers if a business will have to be sold.

This broker is careful to convey a helpful image and is able to quickly discover if there will be a problem and, if so, to begin work to solve it. In some cases, she has shown tenants who to contact for public assistance. In other cases, she has recommended attorneys where she felt the survivor might have a worker's compensation or liability claim. If you are not comfortable with the above approach, don't use it.

WAITING LIST

> *You must be meticulous in following the order of the waiting list of your prospective tenants when taking applications for units and qualifying prospective tenants.*

By not following the proper order of the list could result in charges of discrimination as to a race, age, sex, disability, familial status, etc. However this does not mean that you must accept the tenant at the top of the list. If they would otherwise not qualify because of income or credit history or if they are unable or unwilling to take the unit when it becomes vacant, you can go down the list to another party.

If an apartment consistently has a waiting list and the rents are not limited by rent control, it should be clear that the demand has exceeded the supply and rent increases would be in the best interest of the owner.

TENANT'S RIGHT TO REPAIR

Many states allow a residential tenant to make repairs and deduct the costs from the rent in cases where the repairs are necessary for habitability and the lessor has failed, after reasonable notice, to make the repairs.

California Civil Code Section 1942, allows the tenant to make such repairs and deduct the cost of the repairs from the rent, providing that the cost of the repairs do not exceed one month's rent. The tenant may exercise this right no more than two times in any 12-month period. As to period of time for a notice, 30 days is presumed to be a reasonable period of time but the period could be shorter based on the problem. A tenant who had plumbing repairs on an inoperable toilet in a single-bath apartment would not have to wait 30 days.

A court might consider even 24 hours failure to repair to be a reasonable period.

As an alternative to making a repair the tenant could, after the lessor's failure to correct the problem within a reasonable time, treat the failure as the landlord's constructive eviction and vacate the premises and be discharged from further rent payments and other conditions of the lease.

If a lessor would attempt to evict a tenant who has properly made repairs and deducted the cost from the rent, the tenant would have the defense of retaliatory eviction.

TENANT PAINTING

Many landlords who deal direct with tenants supply the paint and allow tenants to paint their units. In some cases the landlords give tenants rent credit for the work.

From experience, we don't believe it is a good practice. Besides poor workmanship, paint on woodwork and carpeting plus work that may only get half finished, we would want to control the colors and quality of paint used. By limiting interiors to one or two colors, we can often have a maintenance person touch up a paint job with a roller in from 30 minutes to one hour per unit. In areas where there is not a great deal of airborne dirt, this is the norm rather than the exception.

Even where we have supplied tenants with paint, we have had them paint over varnished woodwork and kitchen cabinetry and even change the colors by adding tints. Therefore, we ceased allowing tenants to paint units in properties we have managed.

In small units, such as fourplexes, where we did not have resident managers, we allowed a tenant to have a rent concession by taking care of the lawn, walkways, entry ways and hallways. We have also hired retired tenants with maintenance skills to handle maintenance work within a complex. If you do so, make certain that your contract spells out that they are independent contractors rather than employees.

WASTE

WASTE *is an abuse of property that impairs the value of the property.* Waste could be an alteration of the premises, removal of a structure, removing trees, etc. Waste results in substantial or permanent damage to the property that impairs value. A landlord would be justified in terminating a lease for waste. The landlord would also be entitled to damages.

Chapter 14

Case Example

Freeze v. Brinsin (1991) 4 C.A. 4th Supp 1

Plaintiff brought action against a tenant for unlawful detainer alleging that the tenant had committed waste on the premises. The landlord claimed there was damage to a wall and floor caused by excrement of the tenant's dog. The trial court found for the plaintiff but the Superior Court Appellate Department reversed the decision.

The court held that to declare waste there must be clear evidence of acts that seriously affect the market value of the property. The burden is on the landlord to show that the value was permanently or substantially impaired. While the landlord had shown damage to the premises, there wasn't any evidence to show the value of the premises was substantially or permanently diminished.

EXTENDED TENANT ABSENCE

The property manager should tell tenants that if they will be absent for a long period of time to notify him or her of the absence. Also request in writing that you have the right to enter their unit for inspection purposes and to place any mail papers and deliveries in the unit. The manager must impress upon tenants that they are responsible for any damage caused by failure to maintain utilities when absent. This is particularly important for property in Northern or mountain areas where a freeze could destroy plumbing as well as result in water damage.

If possible, also ask tenants who will be gone for an extended period, where they can be contacted or who to contact in an emergency.

CHANGE IN TERMS/END OF TENANCY

For a month-to-month tenancy, the lessor can change the rent or other terms of the tenancy. However, a notice (usually 30 days) is required to do so.

Similarly, to end a periodic tenancy, either tenant or landlord can generally give the other party a notice for the length of the rent paying period (but no more than 30 days) that the tenancy is to end.

When you raise the rent, it is a good practice to justify the raise. As an example, painting hallways or doing landscaping work just prior to a rent increase will be accepted better than a raise without any improvement of the property or apparent increase in owner costs.

NEVER HAVE SURPRISE CHARGES

Some mobile home parks surprise tenants with a group of hidden charges such as a charge to check the sewer hookups or to connect to the park's cable television system. Some charges are in the nickel and dime category while others are substantial.

All charges should be fully and clearly revealed before a tenant is obligated to the rental. Even a justified change will be resented if it comes as a surprise.

FAILURE TO TAKE POSSESSION

If a tenant fails to take possession after signing a lease, the tenant is liable under the lease even if they never moved in and you have a right and duty to hold them to their agreement. Sometimes they think that they can just forfeit what they paid if they find something they like better. Your duty to your principal is to enforce the lease.

SURRENDER OF LEASE

A **SURRENDER** *of a lease is the lessee giving the premises back to the lessor and the lessor accepting possession with the understanding that the lease is ended.* A surrender ends all lease obligations of the lessee at the time of surrender.

A tenant who vacates the premises prior to the end of the lease is likely to claim that he or she has surrendered the premises, however, the lessor would likely want to consider it an abandonment of the premises with the lessee remaining liable for future lease payments.

While there can generally be a verbal surrender of leases for one year or less, written leases for more than one year should not be surrendered orally.

There should be a written surrender agreement.

THE FIRST EXCUSE

If a tenant calls you to explain that he or she will be late with the rent, ask the tenant when the rent will be paid. Arrive at an agreement as to date of payment and inform the tenant that if the rent is not paid by the agreed date that a notice (three-day) shall be given followed by eviction if the tenant fails to pay or vacate.

If the rent is not paid by the date set, do not take a second promise. Go ahead with eviction proceedings. If the tenant brings in the money, never waive the late charge. Waiver of late charges condones being late.

Never allow the tenant to fall behind a full month's rent. If it happens, the majority of the time rent never becomes current.

THE ELEVEN MONTH YEAR

Owners may turn over property for management with tenants who are over a year in rent arrearage. This rent arrearage isn't necessarily because of a tenant's inability to pay, it is often because of the gullibility of the landlord.

A tenant may pay June rent on June 10th. The tenant may pay rent for July on July 19th. For August, the rent may be paid on August 26th. The tenant may pay rent for September on October 3rd. You soon realize then that the tenant has become one month behind in rent in just a few months. Landlords are unwilling to evict such a tenant because the tenant pays rent, although a little slow. The owner will suddenly realize how far the tenant is in arrearage. Now the landlord believes that if he or she is just patient with the tenant, who appears to be trying, he or she will get caught up on the rent. It is not going to happen.

In management, you have a duty to the owner.

You cannot allow a tenant to get away with less than 12 monthly payments per year. Remember that fairness is a two-way street. While you want to be fair with tenants, they must also be fair with you.

EVICTION

A tenant may be evicted for failure to pay rent or for the breach of a significant lease provision. The first step would be a notice (generally a three-day notice). The notice could be:

Quit or Pay Rent

The tenant can cure such action by paying the rent.

Note: A lessor need not evict a tenant who is delinquent in rent. The lessor, as an alternative, could sue for rent as it becomes due. This alternative would only be feasible where the tenant has financial resources making a judgment collectable.

Quit or Cure

Such a notice would require the tenant to cure the default. As an example, if the notice was based on the tenant having a pet in violation of the law, removing the pet from the premises would cure the default.

Quit

If the default is one that cannot be cured, the three-day notice to quit would be appropriate. As an example, assume a tenant lied about the size of his or her family in order to rent a one-bedroom apartment. If there were six people rather than the two claimed, a three-day notice to quit would be appropriate. (Three-day notices are included in Chapter 5.)

The three-day notice would be followed by an unlawful detainer action. After being served with this action, the tenant has a statutory period (five days in California) to file an answer. The tenant could claim a defense such as retaliatory eviction, the premises were uninhabitable or a denial of the charges. The tenant could also claim a procedural error in that the tenant had not been served with a three-day notice or that the notice was defective. Another possible defense would be a claim that eviction was based upon the race, religion, national origin, sex, etc. of the tenant so it would be a civil rights violation.

If a lessor indicates in an unlawful detainer action, based on nonpayment of rent, that the amount due is greater than the amount the court determines is actually due, then the unlawful detainer action would be faulty and would likely fail.

> *A partial payment accepted after the three-day notice will also invalidate the unlawful detainer action.*

If the tenant answers the unlawful detainer action, the tenant has his or her day in court and the court would decide if a judgement should be entered in favor of the landlord. The court would grant the landlord a judgement if the tenant failed to answer the unlawful detainer action.

If the tenant fails to vacate the premises, the landlord can obtain a Writ Of Possession authorizing the sheriff or marshal to physically remove the tenant and his or her possessions from the premises. In most cases, the tenant will peacefully vacate, although damage to the premises is an all too common occurrence.

Case Example

City of South San Francisco Housing Authority v. Guillory (1996) 41 C.A. 4th Supp 13

A lease contained a "zero tolerance" drug clause. Drugs were found in the closet of the son of the tenant. The family was evicted.

The Superior Court affirmed the Municipal Court's decision that the housing authority had good cause for eviction. Parents can be held for the illegal conduct of their children.

Case Example

Lamanna v. Vagnor (1993) 17 C.A. 4th Supp 4

A tenant was served a three-day notice for rent delinquency on a Wednesday. On the following Tuesday, the day after Memorial Day, the landlord filed an unlawful detainer action.

The Appellate Court held that the unlawful detainer action was invalid because the tenant was not given a three-day notice, as required by California law, to quit or pay rent and retain possession.

In California, the time for a three-day notice is computed by excluding the day of service and including the last day. Therefore, the three days commenced on Thursday and Friday would have been the second day. Since business days only are counted and Monday was a holiday, the third day was Tuesday. The tenant had all of Tuesday to cure the rent arrearage. The unlawful detainer should not have been filed until Wednesday.

Note: Be certain that you count days properly in accordance with state law or your unlawful detainer will fail. You would then have to again give a new three-day notice followed by an unlawful detainer action.

Case Example

Jayasinghe v. Lee (1993) 13 C.A. 4th Supp 3

A lease provided for rent of $2,000 per month subject to annual CPI or 10 percent of gross income. The landlord never asked for or received an income statement but notified the tenant on two occasions of rent increases beyond the CPI increase. The tenant paid the base rent plus the CPI amount.

The landlord served the tenant a three-day notice demanding more rent than was due followed by an unlawful detainer action. The trial court found for the tenant based on the pleadings.

The appellate division found that the trial court did not abuse its discretion. The parties had stipulated to the facts and the landlord's demand for rent was overstated so could not support on unlawful detainer action.

Note: Be certain of the amount due or your eviction action could fail.

RENT AFTER NOTICE

After you have commenced an eviction with a three-day notice and/or unlawful detainer action, should you accept any rent, your notice will be canceled. Any further eviction would mean you must start over. Consider this when a partial rent payment is offered.

Some tenants are well aware of this and are quite sophisticated in their approach. They will bring in a money order or cash and promise the rest in four or five days. If you give them a receipt, you have given them a defense to your eviction action.

CONSTRUCTIVE EVICTION

A *landlord's actions can negatively affect the use and enjoyment of premises to the extent that a tenant could get out of a lease under the doctrine of* **CONSTRUCTIVE EVICTION***.*

If a landlord fails to provide utilities as agreed or cuts off the tenant's utilities, these actions would allow a tenant to rescind the lease. Failing to correct a vermin or sanitation problem could also be grounds for a tenant's ending a lease. Failure to take action against another tenant's activities which materially affected the use and enjoyment of the property by others would also be grounds for a tenant to end a lease.

In order to declare constructive eviction as a defense for leaving the premises prior to a lease expiration, the tenant must do so within a reasonable period after the landlord's actions (or failure to act).

If the tenant stays in possession, the tenant must pay rent. The tenant cannot use the landlord's action as an excuse not to live up to his or her rental obligations.

Case Example

Lee v. Placer Title (1994) 28 C.A. 4th 503

Placer Title moved out of its space in a shopping center prior to the expiration of its lease. In a suit for rent due, Placer claimed constructive eviction since the landlord failed to stop an adjoining dry cleaners from allowing toxic fumes to enter Placer's premises.

The Court of Appeals affirmed the trial courts decision in favor of the landlord since the lease provided that in "no event shall tenant have the right to terminate this lease as a result of landlord's default and tenant remedies shall be limited to damages and/or an injunction." Placer had breached the lease. They had given up any rights to claim constructive eviction.

Note: This case applied to a commercial rental. Such a clause cannot be expected to be upheld for a residential rental.

RETALIATORY EVICTION

RETALIATORY EVICTION *is eviction because the tenant exercised legal rights which have upset the landlord.* Retaliatory eviction can result in not only losing at an attempt to evict but possible punitive damages.

Examples of retaliatory eviction would be eviction because of a tenant complaining to the health department, a rent control board, zoning commission or other agency. It could also be because the tenant attempted to organize a tenant organization or made repeated request for repairs which were the responsibility of the landlord.

You must avoid any appearances that an eviction is retaliatory.

As an example, if you evict a tenant who has made frequent complaints but based your eviction on the fact that the tenant had a dog which was not permitted under the lease, it could be considered retaliatory if you had taken no action against other tenants with dogs who had not made similar complaints. In other words, selective enforcement of lease provisions or rules and regulations could be determined by the court to be retaliatory.

PHYSICAL EVICTION

Many years ago landlords would take evictions into their own hands and remove tenants. Common methods used were to simply remove the front door or turn off utilities. Other owners used physical threats to get a tenant to leave while still others actually carted the tenant's possessions out to the sidewalk.

Don't resort to any of these actions. You are asking for a costly lawsuit.

There are plenty of attorneys who will be happy to sue you for outrageous conduct in the hopes of getting punitive damages.

For cutting off the utilities, damages may be set by state statute.

SEIZURE OF PROPERTY

In most states, a landlord has no lien on personal property of a tenant. The landlord can evict or sue for rent. If the landlord seizes property of the tenant because the tenant owes money to the landlord, the landlord could be exposing himself or herself to substantial damages (both compensatory and punitive) because of wrongful seizure.

PAY THEM TO LEAVE

While it may go against your personal feelings, often the best way to get a tenant to leave is to offer them cash providing they vacate by a particular date and the unit is left in a presentable condition.

More important than the savings of an unlawful detainer, a couple hundred dollars paid to a tenant who may owe you money will reduce the probability of the unit being trashed by an evicted tenant. Ripped out plumbing fixtures, doors ripped off cabinets and holes in the walls and piles of trash are not the norm, but this does not have to happen too many times to realize that a few dollars paid can be well spent.

If a tenant has posted a property damage bond, your agreement could be that you will return the property damage bond and not apply it to rent due, which you would otherwise be entitled to do.

You might also have to agree to forgive past rent that is due. While this could seem like you're giving up a lot, in most cases you will be dealing with judgement-proof tenants where collection is not likely.

> *An advantage to a tenant, in agreeing to leave, is that their credit report would NOT show an eviction.*

Before you pay to have a tenant leave or give up any rights to past due rents, explain the situation to the owner and get the owner's written approval for your action. After the fact, an owner's attorney could make such action appear improper.

MITIGATION OF DAMAGES

When a tenant breaches a lease by moving out before the lease period has expired or he or she has been evicted, the landlord has a duty to **MITIGATE DAMAGES**. *This means that the landlord must use reasonable steps to re-rent the premises.*

In trying to re-rent the premises, if a landlord asked for a higher rent than the defaulting tenant paid, the defaulting tenant would probably be excused as to any subsequent rent because the landlord was not reasonable in his or her attempt to mitigate damages. In the same respect, insisting on different lease terms, such as a longer lease, could also serve to relieve the former tenant of obligations under the lease.

If in trying to re-rent the premises the landlord refused a prospective tenant, the landlord could have relieved the prior tenant from the obligation unless the refusal can be shown to be reasonable.

Chapter 14

If economic conditions require the landlord to rent at a lower figure, the former tenant's obligation would be for the period of vacancy plus the difference in the rent he or she had agreed to pay and the rent actually received.

> *Note: The landlord can sue a former tenant for rent as it becomes due but CANNOT sue for the entire amount that is owed on the lease because the actual damages have yet to be determined.*

Case Example

Zanker Dev. Co. v. Cogito Sys., Inc. (1989) 215 C.A. 3rd 1377

This case involved a landlord who expended $1 million preparing a property for a tenant. As part of the seven-year lease, the landlord gave the tenant nine month's free rent. After the free rent period expired, the tenant never made rent payments on time. The landlord was nearly forced into bankruptcy. The landlord finally evicted the tenant and sought damages for the remainder of the lease. The trial court awarded the landlord $3.6 million in damages.

On appeal, the tenant claimed that the landlord failed to properly mitigate damages since the tenant wanted to renegotiate the lease with different terms. The Court of Appeals upheld the trial court and stated that the landlord had taken reasonable measures to re-let the premises to allow recovery. The court pointed out that a landlord should not have to renegotiate a lease with a tenant who had repudiated the original lease after the tenancy was terminated by an unlawful detainer.

Note: This case indicates that a landlord can refuse a lease with a tenant who has not met prior lease obligations without forfeiting rights for failure to mitigate damages. The landlord can be reasonable as to re-renting.

Owner Relations

COMMUNICATIONS

As previously stated, there should be one contact person in a management office for an owner. This should be the person who directly supervises any onsite personnel and has the responsibility for management decisions involving the owner's property.

The communication lines must be kept open in that negative and positive information must be conveyed to the owner as soon as practical. As an example, if you discover that a major commercial tenant has just gone into Chapter 11 Bankruptcy, let the owner know. Be prepared to explain what Chapter 11 is and its ramifications as to rent owed and future rent.

If the owner lives out of the area, an office "800" number will encourage owner communication.

Owner questions, letters and calls must be promptly acknowledged and questions answered fully and honestly.

At least one annual face-to-face encounter with the owner is desirable. A good time for this would be during delivery of the annual statement. You could then go over operations of the past year and future management plans.

FIDUCIARY DUTIES

In dealings with an owner, you must keep in mind that he or she is your principal and that you have fiduciary duties toward the owner. These duties include the following.

Loyalty

The manager must realize that he or she must be loyal to his or her principal. Loyalty to an owner would mean being faithful to the owner's interests. When a lease expired and the manager persuaded a tenant to move into another property he or she managed because the manager felt the management contract on the property the tenant occupied would not be renewed, then the agent would have breached his or her fiduciary duty of loyalty and could be held civilly liable for damages.

Confidentiality

Information received from the owner must be regarded as confidential unless it is clear that it is to be provided to prospective tenants. Assume that an owner told the property manager that he wanted $1,500 per month for a property but, that if he had to, he could accept less because his payments were only $1,000 per month. If the manager revealed this information to a prospective tenant who offered to lease the premises for $1,000 per month, the property manager would have breached the duty of confidentiality.

Confidentiality is the reason that a property manager should not gossip about an owner, even within his or her office. The problem is that it is hard enough for one person to keep information to themselves.

Once two people have been told something, it is on the verge of becoming public knowledge.

Fair and Honest Dealings

Ask yourself if you would consider your action fair if you were a third party. If you would not, the action would not be fair.

If you told an unsophisticated owner that the management and leasing fees you charge are "customary" when in fact they are quite a bit higher than customarily charged for the type of property and services, you are not only treating the owner unfairly but your action would also be dishonest.

Full Disclosure

> *Failing to inform an owner of any information you had (other than confidential) of a type that an owner could reasonably be expected to want to know would be a violation of your disclosure duty.*

As an example, assume a major franchise has negotiated a lease with another agent for $1.80 per square foot. Assume the franchise is interested in a second location and are interested in leasing a property that you manage. While you're asking $1.60 per square foot, the franchise offers to lease the space for $1.40. The information as to the other lease would be the kind of information the owner would want to know. It would reinforce any desire to hold firm at $1.60 since the owner knew the franchise could pay that much. Failure to tell the owner would be to breach your duty of full disclosure.

Reasonable Care and Skill

> *You have a duty to use the reasonable care and skill that an owner would expect and that a property manager should possess.*

Telling an owner to sign a lease prepared by the tenant without reading it or having it checked by an attorney would not be the exercise of reasonable care and skill. A court would probably determine the manager to be negligent.

Obedience

The duty of obedience means that you must follow the lawful instructions of your principal. That does not mean that you should not disagree or make your opinions known. Failure to inform an owner that you feel that an owner's proposed action is a mistake could be a breach of your duty of due care.

UNDERESTIMATING COSTS AND OVERESTIMATING INCOME

While optimism has its place, realism is what an owner wants when dealing with what the owner holds dear, his or her pocketbook.

LOW-BALLING is a term that has its origin in used car sales. It is an estimate of what a car can be purchased for that is less than what the dealer will actually take. The purchaser is induced to begin the bargaining process with an offer and then later induced to raise it.

> *"Low-balling" has NO place in property management.*

If an estimate is given to an owner or tenant as to what modifications or repairs will cost, it should be based on experience or bids. You should never quote a figure to tease a person to act. In dealing with property owners, it would also be a breach of fiduciary duty.

Did you ever take your car to a garage and sign an original estimate only to later receive a call or calls that it was going to cost considerably more than originally estimated. How did you feel?

On the other hand, if costs are less than estimated, your feelings towards the person who gave you the estimate would probably be positive. You are more likely to recommend to others the person who beat the estimate rather than the person who exceeded the estimate.

This lesson can be applied to property management:

1. Don't low-ball bids or be overly optimistic in estimating property returns, rental periods or expenses.

2. Be realistic. Prepare owners for your best estimate but give them some idea as to what could happen. A worst case scenario can make for a happy owner when it doesn't happen.

RELATIONSHIPS WITH OWNERS

While there can be a conflict of interest when a property manager has a close relationship with a tenant, this conflict would not exist in a relationship with an owner. The agent and the owner are on the same team and their interests should be the same. Many business relationships develop into close friendships.

Our personal preference is that relationships with both owners and tenants be kept on a friendly but business level.

Romantic relationships, however, should be discouraged because breakups often result in resentment or anger. This would mean one or both parties would want to limit future contact with the other. A breakup of a romantic relationship could likely result in a management contract not being renewed.

HOMEOWNER ASSOCIATION MANAGEMENT

Homeowner associations are often hotbeds of politics with groups wanting to usurp the present association management.

As a property manager you should avoid appearing too closely allied with either group. This would include social contacts. You want to be considered as a service provider who will do whatever the board of directors wants but will nevertheless make recommendations which you feel are fair and in the best interests of the owners.

You must avoid gossip with or about any owner and treat every owner with patience and courtesy even if you feel a complaint is frivolous or even mean spirited.

VIOLATING THE LAW

Some property managers have been asked to violate the law or to aid the property owner in violating the law. Generally it is tax laws that are involved. Usually the owner does not say "Help me avoid paying taxes"; it is more subtle. It could be "Please pay this billing" which would be for services or material not supplied or supplied to the owner's personal residence. The check would possibly be made out to a illegitimate firm name or even a foreign firm. This particular tax scam takes the operating profits and turns them into a deductible expense.

A variation of the above was a case where a property manager was asked to put the son of the owner on the property's payroll. The owner simply wanted to make the support of his son a tax deductible expense. There would have been nothing wrong if the son had actually contributed services to the property, but in this case it was simply a scam.

Owners have asked property managers for operating statements that don't reflect the true operations. These could be for lenders, as owners could intend to defraud the lender by obtaining a loan based on false figures.

If an owner asks you to prepare any false document or report, or to pay any bills where the recipient is NOT entitled to the monies as a property expense, don't do it.

This would include paying inflated billings.

You do not want to be a part of any unlawful activity or help to carry out any owner's secret agenda that would tend to deceive. Besides possible criminal and/or civil liability, it would be unethical behavior that would reflect upon your professionalism.

Such activity could also lead to suspension or revocation of your real estate license.

SUING A PRINCIPAL

While you represent an owner and have fiduciary duties toward that owner, you should realize that you have rights under the management contract and that it is not a breach of your fiduciary duty to enforce those rights.

As an example, assume that you have a management contract on a large free standing property and are seeking a tenant. Assume also that you have interested Home Depot in the property and are in the process of negotiating a lease which will provide you with significant leasing fees over the proposed 20-year term. Assume the owner, in an apparent effort to avoid paying the leasing fees, cancels the management contract and negotiates directly with Home Depot, signing a 20-year lease. Good business practice would dictate that you make demands for your commission, and if not forthcoming, seek to collect by legal means.

While suing an owner should be avoided if a dispute can be resolved by agreement, it does not mean you should not vigorously defend your rights when there is an attempt to deprive you of them.

═══ CHAPTER 14 SUMMARY ═══

A great many tenant problems can be avoided by properly explaining to the tenant at the time the lease is signed what the tenant's obligations are under the lease as well as any property rules and regulations for the tenants.

Renting to friends or relatives could create significant problems as they are likely to expect special treatment and your relationship could likely affect your actions if the friend or relative breaches a lease clause or occupancy rule. There could also be an appearance of a possible conflict of interest.

Romantic involvement with tenants not only provides the appearance of a conflict of interest, it could also result in loss of a tenant as well as other complications.

A record should be kept of all tenant complaints and the action taken. The tenant should be informed as to what, if anything, will be done. The property manager should be entirely truthful with the tenant.

There may be problem tenants who have constant frivolous complaints or who bother other tenants. A property manager should consider letting such a tenant out of his or her lease.

After the death of a tenant, by asking if you can help, you can ascertain any problems and possibly avoid problems relating to the tenancy.

The order of a waiting list should be followed without exception to avoid any chance of discrimination claims.

It is not a good policy to allow tenants to paint their own units because of workmanship problems.

A lessor has the right to terminate a lease if the tenant commits waste.

The property manager should ask tenants to notify him or her when the tenant will be absent for a protracted period of time. The manager should also request the right to enter the unit for inspection purposes and to deposit mail and deliveries.

A notice is required to change the terms of tenancy on a month-to-month lease. It is a good policy to provide something extra prior to a rent increase.

Tenants should not be surprised with expenses not revealed at the time of leasing.

Failure to take possession after the lease has been signed would not relieve the tenant from the lease obligations.

A surrender of the premises that is accepted by the lessor would relieve the tenant of all further lease obligations. In accepting the premises from a vacating tenant when the lease has not expired, the lessor should make it clear that this is not a surrender and the lessor will hold the lessee liable for remaining lease obligations.

As a matter of policy, allow only one excuse for late payment and then serve a three day notice. Never allow a tenant not get more than one month behind in rent without commencing eviction action.

The eviction process begins with a three-day notice to quit or pay rent, quit or cure (when other than rent) or quit (when a cure is not possible). The three-day notice is followed by an unlawful detainer action. The tenant has five days to answer or a judgment will be entered for the lessor. Defenses of eviction include retaliatory eviction, uninhabitable premises, a denial of the charges, procedural error, discriminatory eviction, incorrect amount due stated or a payment made after the three-day notice was served.

If the tenant fails to answer or the court finds for the lessor, a judgment would be entered for the lessor. The lessor could get a Writ of Possession and the sheriff could remove the tenant and possessions from the property.

A landlord's actions in interfering with a tenant's rights could be viewed by the tenant as constructive eviction which would allow the tenant to vacate without any further lease obligations.

Retaliatory eviction is not allowed. Examples would be evicting a tenant for exercising a legal right to complain or to organize a tenant's group.

A lessor cannot physically evict a tenant. To cut off utilities would likely subject a lessor to penalties.

A lessor generally has no right to a tenant's property because of failure to pay rent.

Sometimes it can be advantages to pay a tenant to vacate rather than to evict. It saves time, money, and the premises are likely to be left in better condition.

The lessor has a duty to keep the tenant's damages as low as possible. If the tenant has vacated prior to the expiration of the lease, the lessor has a duty to attempt to re-rent the premises.

Owner relations are based on open and full communication. The property manager also has a fiduciary duty toward the owner which includes:

1. Loyalty
2. Confidentiality
3. Fair and honest dealings
4. Full disclosure
5. Reasonable care and skill
6. Obedience

A property manager will have an unhappy owner if the manager tends to underestimate costs and is overly optimistic as to revenue. The property manager should be realistic in his or her estimates.

While a business relationship is best, personal relationships with owners do not create conflicts of interest. Romantic relationships, however, can create numerous problems leading to loss of management.

In dealing with homeowner associations, the manager must avoid owner politics and be fair and friendly to everyone.

The manager should never get involved with owner deceit, fraud or other activities that could be perceived as being illegal even when asked to do so by the owner.

While the manager represents the owner, the manager should make certain that the owner meets his or her responsibilities to the manager. The manager can properly bring legal action to enforce these rights.

CLASS DISCUSSION TOPICS

1. Did the property manager fully explain your obligations at the time you may have signed a lease? What didn't you understand?

2. As a tenant, have you ever complained to a landlord? What was the nature of your complaint?

3. Did you ever have a tenant in a neighboring rental unit who was difficult?

4. Are you familiar with any lessor who had a tenant get way behind in rent? How did it happen and what should the lessor have done?

5. Do you know of any property manager who had a dispute with an owner? If so, what was the dispute about?

CHAPTER 14 QUIZ

1. Which of the following is true as to a lease "surrender" when one year was remaining on the lease?
   - A. The tenant is liable for one month's rent
   - B. The tenant is not liable for the remaining rent
   - C. The landlord must mitigate damages
   - D. The tenant is immediately liable for total rent to the end of the lease

2. As a property manager it is NOT a good business practice to lease to:
   - A. close relatives
   - B. close friends
   - C. a person you are romantically involved with
   - D. any of the above

3. In handling a tenant waiting list you should give preference as to:
   - A. friends
   - B. women
   - C. families with children
   - D. time and date of application

4. Fiduciary duty of a property manager to a property owner includes:

    A. loyalty
    B. confidentiality
    C. full disclosure
    D. all of the above

5. Tenant "waste" refers to:

    A. inefficient management
    B. a high tenant turnover
    C. tenant abuse of the property
    D. the failure to conserve energy

6. A tenant signed a one-year lease and failed to take possession. The maximum tenant obligation would be:

    A. one month's rent
    B. 30 day's rent
    C. rent for one year
    D. none of the above

7. The first notice to evict a tenant who has not paid rent would be a(n):

    A. Quit or Pay Rent notice
    B. unlawful detainer action
    C. Writ of Possession
    D. notice of nonresponsibility

8. If correct, which of the following would be a defense against an unlawful detainer action?

    A. A claim of retaliatory eviction
    B. Partial rent payment after the three-day notice
    C. A claim that the residential premises were uninhabitable
    D. All of the above

9. Which of the following is an example of constructive eviction?

    A. Failure of the landlord to provide contracted for utilities
    B. Failure to take action against a tenant who is interfering with another tenant's use of the premises
    C. Failure to correct a sanitation problem which is the landlord's responsibility
    D. Any of the above

10. Which of the following would be an act to mitigate damages after a tenant vacated the premises?

    A. Changing the use and asking for a higher rent
    B. Bringing legal action as each month's rent is due
    C. Waiting until the lease expires before placing the property on the rental market
    D. None of the above

Answers: 1. B; 2. D; 3. D; 4. D; 5. C; 6. C; 7. A; 8. D; 9. D; 10. D

Management Operations

KEY WORDS AND TERMS

Bonuses
Colorblind Management
Completed Staff Work
Dress Code
Economics of Scale
Employee Contract
Employee Evaluation
Employee File
Employment Application
Employment Interview
Employment Tests
Firing
Health Insurance
Hiring
Immigration Reform and Control Act
Interpersonal Relations

Job Description
Key Money
Leasing Fees
Management Fees
No-Tolerance Drug Policy
Opening a Management Office
Organizational Chart
Policy Manual
Profit Sharing
Staffing
Tenant Gifts
Tenant Exit Interview
Termination Fee
Theft
Training
Vacation Days

LEARNING OBJECTIVES

In this chapter you will tie together much of the material you have previously learned into practical application. You will learn about the organization of a management office and staffing requirements. You will learn about the importance of having a policy manual and some of the items that should be in such a manual.

You will learn about the economics of scale and how size relates to the costs of management and how fees are calculated.

You will learn about the status of a resident manager, attributes of a good manager, what a resident manager's duties are likely to be as well as dealing with managerial problems.

You will understand the hiring process and the importance of a job application and employee interview. You will also learn how to protect yourself from a possible violation of the Immigration Reform and Control Act.

In working with employees, you will learn what should be included in an employee file, the employee evaluation process as well as employee relations to reach a common goal. You will also learn about ways to retain employees.

You will learn about in-house training of employees and the utilization of professional organizations for training. You will also gain an insight into firing procedures.

The problems of opening a management office will be addressed. You will gain an insight into what it will take for success in your own property management office.

The Management Office

ORGANIZATIONAL CHART

The organizational chart of a property management office can vary significantly. In a small office with only a few properties, the chart might look like the following:

The organizational chart of a much larger operation might look like the following:

On-Site Managers

An on-site manager might in turn have under his or her supervision a director of maintenance and a maintenance staff.

Some property management firms have management property in a number of states. A wide geographical service area is possible because of the availability of fax machines, computer modems, cellular telephones, teleconferencing, etc. What formerly took days to resolve can now be done in minutes with better communication and flow of documents.

Most of these multi-state operations deal with large properties allowing a strong on-site team. Nevertheless, regular visits are generally conducted by a management team to evaluate records, leasing activity and leases, maintenance, security, improvement planning, etc. By use of a team approach it is possible to provide a wide area of expertise.

While multi-state management requires licensing in each state, we will see more of this in the future. We know of one firm operating in several states which specializes in managing condominium associations. Large REITs operate nationwide.

Wide spread management operations might alter the organizational chart. A number of REITs have regional offices that appear to be working well.

STAFFING

There is no standard staffing plan for a property management office. Staffing must be based upon the specific needs of an office. This would be based on a number of factors such as:

1. number of separate properties managed;
2. number of individual tenants;
3. physical proximity of units;
4. type of units;
5. types of leases;
6. number and type of on-site employees;
7. duties of on-site employees;
8. advertising budget;
9. management duties contracted for.

There is also no standard staffing plan for an on-site office. During initial lease-up operations there would be more rental agents than there would be after the property had stabilized. Factors affecting staffing of the on-site office include many of those for the property management office.

The number of maintenance employees would be based on:

1. age, construction and quality of the building;
2. number of units and/or total square footage;
3. the amount and type of landscaping;
4. special features such as waterfalls, playgrounds, pools, etc.;
5. the amount and type of work covered by contract labor.

POLICY MANUAL

You should supply all employees, including resident managers, with a policy manual. The *POLICY MANUAL should include the employee's job description as well as how tasks should be carried out and the treatment regarding emergencies.*

Dealings with Owners

The policy manual should point out that the resident manager should NOT have any direct dealings with the owner unless directed to do so by the property manager or unless contacted by the owner.

The property manager should answer any questions fully and honestly if he or she is contacted by the owner. The resident manager should then contact the property manager about the owner's contact and convey any concerns of the owner.

The person who is directly responsible for a property should be the primary contact person with the owner because that person knows the property status better than anyone else. This person might be the on-site manager for a very large project.

However, generally it is the person who has responsibility for the property and directly supervises the on-site manager. If an owner has multiple properties, the same person should be responsible for all of them. However, this might require different levels of expertise where an industrial park and an office building are involved.

Dress Code

Your employees reflect the image of your firm. The employee manual should cover appearances which could specify:

1. clean clothes;
2. for males, a shaved appearance;
3. hair that is short, tied or under a cap;
4. avoidance of body odors or overpowering perfumes.

The dress code in some projects include shirt, tie and jacket for men, dresses for women. The type of property and area where located should dictate the dress code.

> *Basically, the dress code should reflect the way you would expect a professional in the business to dress.*

Interpersonal Relations

Some policy manuals forbid property managers from dating tenants or other employees whom they supervise. This type of policy makes sense because the end of a relationship could lead to loss of a tenant or an employee.

Theft

You can expect some theft and you will probably even condone some pilferage. As an example, there are probably very few parents who haven't given their school age children pencils, pens or other supplies which were paid for by the parents' employers. Actually, this kind of theft will probably be viewed more as an employee benefit than a crime. It is when theft gets out of hand that something must be done. Selling supplies, stealing cash, taking items of considerable value or stealing from tenants cannot be condoned.

> *The policy manual or employee manual should state that such action will result in discharge of the persons involved.*

Completed Staff Work

All employees should be imbued with the principle of completed staff work.

Completed staff work is:

1. **Define the Problem.** What exactly is the problem.

2. **What Are Possible Solutions?** There could be a number of ways that a particular problem could be solved.

3. **What Do You Recommend?** The person presenting the problem should be expected to also provide the solution.

4. **Why is Your Recommendation Best?** The person who presents a problem should be able to defend the recommended course of action over other possible solutions.

Employees who understand "completed staff work" become part of the solution rather than part of the problem.

Neither the property manager, owner or tenant wants to know about problems, they want to know about solutions.

Tenant Gifts to Managers

Some property management firms have a policy that resident managers are not to accept gratuities or gifts from tenants while in some apartment complexes the resident managers regard gifts and gratuities as an entitlement going with the job.

A problem with allowing resident managers to accept gifts or gratuities is that those tenants who give greater amounts expect priority treatment regarding complaints.

The manager receiving the gifts or gratuities generally cooperates. Others who don't receive this kind of treatment feel short changed, are likely to be unhappy and seldom remain long-term tenants. This is not in the best interest of the owner.

In addition, the resident manager who accepts significant gifts or gratuities has priorities being dictated by both his or her supervisor and a tenant who expects something in return. This conflict can result in resources of time and money being expended that may fail to meet the best interests of the owner.

Key Money

When a vacancy arises in a rent controlled area, such as Santa Monica California, there is no problem filling that vacancy. There is such a demand that prospective tenants are often willing to pay extra to get a rental.

Some resident managers have been receiving **KEY MONEY** to give tenancy. This is simply a payment to the manager to give them occupancy. One problem with allowing a resident manager to accept key money is that key money is illegal in many rent-controlled areas because it amounts to rent.

Some resident managers have stocked units with a few pieces of old furniture and required prospective tenants to buy the furniture for thousands of dollars. This is really key money in a different form.

> *You CANNOT allow your resident manager to accept key money.*

You could be viewed as a conspirator in an illegal act. You must demand absolute honesty of your resident managers and cannot allow a "secret profit."

MANAGEMENT COSTS

> *The larger a management complex, the greater the possibilities of operational efficiency.*

For instance, the management costs per unit for a 1,200-unit residential development are likely to be significantly less than the management costs to operate a 100-unit development (management costs not directly reimbursed by the property owner). Therefore, lower management fees are possible on a per unit or gross rent basis when dealing with larger developments.

It also holds true that the more property a property firm manages, the lower the central office overhead costs are per unit. This is because many of the costs are fixed and not directly related to the number of units managed. *Even for variable costs, greater efficiency is possible as the numbers increase. This is often referred to as* **ECONOMICS OF SCALE**.

MANAGEMENT FEES

For Management

> *Most management fees are based on a percentage of the gross income.*

The percentage might vary in a range from around three percent to 10 percent depending upon the type of property, scheduled gross rents, services provided and the leasing fee schedule. As an example, a lower leasing fee might be coupled with a higher percentage of the gross.

Never agree to a percentage of the net because there might not be any net income because of reasons, such as a high debt service, which are beyond the control of the property manager.

For a single-tenant building you would want a minimum fee coupled with a percentage of the gross. The reason for the minimum fee is that a vacant property is likely to require as much or greater management effort than one that is occupied. The property must be protected and maintenance is still required. A percentage fee without a minimum would mean a "zero" management fee for considerable expenditure of management resources.

For some properties managers might negotiate a fee per unit rather than a percentage of the gross. A bachelor apartment building consisting of 140 units would likely take the same or greater management effort than would be required to manage 140, two-bedroom units with a gross rental that might be 150 percent to 200 percent greater than the rents from the bachelor units. A price per unit or a higher percentage would be a fairer approach for the bachelor units.

Leasing Fees

> *"Management fees" and "leasing fees" are related.*

If a manager charged a higher than normal management fee, the leasing fee might be reduced or eliminated. If the management fee were quite low, the leasing fee would probably be higher.

If an owner reimbursed the manager for advertising costs, the leasing fee would likely be significantly lower than if the advertising costs were the responsibility of the property manager. Leasing fees may be one or two month's rent (based on the length of the lease and the type of property), but leasing fees are more likely to be a percentage of the entire lease. The percentage might be flat for the entire lease or it may be structured so that a higher percentage is charged in the first year with lower charges for subsequent years.

> *A management contract that doesn't provide for leasing fees is a disservice to an owner.*

Because there is a leasing fee, many property managers and there agents cooperate with each other in directing prospective tenants to each others properties when management would otherwise be unable to meet the tenant's needs. Without a leasing fee, any fee to a cooperating broker would have to come from the pocket of the property manager. Cooperation is particularly important in nonresidential leasing.

Lease Renewals and Options

The property manager might renew the lease when the lease expires. The leasing commission for the renewal might be the same or less than the original leasing commission.

When a lease contains a renewal option and the tenant exercises the option, the management agreement would likely provide that the commission structure for the original lease would continue.

Termination Fee

Some owners want the right to terminate the management contract. If there were no termination fee, an owner could take advantage of a property manager who had expended a great deal of effort to solve property problems by simply terminating the agreement.

A termination fee is really like liquidated damages agreed to in advance by the manager and owner.

With an agreed termination fee, a property manager does not have to prove the amount of damages for an owner's renunciation of the contract.

Employees

STATUS OF THE RESIDENT MANAGER

Your resident manager is treated by law as an employee.

The resident manager would either be employed by the owner (in most cases) or the property manager. Therefore, the employee would be eligible for worker's compensation and unemployment insurance. The resident manager is also protected against wrongful discharge as is any employee.

Resident managers are subject to minimum wage laws. There have been cases where resident managers won lawsuits entitling them to back pay for minimum wages and payments for far more than 40 hours a week. Thus, you should consider an employment contract which clearly specifies that your resident manager is not to work more than 40 hours per week without specified authorization for the additional hours, except in emergency situations.

If you provide your resident manager with an apartment and the resident manager is required to reside in the unit, then the value of the apartment would not be shown as part of the employee's gross salary for determining withholding tax or social security contributions. However, should the resident manager not be required to reside on the premises then the apartment that is furnished would be part of the wages. Some property management companies collect rent on the apartment managers' units which tends to separate the rental units from the employment contracts.

If you discharge a former apartment manager who is not paying rent, the former manager generally need not be given notice because the manager would not be considered a tenant. An unlawful detainer action would be proper. However, if you give the manager a 30-day notice, the former manager could be considered to be on a month-to-month tenancy and might be able to raise the defense of retaliatory eviction.

Once you give notice you may have created a tenancy.

While large nonresidential properties will often have a management office on the premises, smaller properties as well as some small residential properties, such as single-family homes and duplexes, are unlikely to have resident managers.

Where there are no resident managers the rentals would be handled out of the management office. In order to show a prospective tenant properties at various locations, lock boxes would likely be used.

Case Example

Brewer v. Patel (1993) 20 C.A. 4th 1017

A motel manager was required to remain on the premises 24 hours a day. The manager could remain in his apartment during the hours the office was not open. The manager filed a claim for overtime wages.

The Superior Court ruled that the manager was not entitled to wages during those hours when he was not required to work. The Court of Appeals affirmed the trial court holding that only those hours carrying out employee duties need be compensated.

Note: This decision would apparently apply to resident managers who were required to reside on the premises. However, your contract should specify the hours to be worked and specify authorization requirements as to overtime so that you are protected against a manager who claims to have worked excessive hours.

Case Example

Chan v. Antepenko (1988) 203 C.A. 3rd 21

This case held that a discharged property manager is not a tenant at sufferance but is a licensee. The agreement between the landlord and the property manager only gave the property manager a license, not a tenancy. While the case covered whether or not the discharged manager was protected by San Francisco's rent control ordinance, the reasoning of the court would indicate that a notice is not required to terminate occupancy since no tenancy existed.

The proper action would be one for ejectment since the former property manager is no longer legally in possession of the premises.

QUALITIES OF A RESIDENT MANAGER

There are a number of qualities that make a good resident manager. These qualities include:

People Oriented. The resident manager should like dealing with people and care for their interests. The interpersonal skill of presenting a problem and getting others to help in its solution is important. The property manager must be able to correct behavior without antagonizing and be able to refuse a request without resulting animosity.

Reliable. The resident manager cannot be a procrastinator. When the resident manager states that something will be done, then he or she must be the type of person who will make sure that something will be done. The resident manager should be the kind of person others expect to rely on.

Organized. A good resident manager must organize his or her time and that of others who the resident manager supervises to accomplish the required tasks in order of reasonable priority. The time and resources must be allocated to best meet the needs of the tenants and owners.

Salesmanship. The residential manager must be able to efficiently close a rental by asking for a deposit.

Good Character. The resident manager must be of good character to be bonded. The resident manager can't have any vices which would reflect negatively on the owner or property management firm.

Trade Skills. An important asset is the ability to actually do a job or to understand what is needed so that the manager can adequately prepare purchase orders and/or supervise the work.

Positive Attitude. Attitude is extremely important in a resident manager. Tenants and owners don't want negativism; they want instead to know what can be done and how and when.

RESIDENT MANAGER JOB DESCRIPTION

Your resident manager's job description should outline the responsibilities of the position. They might include many of the following tasks:

1. Showing units to prospective tenants.
2. Taking rental applications and deposits.
3. Faxing or sending applications to credit reporting company and/or the property management office.
4. Making calls to verify employment and check prior rental history.
5. Contacting prospective tenant as to the acceptance or rejection of his or her application.
6. Going over the lease with the tenant and having the tenant sign it.
7. Collecting balance of rent and security deposit.
8. Reviewing property rules and regulations with tenant and having tenant sign and date a copy.
9. Receiving tenant complaints and answering the tenant's questions.
10. Supervising maintenance.
11. Supervising service contracts.
12. Preparing work orders.
13. Tracking work in progress.
14. Conducting move-in and exit inspections.
15. Inventory preparation of furnished units.
16. Serving three-day, 30-day and unlawful detainer notices.
17. Maintaining records.
18. Mediating tenant disagreements.
19. Advising property management office as to problems.

In some cases, the resident manager might also have maintenance and repair duties.

> *The duties of the property manager vary greatly. What is important is that a property manager fully understands his or her duties.*

What the on-site manager should not do is establish rental rates or modify standard leases or contracts without the approval of the property manager.

MANAGERIAL PROBLEMS

When a property has operational problems, it could be related to problems concerning the manager, the communication process or to extraneous factors.

If work is not completed, you want to find out why.

1. Did the manager know what was expected of him or her?

2. Did the resident manager know how to get the job done?

3. Was there an extenuating circumstance beyond the manager's control? It could be the unavailability of a part or problems of a contractor.

4. Was the problem the result of the property manager's action? By giving priority to jobs using resources that could have been allocated elsewhere, it could have resulted in another job not being accomplished.

You must try to avoid using 20/20 hindsight to criticize. If you did not cover how a situation should have been handled, you must be willing to share the blame. It shows your support of the employees.

> *Employees should feel that management supports them when a discretionary decision later turned out to be wrong.*

Consider asking the employee how we can avoid similar problems in the future. You want positive suggestions with open communications. Yelling at employees only creates a me-against-you attitude when you really want a team feeling.

When employees realize that you value their opinions, then they will help you devise the solution to problems and ways to prevent others.

Even if you don't accept an employee's suggestion, you should try to incorporate it into part of the solution. You can then explain how you used the employee's idea. This serves to reinforce the employee's self image.

The tendency of many firms is to overlook problems in more productive employees. Don't do it. Other employees will resent the difference in treatment and the problem will probably only get worse rather than better.

When there is a problem, unless it is a group problem, be private in your discussion with the employee. If an employee feels you were critical of him or her in front of others, then that employee's self-esteem will suffer. You could also place the employee in a position where he or she will act defensively or even offensively and verbally retaliate and later regret the incident.

If a resident manager engaged in a shouting match with a tenant, you could explain to the manager, "If you have any problem in the future, tell the tenant to call me." However, if you wanted to handle the incident through the resident manager then you could suggest, "Count to ten first, be calm and tell it the way it is! If the tenant abuses you verbally, walk away."

If an employee appears to have personal problems or what you suspect is an alcohol problem, ask the employee what's wrong. Ask also if you can help. Let the employee know that you will be supportive. Should he or she resist admitting to what you are reasonably sure is the problem, suggest AA or a similar self-help group. If the employee indicates that the problem is not that bad, you know you're on target. Let the employee know that you want their employment to continue but that they must want to solve their problem. Suggest that they think about it and come and see you the next day.

> *Sometimes good employees begin to slack off. Let them know that you noticed. Ask how you can help them.*

If an employee is continuously late, then point this out to the employee. Again, ask if you can help. If the employee claims it was only once or twice, be prepared to show the employee that it has been more than a few times. End the discussion of the problem on an upbeat tone. Let the employee know that you regard him or her as a valuable asset.

Employee Hiring

APPLICATION

In hiring any employee, you should have the employee complete a job application. Most form companies have general employment application forms. As a matter of policy, you should not hire anyone until an application has been received.

Things of particular interest to you would be:

1. Long gaps in employment.
2. Short periods for the last few jobs.
3. Employers listed who are no longer in business and so can't be checked.
4. Last job or jobs at a significantly lower wage and/or level of responsibility than prior jobs.

The employment application should include the authorization to check references given and to investigate an applicant's work history. Also check on personal traits which could include a credit check. Constant late payments and collection accounts could indicate a reliability problem as well as other problems.

In verifying prior employment and employment dates, ask why the employee left and if they would hire the former employee again. You want a "Why?" with the last question.

Many applications for employment include a statement above the applicant's signature which states that the application is truthful and that the applicant understands that any false representation made shall be considered sufficient grounds for termination of employment.

Don't require a photograph of the applicant with the application. It could be viewed as an attempt to weed out minority applicants without an interview.

You want to go over all employee policies when hiring. You should have an employee handbook that sets forth policies.

You might have a no-tolerance drug policy where the possession or use of drugs during duty hours or on managed property shall result in dismissal and that reporting for work under the influence of drugs and/or alcohol shall be grounds for dismissal.

TESTS

You should avoid giving prospective employees tests.

While they were popular in past years, a number of cases have held that written tests for job applicants were discriminatory when the employer could not show that the knowledge tested was really necessary for performance of the job. The reasoning is that minorities who may have less education and take a test which does not relate directly to the job would therefore be discriminated against.

However, you can test typing and shorthand as these are measurable skills that could be directly job related.

EMPLOYEE INTERVIEW

The interviewing process can weed out possible problem employees but it is not infallible. While an interviewer might lack training in psychology, asking the proper questions can reveal positive and negative features in a prospective employee. Chances are you don't want employees who always have excuses or someone to blame. Some people feel that the whole world is out of step with them rather than vise versa. You don't need a gossip who will tell tenants about other tenants. If all of a prospective employees prior supervisors were idiots, watch out. If an employee is personally defensive over any questioning, watch out!

If a prospective employee expresses unsolicited strong views as to religion, politics or antipathy towards any group of people, watch out! That person could be disruptive to other employees and tenants.

Keep in mind that the interviewee might have his or her guard up. Your questions should be friendly and non-intimidating so that the person will relax and open up to you. Some of the questions you could ask which might reveal the nature of the prospective employee, would be:

1. Tell me about your last supervisor? (If you are told about the supervisor being a drunk, drug user or womanizer, the chances are that the interviewee is a gossip.)
2. What could (your last employer) have done to make you stay?
3. Who was your best boss? Why?
4. Who was your worst boss? Why?
5. What is there about this job that interests you?
6. What is your strongest asset?
7. What is your major weakness?
8. How long do you expect to work for us?
9. What aspects of this job interest you the most?
10. What aspects of this job least interest you?
11. What previous job did you like best? Why?
12. How would previous co-workers describe you?
13. How would (previous employers) describe you?
14. Can you get a recommendation from a (previous employer)?
15. Do you have a current driver's license?
16. If you could do something to improve yourself, what would it be?
17. How many traffic citations have you received in the last three years? For what?

You can also use the interview process to present hypothetical situations relating to interpersonal relationships that relate to the job. The answers could be very revealing.

You might want to include an employee who the new hire would be working with or who has a similar position at another property as a co-interviewer. Allowing other employees to have a voice in hiring will help your employee relations. They realize that you regard their views and the job as being important. In addition, other employees are often valuable in discovering the strengths and weaknesses in prospective employees.

While you will get some half-truths, the interview will give you quite a bit of information about the job applicant. Coupling the interview with the employment application and checking prior employers, you will have a far better chance of hiring a person with whom you will be satisfied than you would hiring at random. You will be fooled; you just don't want it to be too often.

TEMPORARY WORKERS

Some firms will use temporary workers to fill positions when their contracts with the temporary worker firm allows them to convert to employee status.

By taking this approach, a firm can observe the actual performance of the person. They can also ask for other workers or can hire the worker supplied. It allows for a relatively inexpensive trial period without obligations.

COLORBLIND MANAGEMENT

We realize that we should not discriminate in leasing or in hiring yet we see results that do not indicate a colorblind approach as to promotions. While there are a number of minority-owned property management firms, the upper echelon of corporate property management and REITs indicate that few people of color reach the Vice Presidential or Director status.

The authors selected 20 annual reports of Real Estate Investment Trusts (REITs) at random. Most of the annual reports displayed photographs of the officers as well as the directors. From the photographs, it did not appear that any of the officers or directors were African American. Furthermore, women were completely absent at the Director's level and represented only 12 percent of corporate officers. There wasn't one case where a woman was listed as the President of a REIT.

Photographs in the annual reports did indicate a great many African Americans and women in the on-site leasing and maintenance categories.

> *The authors view this as a significant problem which the profession will have to address. It is NOT enough that we "talk the talk." We must "walk the walk."*

ILLEGAL ALIENS

To be protected against any claim that you violated the Immigration Reform and Control Act of 1986 by hiring an illegal alien, you should require employees to complete Immigration And Naturalization Form 1-9 shown as Figure 15-1.

Figure 15-1

EMPLOYMENT ELIGIBILITY VERIFICATION (Form I-9)

1 EMPLOYEE INFORMATION AND VERIFICATION: (To be completed and signed by employee.)

Name: (Print or Type) Last	First	Middle	Birth Name
Address: Street Name and Number	City	State	ZIP Code
Date of Birth (Month/Day/Year)		Social Security Number	

I attest, under penalty of perjury, that I am (check a box):

☐ 1. A citizen or national of the United States.

☐ 2. An alien lawfully admitted for permanent residence (Alien Number A _____).

☐ 3. An alien authorized by the Immigration and Naturalization Service to work in the United States (Alien Number A _____, or Admission Number _____, expiration of employment authorization, if any _____).

I attest, under penalty of perjury, the documents that I have presented as evidence of identity and employment eligibility are genuine and relate to me. I am aware that federal law provides for imprisonment and/or fine for any false statements or use of false documents in connection with this certificate.

Signature	Date (Month/Day/Year)

PREPARER/TRANSLATOR CERTIFICATION (To be completed if prepared by person other than the employee). I attest, under penalty of perjury, that the above was prepared by me at the request of the named individual and is based on all information of which I have any knowledge.

Signature	Name (Print or Type)		
Address (Street Name and Number)	City	State	Zip Code

2 EMPLOYER REVIEW AND VERIFICATION: (To be completed and signed by employer.)

Instructions:

Examine one document from List A and check the appropriate box, *OR* examine one document from List B *and* one from List C and check the appropriate boxes. Provide the *Document Identification Number* and *Expiration Date* for the document checked.

List A Documents that Establish Identity and Employment Eligibility	List B Documents that Establish Identity	and	List C Documents that Establish Employment Eligibility
☐ 1. United States Passport ☐ 2. Certificate of United States Citizenship ☐ 3. Certificate of Naturalization ☐ 4. Unexpired foreign passport with attached Employment Authorization ☐ 5. Alien Registration Card with photograph	☐ 1. A State-issued driver's license or a State-issued I.D. card with a photograph, or information, including name, sex, date of birth, height, weight, and color of eyes. (Specify State)_____ ☐ 2. U.S. Military Card ☐ 3. Other (Specify document and issuing authority) _____		☐ 1. Original Social Security Number Card (other than a card stating it is not valid for employment) ☐ 2. A birth certificate issued by State, county, or municipal authority bearing a seal or other certification ☐ 3. Unexpired INS Employment Authorization Specify form #_____
Document Identification #_____	*Document Identification* #_____		*Document Identification* #_____
Expiration Date (if any) _____	*Expiration Date (if any)* _____		*Expiration Date (if any)* _____

CERTIFICATION: I attest, under penalty of perjury, that I have examined the documents presented by the above individual, that they appear to be genuine and to relate to the individual named, and that the individual, to the best of my knowledge, is eligible to work in the United States.

Signature	Name (Print or Type)	Title
Employer Name	Address	Date

Form I-9 (05/07/87)
OMB No. 1115-0136

U.S. Department of Justice
Immigration and Naturalization Service

Don't assume from a person's accent or appearance that they are NOT a citizen of the United States.

Do not refuse to hire a person because of these reasons since it could amount to a civil rights violation on your part. Simply give all employees the Form 1-9 and have them complete it and return it to you. You are not required or expected to investigate the facts but you should complete part two of Form 1-9 and retain it for three years from the end of employment.

Working With Employees

EMPLOYEE FILE

You should keep a file for every employee. This file should include:

1. employee application,
2. information on employee and pre-employment check,
3. employee's employment contract,
4. copies of all employee evaluations,
5. payroll records,
6. complaints received and any action taken or praise about employee's work and
7. Form 1-9.

The file should not contain hearsay evidence. The information in the file should be as factual as possible.

EMPLOYEE EVALUATION

All employees should be evaluated.

Evaluation serves to point out areas of concern to help in the employee's development. By pointing out strengths and instances of good performance, it also helps to reinforce the employee's self image.

30-Day Evaluation

The initial evaluation period of 30 days allows the employee time to learn the job and be exposed to problems.

You want the employee to tell you about what they like and/or dislike about the job and get their own evaluation before you give any input. It pays to be a better listener than talker.

Subsequent Evaluations

A subsequent evaluation might be at the 90-day or 6-month period. After that, evaluations should be at least on an annual basis and be regularly scheduled as a priority item.

You must convey the attitude that you care about the employee and you want the employee to be both productive and happy.

> *The time to give any salary raise or bonus would be at the close of an evaluation session.*

The employee should be given a copy of a written evaluation at the time of the evaluation meeting. The employee should sign and date the management copy showing the receipt of his or her evaluation.

Tenant Exit Interview

A tenant exit interview can help you in that it can show areas where improvement is needed as to the property and property management.

An exit interview can be a short telephone call. A sample script of such a call, would be:

"[Mrs. Jones] this is [Alice Smith] from [Morgan Management]. I wonder if you could take just a little time to answer a few questions. By knowing why tenants give notice to leave we feel we can better serve tenant needs in the future.

   1. Why did you decide to leave [Allenview Terrace]?
   2. Where will you be moving to?
   3. Why did you choose......?
   4. During the [two years] you have lived here at [Glenview Terrace], how would you rate the cooperation of [the resident manager]? Why?
   5. What did you like about living at [Glenview Terrace]?
   6. What if any were problems that you saw as to the property?

Thank you very much for your time. Your cooperation is appreciated."

EMPLOYEE RELATIONS

You want your employees to feel that they have a common goal and are members of a team where every person is important.

> *You should always address an employee with respect. Never use derision.*

Never gossip with employees about other employees or owners.

If any decision has been made that will affect an employee's work hours or working conditions, you should tell the employee as soon as possible and the reason for the decision.

Occasionally accounts are lost despite excellent management results. Try to relocate the resident manager to another property. When you take care of your own, your people will have greater respect for you.

> *An incentive for resident property managers to excel can be promotion to larger units offering higher earnings and/or better living conditions.*

Many management firms always remember birthdays and anniversaries of employees with a gift. As an example, it might be a certificate for dinner for two at one of the areas better restaurants. Whatever it is, you want your employees to know you care about them.

Besides treating employees with respect on the job, many firms have social events to bring employees from different properties together. Social events might include an annual picnic, a Christmas party or tickets to a circus for employees and families.

You must be careful as to supplying alcoholic beverages. A drunk and loud employee can undo everything you are trying to do. In addition, an accident involving an intoxicated employee could subject you to liability because he or she was drunk at a company sponsored event where you supplied the liquor. Soft drinks and good food is a better way to go.

One property manager who operates in a college community annually hosts a tailgate party complete with grilled hot dogs and hamburgers prior to a football game. He provides every employee and family members with tickets to the game.

Another manager we know invites two resident managers and their spouses to a dinner at his home. This way every resident manager is invited at least once every 18 months. The reason that he uses his home rather than a restaurant is because he feels it helps create a more personal relationship. The managers who ordinarily would seldom meet each other are encouraged to talk about amusing problems, etc. He reports that these dinners have led to managers developing a personal relationship with one another and calling each other to discuss ideas and problems.

EMPLOYEE RETENTION

Owners of property management offices tend to lose qualified employees to other firms who offer higher salaries, higher commissions or a particularly desirable property situation.

There are ways a management firm can keep most of their core employees without getting involved in a bidding war. They can offer:

Health Insurance. The insurance can vary from full coverage to the firm paying just half the premium on a high deductible policy.

> *The better the coverage offered, the more difficult it becomes for an employee to leave.*

Vacation Days. By offering paid vacation days that increase as the length of employment increases, it serves as a disincentive to leave.

Retirement Program. Some firms have a retirement program where the company will match the employees contribution to the plan up to a specified dollar amount or where the employer doesn't require the employee to contribute matching funds. The retention kicker is that the employer's contribution to the plan does not vest with the employee until he or she has been with the firm a stated period, such as three to five years. If the employee leaves before the pension funds have vested, the employee could be walking away from thousands of dollars.

Profit Sharing. A profit sharing program can mean a bonus of several thousand dollars each year for an employee.

> *An employee gets used to this end-of-the-year bonus so it becomes difficult to accept another position where such a bonus is NOT given.*

Management Fees. Many management offices give management responsibility plus a percentage of the management fees to the person who brings in the management contract. As a person builds up his or her portfolio of contracts, his or her monthly check increases. Many managers get several thousand dollars every month from the management contracts in addition to their leasing commissions. If a person has $40,000 a year coming in for management contracts and is averaging $50,000 per year in leasing fees, it is difficult to walk away from the job.

Contract Rights. Most offices provide employees with a contract which spells out their rights and commissions.

One firm that we know of gives retiring management employees 40 percent of the management fee that they would receive for handling properties that they signed up for as long as the firm retains management. The other 60 percent is given to the manager who is assigned the management responsibility for the property. In addition, this particular firm encourages retirees who remain in the area to attend staff meetings and social functions and to sign up new management accounts so that their income flow increases rather than decreases.

Seeing affluent retirees attending staff meetings and social functions makes managers realize that this is more than a job, it is a career with a firm that cares.

Bonuses. In property management, we try to arrive at a reasonable annual operating budget for repairs and maintenance. Rewarding property managers who are able to maintain the property but come well below budget estimates can be good business. One property manager told us that he has given annual bonuses of over $4,000 to resident managers with the concurrence of the property owner. He gives the managers a percentage of the savings for costs below the budget. According to the property manager, the reason for the savings realized is that his resident managers are more aware of what the maintenance personnel can do and they have cut down the number of purchase orders for outside contractors.

TRAINING

Employee training can involve new employees as well as all employees in various categories.

One large management firm schedules several full day sessions for resident managers each year. The sessions cover cost-saving methods, computer programs to aid the resident manager and other topics of interest. A benefit of bringing the managers together is that they get to know each other and build a professional rapport. Resident managers tend to contact other resident managers to brainstorm ideas and solutions to problems.

New resident managers should work several days with another resident manager for initial indoctrination. There should also be formal training that would include:

Job Description. By discussing the job description with the resident manager and asking questions, you will ascertain the manager's understanding as to what is expected. You should also go over the job descriptions of any maintenance personnel who will be supervised by the resident property manager.

Service Contracts. The property manager and resident manager should review all service contracts, purchase order procedures and preferred contractors.

Office Policy Manual. Discussing and asking questions will insure that the employee fully understands office policy.

Property Rules and Regulations. Discussing with and questioning the resident manager about the tenant rules and regulations concerning specified properties will insure that the new resident fully understands what is required.

Telling. The first step in learning any procedure is to tell the person how to do it. For instance, you could tell the resident manager how to fill out a rental application.

Demonstration. The learning process is enhanced by watching the application being filled out by another.

Doing It! This is the most important step of training. The resident manager at this stage would actually fill out the application.

Paper Backup. The process of telling, demonstration and performance should be backed up by a policy manual or other written material that clearly shows how the task should be performed.

> *Proper training of new hires and an understanding of what is expected is well worth the few days needed for training.*

During the first few weeks, the property manager should make numerous visits to the resident manager to ascertain how the resident manager has been doing his or her job. Suggestions for improvements should be given as required.

Professional Organizations. As indicated in Chapter 1, many professional organizations offer educational opportunities for professional advancement.

You should encourage resident property managers to take applicable courses. Many management offices pay for these courses. It is good employee relations and makes for better employees.

FIRING AN EMPLOYEE

You should document the reasons with written statements of others, if applicable,before you fire an employee. Be factual, not subjective. After the fact, former employees could claim the reasons for firing were because of race, sex, etc., or because of retaliation against a whistle blower. You can't stop the claims but you can have a file to support your actions.

It is unfortunate but unsubstantiated claims could place you in a situation where you are forced to let an employee go even if you don't really believe the claims. A property manager we know fired a resident manager because a tenant claimed that her child said that the manager "talked dirty" to her. While the manager denied the charges, the property manager felt he had no alternative but to fire the resident manager. If the manager was not fired and later assaulted a child, the property manager could be facing a lawsuit seeking significant damages.

From the National Fair Housing Advocate: April 1997:

It cost a building owner $200,000 plus an agreement to terminate the building superintendent to settle a sexual harassment suit in Washington, D.C. (continued)

According to the lawsuit, which was brought by a preschool teacher, the supervisor grabbed her in an elevator and later pinned her against a table rubbing himself against her. She reported the facts to the management company. After the management company failed to reprimand or fire the building superintendent, she began legal action.

Note: This case points out the necessity of taking sexual harassment charges very seriously.

It is unfortunate, but in most of these cases the charges are denied and the property manager does not know who is telling the truth.

> *Firing an employee should be done on a face-to-face basis if at all possible.*

The firing might be based on other than employee performance or employee problems. In this type of situation, the employee should be told and offered a letter of recommendation.

If you fire an employee because of job performance, interpersonal problems or unacceptable behavior, you don't want to go into a litany of transgressions. You don't want to argue fault or even the truth of allegations made against an employee if the employee is aware of such allegations.

You should have the employee's check available to pay them. In some instances, you might want to give severance pay.

At the time of the firing, you want the employee to surrender all keys to property or vehicles and any other company property.

If the firing is for cause, you can dispute the employee's entitlement to unemployment insurance. However, you may not wish to do so, depending upon the circumstances.

Opening a Management Office

Property management requires analysis and planning. Going into the property management business also requires analysis and planning. The following should be done before you consider opening a management office:

YOUR COMPETITION

Property Type. What type of property do property managers in the area manage? Do they specialize in particular types of property?

Fees. What are the fee ranges for property management and leasing in our area?

Success (Financial). Do the property managers in the area appear to be doing well economically?

Meeting Needs. What owner needs are there which local property management firms have not or only partially fulfilled? Can you do the job as good or better?

YOURSELF

Owner Contacts. What owner contacts do you currently have that could aid you in obtaining property management?

Broker Contacts. Do you have broker contacts which will help you obtain property management?

Type of Property. What type or types of property are you most capable of managing? Ask yourself: Why?

Personal Attributes. What important personal attributes do you have to be successful in property management?

Experience. What experience do you have as to:

1. property management in general,

2. specified areas of property management,

3. computer use for property management accounting and recordkeeping,

4. supervisory experience in maintenance and management personnel and

5. are you willing to obtain experience or training to augment what you have?

Financial Resources. What financial resources can you bring to property management including personal and borrowed funds?

Financial Risk. Are you willing to risk your financial resources for your success?

YOUR PLAN

You must plan a business. However, your plan should not be cast in concrete. Changing circumstances should allow flexibility. Your plan should include:

Type of Management Activity. Are you going to specialize in an area or areas of management or take a general management approach?

Office.

1. Location for the office.
2. Equipment, supplies, telephone service, utilities, signage, furniture, computers, programs, etc., required to open the office.

Staffing. Initial staffing that will be required to open the office. Do you have experienced people willing to join you?

Insurance. Will you have adequate insurance coverage when you open your office?

Initial Management. Will you have any management contracts when you open your office?

Contractors and Service Providers. Have you assembled a group of contractors and service providers who you feel will meet owner needs?

Financial.

1. Estimated costs to open the office. (Historically, most brokers underestimate costs by about 50 percent.)
2. Estimate your monthly fixed operational costs. Be certain to include any monies you require for personal living expenses.
3. How much must you generate in monthly fees to reach your break-even point?
4. Plot your planned revenue growth month-by-month until you reach your break-even point. Your financial reserves must allow you to comfortably reach this point.

Goal Setting. Your goals should be set forth in writing. They should be divided into short-term (1 to 12 months), intermediate-term (1 to 5 years) and long term (over five years).

Your short-term goals would include weekly and monthly goals as to contacts to make and things that you will be doing to obtain management contracts and service the contracts you have.

Intermediate-term and long-term goals might be based on measurable number of units or dollar volume. Your short-term goals should be constantly revised as they are accomplished. The short-term goals should lead to the intermediate term goals which are milestones on the way to your career goal.

> *Just setting a direction to your career will NOT guarantee success. However, success is more likely when planned than managing by crisis where the first telephone call of the day determines the direction of your efforts.*

CHAPTER 15 SUMMARY

The organizational chart for a property management firm will vary based on the number of properties managed, the number of employees, and even geographical distribution of management properties.

Staffing of a management office would be based on the number of properties managed, number of tenants, types of properties, types of leases, on-site employees supervised, duties of on-site managers, advertising budget, and management duties contracted for.

The policy manual should cover the employees' job descriptions and how tasks are to be carried out. Other areas to be addressed are dealing with owners, dress codes, interpersonal relations with subordinates and tenants, theft by employees, the necessity of never having a supervisor handle a problem without providing a supportive solution, and the prohibition on accepting gifts from tenants or key money.

Management costs of larger properties go down per unit, which in turn allows for lower management fees. Management fees include a percentage of the gross and leasing fees. The fees are interrelated because a lower management fee could be offset by a higher leasing fee. Lower leasing fees are probable when owners pay the advertising costs. Besides fees for initial leasing, fees are customarily charged for lease renewal and the exercise of options to extend leases.

The resident manager is an employee, and is subject to minimum wage laws. If the resident manager must reside on the premises, then the apartment furnished is not considered part of the wages. In such a case, the resident manager is not regarded as a tenant, so a notice to vacate is not required for an unlawful detainer action.

The resident manager's duties vary by owner requirements and the property being managed. It is important to discover the "Why?" when evaluating problems with managers.

All new hires should complete an employment application. You should be interested in gaps in employment, short periods with employers, employers listed who are no longer in business and, therefore, cannot be checked, and acceptance of jobs having a lower wage or lower level of responsibility.

The employment interviewing process can tell you positive and negative things about a potential employee. You want to search for the true person by asking inquiring questions.

By hiring temporary workers who then could become permanent employees, you really have a trial employee.

You must strive to hire without any element of discrimination.

By having new hires fill out a citizenship form, you can be protected against liability for hiring an illegal alien.

The employees' file should include employment application and pre-employment checks, employees' contracts, employee evaluations, pertinent correspondence, payroll records, complaints and commendations.

Employees should be evaluated to assist the employee's development and point out areas of strength and areas that require more attention. Tenant exit interviews can reveal positive and negative areas of management, the problems and strengths of individual managers and the property.

You want employees to feel that they are worthwhile persons. They should be treated with respect and kept informed. Remembering birthdays and anniversaries and social events can be used to reinforce employee morale.

Employee retention can be aided by health insurance, vacation days, a retirement program, profit sharing, sharing in fees and the use of bonuses.

Training of new hires should include:

1. job description,
2. understanding of service contracts,
3. understanding the office policy manual,
4. understanding property rules and regulations.

The training process should involve telling, showing and the employee performing the task. Additional training is available through professional organizations.

Before you fire an employee, document your reasons. Don't get into an argument. Pay the employee any amount owed at the time of firing and get any keys or property belonging to your firm.

Before a person starts a property management business, they should analyze their competition and themselves as to:

1. owner contacts they have,
2. broker contacts for referrals,
3. the type of property they wish to manage,
4. their experience,
5. available financial resources,
6. if they are willing to risk their resources.

For success, a property manager should have a plan as to where they will locate, the type of management activity that they will engage in, preliminary staffing requirements, what management contracts that they will have to start with, what service providers and contractors will be used, an estimate of start-up costs, an estimate of fixed monthly costs, and what it will take to reach a break-even point as to fees and time.

Success should be planned and one element of planning is goal setting. Setting measurable goals of short-term, intermediate-term and long-term duration that leads to what you are after is a plan for success.

CLASS DISCUSSION TOPICS

1. Select a major brokerage firm in the area that you are familiar with and draw an organizational chart. How does your chart compare with the charts in this Chapter?

2. Does your brokerage office have a policy manual? If so, what does the manual cover?

3. How do large real estate offices in your area manage to keep key personnel?

4. How do the hiring procedures in your office compare with the procedures covered in this chapter?

5. Assume you are going to open a management office with yourself and one clerical/computer support person. Estimate what you would consider to be all expenses to open your office.

CHAPTER 15 QUIZ

1. As used in this chapter, "Key Money" refers to:

    A. a form of security deposit
    B. a lease deposit
    C. a payment to be given occupancy
    D. none of the above

2. Management costs per unit managed:

    A. increase as the number of units increase
    B. decrease as the number of units increase
    C. decrease as the number of units decrease
    D. are not related to the number of units

3. As to management and leasing fees, which of the following is a true statement?

    A. Larger complexes would probably have a lower percentage of the gross as management fees

    B. Below-normal management fees could be compensated for with higher leasing fees

    C. When the owner pays for advertising costs, leasing fees will probably be lower

    D. All of the above

4. A resident manager lives in the complex she manages but does not pay any rent. Which of the following is true?

    A. If she is not required to live there, the value of the apartment counts as wages

    B. If she is required to live there, the apartment value does not count as wages

    C. Both A and B

    D. Neither A nor B

5. A property manager would probably be worried about hiring an individual if the application showed:

    A. a history of work going to more and more responsible positions

    B. the employee had not worked for one employer more than two months

    C. no period of unemployment greater than three weeks

    D. any of the above

6. A prospective employee looks foreign and speaks with an accent. You should:

    A. assume that he or she is an illegal alien

    B. offer below minimum wages

    C. have the person complete a government form to show citizenship or alien status

    D. refuse to interview or hire the person

7. The main purpose of an employee evaluation is to:

    A. justify firing the employee

    B. help the person to be a better employee

    C. comply with the law

    D. both A and C

8. Ways to discourage employees from accepting a position with another broker would be to offer:

    A. health insurance coverage

    B. a retirement program

    C. profit sharing program

    D. all of the above

9. By contributing to an employee's retirement program where your contribution will not vest for five years, you:

    A. need not part with any money

    B. make it difficult for the employee to leave before five years

    C. encourage job-hopping

    D. avoid minimum wage restrictions

10. Before you go into your own property management business, you should consider:

    A. your financial resources

    B. the cost to open an office

    C. your contacts who will help you gain management business

    D. all of the above

Answers: 1. C; 2. B; 3. D; 4. C; 5. B; 6. C; 7. B; 8. D; 9. B; 10. D

Accredited Management Organization (AMO): A professional designation available to a management firm that meets IREM specifications.

Accredited Resident Manager (ARM): A professional designation of the Institute of Real Estate Management (IREM).

Accredited Marketing Director: A professional designation of the International Council of Shopping Centers.

Accredited Shopping Center Manager (ASM): A professional designation of the International Council of Shopping Centers.

Agent: A person who acts for another such as a property manager.

American Industrial Real Estate Association: An organization that provides educational material including lease forms.

Americans With Disabilities Act: An act prohibiting discrimination, as well as allowing and requiring modifications for handicapped.

Anchor tenant: The major tenant(s) who act(s) as an attraction in a shopping center.

Appreciation: An increase in value.

Arbitration: Nonjudicial process of a dispute resolution before a party agreed to by the parties (arbitrator).

Assignment of lease: Transfer of all lease interests by the lessee. Assignee becomes the tenant of lessor.

Association Management Specialist (AMS): A professional designation of the Community Associations Institute.

Attornment: A tenant agrees to be the tenant of a prior lienholder who forecloses.

Automatic renewal: A clause that the lease renews itself unless notice of termination is given.

Binder: Authorized insurance coverage prior to the issuance of a policy of insurance.

Boiler insurance: Insurance that covers losses from a boiler explosion.

Budget: A financial plan for operation.

Building Owners and Managers Association International (BOMA): A major property management organization.

Built-up roof: A layered roof of hot tar and roofing paper.

Cal OSHA: California Occupational Safety and Health Act

Capital gains: Gains on the sale of a capital asset (Real Estate) that are subject to a preferred tax rate.

Cash flow: Cash left over from all cash receipts after cash expenses (net spendable).

Certified Leasing Specialist (CLS): A designation of the International Council of Shopping Centers.

Certified Manager of Community Associations (CMCA): A professional designation of the Community Associations Institute.

Certified Property Manager (CPM): The highest professional designation of the Institute of Real Estate Management (IREM).

Certified Shopping Center Manager (CSM): A professional designation of the International Council of Shopping Centers.

Civil Rights Act of 1866: The first federal civil rights act. The act applies to racial discrimination.

Civil Rights Act of 1968: THis is our Federal Fair Housing Act.

Class A building: The best quality of office building.

Class B building: An older quality office building.

Class C building: Older office building of lesser desirability in a less than prime area.

Class D building: The least desirable category of office buildings.

Clothing optional: Developments catering to nudists.

Co-Insurance: An insurer requirement that the insured carry a set percentage of replacement valu (usually 80 percent) to be fully covered up to policy limits.

Commingling: Mixing broker funds with funds of others.

Community Associations Institute (CAI): An association of persons having an interest in commo ownership developments.

Community shopping center: A shopping center where the anchor tenant would be a department stor

Condominium: An ownership in common of common areas with each unit owner owning his or h own air space.

Consumer Price Index (CPI): A government index often used for rent increases in a lease subject rent adjustments.

Constructive eviction: An action by the lessor that can be treated by the tenant as an eviction to e lease obligations.

Contract of adhesion: A take-it-or-leave-it contract or lease offered by one who has great bargaining pow

Covenant to remain in business: Tenant on a lease agrees that he or she will not terminate business during the term of the lease.

Depreciation: A noncash expense taken for tax purposes to shelter income from taxation.

Development fees: Fees charged for new developments to cover infrastructure costs.

Dram shop liability: Liability of a property owner for injuries resulting from an intoxicated custome a tavern.

Earthquake insurance: A high deductible policy covering earthquake damage.

Elevator insurance: A liability coverage policy for losses due to elevator malfunctions.

Eminent domain: The taking of property by a public entity.

Equal Credit Opportunity Act: Prohibits lessor discrimination as to source of income (public assistance).

Errors and omission insurance: Protects a property manager as to liability for mistakes.

Escalation clause: A clause in a lease calling for rent increases.

Estate for years: A lease having a definite termination date.

Estoppel Certificate: Certificate by lessee (or lessor) setting forth all rights under a lease.

Excess parking: Parking space that exceeds normal needs.

Facilities Management Administrator (FMA): A professional designation of BOMA.

Factory outlet centers: Shopping centers where the tenants are manufacturers or off-price merchandisers.

Familial status: Family status as to married, children and age.

Fidelity bond: A bond that protects against employee theft.

Fiduciary duty: Duties owed by a property manager to an owner client.

Fixtures: Items that were personal property which have become real property.

Flood insurance: Insurance coverage for flood damage.

Footloose industry: A business that can locate anywhere.

Garden office buildings: Single-story office structure.

Gentlemen farms: Farms where appearance is more important than profit.

Good funds: Cash, cashiers checks or other checks that have cleared the makers bank.

Gross lease (Flat lease): A level payment lease. The owner pays taxes, insurance, etc.

Gross multiplier: The relationship between gross income and the sale price determined by dividing the sale price by the gross income.

Ground lease: Lease of the land. Tenant builds improvements.

Guarantor: A party who guarantees a lease by agreeing to be liable.

Hazardous substances: Substances declared hazardous by governmental agencies.

Hold Harmless Clause: A clause whereby the lessee agrees that they will not hold an owner liable for personal or property losses.

Holdover clause: Clause in a lease that increases rent should a tenant hold over after the end of the lease.

Homeowner Association: The managing association of a common interest development.

Homeowner policy: A fire, liability policy that covers a wide range of perils.

HVAC: Heating, ventilating and air conditioning.

Improvements: Improving a property by providing something the property did not have before.

Independent contractor: A contractor hired for results who is not directly supervised by his or her principal.

Independent living facilities: Elderly housing where tenants live independently of one another.

Industrial parks: Industrial subdivisions.

Inland marine insurance: Insurance for property in transit or storage as well as for specific items of personal property.

International Council of Shopping Centers (ICSC): An organization of Shopping Center operators.

International Real Estate Institute: An international association that includes property managers.

Institute of Real Estate Management (IREM): The property management association of the National Association of Realtors®.

Joint and several liability: Parties agree to be both jointly and separately liable under a contract.

Key man insurance: Life insurance on the life of a key employee payable to the employer.

Labor oriented business: Manufacturer located close to labor supply.

Late charges: A charge for a late rent payment.

Lead-based paint: Oil based paint containing lead.

Lead-based paint disclosure: Federally mandated disclosure required for residential property built prior to 1978.

Lease: The occupancy and possession contract between an owner and a tenant.

Letter of intent: While not a lease it is an agreement to negotiate for a lease.

Liability insurance: Insurance that covers injuries to third parties and their property.

Libel: Written false statement that injures another.

Life-care facilities: Facilities where the management agrees to provide the degree of housing or care required for life (from independent living units to nursing facilities).

Low-rise: Buildings of two to three stories.

Maintenance: The care and repair of property.

Management contract: The agency agreement between the owner and the property manager.

Management plan: An operation plan for property management of a property.

Market oriented business: A manufacturer located close to market for its goods.

Master lease: The lease of the entire premises to a tenant who will sublease all or part.

MAXI Award: An award given by the International Council of Shopping Centers.

Mechanic's lien: A lien by a contractor, subcontractor or material provider who has not been paid for the

Medical-pay insurance: An insurance policy that covers medical expenses of persons injured on property without regard to liability.

Mid-rise: Buildings of four to eight stories.

Mini-mall: Small centers with a convenience or fast food store as the anchor tenant.

Mini-storage: Small warehouse rental units.

Mitigation of damages: A duty of a lessor to keep damages as low as possible by trying to re property vacated prior to the end of a lease.

Mobile home: A manufactured home that is transported on its own chassis.

Motion sensor: A sensor that turns on lights or an alarm if the sensor detects motion.

Negative cash flow: A loss operation where cash expenditures exceed cash receipts.

Negotiation: The process of give and take where lease terms are arrived at.

Neighborhood shopping center: A shopping center where the anchor tenant is a major food store.

Net lease: A lease where the tenant pays a set rent plus taxes, insurance and maintenance.

Nondisturbance clause: Prior mortgage holder agrees not to terminate tenancy if the mortgage is foreclosed.

Notice of nonresponsibility: Notice posted by lessor that lessor will not be obligated for work authorized by tenant.

Occupational Safety and Health Act: Federal act that sets safety standards and provide for reporting of injuries and illnesses of employees.

Option to purchase: A right given to purchase property at an agreed price.

Option to renew: A right given a tenant to renew a lease.

Overimprovement: An improvement that is not economically justified.

Partnership insurance: Term life insurance on all partners payable to the surviving partners in order to buy out the deceased partner's interests in the business.

Percentage lease: A lease where the rent is set at a percentage of gross income.

Periodic tenancy: A tenancy from period to period that renews itself unless notice is given to terminate.

Pitch (roof): The vertical drop per horizontal foot.

Proactive guard patrol: A patrol whose job is to prevent crime.

Professional Community Associations Manager (PCAM): The highest professional designation of the Community Associations Institute.

Pro-Forma Statement: An estimated operating statement.

Property Management Association (PMA): A professional management organization.

Proximate cause: An action must be the cause of the injury to make the perpetrator liable.

Psychic income: The benefit of pride of ownership.

Qualifying tenants: The process of determining if a tenant has the income, credit and character to be good tenant.

Quiet enjoyment: Lessor agrees not to interfere with the tenants use of premises or permit others to do so.

R Factor: Resistance factor used to measure effectiveness of insulation.

Radius clause: The tenant agrees not to open a competing location within a stated distance.

Reactive guard patrol: A patrol that responds to alarms in order to catch a criminal.

Real Estate Investment Trust (REIT): A publicly traded ownership that avoid double taxation of corporations.

Real Property Administrator (RPA): A professional designation of BOMA.

Recapture clause: Clause in a percentage lease providing that the lessor can terminate the lease if a stated volume of sales is not reached.

Recreational vehicle park: Park where spaces are rented to mobile units.

Recording: Process of filing a document with the country recorder so constructive notices may be given of an interest.

Regional shopping center: A major shopping center anchored by several department stores.

Registered Property Manager (RPM): A designation of the International Real Estate Institute.

Rent: Compensation for possession.

Rent control: Political limitations on rents and/or rent increases.

Rent incentives: Free or reduced rent given to a tenant to induce the tenant to sign a lease.

Rental interruption insurance: Insurance covering rent loss due to a casualty loss.

Research and development buildings: Office and laboratory structures that might conduct prototype manufacturing.

Resident manager: Manager who lives in the managed property.

Residential property: Property where people live.

Restoration: Return of premises to an original condition.

Retaliatory eviction: Unlawful eviction for making proper complaints to public authorities or for organizing a tenant organization.

Right of first refusal: The right to buy or lease at terms offered by another by agreeing to meet those terms. It is a preemptive right.

Rumford Act: California's Fair Housing Act.

Security deposit: A deposit that insures the lessor against tenant damage or default.

Self insured: A party bearing the risk without insurance company protection.

Semi-independent living: Elderly housing where services are provided but tenants have their own apartments.

Sick buildings: Buildings associated with tenant illnesses from fumes or bacteria.

Single Room Occupancy (SRO): Motel and hotel facilities converted to permanent housing.

Slander: Verbal false statement that injures another.

Smart building: A building equipped with electronic and communications equipment for tenant use.

Square footage: Measurement of floor space to compute rents.

Stabilization: The process of renting a new or vacant property to the point where vacancy factor reduced to a reasonable level.

Standard policy (Fire insurance): A policy covering loss by fire, lightning and removal of proper because of those perils.

Glossary

Statute of Frauds: The requirement that certain agreements must be in writing to be enforceable.

Steering: The illegal process of directing prospective tenants based on race, sex, marital status, etc.

Stigmatized property: Property with an undesirable reputation.

Storage yards: Outside storage areas.

Strip center: A line of shops catering to vehicular traffic.

Sublease: A lease by the lessee. The sublessee is the tenant of the original lessee.

Subordination: An agreement to be secondary to another agreement.

Subsidized housing: Below market rent housing subsidized by government ownership or low interest financing.

Supply oriented business: A manufacturer located close to supply of material used.

Surrender: Turning over the premises that terminates the lease obligations.

Systems Maintenance Technician (SMT): A professional BOMA designation.

Theme buildings: Buildings where all tenants have similar businesses.

Thirty-day notice: Notice given on a periodic tenancy to terminate or change tenancy terms.

Three-day notice: A notice given prior to an unlawful detainer action to quit or pay rent, quit or cure or quit.

Time is of the essence: An agreement that dates set are material and are not approximate.

Time share: A divided-unit ownership where each owner is entitled to occupancy of a unit during a specified time period.

Trade fixtures: Fixtures installed for a business or trade. They remain personal property.

Trophy building: A pride of ownership structure.

Trust account: Account holding funds of others prior to disbursement.

Unlawful detainer: The legal eviction notice.

Unruh Act: California act that prohibits a business from discriminating.

Urban Land Institute (ULI): A research and publishing organization with emphasis on development.

Urban pedestrian mall: A foot traffic only open mall.

Utility oriented: Manufacturer that wants to be located where utility costs are low.

Vacancy factor: The percentage of vacancies.

Waiver of subrogation: An insurer giving up rights to make a claim for a covered loss against the property manager.

Waste: Tenant causing damage to property.

Workers Compensation Insurance: Required coverage covering employee job related injuries.

Zero-based budgeting: Budgeting based on the idea that every expense must be justified.

Index

A

Accredited Management Organization (AMO): 18
Accredited Marketing Director (AMD): 23
Accredited Residential Manager (ARM): 17
Accredited Shopping Center Manager (ASM): 23
Administration of Lease Clauses: 98
Advertising: 48, 412
After Occupancy: 163
   30-Day Notice: 165
   Change in Rent/Covenants: 165
   Confirmation of Lease: 167
   Enforcement of Contract Provisions or Rules and Regulations: 165
   Rent Collections: 163
     Three-Day Notice: 163
     Unlawful Detainer Action: 163
Agency Termination: 53
AIDS: 91
American Industrial Real Estate Association: 22
Americans With Disabilities Act: 418
   Enforcement: 418
   Penalties: 418
Anchor Tenants: 176
Annual Statement (Owners): 357
Appraisals: 152
Appreciation: 33
Arbitration: 100
Assignment: 68
Assignment and Subleasing: 100
Assignment and Subletting: 68
   Assignment: 68
   Sublease: 68
Attractive Nuisance Doctrine: 299

Attributes of a Successful Manager: 10
   Ability to Delegate: 12
   Ability to Prioritize: 11
   Accept Responsibility: 13
   Agency Focused: 14
   Be Part of the Solution: 13
   Benefit Oriented: 13
   Bravery: 11
   Communication Skills: 12
   Flexibility: 13
   Goal Oriented: 12
   Integrity: 11
   Mental Stamina: 10
   Money Manager: 14
   Organizational Skills: 11
   People Skills: 11
   Team Oriented: 12

B

Bad Checks: 104
Bankruptcy: 104
Binders: 261
Bird Dogs: 379
Bonding: 264
Building Owners and Managers Association International (BOMA): 19
   Additional Designations: 20
   Facilities Management Administrator (FMA): 20
   Real Property Administrator (RPA): 19

C

California Recreational Vehicle Park Occupancy Law: 239
Capacity: 64

Carbon Monoxide Detectors: 301
Career Opportunities in Property Management: 4
  Corporations: 6
  Employees of Private Owners: 7
  Financial Institutions: 6
  Franchises: 7
  Government: 4
    General Services Administration: 4
  Independent Property Manager: 4
  Minorities in Property Management: 8
  On-Site Management: 7
  Private Management Firms: 7
  Real Estate Investment Trusts (REITs): 4
  Resident Manager: 4
  Women in Property Management: 8
Cash Flow: 32
CC&Rs: 220
Certified Leasing Specialist (CLS): 22
Certified Property Manager: 17
  Criteria: 17
Certified Shopping Center Manager (CSM): 23
Civil Rights Act of 1866: 402
Civil Rights Act of 1870: 403
Civil Rights Act of 1964: 403
Civil Rights Act of 1968: 403, 423
  Discriminatory and Nondiscriminatory Advertising Language: 414
  Enforcement: 413
  Equal Housing Opportunity Poster: 413
  Exemptions: 403
  Prohibitions: 404
Class A Office Buildings: 188
Class B Office Buildings: 188
Class C Office Buildings: 188
Class D Office Buildings: 188
Clothing Optional: 221
Code Violations: 40
Commercial Leases: 185
Commercial Property: 174
Commercial Property Management: 174
  Commercial Leases: 185
  Commercial Property: 174
  How Much Commercial Space?: 174
  Overbuilding: 185
  Parking: 184
  Rent Setting: 182

  Bargain Rents: 183
  Determining Rents: 182
  Don't Be Unreasonable: 183
  Tenant Selection: 180
  Tenant Mix: 180
  Tenant Quality: 181
  Types of Properties: 175
  Anchor Tenants: 176
  Community Shopping Center: 176
  Factory Outlet Centers: 179
  Large Freestanding Retailers: 180
  Mega Malls: 178
  Mini-Malls: 176
  Neighborhood Shopping Center: 176
  Pedestrian Shopping Streets: 175
  Regional Shopping Center: 177
  Strip Centers: 176
  Symbiotic Relationship: 176
  Urban Pedestrian Mall: 176
  Wholesale Operations: 180
Commingling: 349
Community Associations Institute: 24
  Association Management Specialist (AMS): 25
  Certified Manager of Community Associations (CMCA): 24
  Professional Community Association Manager (PCAM): 25
Community Shopping Center: 176
Completed Staff Work: 13
Computer Management Software: 364
Computerized Buildings: 338
Condominium Management: 214
  Board of Directors: 214
  CC&Rs: 220
  Compensation: 220
  Management Duties: 215
  Personal Relationships: 219
Consideration: 64
Constructive Eviction: 441
Contracts of Adhesion: 77
Corporation Leases: 67
Corporations: 6

D

Dead Bolts: 286
Deep Pocket Laws: 257

Depreciation and Capital Gains: 33
Disclosures: 90
 AIDS: 91
 Death: 91
 Flood Hazard Area: 90
 Hazardous Substance: 90
 Lead-Based Paint: 90
 Military Ordnance: 90
 Stigmatized Property: 91
Docking Facilities: 241
Drafting Leases: 76
 Contracts of Adhesion: 77
 Expiration Date: 78
 Leases Prepared by Lessees: 77
 Length of The Lease: 78
 Title of Lease: 77
 Use of Standard Forms: 76

E

Economics of Scale: 461
80 Percent Coinsurance: 270
Elderly Housing Projects: 224
 Alternative Elderly Housing: 226
 Independent Living: 225
 Life Care Facilities: 226
 Nursing Facilities: 225
 Security for the Elderly: 226
 Semi-Independent Living: 225
 The Property Manager For Elderly Housing: 226
Electronic Gates: 289
Eminent Domain: 107
Employee Hiring: 468
 Application: 468
 Colorblind Management: 471
 Employee Interview: 469
 Illegal Aliens: 471
 Temporary Workers: 471
 Tests: 469
Employees: 463
 Managerial Problems: 467
 Qualities of a Resident Manager: 465
 Resident Manager Job Description: 466
 Status of the Resident Manager: 463
Energy Conservation: 331
 Automatic Damper Control: 332
 Computerized Buildings: 338

Electric Use Controls: 332
Fireplaces: 332
Going to Individual Units: 331
Heating and Air Conditioning Engineers: 331
Insulation: 335
 R Value (Resistance Value): 335
Lights: 332
Solar Heat: 333
Solar Lights: 333
Venting: 334
 Power Vents: 335
Water Conservation: 333
Water Heaters: 332
English Doctrine of Respondeat Superior: 251
Environmental Protection Agency (EPA): 113
Equal Credit Opportunity Act: 419
Equal Housing Opportunity Poster: 413
Escalator Clause: 108
Estate for Years: 65
Ethics: 421
Eviction: 438
 Quit: 439
 Quit or Cure: 438
 Quit or Pay Rent: 438
Exterminators: 325

F

Facilities Management Administrator (FMA): 20
Factory Outlet Centers: 179
Fair Housing (Federal): 402
 14th Amendment: 402
 1988 Fair Housing Amendment Act: 406
 Advertising: 412
 Americans with Disabilities Act: 418
 Civil Rights Act of 1866: 402
 Civil Rights Act of 1870: 403
 Civil Rights Act of 1964: 403
 Civil Rights Act of 1968: 403
 Equal Credit Opportunity Act: 419
 Executive Order 11603: 403
Fair Housing (State): 419
 Rumford Act: 420
 Unruh Act: 419
Farm/Ranch Management: 240
 Corporate Owned Farms/Ranches: 240
 Gentlemen Farms: 241
 Lender-Owned Farms: 240

Federal Deposit Insurance Corporation (FDIC): 347
Federal National Mortgage Association (Fannie Mae): 384
Fiduciary Duties: 445
    Confidentiality: 445
    Fair and Honest Dealings: 446
    Full Disclosure: 446
    Loyalty: 445
    Obedience: 446
    Reasonable Care and Skill: 446
Financial Institutions: 6
Fire Insurance: 262
    Earthquake and Flood Coverage: 262
    Homeowner Policies: 262
    Standard Policy: 262
Fireplaces: 332
Firing an Employee: 478
Fixtures: 108
    Adaptability: 108
    Attachment: 108
    Intent of the Parties: 108
Fixturing Allowance: 195
Flood Hazard Area: 90
Force Account: 311
"For Lease" Signs: 388
14th Amendment: 402
Franchises: 7
Furnished Units: 148

G - H

Garden Office Buildings: 189
Gentlemen Farms: 241
Good Funds: 351
Graffiti: 324
Gross Lease: 66
Ground Lease: 67
Handicapped: 406
Hazardous Substances: 90, 109, 258
Hazardous Waste: 257
High-Rise Office Buildings: 189
History of Property Management: 2
    Electric Elevator: 3
    Industrial Revolution: 3
    Moldboard Plow: 3
    Structural Steel: 3
    The Great Depression: 3

Homeowner Association Management: 448
Hotel/Motel Management: 224
    Elderly Housing Projects: 224
Housing and Urban Development (HUD): 114, 227, 412, 413
HVAC: 193, 319

I

Illegal Aliens: 471
Immigration Reform and Control Act of 1986: 471
Independent Contractor: 52
Industrial Leases: 203
Industrial Parks: 202
Industrial Property Management: 197
    Changing Uses: 203
    Evaluating a Site: 202
    Industrial Leases: 203
    Industrial Parks: 202
    Locational Needs: 197
    Preparing to Lease: 203
    Special Use Structures: 202
    Structural Needs: 201
      Historic Structures: 201
      One-Story Factories: 201
    Warehouse Space: 202
Institutional Management: 227
Insulation: 335
    Basement Windows: 337
    Caulking and Weatherstripping: 336
    Ceiling: 335
    Duct Work: 338
    Insulation Paint: 338
    Walls: 336
      Basement Walls: 337
    Windows: 337
Insurance Register: 359
Intelligent Building: 191
International Council of Shopping Centers (ICSC): 22
    Accredited Marketing Director (AMD): 23
    Accredited Shopping Center Manager (ASM): 23
    Awards: 23
    Certified Leasing Specialist (CLS): 22
    Certified Shopping Center Manager (CSM): 23
    Senior Level Accreditation: 23

International Facility Management Association: 25
International Real Estate Institute: 21
Internet: 389
Interpleader Action: 351

K - L

Key Man Insurance: 268
Lead-Based Paint: 90
Lead-Based Paint Disclosure: 113, 156
    Environmental Protection Agency (EPA): 113
Lease: 64
    Capacity: 64
    Consideration: 64
    Legal Purpose: 64
    Mutuality: 64
Lease Clauses: 98
    Arbitration: 100
    Assignment and Subleasing: 100
    Bad Checks: 104
    Breach by Lessor: 104
    Competition Clause: 105
        Radius Clause: 105
    Destruction of Premises: 106
        Option to Rebuild: 107
        Partial Destruction: 107
        Rent Tolled: 107
        Termination: 106
    Eminent Domain: 107
    Escalator Clause: 108
    Fixtures: 108
    Hazardous Substances: 109
    Hold Harmless Clause: 110
    Lead-Based Paint Disclosure: 113
    Mitigate Damages: 109
    Option to Purchase: 115
    Quiet Enjoyment: 119
    Recapture Clause: 120
    Renewal: 120
    Renewal of Lease: 119
    Right of First Refusal: 122
    Security Deposit: 124
Lease Negotiations: 80
    Dealing With Impasse: 88
    Disclosures: 90
    Foreign Language Negotiations: 89

Lease Renewals: 87
    Recording Leases: 89
    Rent Incentives: 85
        Free Rent: 85
    Understanding Positions and Expectations: 80
Lease Period: 147
Length of Lease: 78
Liability: 250
    Criminal Activity: 253
    Dram Shop Liability: 257
        Deep Pocket Laws: 257
    Hazardous Waste: 257
    Injury and Property Damage: 250
    Liability as to Independent Contractors: 252
    Liability for Actions of Other Tenants: 253
    Liability for Employees and Agents: 251
        English Doctrine of Respondeat Superior: 251
        Slander and Libel: 251
        Within the Scope of Employment: 251
    Liability Off The Premises: 253
    Strict Liability: 250
Libel: 251
Licensing Requirements: 14
    Hotel Manager: 16
    Owners: 14
    Power of Attorney: 15
    Resident Managers: 16
    Transient Occupancy: 16
    Without Compensation: 14
Logo: 377
Low-Balling: 447
Low-Rise Office Buildings: 189

M

Maintenance Program: 310
    10-Day Week: 315
    Developing Contractor Relations: 313
    Employee Versus Contract Services: 311
        Force Account: 311
    Identify Your Maintenance Personnel: 316
    Maintenance Records: 316
    Patch-and-Hope Repairs: 315
    Priority of Repairs: 313
    Recommended Priority of Repair: 314
    Staffing: 317
    Standardization: 313
    Your Own Maintenance Company: 312

Management Office: 456
  Management Costs: 461
    Economics of Scale: 461
  Management Fees: 461
    For Management: 461
    Lease Renewals and Options: 463
    Leasing Fees: 462
    Termination Fee: 463
  Organizational Chart: 456
  Policy Manual: 458
  Staffing: 457
Management Records and Controls: 358
  Eviction Register: 360
  Inactive Files: 361
  Insurance Register: 359
  Inventory File: 360
  Lease Files: 358
  Mortgage File: 359
  Move-Outs Who Owe: 360
  Payroll Records: 361
  Percentage Lease Verification: 359
  Purchase Orders Files: 361
  Rent Rolls: 359
  Utility Files: 360
  Vendor Files: 360
Marketing Plan: 37
Mechanic's Liens: 330
  Notice of Nonresponsibility: 330
Medical Offices (MDs): 242
Mega Malls: 178
Mid-Rise Office Buildings: 189
Military Ordnance: 90
Mini-Malls: 176
Mini-Storage: 242
Minorities in Property Management: 8
Mitigate Damages: 109
Mitigation of Damages: 443
MLS: 380
Mobile Home Park Management. 232
  Condo - Mobile Home Park: 239
  Court Determinations: 238
  Mobile Home Residency Law: 232, 237

J - O

National Association of Realtors® (NAR): 350
Negative Cash Flow: 40

Neighborhood Shopping Center: 176
Net Lease: 66
1988 Fair Housing Amendment Act: 406
  Familial Status: 410
  Handicapped: 406
  Reverse Caregiver Laws: 410
Notice of Nonresponsibility: 330
Occupational Safety and Health Act (OSHA): 301
  State OSHA: 302
Office Leases: 196
Office Property Management: 185
  Categories of Office Buildings: 188
    Class A Office Buildings: 188
    Class B Office Buildings: 188
    Class C Office Buildings: 188
    Class D Office Buildings: 188
    Garden Office Buildings: 189
    High-Rise Office Buildings: 189
    Low-Rise Office Buildings: 189
    Mid-Rise Office Buildings: 189
  Combination Buildings: 192
  Computing Square Footage: 194
    Usable Square Footage Method: 195
  Demolition of Serviceable Office Buildings: 193
  Fixturing Allowance: 195
  Intelligent Building: 191
  Keeping Tenants Happy: 196
  New Construction: 194
  Office Leases: 196
  R & D Facilities Management: 192
  Repositioning Office Buildings: 189
    The Charm of History: 189
    Theme Buildings: 190
  Trophy Buildings: 190
  Vacancy Factor: 194
On-Site Management: 7
Opening a Management Office: 479
  Your Competition: 479
  Your Plan: 480
  Yourself: 480
Owner Relations: 444
  Communications: 444
  Fiduciary Duties: 445
  Homeowner Association Management: 448
  Relationships with Owners: 447
  Suing a Principal: 449

Underestimating Costs and Overestimating Income: 447
   Low-Balling: 447
  Violating the Law: 448
Owner Reports: 356
  Annual Statements: 357
   Addendums: 358
   Average Rents: 357
   Balance In Account: 357
   Comparative Operating Statement: 357
   Multiple Owner Properties: 357
   Occupancy Factor: 357
  Monthly Statement: 356
Owners, Landlords and Tenants Liability (OLT): 263

P

Partnership Insurance: 268
Payroll Records: 361
Pedestrian Shopping Streets: 175
Percentage Lease: 67, 121
Periodic Tenancy: 65
Physical Eviction: 442
Policies (Rental): 145
  Furnished Units: 148
  Lease Period: 147
  Occupancy: 148
  Pets: 146
  Qualification Requirements: 148
  Security Deposits: 145
  Uniform Residential Landlord and Tenant Act: 146
  Who Not To Rent To: 148
Policy Manual: 458
  Completed Staff Work: 459
  Dealings with Owners: 458
  Dress Code: 459
  Interpersonal Relations: 459
  Key Money: 460
  Tenant Gifts to Managers: 460
  Theft: 459
Power of Attorney: 15
Private Management Firms: 7
Pro- Forma Statement: 36
Problem Property: 381
  Code Violations: 381
  Evictions: 382
  Poor Maintenance: 382
  Tax Delinquent Properties: 382

Professionalism in Property Management: 16
  Accredited Management Organization (AMO): 18
  Accredited Residential Manager (ARM): 17
  American Industrial Real Estate Association: 22
  Building Owners and Managers Association International (BOMA): 19
  Certified Property Manager (CPM): 17
  Community Associations Institute: 24
  Educational Courses: 18
  Institute of Real Estate Management (IREM): 16
  International Council of Shopping Centers (ICSC): 22
  International Facility Management Association: 25
  International Real Estate Institute: 21
  Property Management Association (PMA): 20
  Urban Land Institute (ULI): 21
Promoting Rental Space: 387
  "For Lease" Signs: 388
  Advance Fee Rental Agencies: 387
  Billboards: 389
  Chambers of Commerce: 389
  Classified Ads: 390
  Display Ads: 391
  Fee Splitting: 387
  Flags, Balloons and The Open House: 389
  Further Ad Help: 393
  Internet: 389
  Movie Screen Ads: 392
  Neighborhood Walk-Around: 393
  Personnel Offices: 389
  Public Transit Ads: 390
  Radio: 393
  Rental Magazines: 392
  Selection of Newspapers: 391
   Daily Newspapers: 391
   Foreign Language Papers: 392
   Special Interest Papers: 392
   Weekly Throwaway Papers: 391
  Talking Signs: 388
  Telephone Solicitations: 393
  Television Ads: 393
  Use Other Tenants: 387
Promoting Your Firm: 374
  Institutional Advertising: 378
  Leased Signs: 377
  Logo Identification: 377
  Management Signs: 377

Meeting Owners: 374
  Membership In Property Owners Groups: 374
  Organization Membership: 375
  Public Speaking: 374
  Religion: 375
  Teaching: 375
Newspaper Columns: 376
Personal Promotion: 376
Press Releases: 375
Professional Associations: 377
Professional Journals: 377
Yellow Pages: 378
Property Improvements: 328
  Economic and Uneconomic Improvements: 328
Property Management Association (PMA): 20
Property Management Contract: 42
  Article I: 42
  Article II: 42
  Article III: 48
    Advertising: 48
    Compensation: 49
    Lease Negotiation: 48
    Rental: 48
    Rental Rates: 49
  Article IV: 49
    Bonding of Employees: 50
    Collection and Segregation of Funds: 50
    Compensation: 51
    Employees: 50
    Expenditures: 50
    Interest and Tax Payments: 50
    Legal Proceedings: 51
    Management of Building: 49
    Monthly Statement: 50
    Reimbursement: 50
    Repairs: 49
    Service Contracts: 49
    Special Services: 50
  Article V: 51
    Compliance With Laws: 51
    Indemnification: 51
    Insurance: 51
    Waiver of Subrogation: 51
  Article VI: 52
  Article VII: 52
    Assignment or Amendment: 52
    Bankruptcy and Insolvency: 52

    Independent Contractor: 52
    Notice: 52
    Suit or Action: 52
  Schedule 1: 52
    Description of the Property: 53
    Employees of Owner: 53
    Management Commission: 53
    Manager Compensation for Leasing: 53
    Payments by Manager: 53
    Sale Commission: 53
Property Management Insurance: 267
Property Owner Benefits: 32
  Appreciation: 33
  Combination of Benefits: 34
  Depreciation and Capital Gains: 33
  Income: 32
    Cash flow: 32
  Maintaining the Property: 33
  Psychic Income: 34
  Security: 33
Proposal to Lease: 72
Psychic Income: 34

Q - R

Qualifying Tenants: 69
  Character: 71
  Income Determination: 70
Qualities of a Resident Manager: 465
Quiet Enjoyment: 119
R Value (Resistance Value): 335
Real Estate Investment Trusts (REITs): 4, 179, 378
Real Estate Investors: 383
Real Property Administrator (RPA): 19
Recapture Clause: 120
Recording Leases: 89
Recreational Vehicle Parks: 239
  California Recreational Vehicle Park Occupancy Law: 239
Refusing Management: 38
  Code Violations: 40
  Negative Cash Flow: 40
  Slumlording: 39
  Specialization: 39
  Unrealistic Fees: 39
Regional Shopping Center: 177
Rent Control: 137

Rent Incentives: 85
Rent Rolls: 359
Rental Process: 154
   Lease Signing: 156
   Lessor Disclosures: 156
     Lead-Based Paint Disclosure: 156
   Preparing To Lease: 154
   Prequalifying Your Prospective Tenants: 154
   Qualification Process: 155
   Showing to Prospective Tenants: 155
Research and Development (R&D) facility: 192
Resident Manager: 16, 214
Residential Defined: 134
Residential Housing Need: 134
   Economic Conditions: 134
   Family Units: 134
   Interest Cycles: 135
   Political Changes: 135
     Development Fees: 136
     Moratoriums and Limits: 136
     Rent Control: 137
     Taxes: 135
     Zoning: 138
   Population Bulges: 135
   Society Changes: 135
   Stratified Need: 139
   Time for Development: 139
Residential Management Contracts: 140
   Additional Owner Obligations: 144
   Additional Terms: 145
   Attorney Fees: 145
   Authorities and Obligations of Brokers: 140
   Entire Agreement: 145
   Notice: 144
   Owner's Obligations: 143
   Time: 145
     Time is of the essence: 145
Resort Area Management: 221
Retaliatory Eviction: 442
Reverse Caregiver Laws: 410
Risk Administration: 260
Risk Management: 258
   Binders: 261
   How Much Insurance?: 269
     80 Percent Coinsurance: 270
     Deductibles: 269
     Lender Requirements: 269

Identifying and Administering Risks: 260
Partnership Insurance: 268
Property Management Insurance: 267
   Automobile Coverage: 268
   Errors and Omissions: 267
   Key Man Insurance: 268
   Records Insurance: 267
   Surety Bonds: 268
Risk Administration: 260
Self-Insured: 260
Types of Owner-Insurance Policies: 261
   Additional Insurance: 265
   Boiler Insurance: 263
   Earthquake and Flood Coverage: 262
   Elevator Insurance: 263
   Fidelity Bonds: 264
   Fire Insurance: 262
   Inland Marine Insurance: 264
   Liability Insurance: 263
   Medical Pay Coverage: 264
   Owners, Landlords and Tenants Liability (OLT): 263
   Rental Interruption Insurance: 264
   Worker's Compensation Insurance: 265
Types of Tenant Insurance Policies: 265
   Business Interruption Insurance: 266
   Extra Expense Coverage: 266
   Fidelity Bonds: 266
   Fire and Extended Coverage: 265
   Inland Marine Coverage: 266
   Leasehold Insurance: 266
   Liability Coverage: 266
   Medical Pay Coverage: 266
   Residential Tenant Coverage: 267
Rumford Act: 420

S

Sale-Leasebacks: 67
Security and Safety: 281
   Bomb Search: 296
   Carbon Monoxide Detectors: 301
   Doors: 284
     Dead Bolts: 286
   Electronic Gates: 289
   Electronic Security Alarms: 292
     Alarm Box: 295

Closed-Circuit Alarm: 293
Entry Alarms: 292
Interior Alarms: 294
Emergency Oxygen Units: 297
Emergency Telephones: 297
Employee Background Checks: 297
Employee Name Tags: 298
Fences and Walls: 284
Fire Doors: 300
Fire Extinguishers: 299
Fire Suppression: 300
Guard Dogs: 292
Guard Gate Services: 290
Guard Patrols: 291
Proactive Patrol: 291
Reactive Patrols: 291
Guard Services: 290
Injuries on Premises: 301
Landscaping: 283
Lighting: 282
Locks: 285
Occupancy Rules: 298
OSHA (Occupational Safety and Health Act): 301
Rent Collection Security: 296
Resident Manager: 296
Safety Rules: 301
Security Committees: 298
Showing Units: 297
Smoke Detectors: 301
Staff Supervision: 298
Television Cameras: 295
Vacant Units: 298
Attractive Nuisance Doctrine: 299
Windows: 288
Security Deposits: 124, 145
Security: An Overview: 278
Security Defined: 278
Security Obligations: 278
Advertising Security: 279
Foreseeability of Harm: 278
Security Disclosure: 280
Service Contracts: 49
Setting Rents: 149
Ideal Rent: 151
Inflation and Rent: 153
Raising Rent: 152
Supply and Demand: 150

Using Comparables: 149
What Not to Use in Setting Rents: 151
Appraisals: 152
Owner Costs: 151
When Rents Are Too High: 152
Short-Term Residential Properties: 223
Sick Buildings: 192
Single Family Dwellings: 222
Maintenance: 222
Management Fees: 223
Owners' Goals: 222
Rent Problems: 223
Renters: 223
Utilities: 223
Single Room Occupancy (SROs): 210
55 and Older: 213
Furnishings: 212
Housekeeping: 212
Laundry Room: 212
Lease: 211
Occupancy: 211
Public Rooms: 213
Rental Period: 211
Resident Manager: 214
Restaurants/Bars: 213
Security: 211
Tenant Qualifying: 210
Utilities: 212
Slander: 251
Slumlording: 39
Smoke Detectors: 301
Solar Heat: 333
Sources for Obtaining Management: 378
Banks: 380
Bird Dogs: 379
Consulting Contracts: 385
Developers: 383
Fannie Mae: 384
Getting Owners to Buy: 380
Leasing: 385
Neighbors: 380
Newspaper Ads: 382
Ads for Trade: 382
For Sale by Owner: 383
Rental Ads: 382
Problem Property: 381
Property Sales: 380

Real Estate Investors: 383
Referral Fees for Management: 379
Referrals From Owners: 379
Speculators: 384
Vacant Property: 381
When There is a Manager: 384
Special Use Structures: 202
Specific Maintenance Tasks: 317
  Air Filters: 324
  Aluminum Wiring: 327
  Carpeting: 322
  Cleaning: 327
  Exterminators: 325
  Furnaces and Air Conditioners: 319
  Graffiti: 324
  Gulls, Ducks and Geese: 326
    Rocket Nets: 326
  Paint: 322
  Pigeons: 325
  Plumbing: 319
  Pressure Washing: 324
  Roofs (New): 317
  Roofs (Repairs): 318
  Temporary Clean-Up Work: 327
Speculators: 384
Statute of Frauds: 65
Stigmatized Property: 91
Storage Yards: 242
Strip Centers: 176
Sublease: 68
Subsidized Housing: 227
  Problems of Subsidized Housing: 227
  Solutions to Problems in Public Housing: 228
Supply and Demand: 150
Surety Bonds: 268
Surrender (of Lease): 437

T

Takeout Checklists: 54
Taxes: 135
Tenant Complaints: 432
Tenant Relations: 431
  Change in Terms/End of Tenancy: 436
  Constructive Eviction: 441
  Death of a Tenant: 433
  Eleven Month Year: 438

Eviction: 438
Extended Tenant Absence: 436
Failure to Take Possession: 437
Let the Tenant Go: 433
Mitigation of Damages: 443
Never Have Surprise Charges: 437
Pay Them to Leave: 443
Physical Eviction: 442
Rent After Notice: 441
Renting to Friends and Relatives: 431
Retaliatory Eviction: 442
Romantic Entanglements: 432
Seizure of Property: 442
Surrender of Lease: 437
Tenant Complaints: 432
Tenant Education: 431
Tenant Painting: 435
Tenant's Right to Repair: 434
The First Excuse: 437
Waiting List: 434
Waste: 435
Tenant's Right to Repair: 434
The Management Plan: 34
  Cost Savings: 37
  Economic Changes: 37
  Goals: 36
  Management Plan Prior to Construction: 38
  Marketing Plan: 37
  Pro-Forma Statement: 36
  Property Analysis: 35
    Area Analysis: 35
    Current Tenants: 35
    Grounds and Parking: 35
    Location of The Property: 35
    Other Possible Uses: 35
    Photos: 35
    Physical Structure: 35
  Reserve Requirements: 37
  Staffing: 37
  Zero based budgeting: 37
30-Day Notice: 165
Three-day Notice: 163
Time Shares: 229
  Management Duties: 230
  Management Problem Areas: 231
Trust Account: 347

Trust Fund Accounting: 346
 Broker Funds in Trust Account: 350
 Checks Held Uncashed: 347
 Commingling Trust Funds: 349
 Conflicting Claims on Trust Funds: 351
   Interpleader Action: 351
 Deposits Received by Property Manager: 346
 Disbursements from Trust Account: 348
 DRE Audits: 356
 Funds Received by Employees/Agents: 347
 Interest Bearing Trust Accounts: 347
 Offset of Trust Funds: 351
 Reconciliation of Trust Account: 352
 Retention of Trust Records: 356
 Return of Trust Funds: 350
   Good Funds: 351
 Trust Account: 347
 Trust Fund Records: 352
Trust Funds: 346
 Non-Trust Funds: 346
Types of Leases: 65
 Corporation Leases: 67
 Estate For Years: 65
 Ground Lease: 67
 Periodic Tenancy: 65
 Rent-Paying Provisions: 66
   Gross Lease: 66
   Net Lease: 66
   Percentage Leases: 67
Types of Owner-Insurance Policies: 261
Types of Tenant Insurance Policies: 265

U - V

Uniform Residential Landlord and Tenant Act: 156
 General Provisions: 160
 Lessor's Duties: 161
 Tenant's Duties: 162
Unlawful Detainer Action: 163
Unruh Act: 419
Urban Land Institute (ULI): 21
Urban Pedestrian Mall: 176
Usable Square Footage Method: 195
Vacancy Factor: 194

W

Warehouses: 202
Water Conservation: 333
Water Heaters: 332
Wholesalers: 180
Why Owners Choose Management: 8
 Economic Reasons: 8
 Main Financial Benefits: 9
 Personal Reasons: 10
Women in Property Management: 8
Worker's Compensation Insurance: 265
Working With Employees: 473
 Employee Evaluation: 473
   30-Day Evaluation: 473
   Subsequent Evaluations: 474
   Tenant Exit Interview: 474
 Employee File: 473
 Employee Relations: 474
 Employee Retention: 475
 Firing an Employee: 478
 Training: 477

Y - Z

Your Own Records and Controls: 361
 Ad Register: 362
 Audit: 363
 Employee File: 363
 Management Office Insurance File: 362
 Operation Costs and Expenses: 361
 Telephone and Walk-In Records: 362
Zero-Based Budgeting: 37
Zoning: 138

Order Department

Sometimes our textbooks are hard to find!

If your bookstore does not carry our textbooks, send us a check or money order and we'll mail them to you with our 30-day money back guarantee.

The Exceptional Books From Educational Textbook Company:

California Real Estate Principles, 9th ed., by Huber ·······························$50.00 _____
How To Pass The Real Estate Exam (850 Exam Questions), by Huber·······$50.00 _____
California Real Estate Law, by Huber & Pivar·····································$50.00 _____
Financing California Real Estate, by Huber ····································$50.00 _____
Real Estate Economics, by Huber & Pivar·······································$50.00 _____
Real Estate Appraisal, by Huber & Pivar ·······································$50.00 _____
Mortgage Loan Brokering, by Huber & Pivar ····································$50.00 _____
Property Management, by Huber & Pivar···$50.00 _____
Escrow I: An Introduction, by Huber···$50.00 _____
California Real Estate Practice, by Huber & Bond ·····························$50.00 _____
California Business Law, by Huber, Owens, & Tyler····························$65.00 _____
Six-Hour Survey, Continuing Education, by Huber ·····························$15.00 _____

Subtotal _____
Add shipping and handling @ $5.00 per book _____
Add California sales tax @ 8.25% _____
TOTAL _____

Allow 2-3 weeks for delivery

Name: _____
Address: _____
City, State, Zip: _____
Phone: _____

Check or Money Order:
Educational Textbook Company
P.O. Box 3597, Covina, CA 91722
626-339-7733 . 626-332-4744 (Fax)